The Gerson Institute keeps this book in print in its efforts to keep Dr. Gerson's work alive.

The Gerson Institute is a non-profit organization located in San Diego, California, dedicated to providing education and training in the alternative, non-toxic treatment of cancer and other diseases, using the Gerson Therapy.

Some of our programs and services include:

Information and Referral Service: Our toll-free helpline provides information about the Gerson Therapy, Gerson clinics, referrals to Home Set-up Trainers and recovered patients and other resources.

Patient Support: We assist patients with the process of applying to licensed clinics and follow up with patients' progress after they left the clinic.
Training Programs: We train medical professionals to become licensed Gerson Practitioners.

We conduct lectures, workshops and media interviews about the Gerson Therapy.

We also train individuals to assist Gerson patients in their homes.

Education: We conduct lectures, workshops and media presentations about the Gerson Therapy. We also publish and distribute materials by and about Dr. Gerson and his therapy, including books, DVDs and the *Healing News* newsletter for our members.

Bookstore: We publish and distribute educational materials about the Gerson Therapy. We sell books, DVDs, audio CDs and other Gerson products.
Contact The Gerson Institute to:

• Start the Gerson Therapy at a Gerson Clinic or at home • Order educational materials

• Obtain referrals and information

• Sign up for a training program or workshop

• Join as a member and receive our bi-monthly newsletter

• Volunteer at the Gerson Institute

• Make a donation to help us bring hope and healing to more people

  around the world

Visit our online store at **www.gerson.org/store** for additional educational materials

www.gerson.org
info@gerson.org
(888)443-7766 Toll Free U.S. & Canada
(800)838-2256 Toll Free U.S. Only
(619) 685-5353 International
PO Box 161358
San Diego, CA 92176

12/2014

A Cancer Therapy

Results of Fifty Cases

and
The Cure of Advanced Cancer
by Diet Therapy

A Summary of 30 Years
of Clinical Experimentation

Max Gerson, M.D.

Gerson Institute

The Gerson Institute
1572 Second Avenue
San Diego,CA 92101
Telephone: 619-685-5359, or 1-888-4-GERSON
email: mail@gerson.org / web: www.gerson.org

Library of Congress Cataloging-in-Publication Data

Gerson, Max
    A cancer therapy: results of fifty cases: a summary of 30 years
    clinical experimentation / Max Gerson.
    p. Cm.
    Originally published: New York : Whittier Books, [c 1958]
    ISBN 0-88268-203-2 (pbk : alk. paper)
    I. Cancer-Diet Therapy-Case Studies 1. Title
    [DNLM: 1. Neoplasms- therapy. Not Acquired]
RC271.D52G47 1997
616.99'406-DC21
DNLM/DLC
for Library of Congress
                              96-50956
                              CIP

Printed in the United States of America

The names Gerson® and Gerson Therapy® are worldwide trademarks, service marks, and/or registered trademarks or servicemarks of the Gerson Institute. All Rights Reserved. Used by permission.

The information contained in this book is for educational and scientific purposes only. Do not undertake any medical treatment or dietary changes without the advice and support of an appropriately licensed healthcare practitioner.

Preface to the Sixth Edition

Max Gerson, M.D. had the wisdom, foresight, and courage to look beyond the prevailing medical views of his day. Out of 30 years of clinical experimentation, he arrived at some then-radical concepts:

- Diet has a considerable effect on almost all diseases
- The human body can heal itself given the appropriate nutrients
- Any effective treatment for degenerative disease must treat the whole person
- People with serious illnesses must help their body detoxify

While these ideas sound sensible today, they were almost blasphemous in the 1940s and 1950s.

More than 40 years have passed since Max Gerson, M.D. died in March of 1959. At that time, most cancers were not considered curable by orthodox medicine, and the American Medical Association and American Cancer Society both flatly rejected the notion that diet could have any effect on either the prevention or treatment of cancer.

In spite of the fierce resistance to his ideas and methods, Max Gerson worked virtually alone to treat and heal many cancers considered to be terminal, as well as numerous other diseases. He worked to publish and share information as best he could about the methods he had developed. At the time of this printing in 1999, cancer survival rates remain virtually unchanged, and the number of new cancer diagnoses has continued to increase each year. Certain diseases (cancers of liver, lung, and pancreas, among others) are still virtual death sentences. New diagnoses of previously rare diseases are growing at an alarming rate. The "War on Cancer" declared by then-president Nixon in 1971 has, for most cancers, neither decreased the number of new diagnoses, nor improved survival for those already diagnosed.

For over 20 years, the Gerson Institute has worked to help patients recover from these otherwise "incurable" diseases, and to share knowledge of, and continue research and development of the safe, effective Gerson Therapy approach to healing cancer and other degenerative diseases. When we started in 1977, almost no one would listen to what we had to say. We were unable to treat patients in the United States because medical boards threatened the licenses of physicians who deviated from conventional treatment methods. Only the desperately ill and dying, "given up" by their doctors, sought our help. In spite of the difficulties, we succeeded in helping hundreds of patients recover from otherwise terminal diseases, teaching thousands more to take steps to improve health and prevent the development of disease.

Today, fortunately, much has changed. Many patients are now demanding (and receiving) from their insurance companies the option of pursuing holistic treatment. A growing number of states have established separate, independent licensing boards for practitioners using natural methods. Other states have passed laws requiring insurance companies to pay for alternative care, or specifically protecting practitioners using natural methods from reprisals by their medical boards. The National Institutes of Health has established an Office of Alternative Medicine, dedicated to research and validation of holistic methods of treatment. Independent medical researchers have documented and verified the biochemical basis for many important elements of the Gerson Therapy in more than 300 articles in the peer-reviewed medical literature.

All of these factors have led to a dramatic increase in interest in Gerson Therapy treatment. Today, our staff handles as many as 300 inquiries a day from those seeking information on Gerson Therapy medical education programs, referrals to practitioners, treatment centers, halfway houses, and therapy assistants. Patients are seeking Gerson treatment as a first choice, rather than a last hope. For those interested in medical training, the Gerson Institute maintains certification programs for physicians, treatment centers, and home care assistants. We are actively working to establish certified treatment centers and medical practitioners worldwide. Contact us for current offerings.

While there are many paths to wellness, the Gerson Therapy is, in our opinion, the most complete, all-encompassing approach for comprehensive healing. Our continuing research is designed to ensure that we maintain and improve our ability to heal and prevent diseases, enhance well-being and longevity, and help individuals operate at their peak potential for a long and satisfying life into the 21st century and beyond.

Charlotte Gerson
Founder, Gerson Institute
June 1999

DEDICATED TO MY WIFE
MARGARET

Acknowledgments

I FEEL INDEBTED to express my deep gratitude first to my daughter, Gertrude Selten, for her active cooperation as the manager of the Cancer Clinic and her untiring help in the further development of this new therapy.

Among the physicians, I wish to express my indebtedness to Dr. Joseph Ziegler, Roentgenologist, for his loyal help in preparing valuable X-ray pictures and objective explanations; Dr. Kurt Heinrich for his exact urological and cystoscopic findings; the late Dr. James V. Ricci for his precise gynecological reports and the late Dr. Jonas Borak for his enthusiastic intellectual stimulus; and Professor Dr. Werner Kollath, Germany, for his ideal manner of transforming problems into realistic biological material.

My eldest daughter, Johanna Oberlander, helped energetically in the translation and organization of this work. My youngest daughter, Lotte Straus, helped wherever she could with great interest and understanding encouragement. My secretary, Erna Harding, worked diligently with enduring perseverance in typing this manuscript.

I wish to acknowledge with deep gratitude the cooperation and encouragement received from the Foundation for Cancer Treatment, Inc., a non-profit organization formed many years ago by grateful patients for the purpose of perpetuating the treatment as described in this book. To the following directors of the Foundation, I would like to express my special thanks: Professor Dr. Albert Schweitzer, Professor Henry Schaefer-Simmern, Mr. Carl Gropler, Rev. Dr. Erwin Seale, Professor Fulmer Mood, Mr. Louis J. Rosenthal and Mr. Arnold J. Oberlander.

Without the aid and encouragement of my wife, Margaret, I could not have written this book. To her, I have dedicated this work.

MAX GERSON, M.D.

This publication is an exemplification of the work of Max Gerson, M.D., on his treatment of cancer as disclosed to the United States Senate in public hearings held July 1, 2 and 3, 1946. It is designed as a report on his continued work in cancer treatment, and will be filed with the United States Senate when it again resumes hearings on means of curing and preventing cancer. The title page of the U. S. Senate Committee report, containing 227 pages, follows:

CANCER RESEARCH

HEARINGS

before a

Subcommittee of the

COMMITTEE ON FOREIGN RELATIONS
UNITED STATES SENATE
SEVENTY-NINTH CONGRESS
Second Session
on
S. 1875

A Bill to authorize and request the President to undertake to mobilize at some convenient place in the United States an adequate number of the World's Outstanding Experts, and coordinate and utilize their services in a Supreme Effort to Discover Means of Curing and Preventing Cancer.

July 1, 2 and 3, 1946

———

Printed for the use of the Committee on Foreign Relations

———

UNITED STATES
GOVERNMENT PRINTING OFFICE
WASHINGTON: 1946

89471

Contents

PART II

PART
I

Introduction

THIS BOOK has been written to indicate that there is an effective treatment of cancer, even in advanced cases. For that reason it is necessary to acquaint the reader with observations and data in the cancer problem which are used in the accepted cancer treatments. The history of medicine has shown that many physicians adhere to their accustomed treatment with great tenacity, and often evidence very strong "allergic" reactions against everything that could possibly change their customary therapeutic methods.

It is very well known that great difficulties exist, and that many objections may be raised against publication of a cancer therapy which differs from the accepted methods. The time is ripe, however, to wipe out the deep pessimism which most physicians have about everything that assumes to be therapeutically effective in degenerative diseases and especially in cancer.

At this time, of course, it is not possible to replace a century-long pessimism with an overwhelming optimism. We all know that everything in biology is not as precise as in mathematics or physics. I fear that it will not be possible, at least in the near future, to repair all the damage that modern agriculture and civilization have brought to our lives. I believe it is essential that people unite, in the old conservative manner, for the humanitarian purpose of producing nutrition for their families and future generations as natural and unrefined as possible.

The coming years will make it more and more imperative that organically grown fruit and vegetables will be, and must be, used for protection against degenerative diseases, the prevention of cancer, and more so in the treatment of cancer.

3

According to present government statistics, one out of every six persons in our population will die of cancer. It will not be long before the entire population will have to decide whether we will all die of cancer or whether we will have enough wisdom, courage, and will power to change fundamentally all our living and nutritional conditions. For "Cancer is a phenomenon coexistent with the living process . . ."[1]

We will again need real housewives, not eager to save kitchen time, but homemakers who will devote their lives to the benefit of all, especially the task of developing and maintaining a healthy family. Babies would no longer be fed by a formula but would have the natural mother's milk; they would grow up without being afflicted with a fatal disease such as leukemia, and without being mentally retarded, both conditions which are increasing rapidly at present.

For the future of coming generations, I think it is high time that we change our agriculture and food preservation methods. Otherwise, we will have to increase our institutions for mental patients yearly, and we will see the hospitals overcrowded with degenerative diseases even more rapidly and in greater numbers than the hospitals themselves can be enlarged. Seventy years ago, leukemia was unknown in the United States. Fifty years ago, lung cancer was so seldom observed in clinics and autopsies that every case was worthy of publication. But today—what a change for the worse. (*O quae mutatio rerum.*)

The practice of the treatment is a difficult task. The treatment in the hospital as well as in the home requires somebody's help all day long, particularly in advanced cases where a life is at stake and the patient is very weak. The family has to give up some of the social life and do this humanitarian work with deep devotion. The decline in our modern life is evident by this lack of devotion for the sick members of the family.

This is a short outline of the contents of this book.

Facts and proofs of fifty cancer cases have been placed in the foreground, while theories and explanations have been shortened.

---

[1] Jesse Greenstein, *Biochemistry of Cancer*, p. 598, 1954.

CHAPTER I

The "Secret" of my Treatment

OF COURSE, there is none! The heading is used because I am asked frequently, often reproachfully, by physicians about it.

The harmony in the metabolism of all internal organs and systems must be maintained; it reflects the eternal mystery of life, expressed in our health and continuance. "Each form of life is a biologic entity. Each has only one purpose: to grow and reproduce with the aid of the food to its disposal."[2] The onset of metabolic disturbance constitutes the beginning of disease.

"The Eternal Life has been developed over millions of years," Kollath said, "and it will continue to develop endlessly. Each of its parts is important. None is privileged, for the internal equilibrium may not be disturbed."[3]

Following historical analysis, we see in Kollath's presentation that it was mainly science and technology which have brought about the evil, a part of it is "oversimplification."

"Symptomatic treatment is harmful wherever in nature it is applied to the soil, plants, animals or human beings, or in medicine.

"Each part is important, but the whole in its infinitely fine order is more important."[4]

History shows that, from time to time, men are swayed too easily by new thoughts and theories and by new developments in technology and chemistry, which they use as their bases in medical practice.[5] This leads them too far away from nature.

---

[2] Quote of J. F. Wischhusen, Cleveland, Ohio.

[3] See Introduction to Dr. Werner Kollath's book *Die Ordnung Unserer Nahrung.* Hippokrates Verlag, Stuttgart, Germany.

[4] Ibid.

[5] The Reverend Juenger, *Failure of Technology.*

Therefore, it becomes necessary from time to time to bring medical doctrine back nearer to nature. (See chapter on Paracelsus.)

Seeking an explanation for the negative attitude of the majority of physicians toward the idea of an effective cancer treatment, I have come to several conclusions. First, we are all trained to believe that cancer is an incurable disease. Secondly, several previous attempts to introduce a new cancer treatment, including theories and promises, have failed. The great fallacy lies in the manner in which dietary tests are proposed and made, that is, by the use of one special substance at a time, observing its effect on the body, followed by another substance, and so forth.

A long time ago, I worked along the same lines. The result was a failure. Thereupon I started to use almost the same dietary regime developed through years of experience, which I had previously applied in my work in tuberculosis. (*Diättherapie der Lungentuberkulose*, 1934) To observe externally the reactions of the diet and its changes I chose skin tuberculosis, so-called *lupus vulgaris*. Later I used the same procedure in cancer patients by observing the reactions of the diet and its changes in involvements of the skin. These observations showed the treatment inadequate for malignancies of the intestinal tract; these need more intensive treatment. The medication for the tuberculosis treatment and that for cancer treatment were developed in a similar manner, but they are not the same.

From the beginning, the fundamental idea was and still is the following: A normal body has the capacity to keep all cells functioning properly. It prevents any abnormal transformation and growth. Therefore, the natural task of a cancer therapy is to bring the body back to that normal physiology, or as near to it as is possible. The next task is to keep the physiology of the metabolism in that natural equilibrium.

A normal body also has additional reserves to suppress and destroy malignancies. It does not act in that manner in cancer patients, where the cancer grew from the smallest cellular unit freely, without encountering any resistance. What forces can suppress such a development? My answer is that this can be accomplished by the oxidizing enzymes and the conditions which maintain their activity. The best known oxidizing enzymes are: arginase, catalase, xantine dehydrogenase, esterase, the urea oxidizing systems, cystine-desulfurase, cytochrome-c, cytochrome oxidase and amino acid oxidase and flavin. All these are lower in activity in both fetal liver and hepatoma than in normal or regenerating liver. Otto Warburg[6] was the first who found the metabolic deviations of malignant tissue from normal tissue and formulated

it by the co-efficient $\dfrac{\text{anaerobic glycolysis}}{\text{cell respiration}}$

In normal tissue it is zero.

In embryonic tissue   0.1

In benign tumors   0.45 to 1.45

In malignant tissue up to 12.

On the contrary, alkaline phosphatases and the deaminases are higher in activity in fetal liver and hepatoma than in normal and regenerating liver. The very frequently expressed view is that fetal and neoplastic hepatic tissue show a similar oxidizing pattern to embryonic, more primitive, and less differentiated tissue.

It is known that in primitive forms of life the energy of the cells is derived almost entirely from anaerobic conditions or through fermentation. In higher animals, the lower fermentative anaerobic systems are mixed with oxidation systems, whereby more and more molecular oxygen is utilized, transported from the respiration of the lungs. The malignancies in human beings continuously fall back deeper and deeper into fermentation. The major general part of the body becomes more poisoned and more reduced in its defense and healing power.

The ideal task of cancer therapy is to restore the function of the oxidizing systems in the entire organism. This, of course, is difficult to accomplish. It involves the following: 1) detoxication of the whole body, 2) providing the essential mineral contents of the potassium group, 3) adding oxidizing enzymes continuously as long as they are not reactivated and built in the body (in the form of green leaf juice and fresh calf's liver juice*). This will create a near normal condition of the oxidizing system in the body, to which malignant cells with the fermentation system cannot adapt.

Nutrition is generally an exogenous factor, but the intake of food, slightly toxic, below the level of a stimulant, brings about

---

[6] Otto Warburg, *The Metabolism of Tumors*, Constable & Co. Ltd London, 1930.

* See Appendix III. page 421

a disposition in the organism, which may be regarded as premorbid. "Diet, however, appeared to have no influence on liver tumors in rats produced by 2-acetylamino-fluorene. The manner in which diet produces procarcinogenic or anticarcinogenic effect is unknown. Chemical differences between mitochondria of normal liver and mouse liver hepatoma have been reported by Hogeboom and Schneider.

"Some interesting observations in regard to the influence of diet on the development of spontaneous hepatomas in inbred C_3H mice were made by Tannenbaum and Silverstone. These investigators have shown that increase of fat in the diet from two per cent to 20 per cent increased the rate of hepatoma formation from 37 per cent to 53 per cent. Low riboflavin intake resulted in a decrease of hepatoma formation. This can be attributed to the reduced caloric intake, which has been shown to inhibit growth of hepatomas in this species. It has likewise been shown that, contrary to the experiences with induced hepatomas in rats, the spontaneous tumors in mice are not accelerated by a rice diet but on the contrary are accelerated by increased casein content. Methionine has likewise been shown to accelerate the development of these tumors in mice. The conclusion is drawn that the sulphur-containing amino acids, which are necessary for normal growth, are also necessary for growth and development of these neoplasms. Again a startling indication of the similarity between physiologic growth and neoplasia!"[7]

Our modern civilization brings about a premorbid disposition in almost all human beings, differing only in degree. It may be regarded (in some of us) as a pre-neoplastic condition: According to government statistics, this applies to one out of six. The percentage has accelerated in the last 25 years; carcinomas and undefined cancers in mankind are increasing yearly.

Before I was ready to demonstrate my tuberculosis results in the Medical Society of Berlin, H. Zondek asked me to discuss the diet and its effects with the best known nutritional biologist, Professor E. Abderhalden, University Halle a/S . . . After a short discussion his advice was: "It is impossible to explore one or another substance alone. We need, as you did, a simple nutritional groundwork. On this basis you can work out the therapy by

---

[7] Mitchell A. Spellberg, *Disease of the Liver*, Grune and Stratton, 1954, p. 136.

adding or subtracting one or another substance and observe the effect. Having such results I would not change anything. The same thing is true for medication. Most of it we cannot explain, the result is decisive."

"Nutrition is primarily an exogenous factor, but a constantly changed unnatural nutrition brings about in our organism that internal premorbid disposition."[8] I may add: It is a slowly progressive internal adaptation which the body performs, as *each daily poisonous irritation* level is most probably too low to cause a defensive reaction until a tumor can grow while the body is undefended and poisons continue to accumulate.[9]

After my second lecture at the International Cancer Congress in Germany in October, 1952, Professor Werner Kollath handed me his latest book *Die Ordnung Unserer Nahrung* (The Order of Our Nutrition 1952) with the inscription: "With gratitude for your Doctrine: INCURABLE IS CURABLE."

The secret of my treatment is that the nutritional problem is not well enough understood in view of the knowledge and information on hand at present. Abderhalden's and other scientists' advice helped a great deal to solve the problem in clinical practice. I think the medication is a little more subject to medical argumentation. Both may be two other unsolved problems in medicine; our task is to acknowledge this and to present the favorable results of the treatment.

In a normal body all is alive, especially the basic substances built by the minerals, they have ionized or activated potassium and minerals of the potassium group with positive electrical potentials.

In a sick body—mainly in cancer—potassium is *inactive*—sodium and minerals of the sodium group are ionized with negative potentials. On this basis all other abnormal processes develop as consequences. For healing purposes the body must be detoxified—activated with ionized minerals, natural food so that the essential organs can function again.

For healing the body brings about a kind of inflammation. That is a tremendous transformative reaction. This renders the body hypersensitive or allergic to a high degree against abnormal

---

[8] Professor Siegmund, p. 277. *Ganzheits behandlung der Geschwulsterkrankungen*, 1953. Hippokrates Verlag.
[9] See Leonhard Wickenden's *Our Daily Poison*, Devin-Adair Co., 1955.

or strange substances (including bacilli, cancer cells, scars, etc.). Consequently the more malignant the cells are the more effective is the treatment. I think this is "the end effect or secret of the treatment." The school of von Bergmann did reveal some of the features of the allergic reaction.[10]

A mechanical method and several types of stimulation could not accomplish such a purpose. The attempts of August Bier,[11] H. Lampert, Germany and O. Selawry, Buffalo[12] and others did not succeed in helping degenerative diseases or cancer.

---

[10] See chapter seventeen.

[11] *Hyperaemie als Heilmittel.*

[12] *Tumorbeeinflussung durch Hyperthermie und Hyperaemie.* Karl F. Haug Verlag, Ulm a.d. Donau, 1957.

CHAPTER II

The Concept of Totality-Decisive in Cancer and Other Degenerative Diseases

CANCER IS a chronic, degenerative disease, where almost all essential organs are involved in the more advanced cases: The entire metabolism with the intestinal tract and its adnexa, the liver and pancreas, the circulatory apparatus (the cellular exchange supporter), the kidneys and bile system (as main elimination organs), the reticulo-endothelial and lymphatic system (as defense apparatus), the central nervous system and especially the visceral nervous system for most metabolic and motoric purposes.

Dr. Nichols was probably one of the first in our time who recognized the "concept of totality" as applied to disease. He combined the following clinical appearances: Emotional, nutritional, poisons, infections, accidents and inheritance as underlying causes for diseases: "No wonder we are all sick . . . and science is no longer science when it attempts to violate God's natural law."[13]

He did not mention degenerative diseases in general, and did not approach the cancer problem in his article. However, his idea shows in many respects progress in the concept of acute and chronic diseases.

Some cancer biologists are of the opinion that "cancer is a phenomenon co-existent with the living processes," "that the cancer cell is not something living exclusively from the body," and that the cancer cell is not a special "system isolated from the living organism." *They are united with and part of the whole*

---

[13] See *The Texas Bankers Record* for May, 1952, Lee Fdt., No. 58.

body. There, all is arranged according to the fundamental rules of nature, where dynamic forces are combined and arranged *in harmony in a well functioning body.*

The vitamins work together with the enzymes; therefore, they are called co-enzymes. The enzymes function only when the other conditions in the cell are normal and active. They are combined with reactivated hormones and united with the right mineral composition.

It has been emphasized before that cancer develops in a body which more or less has lost the normal functions of the metabolism as a consequence of a chronic daily poisoning accumulated especially in the liver.[14] It is important to realize that in our body all the innermost processes work together, depend on each other, and will be deranged with each other in diseases. That is the reason why all of them together have to be attacked for healing purposes at the base and in combination. My clinical experiences revealed that this is the surest way to the success of a therapy. Most parts of the general metabolism can be found concentrated in the liver. The biological function of the liver itself, however, depends on the proper activity and correct cooperation of many other essential organs.

I found the ideas of totality more profoundly developed in the ancient work of Paracelsus, and many other physicians of long ago.

It is not only in biology where the idea of totality is to be regarded as an entity of the natural processes; it is also the rule in art, in philosophy, in music, in physics, where the most learned scholars found the concept of totality alive in their fields of research and work. As a few samples, I would like to mention first Henry Drumond's philosophical work *Natural Law in the Spiritual World* (1883). The basis of it is expressed in his words: "The continuity of the physical world to the spiritual." This means the coherence of the physical inorganic powers as they are transferred basically into the organic world of plants and animals. In man, there are the electrical potentials outstanding in the life of the cells. They are especially accumulated in the nervous system, which is ultimately our "spiritual organ" capable of creating progress and great accomplishments.

---

[14] *Our Daily Poison* by Leonard Wickenden, Devin-Adair Co., New York, 1955.

In physics, Albert Einstein's first great work was *Relativity of Space and Time*. At first the theory was considered fantastic. Later it was generally accepted. Einstein's advanced studies dealt with a transformation of light and the photoelectric effect. Finally, his "transformation theory" attempted to include gravity, magnetism, and electricity into one basic physical system, which he called the Unified Field View—*most difficult to prove*.

In art, as an example of this concept, is the work of Schaefer-Simmern, who took the explanation of art out of the narrow limitations of the old rational principles and demonstrated that art is a "creative power," inherent in our brain functions, developing according to the body's growth, mental, emotional and intellectual maturity. Schaefer-Simmern said that "The creative potentialities in men and in women, in business and the professions, are always present as an entity," united with all other powers of the body. Schaefer-Simmern used art to "unfold the inherent artistic ability in the education of children," since it may become the decisive factor in the groundwork of a culture that rests on the creative nature of man.[15]

Norbert Wiener, Professor of Mathematics at M.I.T., writes: "There are fields of scientific work which have been explored from the different sides of pure mathematics, statistics, electrical engineering and neurophysiology, in which each single notion receives a separate name from each group, and in which important work has been triplicated or quadruplicated; while still other important work has been delayed by the unavailability in one field of results that may have already become classical in the next field."[16]

Medical science has eliminated the totality of the natural biological rules in the human body, mostly by dividing research and practice into many specialities. Doing intensive, masterly specialized work, it was forgotten that every part is still only a piece of the entire body.

In all textbooks, we find that single biological processes have been studied and overestimated statements made about them. The symptoms of a disease have become the main problem for research, clinical work and therapy. The old methods which

---

[15] See Schaefer-Simmern's *The Unfolding of Artistic Activity*, 1950. University of California Press. Berkeley and Los Angeles.
[16] Norbert Wiener, *Cybernetics*, 1953, p. 8.

sought to combine all functional parts in a body into a biological entity, have been pushed aside almost involuntarily, in the clinic, and especially in institutions of physiology and pathology. Finally, that idea became very remote in our thinking and therapeutical work. The opinion of the best cancer specialists is, as Jessie Greenstein stated, "Emphasis must be laid on a *direct* study on the side of malignancy itself,"[17] despite the fact that his book is an excellent collection of physiological changes in the other organs, especially the liver. In my opinion, the application of the concept of totality can help us find the true cause of cancer; it could be best worked out in practical examples, not in animal experiments where every little symptom is observed singly (by itself).

In the nutritional field, observations for centuries have shown that people who live according to natural methods in which plants, animals and human beings are only fragments of the eternal cycle of Nature do not get cancer. On the contrary, people who accept methods of modern nutrition on an increasing scale become involved in degenerative diseases, including cancer, in a relatively short time.

In later medical history, the best known cancer-free people were the Hunzas, who live on the slopes of the Himalaya mountains and who use only food grown in their own country and fertilized with natural manure. Imported food is forbidden. Very similar is the story of the Ethiopians who also have natural agriculture and living habits which seems to prove that this type of agriculture keeps people free of cancer and most of the degenerative diseases.

The damage that modern civilization brings into our lives begins with the soil, where artificial fertilization leads to the displacement of mineral contents and changes in the flora of microbes combined with the exodus of the earthworms. Consequently, frequent erosion of arable land takes place. These changes bring about, at the beginning, an irritation of the plants; later they cause their degeneration. Spraying with poisonous substances (insecticides) increases the poisons in the soil, and these poisons are transferred to plants and fruits.

We must conclude from these and many other observations that the soil and all that grows in it is not something distant

---

[17] Jesse Greenstein, *Biochemistry of Cancer*, p. 598, 1954.

from us but must be regarded as *our external metabolism,* which produces the basic substances for our internal metabolism. Therefore, the soil must be cared for properly and must not be depleted or poisoned; otherwise, these changes will result in serious degenerative diseases, rapidly increasing in animals and human beings. The soil needs activity—the natural cycle in growth and in rest— and natural fertilizer, as we have to give back that which is necessary to replenish the consumed substances. This is the best protection against erosion; it also maintains the soil's microbic flora, productivity and life. Food planted and grown in this way must be eaten partly as living substances and partly freshly prepared, for "life begets life." Very significant are reports about Eskimos who get degenerative diseases and cancer in those parts of their country where canned food and unnatural nutrition were introduced and accepted.

Dr. Albert Schweitzer, who built a hospital in Lambarene, Central Africa, 40 years ago, reported in his letters of October, 1954, the following:

"Many natives, especially those who are living in larger communities, do not live now the same way as formerly—they used to live almost exclusively on fruits and vegetables, bananas, cassava, ignam, taro, sweet potatoes and other fruits. They now live on condensed milk, canned butter, meat- and fish-preserves and bread." Dr. Schweitzer observed in 1954 the first operation on appendicitis on a native of this region. ". . . The date of the appearance of cancer and other diseases of civilization cannot be traced in our region with the same certainty as that of appendicitis, because the microscopic examinations have only been in existance here for a few years. . . . It is obvious to connect the fact of increase of cancer also with increased use of salt by the natives. . . . Curiously enough, we did not have any cancer cases in our hospitals before."

Dr. Salisbury reported, concerning the Navajo Indians, that he had, in 23 years, 35,000 Indian admissions in the hospital, with only 66 cases of cancer. The death rate among these Indians is one out of 1,000, while it is about one out of 500 among Indians who have accepted part of the nutrition of modern civilization.

The Bantu population of South Africa has 20 per cent primary liver cancers. Their diet, of a very low standard, consists chiefly of cheap carbohydrates, maize and mealy meals. Seldom do they have fermented cow's milk. Meat is eaten only at ceremonies. Two physicians, Drs. Gilbert and Gilman, studied their nutrition habits in animal experiments and placed stress on the diet of the Bantus as a cause of cancer. The result was that in almost all animals the liver was affected and 20 per cent developed a cirrhosis of the liver later. When an extract of the liver of a Bantu man was painted on the back of mice, benign or malignant tumors developed.

At the conclusion of this chapter, the reader may well ask: "What should I do with the idea of the concept of totality in understanding the cancer problem and treatment?" The answer is: the "premorbid damage" goes down to the basic vital processes by poisoning the entire metabolism as it was acknowledged in Germany at the International Congress for *Ganzheitsbehandlung der Geschwulsterkrankungern.*[18] Professor Siegmund, of the University of Muenster, explained that this poisoning occurs *now* as a general constitutional condition which is caused by modern civilization and which is not only a preneoplastic stage but also a premorbid general condition of the human body.[19]

Therefore, the treatment also has to penetrate deeply to correct all the *vital* processes. When the general metabolism is corrected, we can influence again retrospective functioning of all other organs, tissues, and cells through it. This means that there should be a treatment applied which will fulfill the task of totality in every respect, taking care of the functions of the whole body in all its different parts, thus restoring the harmony of all biological systems. The treatment which will fulfill this complex problem is described in detail later. Here it should merely be emphasized that the treatment has to fulfill two fundamental components. The first component is the detoxication of the *whole* body which has to be carried out over a long period of time, until all the tumors are absorbed and the essential organs of the body are so far restored that they can take over this important "cleaning function" by themselves. If that is not effected to the necessary degree, the entire body becomes the victim of a continuously increasing poisoning with dire consequences (coma hepaticum). Secondly, the entire intestinal tract has to be restored simultane-

---

[18] Professor W. Zabel, *Totality Treatment of Tumorous Diseases,* Hippokrates Verlag, 1953.
[19] Professor Siegmund, *op. cit.,* p. 277.

ously; with the restoration of the intestinal tract, the most important secretory functions will be repaired, as well as its circulation and motility regulated by the visceral nervous system. In that way we can activate, together with other functions, defense, immunity and healing power in the body. Immunity does not mean here that the body is protected against a special bacterium; as in an infectious disease, it means that no abnormal cell can grow or develop in the body with normal metabolism. For that purpose, the degree of restoration of the liver plays a decisive role. We should not forget that a body detoxified constantly through the liver and the best nutrition can maintain an active metabolism with the help of the liver. Thus, the concept of totality will be obeyed in medicine as it is active in other living and non-living processes of nature. The same is true in the field of nutrition.

According to a report at the third International Congress of Biochemistry, "A knowledge of the interrelationships among nutrients in a diet is essential for an understanding of their quantitative requirements for the animals. Utilization of one nutrient may be profoundly affected by the presence or absence of another. For instance, under certain circumstances the toxicity of zinc in rats may be corrected by copper, the presence of both molybdenum and zinc in any diet may result in significantly poorer growth than was caused by the addition of these elements separately (20). Selenium poisoning may be reduced by arsenic (7); molybdenum poisoning in cattle may be corrected by copper (12). Intravenously administered methionine prevented the toxicity of high doses of cobalt (21). There is less absorption of iron from the gastro-intestinal tract in rats deficient in copper than in rats supplied with copper (22).

"These observations and many others reaffirm the finding that an abnormal condition of the animal may not reflect merely a low or a high level of dietary essential, but an excess or a shortage of one or more other nutrients which interfere with the normal metabolism of the essential dietary constituent.

"One of the most striking examples of this kind concerns the assimilation and storage of copper in sheep (23). It was found in Australia that the addition of ferrous sulphide to the diet lowered the expected copper accumulation in the liver by 75 per cent. Zinc given in an amount of 100 mg. a day had an effect which was significant at the five per cent level, but when added in smaller amounts which would be available to sheep grazing normal pastures, it had no effect on copper retention.

"Molybdenum given in the form of ammonium molybdate was found to have a severly limiting effect, but this effect was only observed when the diet also contained a sufficient quantity of inorganic sulphate. . . .

"The nature of the interrelationship of one microelement with another and with other food constituents is still imperfectly or not at all understood. It is my opinion that it is within the scope of the biochemists' and nutritionists' major duties to clear up the obscurity in this domain as soon as possible."[20]

These examples are chosen to illustrate the biological fact that not one factor alone or a combination of single factors is decisive, but what is decisive is how they influence the *whole body, mind and soul in their entirety.*

To the great complexity of the biological functions of the body belongs also its *capacity of adaptation.* A healthy body can adapt itself to different types of nutrition. It reabsorbs the necessary minerals, vitamins and enzymes as we know from experiments to determine the time for the clinical appearance of one or another vitamin deficiency. A sick body has lost this capacity. The deficiencies cannot be restored as long as the essential organs are poisoned. That is true in cancer also, as demonstrated by clinical observations.

Cancer, the great killer, will be prevented and can be cured if we learn to understand the eternal laws of totality in nature and in our body. Both are combined and have to be united in an effective treatment for cancer; in that way we can learn to ⁻ure cancer in a higher proportion, even of advanced cases. The imitations of the totality of functions of the whole body, however, also come into action here. The totality of functions is lost if *one or another* vital organ is too far destroyed. I saw, in several patients, tumors in the abdomen absorbed, and in others, hundreds of nodules and nodes on the skin and some at the base of the brain eliminated, but the patients died of cirrhosis of the liver in a period of one to three and a half years afterwards.

The role of the liver in cancer, according to Ewing, is seen in the fact that there are about 85 per cent of primary hepatomas

---

[20] L. Seekles in *Proceedings of the Third International Congress of Biochemistry,* Brussels, 1955, p. 47.

and 50 per cent of primary cholangiomas associated with cirrhosis of the liver. The majority of authors think these changes in the liver have arisen independently of, and probably before the growth of neoplasm, as changes are diffuse and far removed from the local tumor. Dr. Ewing states, furthermore, that there is a uniform gradual process between nodular hyperplasia of the liver, multiple adenomas, and multiple carcinomas. The usual progress from adenoma to carcinoma is abundantly supplied in literature. These observations were verified in experimental work with carcinogens which brought about an apparent progression from regenerative tissue of the liver to hyperplasia and finally to neoplasia. Rats fed butter-yellow with a rice diet showed cirrhosis of the liver in sixty days and benign cholangiomas and hepatomas in ninety days, and, in 150 days, carcinomas in nearly all rats, damaging especially the liver, producing high anaerobic glycolysis, alkaline phosphatase and other abnormalities. The protective effect of a diet, consisting of B vitamins and casein on formations of experimental hepatic carcinoma, may permit some comparison with the human disease. It was found, however, that all these results greatly vary with the type of animal and also whether tumors were grown as induced or appeared as spontaneous hepatomas, and vary even more so in human hepatomas. Therefore, it became impossible to find a decisive factor in the vast literature of the production of these malignancies, as physicians looked and are still looking for one specific factor only. The solution is that it is not a single factor but generally one of many factors or an accumulation of one poisoning for a long period of time as the experiments of Itchikawa and Yamagiva show. They needed about nine months first to damage the liver, kidneys, etc.—another proof of reactions in their totality. That a very strong poison can damage the liver in a few days and produce a hepatoma in ten days does not speak against it. This cannot be compared with the slowly progressive deterioration in our system caused by modern civilization.

From work in our clinic, we know that many diseases do not appear independent of each other, but more as "nosological entities." A few examples: (A) Sinus inflammation is frequently combined with chronic bronchitis or bronchiectasis, also with laryngitis, nephritis, and other distant infections. (B) Chronic cystitis is frequently united with appendicitis. Surely, cystitis is associated with a combination of disturbances in the digestive organs. (C) Gall-bladder diseases, mostly combined with liver alterations, appear together with myocardial changes and later cause cirrhosis of the liver. Consequently, where the defense of the body is essentially reduced there frequently are bacterial infections of one or several organs. These clinical findings bring us to the conclusion that several different types of pathological changes may occur as the consequence of a deep general cause in the body which we can subordinate under one leading idea, the law of totality or the loss or diminished degree of "healing power" in a more clinical sense. Despite our great progress in modern biochemistry, we cannot depart from the old Hippocratian doctrine of direct and objective clinical observation: to coordinate them under one clinical picture. In infectious diseases, there would not have been transmissions to neighboring or distant organs, in malignancies not metastases, if there were enough healing power present. Thus, the development of disease, its course and healing process, do not depend so much on the type of tissue or organ involved, but more on the general healing power of the entire organism, united or centralized in all its metabolic processes for the most part concentrated in the liver.

Contrary to this concept, our textbooks and journals have separated different diseases and even cancers as malignant tumors of the nose and paranasal sinuses, malignancies of the stomach or the kidney, cancer of the lungs, etc. There are, of course, differences in the type, development, complications, prognosis, etc., but the basic idea must be maintained that the defense and healing power is an essential part of the *whole* body and must be *restored*, whatever organ or organs may be involved or whatever cause the malignancy may have had. I repeat: In general, the recovery from a malignancy means the restoration of the whole body from a kind of degeneration. In some cases of external cancers—skin and breast—the local treatment may be sufficient, but the concept of totality is a superior and farther-reaching approach as the facts indicate in cases listed in this volume. (See part II)

CHAPTER III

Directions for General Nutrition

IN FORMER times, nutrition was traditionally developed by the conditions of the particular country and historic events. It was controlled by religion or states, and materially adapted to the finances of families or individuals. The modifications in our culture and the progress in science and technique are altering our food constantly by its production in agriculture, by preservation and distribution, and also by adaptation to the improvements of living conditions. These problems[21] must be disregarded here, since I can give only the essential general directions.

To describe the fundamentals of a general nutrition for healthy people which guarantees an uninterrupted daily flux of energy, strength and reserves for work and other duties, is a responsible task and difficult to formulate in a comprehensive form without many tables, literature and explanations. The way in which the fundamentals are described here is derived from many long years of experience with people rejected from military service or denied life insurance.

They were made acceptable by following these directions. Thousands of patients were given this advice after their recovery from chronic sicknesses, and most of them included their families in this pattern of nutrition for many years. The results were satisfactory. The majority remained in good health, were acceptable for life insurance and other services and increased their strength and working power. My family and I, too, have followed these directions for more than thirty years.

---

[21] See *History of Nutrition* by Alfred W. McCann, Science of Eating, Dresden, 1927 and *Die Geschichte Der Ernährung*, by Prof. Lichtenfelt, Berlin, 1913.

This outline permits sufficient margin for personal living habits, family feasts and holidays, as one-quarter of all of the food should be to one's choice; the remainder should be taken for the purpose of protecting the functions of the highly essential organs—liver, kidneys, brain, heart, etc.—by storing reserves and avoiding an unnecessary burden on these vital organs. To save our body from extra work in the disposal of excessive food, especially fats which are difficult to digest, the destruction of poisons, etc., is a precaution that may prevent many kinds of early degeneration, premature old age, and all kinds of acute and chronic sickness in organs somewhat weaker in origin and development or previously damaged. That this outline is written to prevent sickness, not to cure it, must be stressed beforehand. The purpose of healing demands a much deeper dietetic encroachment and a medication directed to the pathology of the body's chemistry after a diagnosis is established.

The fundamentals will not be presented as an enumeration of carbohydrates, fats, proteins, vitamins, hormones and enzymes as they are described in physiology textbooks, together with the necessary amount of grams or calories. These old textbook arrangements meet only the needs of a metabolism based largely on the entire amount of elimination, taking into account only some less essential requirements. As science is not yet developed to the point of knowing all the enzymes, vitamins and many biological functions of hormones and minerals, it is safer to use foods in the most natural form, combined and mixed by nature and raised, if possible, by an organic gardening process, thus obeying the laws of nature. This observation helped the human race for thousands of years before any science was developed. In this way we bring in all known vitamins and enzymes, both the discovered and the undiscovered ones, and especially the unknown, to quote Professor Kollath, "life stimulating substances," given best as fresh as possible and not damaged by refining or preserving processes, such as canned food. These contain all of the necessary substances in their proper quantity, mixture and composition, and are regulated by instinct, hunger, taste, smell, sight and other factors.

Three-quarters of the food which should be consumed include the following:

All kinds of fruits, mostly fresh and some prepared in different ways; freshly prepared fruit juices (orange, grapefruit, grape, etc.); fruit salads; cold fruit soups; mashed bananas, raw grated apples, applesauce, etc.

All vegetables freshly prepared, some stewed in their own juices and others either raw or finely grated, such as carrots, cauliflower or celery; vegetable salads, soups, etc.; some dried fruits and vegetables are permitted but not frozen ones.

Potatoes are best when baked; the contents may be mashed with milk or soup; they should seldom be fried and preferably boiled in their jackets.

Salads of green leaves or mixed with tomatoes, fruits, vegetables, etc.

Bread may contain whole rye or whole wheat flour, or these may be mixed; it should be refined as little as possible. Oatmeal should be used freely. Buckwheat cakes and potato pancakes are optional, as are brown sugar, honey, maple sugar and maple candy.

Milk and milk products, such as pot cheese and other kinds of cheese which are not greatly salted or spiced, buttermilk, yoghurt and butter. Cream and ice cream should be reduced *to a minimum* or restricted to holidays (ice cream is "poison" for children).

The remaining one-fourth of the dietary regime, which allows for personal choice, may consist of meat, fish, eggs, nuts, candies, cakes, or whatever one likes best. Nicotine should be avoided; liquors, wine and beer should be reduced to a minimum in favor of fresh fruit juices; coffee and tea should be cut to a minimum with the exception of the following teas: peppermint, camomile, linden flower, orange flower, and a few others.

Salt, bicarbonate of soda, smoked fish and sausage should be avoided as much as possible, as should sharp condiments such as pepper and ginger, but fresh garden herbs should be used— onions, parsley leaves, chives, celery and even some horseradish.

As for vegetables and fruits, they should, I repeat, be stewed in their own juices to avoid the loss of minerals easily dissolved in water during cooking. It seems that these valuable minerals are not so well absorbed when they are out of their colloidal state.

All vegetables may be used. Especially recommended for their mineral content are carrots, peas, tomatoes, Swiss chard, spinach, string beans, Brussels sprouts, artichokes, beets cooked with apples, cauliflower with tomatoes, red cabbage with apples, raisins, etc.

The best way to prepare vegetables is to cook them slowly for one and one-half to two hours, without water. To prevent burning, place an asbestos mat under the saucepan. You may also use some stock of soup (see Diet: special soup) or else sliced tomatoes may be added to the vegetables. This also will improve the taste. Spinach water is too bitter for use; it generally is not liked and should be drained off. Onions, leeks and tomatoes have enough liquid of their own to keep them moist while cooking. (Beets should be cooked like potatoes, in their jackets and with water.) Wash and scrub vegetables thoroughly, but do not peel or scrape them. Saucepans must be tightly covered to prevent steam from escaping. Covers must be heavy or close fitting. Cooked vegetables may be kept in the refrigerator overnight. To warm them, heat slowly with a little soup or fresh tomato juice.

An explanation for the importance of the absorption of these minerals was propounded by V. Bunge, who said that there must be more K or potassium in the organs in general than Na or sodium, and that a certain relationship between K and Na must be maintained.

K has to be predominant chiefly within the cells (called, therefore, intracellular) while Na has to stay outside the cells in serum, lymph, connective tissue (therefore called extracellular). Later observations led to the opinion that the minerals do not react singly but in groups. As a consequence, Dr. Rudolph Keller established the doctrine of two mineral groups, the intracellular (potassium) or anodic group traveling to the anode, and the extracellular (sodium) or cathodic group traveling to the cathode under biological conditions. A further consequence was the discovery that hormones, vitamins and enzymes obey the same rule as the two mineral groups; this means that their function depends upon the prevalence of the K-group within the cells of the organs and tissues such as the liver, muscles, brain, heart, kidney cortex, etc., whereas the Na-group remains outside of them. The Na-group is stationed in fluids and tissues: serum, lymph, connective tissue, thyroid, bile ducts, etc. Here are also the cathodic or negative vitamins and enzymes, of which the main functions, metabolism and storage, are confined to this extracellular group.

It is impossible to visualize a metabolism without the mentioning of hormones, vitamins and enzymes; their particular functions shall not be itemized. Generally hormones give individuality to tissues and cells; vitamins, or co-enzymes, help metabolic differentiation and vitality, and enzymes bring about, step by step, metabolic activity and specific digestive processes (general dehydrogenation and oxidation), prevent intermedial metabolites of which some are poisonous and may lead to cataract, stone formation or chronic inflammations. The normal metabolism depends upon the combined function of all of them, even if each of them possesses various ways and means of functioning.

To the K-group belong about 60 per cent of body tissues and to the Na-group 30 per cent; 10 per cent are on the borderline. All of them are kept in their proper place, probably by means of their electrical potentials. During the day, some Na penetrates the potassium tissues, and this is followed by chloride and water, a process which brings on fatigue, a little heaviness or swelling. At night, it is reabsorbed and in the morning it is eliminated in urine, and the person feels refreshed.

TABLE I—Mineral Content per Kilogram of the Whole Body at Different Ages[22]

Whole Body	Extracellular							Intracellular		
	Na Gm	Meq	Cl Gm	Meq	Water %	K Gm	Meq	P Gm	mM	Fat %
Fetus, 3-4 months	—	—	2.7	76	93	—	—	2.14	69	0.5
Fetus, 5 "	2.58	112	2.5	70	91	2.00	51	3.58	115	1.2
Fetus, 6 "	2.16	94	2.5	70	87	1.62	41	3.82	123	2.5
Fetus, 7 "	2.14	93	2.6	73	86	1.88	43	3.82	123	2.5
Premature, 7 "	2.42	105	2.7	75	85	1.71	44	3.82	123	3.0
New-born	1.78	78	2.0	56	80	1.90	49	3.40	174	12.0
Adult	1.09	48	1.56	42	72	2.65	68	11.6	374	18.0

These biological rules are vital for the *maintenance* of *health* inasmuch as a deficiency, defect or change means sickness. Almost all acute and chronic sicknesses begin with an invasion by Na, chloride and water of the anodic organs, causing the so-called edema produced by poisons, infections, trauma, etc. It seems to me, therefore, that some tables with short explanations are indispensable to mark how deeply the functions of the minerals are implanted in the animal's body.

[22] A. Shohl, *Mineral Metabolism*, 1939, pp. 19-20.

Table 1 represents the mineral groups in the development of the body from fetus to adult, proving that the fetus, taken as a whole, is first an animal prevalent in Na-group but later Na, chloride and water decrease from 112 milliequivalents Na to 48, while from the K-group, K increased from 51 meq. to 68; phosphorous increases from 69 to 374, etc. This relationship has to be maintained throughout our life because, as mentioned above, the function of the essential hormones, vitamins, and enzymes is adapted and based on that $\dfrac{K}{Na}$ relationship or better, on the two groups of K and Na, the pH content, co-enzymes, etc.

Table 2 indicates the great importance of the $\dfrac{K}{Na}$ relationship in woman's milk compared with the milk of rats and cows:

TABLE II—Comparison of K/Na Ratio of Rat's, Cow's and Woman's Milks[23]

	Rat's Milk Meq./L	Cow's Milk Meq./L	Woman's Milk Meq./L
$\dfrac{K}{Na}$	$\dfrac{43}{33} = 1.30$	$\dfrac{39.5}{26.5} = 1.49$	$\dfrac{12.2}{5.0} = 2.44$

TABLE III—Retention of Na and K in Daily Mineral Balance of Artificially Fed Infant[24]

	Intake		Excretion				Retention	
			Urine		Feces			
	mg.	meq.	mg.	meq.	mg.	meq.	mg.	meq.
From extracellular —								
Sodium	422	18	300	13	78	3	43	2
Chloride	788	22	651	18	13	1	123	3
From intracellular —								
Potassium	1182	30	785	20	104	3	293	7
Phosphorous	804	42	457	26	210	10	137	8

Tables 4 and 5 may prove that this relationship is reversed in sickness. While the tissues lost the power to retain the K-minerals and glycogen, these decreased (see Table 4) from 20.6 to 5.08, then sodium chloride and water invade the tissue cells from extracellular fluids, thus causing an increasing rise in the milk of Na from 13.02 to 42.37:

---

[23] Ibid., p. 73.
[24] Ibid., p. 327.

TABLE IV

	K-Group				Na-Group		
	K_2O	P_2O_5	MgO	CaO	Na_2O	Cl	SO_3
Normal Milk	20.6	26.4	2.72	21.55	13.02	15.58	3.66
"Salzige Milch" Bofold and Stein (pathological)	10.96	15.63	2.16	11.7	33.77	25.23	6.73
Hashimoto	8.94	17.38	1.74	7.44	36.54	33.63	1.34
Udder Catarrh Schrodt	10.56	24.56	2.7	16.77	24.92	24.52	1.56
Tuberculous Cows Storch	10.87	7.1	1.27	4.34	40.6	—	5.08
a) Normal udder	12.64	22.22	2.1		21.79	27.99	—
b) Tuberculous udder	5.08	8.76	0.79		42.37	44.64	—

TABLE V[25]

	Normal Lens	Cataract Lens
from intracellular		
K	5.1	0.6
P	2.0	1.1
from extracellular		
Ca	0.25	1.0
Na	5.5	12.0

The human body has a wonderful reserve power and many possibilities of adjustment, but the best defense apparatus is a 100 per cent functioning metabolism and reabsorption in the intestinal tract in combination with a healthy liver. People may conclude, needlessly, that it is not important to place so much emphasis on nutrition. This may be so under normal conditions and if these persons are not damaged through heredity, civilization, sickness, trauma or other accumulations (nicotine and other poisons).

Civilization has partially taken away this natural bestowal. Experiments on test groups to produce different vitamin-deficiencies by omitting food containing these vitamins showed that one third can be made deficient in about four months and two thirds in six months; only five to six per cent resisted ten months of deficient feeding here in the United States. These nutritional experiments and others show that only a minority possesses a complete intact reabsorption apparatus and at the same time

[25] E. P. Fischer, *Ophthalmologica*. 114:1, 1947.

enough adjustment and reserve power for healthy and unhealthy periods in their lives.

It is not necessary for healthy persons to care so much about enough or too many carbohydrates and proteins, and their caloric value should be ignored. However, one cannot ignore the absolutely necessary minerals, vitamins and enzymes in their most natural composition and in sufficient amounts for a relatively long term and remain unpunished. The minerals have to be in the tissues where they belong, as they are the carriers of the electrical potentials in the cells; and there they enable the hormones, vitamins and enzymes to function properly. This gives the body the best working power and reserves for a sound metabolism and life.

SUMMARY

The best advice is to use fresh vegetables and fruit organically grown as much as possible. Mothers should pay more attention to their children and their kitchen. One's own garden would be a great help in summertime.

Valuable and practical information can be found in the following publications:

"Soil and Men." *Yearbook of Agriculture*, 1938
"Food and Life." *Yearbook of Agriculture*, 1939
Organic Gardening, J. I. Rodale, Hanover House, Garden City, N. Y., 1955
Our Daily Poison, Leonard Wickenden, The Devin-Adair Co., N. Y., 1955
Our Plundered Planet, Fairfield Osborn, Little Brown & Co., Boston, 1948
The Living Soil, E. B. Balfour, Faber & Faber Ltd., London, 1948
Hunsa, Ralph Bircher, Hans Huber, Bern, Switzerland, 1952
Road to Survival, William Vogt, Wm. Sloane Associates, N. Y., 1948
Handbuch der Diaetetik, Johannes Scala, Franz Deuticke, Wien, 1954
Studies in Deficiency Diseases, Robert McCarrison, M.D., Lee Foundation, Milwaukee 3, Wis., 1945
Degeneration Regeneration, Melvin E. Page, D.D.S., Page Foundation, St. Petersburg, Fla., 1951
What Price Civilization? Charles Eliot Perkins, Modern Science Press, Washington, D.C., 1946
The Drama of Fluorine, Arch Enemy of Mankind, Leo Spira, M.D., Lee Foundation, 1953
Prolongation of Life, Dr. Alexander A. Bogomolets, Duell Sloan & Pearce, Inc., N. Y., 1946
Nutrition & Physical Degeneration, Weston A. Price, Paul B. Hoeber, 1949
Hunger Signs in Crops, A Symposium. American Society of Agronomy
W. Kollath, *Zur Einheit der Heilkunde*. Hippokrates Verlag, Stuttgart. 1942
W. Kollath, *Die Ordnung Unserer Nahrung*, Hippokrates Verlag, Stuttgart, Zweite Auflage, 1950

G. v. Wendt, *Kost und Kultur*. Thieme, Leipzig 1936

M. Bircher-Benner, *Ernaehrungskrankheiten*. Wendepunkt-Verlag. Zuerich und Leipzig. Fuenfte Auflage. 1943.

D. Lichti-v. Brasch und A. Kunz-Bircher, *Die Klinische Bedeutung der Frischkost*. Hippokrates Zeitschrift. 30.11. 1956

Duane W. Probst, M.D. "The Patient is a Unit of Practice," Part One, *Nature of Disease*. Charles C. Thomas, Springfield, Ill. 1938

Handbook of Nutrition. A Symposium. American Medical Association. 1943

The Vitamins. A Symposium. American Medical Association. 1939

A Symposium On Respiratory Enzymes. The University of Wisconsin Press. 1942

Edward Howell, *The Status of Food Enzymes in Digestion and Metabolism*. National Enzyme Company. 1946

Karl Myrbäck, *The Enzymes*. Academic Press Inc., New York. 1951

A. I. Oparin, *The Origin of Life on the Earth*. Academic Press Inc., New York 1957. See especially The work of Pasteur, p. 28, Conclusion, p. 487

Max Gerson, M.D., "Feeding the German Army," *New York State Journal of Medicine*. 1471. 41. 1941

——. "Dietary Considerations in Malignant Neoplastic Disease," *Review of Gastroenterology*. Vol. 12, No. 6, pp. 419 to 425 Nov.-Dec. 1945

——. "Effect of a Combined Dietary Regime on Patients with Malignant Tumors," *Experimental Medicine and Surgery*. New York, Vol. VII, Nov. 4, 1949

——. "No Cancer in Normal Metabolism," *Medizinische Klinik*, Munich, Jan. 29, 1954, No. 5, pp. 175-179

——. "Cancer, a Problem of Metabolism," *Medizinische Klinik*, Munich, June 25, 1954, No. 26

——. "Cancer Research," Hearings before a Subcommittee of the United States Senate, S. 1875. July 1, 2, and 3, 1946

CHAPTER IV

Development of the Combined Dietary Regime in Cancer (Survey)

THE HISTORY of the development of the combined dietary regime in cancer follows briefly: After the dietetic treatment of lung tuberculosis was established (1927-1928) I treated, during 1928-29, my first three cancer cases all with favorable results. The dietary regime as it was used in tuberculosis consisted essentially of a saltless, properly prepared diet of fresh fruit and vegetables, predominantly raw, finely grated, and many freshly prepared juices, such as orange, grapefruit, and especially, apple and carrot juices. Frequent enemas were applied and Mineralogen (a composition of minerals) was administered. Later there was added daily: buttermilk, pot cheese, yoghurt and two raw egg yolks, stirred up in orange juice.

My first cancer case was a carcinoma of the bile ducts with two small metastases of the liver. Jaundice and high fever were present. The next two cases were both stomach cancers with adhesions and metastases in the surrounding glands. In all three cases, surgery had been tried in vain and biopsies had been made. One of the cancer patients died of an accident by sliding in the mountains two years later. She was brought to a small mountain village hospital in Quedlinburg and operated on for a ruptured spleen. The organ did not show any bleeding. Professor Lange-Bremen, who had operated on her the first time for cancer came the next day, found the ruptured left kidney but could not save the patient. The autopsy proved that she was free of cancer.

In Vienna during 1933-1934, six cancer cases were treated by me. All six were failures despite the fact that I had added the valuable liver injections. The kitchen of the Sanatorium was not adequately equipped for such a strict regime. All the other patients were treated for other diseases, without much regard to diet. It was difficult to overcome the objections on the part of the physicians, the nurses, the kitchen personnel and others.

In Paris during 1935-1936, I saw three favorable results in seven cancer cases. There I applied the same dietary regime as in my first cases, but with the addition of liver injections and three to four glasses a day of green leaf juice.

In New York I had to treat all my patients, including cancer cases, ambulant until 1943. Since 1938, after several setbacks, I have been able to develop a more successful therapy by adding other medications. At first I recognized that the B.M.R. was very low in a number of cancer patients; I interpreted this as a clinical symptom indicating a loss of iodine. Therefore I applied iodine-medication, first in organic form as thyroid, and later also in inorganic mineral, in lugol solution, half strength, starting with three drops three times daily; later, the dosage was increased to 6x3 drops in the first two to three weeks, and still later the dosage was decreased until the metabolism continued to stay at plus six to plus eight. I found this the best range for the healing power. Iodine is a decisive factor in the normal differentiation of cells, and can be used in order to counteract the decrease of cell differentiation as seen in the cancerous tissues. Iodine is also regarded as counteracting some adrenal hormones.

The results can be further improved by adding niacin which dilates the capillaries (Zwiegebäck) and in that way is helpful in the exchange between serum and cells. Niacin is also necessary for the function of the oxidation system. These additional medications helped remarkably in checking the cancerous growth and aiding the surrounding tissues to regain their electrical potentials and resistance. Finally, it was observed in more advanced cases that potassium in special composition stimulates the visceral nervous system (Kraus-Zondek) and helps to restore the functions of the organs of the intestinal tract. At the same time it counteracts some adrenal hormones.

The more I treated cancer cases the more the patients and their relatives recognized that something could be accomplished for those advanced cases who had been sent home. Gradually the number of so-called terminal cases among my patients increased to more than 90 per cent of the total, having come to me after the applied treatments had failed. As a result of having attracted such a large number of greatly advanced cases, I was urged to explore the cancer treatment in many directions and to improve it as far as possible. About 50 per cent of these cases could be improved and saved; this percentage could be higher if there were better cooperation from the family physician, the patient himself and less resistance from the family against such a strict regime—one which had to be carried out over a rather lengthy period. The initial percentage of improvement is higher, but often with a period of one to two months—a number of patients present clinical symptoms which indicate that the liver and/or other vital organs are too damaged to be sufficiently reactivated to maintain the healing process.

A major portion of the day is needed to prepare this treatment; it is also more expensive than the normal three meals. Where affection and devotion in the family exist, all difficulties are disregarded for the sake of saving a life.

CHAPTER V

The Theory

MY THEORY is not presented to give a general scientific explanation of the cancer problem, nor to compare it with the many existing theories and explanations. It is supposed to be a guide which helps physicians to apply the treatment properly. The theory was derived from clinical observations during which was recorded what was most characteristic of the disease and what seemed to be most decisive in the course of the treatment. In short, it is this: What is essential is not the growth itself or the visible symptoms; it is the damage of the whole metabolism, including the loss of defense, immunity and healing power. It cannot be explained with nor recognized by one or another cause alone.

In my opinion, cancer is not a problem of deficiencies in hormones, vitamins and enzymes. It is not a problem of allergies or infections with a virus or any other known or unknown microorganism. It is not a poisoning through some special intermedial metabolic substance or any other substance coming from an outside, so-called carcinogenic substance. All these can be partial causative agents in man, contributing elements, called secondary infections, etc. Cancer is not a single cellular problem; it is an accumulation of numerous damaging factors combined in deteriorating the whole metabolism, after the liver has been progressively impaired in its functions. Therefore, one has to separate two basic components in cancer: a general one and a local one. The general component is mostly a very slow, progressing, imperceptible symptom caused by poisoning of the liver and simultaneously an impairment of the whole intestinal tract, later producing appearances of vitally important consequences all over the body. The process in the pre-stage of cancer has not been proven clinically. That may be very difficult, even impossible, as liver damage is most probably a predisposition of many other degenerative diseases. In cancer, one or the other liver function may be predominantly more damaged or combined with some other disturbance in another organ. However, we should keep an eye on the liver as the first experiments of Yamagiva and Itchikawa demonstrated that cancer developed, after the *liver*, the kidneys and lymph glands showed pathological changes. In the poisoning of the liver, clinical symptoms are not noticeable for a long period of time, even for many years.

"The liver is the largest single organ in the body and is surpassed by none in the multiplicity and importance of its various physiologic activities. Accordingly, the state of the liver and level of its functional efficiency are of great significance to the general bodily economy both in health and in disease."[26] The liver weighs seven to ten pounds and has a functional capacity far in excess of ordinary needs. Before the functional reserves are used up, it is very difficult to detect a deterioration of liver function. The liver is a dynamic, active organ, and has manifold functions. Most of these are intimately associated and correlated with the activities of the other organs. It is impossible to test a liver by a single function, even by several, to find the degree of hepatic deterioration. That is the reason why the initial development of cancer remains hidden for such a long time; this interval may be called the "pre-cancerous or pre-symptomatic period." If a person gets nervous, feels weaker, has less energy and loses weight during that time, no physician can make a specific diagnosis as a cancer test does not exist and there is no early specific symptom complex. Physician and patient have to wait until a tumor is far enough developed in one or another area of the body to show local symptoms or signs which can no longer be overlooked clinically. This is when we use all modern equipment such as X-ray examinations, bronchoscopy, cystoscopy, and Papanicolaou tests at every spot where we can reach the different organs. Such symptoms can be caused by smaller or larger destructions with secretions or bleedings from the lungs, stomach, intestinal tract, kidneys, bladder, uterus and other organs or metastatic glands. There may be a

---

[26] W. A. D. Anderson, *Pathology*, 1948, p. 861.

great variety of special signs from the brain, spinal cord, bones and other symptoms. Finally, in some cases, a diagnosis can be established only with the help of exploratory operations.

The scientifically accepted method is that these symptoms alone will be treated *locally* wherever they appear. That is what we physicians learn and how we are trained in university clinics. All research work adheres mostly to these local symptoms. This is, in my opinion, the reason why decisive progress in cancer treatment has been impeded, especially in the last 50 years, during which modern medicine made remarkable progress in many other fields.

The local component is caused, in my opinion, by abnormal cells, immature cells, formerly damaged cells, transitional cells when they fall back or are forced to fall back into a type of embryonic life, because they are no longer supported sufficiently by the activated (ionized) minerals of the potassium group and a sufficient amount of reactivated oxidizing enzymes simultaneously united with the normal regulations of hormones, vitamins and the impulse of a normal functioning visceral nervous system. Finally the functions of subcutaneous, reticular lymph cell tissue and reticulo-endothelial system are diminished in function and defense power.

As mentioned above, the general component is important, and it will be treated. It comprises mainly the deterioration of the essential organs of the digestive tract, chiefly the liver. There, the damage is done by a permanent daily poisoning brought about by our modern civilization. This starts with the soil which is denaturalized by artificial fertilizers and depletion, thus gradually reducing the top soil. In addition, the soil is poisoned by sprays with DDT and other poisons. As a consequence, our nutrition is damaged by a decrease in the important K-group content of fruit and vegetables grown on such poisoned soil. Furthermore, the food substances are damaged as they are refined, bottled, bleached, powdered, frozen, smoked, salted, canned, and colored with artificial coloring. Carrots are sold in cellophane bags after having been treated for better preservation. Other foods contain damaging preservatives; finally, cattle and chickens are fed or injected with stilbestrol to accumulate more weight and be quickly "ready for market."

If we approach the cancer problem from a more practical

viewpoint—the clinical side—based on the concept of totality, we learn two things: firstly, we have to live near nature,[27] according to our natural development. Secondly, science cannot help us to solve the deep, underlying cause of cancer.[28]

"The most basic property of the heart is that it is a muscle, and the chief property of muscle is that we do not understand it. The more we know about it, the less we understand and it looks as if we would soon know everything and understand nothing." The situation is similar in most other biological processes and pathological conditions, such as the degenerative diseases (cancer). This suggests that some very basic information is missing. The story of myosin may illustrate this point. It seems as if we know too little about the "life promoting substances" Lebensstoffe —as W. Kollath has called them,[29] recognizing their enormous importance.

Albert Schweitzer recognized the greatness of the "awe for life" or the need to have the deepest respect for everything that is alive ("Die Ehrfurcht vorm Leben"). The living being, whether large or small, plant or animal, is in every respect perfectly created or developed, in all its functions and in all its parts, best in its totality.

Everybody respects and needs science, research, and laboratory work, but their conclusions should not be overestimated. Particularly, the direction of therapeutic action should always be based on the idea of the body as an entity, which has to be supported and restored in its silent perfection.

It is unnecessary to understand the whole life in its minute biological particles and effect—but it is necessary that, for the problem of therapy, the entire sick human organism be attacked in its totality, especially in degenerative diseases. It would be a great mistake to apply the therapy only as far as we understand the corresponding biological reactions or as far as they can be proven in animal experiments. In particular, in degenerative diseases and in cancer, we should not apply a symptomatic treatment or only one that we can fully understand; we need a treatment that will comprise the whole body as far as we know or

---

[27] See G. W. Beadle, *Science*, Jan. 4, 1957, Vol. 125, No. 3236.

[28] See Albert Scent-Gyorgyi, "Bioenergetics," *Science*, Nov. 2, 1956, Vol. 124, No. 3227.

[29] See Kollath's *Die Ordnung Unserer Nahrung*. Hippokrates-Verlag 1952, pp. 15-18.

can imagine it. These thoughts were well known by the physicians of Greece and Rome; the ancient physicians knew that there are no sicknesses but only sick human beings (see chapter on Paracelsus). The best pharmacologists realize how difficult it is to understand the actions of the pharmaca and often must use practical or clinical experience.

Modern technology has almost unlimited possibilities but it cannot transfer these accomplishments into the biology of the human being. In *The Failure of Technology*, Rev. Juenger views our modern civilization as disastrous, almost opposite to the viewpoint of Dr. Norbert Wiener, who hopes for far greater accomplishments.[30] He says, however, at the end of his book, "there is much which we must leave, whether we like it or not, to the un 'scientific' narrative method of the professional historian."

This book does not propose to discuss other cancer theories, but I would like to mention the viewpoint of Jesse Greenstein.[31] Greenstein comes nearer to a general assumption that "cancer is a phenomenon coexistent with the living process, that will be present for some time to come" or, in other words, "cancer is not a system isolated from the living universe." Despite all these general conceptions, he comes to a somewhat contrary-sounding conclusion for the research work—namely, "that emphasis must be laid on a direct study on the site of malignancy itself." In the edition of 1947, he is very pessimistic about the future in saying that "cancer may only be prevented by preventing human beings."[32] No wonder that such viewpoints, which are more or less generally accepted hinder physicians in seeing the cancer problem other than behind the wall of the symptoms—wrapped up in eternal darkness.

A few cancer experts start to explore every new method of investigation, then cling to the old scientific research studies. Alexander Haddow, reporting on findings at the Royal Cancer Hospital in London, finally concluded, after being unable to find any promising solution, "As in every other field, cancer research is not only dependent upon a long-range strategy—in this case centered upon patient investigation of the carcinogenic mechanism—but is also affected by chance, the accidental observation,

---

[30] Dr. Norbert Wiener, *Cybernetics*, edition 11, 1953.
[31] Jesse Greenstein, *Biochemistry of Cancer*, 1954, p. 589.
[32] See Greenstein, 1947 edition, p. 373.

or the unanticipated simplifying principle. Which is likely to be more decisive, it is impossible to tell, yet each is complementary to the other, and both are essential in the advancement of our knowledge of the cancer cell.[33]

Here, as elsewhere in the book the assumption is expressed that cancer is one of the degenerative diseases. This is difficult to prove and it is even more difficult to find out why one organism develops this degenerative disease and the other organism develops one or several different types of a so-called degeneration at the same time. In cancer patients, frequently, a combination of several degenerative diseases is observed. I found cancer frequently combined with chronic osteo-arthritis, high or low blood pressure, chronic sinus trouble, or other chronic infections although seldom with arteriosclerosis, except in older people, or associated with coronary disorders, diabetes and rarely with tuberculosis, asthma, skin diseases, gout, etc.

I think that the origin of the cancerous disease is more probable where the reactivation of the oxidizing enzymes, one of the finest developed functions in the liver, is impaired.[34]

This may be the reason why individuals who have inherited a weaker liver-intestinal system get cancer in earlier years, of a more acute or malignant type, with severe allergic reactions, more edema, less tendency to protect the surrounding tissue by a lymphocytic wall or build scar formation later, with and without calcification.

The experimental causation of cancer, first accomplished by Yamagiva and Itchikawa, through rubbing tar substance on the ears of rabbits for about nine months, is of importance insofar as they found that before the cancer started to appear, the liver was damaged and showed pathological changes, together with the kidneys, spleen and the lymphatic apparatus. The long period was required to poison the liver, before the damaged cells could perform the "mutation" into cancer.

Another experiment proved that cancer is not a contagious disease. Later, we learned to transplant cancer under special

---

[33] See survey article of Alexander Haddow, "The Biochemistry of Cancer," in the *Annual Review of Biochemistry*, Vol. 24, p. 689.

[34] See Rudolf Schoenheimer, *The Dynamic State of Body Constituents*, Harvard University Press, 1942.

conditions in animals. Leo Loeb was the first who succeeded in inoculating rat sarcoma of the thyroid gland to several generations of rats.[35]

The question whether human beings can be immunized against cancer has to be answered negatively. There is no active nor passive immunization thinkable in a body where cancer is growing by itself as a part of its own organism. The type of cancer (mostly virus tumors) against which immunization succeeded do not exist at all in human beings.[36]

The first physician who tried to transplant cancer was most probably Dr. J. L. Alibert, a famous surgeon in Paris at the time of Napoleon. On October 17, 1808, Dr. Alibert performed an extraordinary operation at the Hospital of St. Louis in Paris. He took cancerous material from a female breast tumor, broke it into small particles and finally made an emulsion which he injected into himself and three of his students. A severe feverish inflammation appeared and lasted a few days; there was no other reaction. A few days later, Dr. Alibert repeated the same experiment on himself and a colleague—again no other results.

We know that Napoleon, whose father died of cancer of the stomach, was very much interested in the cancer problem and assumed that he would die of the same disease, which he did. He discussed the subject very often with his physician Dr. Lucien Corvisart.

In recent years, Dr. E. Weiss of Chicago tried to inject a small amount of watery extract obtained from human cancerous tissue into cancer patients, once a week for six consecutive weeks. The result was an increase in appetite and a slight gain in weight for a short time only.

From these first experiments and from numerous later ones, we learned how difficult it is to make cancer transplantations effective in the same type of animal and how much more difficult it is to transplant it into other types.

The question whether the *healthy* body has the power to prevent its "taking" (incorporation) was neglected for a long time, in the following respect: in general we know that the healthy body has the power to defend itself against invasion by foreign

---

[35] J.M. Research 28:15. 1901.
[36] See K. H. Bauer, *Das Krebsproblem*, 1949, pp. 438-441

bodies or living bacteria, cocci, viruses, etc. by a defense reaction, or to destroy them after they have entered the body, by an inflammatory reaction as a means of healing.

I repeat—a defense or healing reaction occurs in the *healthy* body when cancer tissue or extracts of cancer tissues are injected. However, the reaction was different in cancer patients. There, all different types of experiments had only a minimum or temporary effect, as the cancerous body had lost its defense and healing power.

Several outstanding authors, such as August Bier, Pirquet, and von Bergmann, thought the malignancies could be included in the problem of the inflammation, since the cancer body could no longer bring about a normal inflammatory healing reaction. In the beginning, Rudolf Virchow thought that the chronic inflammation was also a process of degeneration, while today the inflammatory process is recognized as a mesenchymal reaction, which may turn out to the advantage or disadvantage of the body.

G. von Bergmann, head of the Medical University Clinic in Berlin and President of the Berlin Medical Association, was the first to examine at his clinic the functional chemical changes in cancerous tissue and cancer-bearing bodies in their reactions, but he did not dare to use these findings for therapeutical experiments. He explained in his book that there are differences in the various types of inflammatory metabolism which were studied in details at his hospital.[37] The cells in an inflammatory exudate have aerobic glycolysis even greater than the normal blood leukocytes, while the leukocytes in leukemia have only an anaerobic metabolism.[38]

Because of the importance of these findings for the new approach to the cancer problem, i.e., regarding it as a disturbance of the *total* metabolism and its essential functions, I should like to quote a passage from Dr. von Bergmann's book:

"Even if a systematic therapeutic use of this idea is impossible at this time, a cancer metabolism starts where the body is no longer able to produce a healing inflammation. It is possible to show distinctly antithesis of the two metabolisms in their reac-

---

[37] G. von Bergmann, *Funktionelle Pathologie*, pp. 173-174.
[38] See Peschel "Stoffwechsel leukemischer Leukocyten," Klin. Wo., 1930, No. 23, and Ruth Lohmann "Krebsstoffwechsel," Klin. Wo., No. 39.

tions. Experiments are made by Ruth Lohmann under supervision of Dr. Kempner which prove that slices of tissue, taken from malignant rat tumors or human cancer tissues, are killed fast in an inflammation exudate simply because the specific metabolism of the cancer cell cannot be maintained in those surroundings. The exact values for sugar, bicarbonate and the acid-degree measured by the pH figure show that no cancer cell can live there any longer. (See Table II, No. 1)

"Table 2 clearly shows the quick elimination of the cancer cells in inflammation fluid after a few hours, while they were perfectly able to live in serum. It means that where the inflammation metabolism begins, the cancer metabolism stops and the cancer cells have to die in the area of such a favorable inflammation metabolism with high oxidation power."

TABLE II—Metabolism of sarcoma tissue after different periods of time in serum and inflammation fluid under aerobic conditions

1	in serum		in inflammation fluid	
	QO_2	QH^{02}	QO_2	QH^{02}
0 hours	10.8	23.4	11.2	21.8
6 hours	10.2	21.8	6.9	13.3
10 hours	9.7	18.9	2.8	2.9
14 hours	9.6	17.5	0	0
2				
0 hours	11.3	17.6	12.0	21.1
12 hours	8.8	16.6	0	0

Fehleisen (1823), Coley (1892-1919) and others could not enforce a sufficient inflammatory reaction by inoculating infections or infectious material in cancer patients which would produce enough high fever for healing reaction. Drs. Alibert, Weiss, Durovic, (Krebiozen) and others did partially succeed in their long endeavors to produce a sufficient defense reaction in the body by inoculating cancerous tissue or extracts from cancer tissues, infectious materials, etc.

Thus, we begin to recognize the disease of cancer as a pathological degenerative variation of the total metabolism, similar to variations of other degenerative diseases.

The therapeutical endeavors concentrate on three essential items:

(1) A far-reaching and maintained detoxication.
(2) A Restoration of the whole enteral metabolism, including the liver, as far as possible.
(3) The restoration of the whole parenteral metabolism necessary for inflammatory reactions and healing power.

The treatment is effective only as long as the liver with the metabolism is restorable.

CHAPTER VI

A Few Similar Cancer Theories

THE INTERNATIONAL CONGRESS for Totality-Treatment in Malignant Diseases (in Berchtesgaden, Hippokrates Verlag, 1953. Stuttgart) revealed that many authors and particularly Professor Zabel, chairman, held to the statement that "before the growth starts, the function of the organism must have been abnormal. . . . This is a real blow to the conception that the tumor is a locally limited disease."

Professor Lambert came to the following conclusions: "In the tissue culture the cancer cell will be damaged by a temperature of 39° C. and dies at 42° C.; the normal cell will be damaged by 43° C. and dies at 46-47° C. The findings of several authors show later aberrations—most probably caused by different methods."[39]

. . . "the next task of our work will be first the increase of our knowledge about the direct influence of temperature on the growth, and second, an intensive study about the connection of indirect influence of higher temperature on the reactions of the local and general bodily difference, especially on the reaction of the neighboring tissue of the tumor. The factors of the disposition and constitution should not be neglected."[40]

Dr. Johannes Kuhl reported: "I started from the fundamentals of the cell metabolism, the oxidation and the glycolysis, the burning down and the spreading of the end products. I found in the ferments, vitamins, hormones and other vital substances only secondary means."[41] Dr. Kuhl regarded the cancer cell end prod-

---

[39] Professor Lambert, *Bodily Resistance and Malignant Growth*, Karl Haug Verlag, Ulm/Donau, 1957, p. 11.

[40] Ibid., p. 160.

[41] Dr. Johannes Kuhl, *Successful Medication and Dietary Regime in the Treatment of Benign and Malignant Growth*, p. 164.

uct, the lactic acid, as a stimulant of growth. He recognized "the constant majorities of oxidation at the development of the cell and its levels. That means the constant majority of glycolysis in the pathological regenerative growth." He saw in addition, "the transition of the stronger glycolysis to major oxidation at the end of the normal regenerative growth."

Kuhl's theory is built on von Euler's finding that the total lacking of the cytochrome system in the cancer cell is significant for the carcinomatous enzyme system. That means that the cancer cell is a so-called cytochrome deficient cell. This is the reason why the cancer cell is not normally differentiated and could only develop a breathing fermenting system, otherwise it is a real body cell without mutation and without other structural changes. One of the leading cancer-biologists, Professor Little says: "Cancer develops in a body where there is a general breakdown of the whole body." And in another statement, Little says: "The cancer problem will not be solved by specialists, rather by a practitioner." This means by a physician who constantly observes the whole body and tries to help the entire system. The practioner is not so much burdened with an immense literature on special cancer fields and is more open to reasonable argumentation.

Professor Ernest Leupold has stated (translation): "all cells in the body, the normal and the tumor cells, stay biologically in contact and exchange reaction to the general metabolic processes which are fundamentally all the same for all cells, whether they produce normal cells or simple proliferations. *Tumors are,* therefore, *only systems of a general disease* which are different in their degree and temporary course from other proliferate producing metabolic processes."[42] He also thinks that the general disease is present *before* the tumor appears as Professor Zabel assumes.

"We should not regard the tumor as a special type of disease. That cannot be proven by the fact that not only the ripe and unripe tumor cells can be influenced by the same conditions of the metabolism, but also many other segments are influenced at the same time and in the same way." I observed the same clinical appearances in cancer patients who also improved or restored completely several chronic diseases in the organs during the

---

[42] Prof. Ernest Leupold, *The Significance of Blood Chemistry in Regard to Tumor Growth and Tumor Destruction,* Georg Thieme Verlag, Stuttgart, 1954, p. 202.

treatment: such diseases as chronic arthritis, chronic sinusitis, chronic gall bladder disorders, arteriosclerosis, asthma, craurosis vulvae, eczemas, etc.

Some chronic or degenerative diseases, including cancer, have been neglected in the last 30 years. Cancer was considered incurable in the minds of physicians; therefore, it almost seemed not worthwhile to put intensive work into it. Internal physicians left cancer work to surgeons, biologists, and pathologists. These, however, were deeply interested in finding out what causes cancer and what it does in animals and human beings in the field of their competence, biological or chemical specialty.

Patients have reported that after unsuccessful operations and X-ray treatments that physicians gave them sedation only, thereby adding new poisons to the large amount which the disease is continuously producing.

When papers report that a surgeon recommends more operations for the purpose of preventing the loss of the patient to the non-physicians, we all should feel gravely concerned. Such aberrations from scientific behavior should be an incentive to apply any promising treatment, regardless of who worked it out or how difficult it may be. Where lives are at stake our surgeons and physicians should not recommend only surgery or non-surgery, but should consider all meritorious possibilities. Of course, this book describes many obstacles which have to be overcome in this modern civilization.

CHAPTER VII

Paracelsus' Dietary Regime*

In his works, Paracelsus (1490-1541) emphasizes that man is a microcosm in the macrocosm of the universe, depending on all the laws working therein. Both men and nature have a frequent and reciprocal influence upon one another which reaches into the smallest particles through water, earth, sun, season, movement of stars, food, soil, etc. Above all we must realize that there is nothing in heaven or on earth that does not also exist in man himself. We can say, therefore, that the system which governs the human being itself is "Great Nature." (Vol. I, p. 25) The body needs nutrition through which it is bound to nature. However, that which we have to give to the body as nutrition *also* contains toxins and damaging substances. In order to deal with the harmful things which we have to use to our disadvantage, the Lord gave us an alchemist (stomach) not to absorb the poisons that we eat together with the good nourishing food, but to separate it from the favorable substances.

The human being has to acquire knowledge of what to eat and drink, and what he has to weave and wear, because nature gave him the instinct of self-preservation. For the things that one does for the prolongation of one's life are ordained by Great Nature. If someone eats what is useful for his health and avoids other things that may shorten his life then he is a man of wisdom and self-control. All that we do should serve to prolong our life.

Many undiscovered qualities are hidden in our nutrition and

---

* Taken from the translation by Dr. B. Aschner, New York—Verlag von Gustav Fischer. Stuttgart, 1930.

they are able to counteract the damaging forces of the stars (such as sunburn). According to Paracelsus, some of the Great Nature's forces help produce animal urges and bad instincts in man which God-given reason and judgment can counteract and overcome. Food and drink can cause morbid conditions; he believes that nutrition aids the development of all characteristics: good or bad, gentle or cruel. Man in his character and disposition reacts to his food like the soil to fertilizer. As a garden can be improved with the right fertilizer so can man be helped with the right food. In the hand of the physician nutrition can be the highest and best remedy. (Arcanum) *Diet must be the basis of all medical therapy, yet diet should not be a treatment in itself.* But it will enable Great Nature to develop and fully unfold its own healing power. But even nutrition is subject to the influence of heaven and earth; therefore, the physician must study its combinations in order to apply them at the right time and break the power of the disease. (II, p. 699)

Diet should also be prescribed differently for each sex, for it should not serve to accumulate blood and flesh. It should rather effect the elimination of the foodstuffs which have spoiled and poisoned blood and flesh. Therefore medication and special nutrition are necessary. In the treatment of a patient the physician must consider that the nutrition as well as the medication is in agreement with the patient's sex, this is not necessary in the case of a healthy person.

Paracelsus gives greatest consideration to diet in constitutional diseases which, in the widest sense, could also be called diseases of the metabolism (he calls them the tartaric acid or stone-forming diseases). Tartaric acids are contained in our food but they do not belong in human beings. These particles are tiny pieces of minerals, sand, clay or glue which in the human body turn into stone. The human stomach is not created with the ability to separate these substances. This separation is achieved by the "subtile stomachs" which are built into the messenterium, liver, kidney, bladder and all other intestines. If their function ceases, various diseases will result in the organs concerned through the coagulation of these tartaric substances by the animal spirits of man (the sperma or "Spiritus des Salzes"). Therewith Paracelsus puts into this group of diseases the stone-forming ones, as well as the Phleboliths, vascular cramps, dental diseases, chronic digestive disturbances, stomach and intestinal ulcers, diseases of the liver and spleen, gout and arthritis, bronchiectasis and bronchitis, (not tuberculosis), for he separates it from this group, at least in its more serious forms) and finally brain diseases. At that early period Paracelsus had recognized that the endogen and exogen stimulants are very closely connected in constitutional diseases. He places the exogen stimulants exclusively into nutrition and with that he comes close to our modern thoughts in respect to a therapy of nutrition. We consume tartaric acid mainly in leguminous plants and grains, stalks and roots. Those transform into a tough sweet slime, while milk foods, meat and fish contain a clay-like mass, wine forms a tartar (winestone) and water a slimy stone.

As prophylaxis against tartaric diseases, the physician must pay special attention to the preparation of the food. (I, p. 138) "The nutrition of man—food and drink—should be especially cleansed from tartar." Furthermore, the specifically guilty tartars in the *different* regions should be ascertained and excluded from the food. For instance, the "Kehlheimer wine would cause the body a large amount of tartaric separation work but not the Neckar wine, therefore the Kehlheimer should be forbidden."

From many observations I would like to mention one: "as far as I am concerned, I have never seen a country where there are so few tartaric diseases as in 'Veltlin' (a valley in the Italian Alps, south of Lake Como) where there are less than in Germany or Italy, France or the Occidentor, the European Orient. In this country, Veltlin, the inhabitants have neither podagra nor colicam, contracturam nor calculum. It is such a healthy country that even that which grows there is healthy, and not many better, healthier locations could be found in all my far travels." (I, p. 600)

For the cure of some diseases Paracelsus suggests special dietary prescriptions. First for the bladder and kidney stones (I, p. 849) the following are forbidden: milk products, cheese, alkaline or lead-containing waters, rain water, sour sea slacks, sour wine, meat crabs and fish. Substances of rich mineral and purin content are intuitively forbidden to prevent phosphatic and uric acid stone formations. (When pains are present poppy seed (morphine) is recommended to render the bladder insensitive.) On the other hand, there are the following remedies (I, p. 152) which reduce and do not transmute or precipitate, for prevention of bladder and gall stones: "There is nothing so much to recommend as butter and olives." Heartburn (II, p. 593) derives from wine, salty meat and venison. These should be avoided; as a remedy he suggests much milk, St. John's bread, chalk (alkali!), "sealing earth" (magnesium?), armenic clay and ocean chalk. Then he prescribes daily vitamin doses through consumption of melon juice and fruit, continuous usage of which should prevent the formation of stones in the intestinal tract.

In a consilium, (II, p. 472) Paracelsus recommends against Podagra and imminent stroke besides the medical cures of the watering places such as Pfeffers and Wildbad (Gastein) as the following: "when you are taking the baths you should be abstemious with food and drink, and with women you should have little or no intercourse." Fish is forbidden—but when fried it does the least damage; no tough, hard meat and nothing from the pig is permitted. As drink, an old, mild, clear red wine would serve best; beer should be taken only rarely and then it should not be consumed without nutmeg and fermented bread." As prophylaxis, he recommends: (II, p. 487) "this is my advice how you can protect yourselves, namely, four things should you avoid—strong smelling wine—lascivious food—anger—women; and the more abstemious you shall live in these things the better." For prevention against stroke of brain or spinal cord, dizziness and pleurisy, he advises that the following foods should be avoided as much as possible: spices, strong wine, herb wine, garlic, mustard, vinegar and fish, especially the fried foods. Abstention is good, but one must not suffer hunger or thirst and should stick to one's daily habits at all hours. This is not a recommendation for fasting—cures.

In a certain aetiological contrast to the tartaric diseases he puts the infectious diseases. In Paracelsus' time an attack of disease through infection by bacilli was not yet known; in his astrological kind of conception he traces the origin of infectious diseases back to the effect of the stars. These consume the patient through their fires, they cause the body to dry up and wither; therefore, the arcanum in these patients is moist food and consumption of large amounts of moisture. For the patient sick with the plague, he says (I, p. 729) that one should not give them any meat, eggs, fish and nothing fried. For drink, they should be given only soup of water or barley sauce with rose vinegar. The most useful drink is barley water (most of this is the original teaching of Hippocrates).

CONCLUSION

In themselves, the statements of Paracelsus about diet are not uniform but one can notice everywhere in them the thought that combines them; their chemical effect. Everywhere in his writings it can be perceived how he would like to dissect everything into the finest particles (atoms) and find an interpretation; it seems as if he would like a penetrating power to enable him to look into things microscopically. The layman only sees the surface; the physician must be able to visualize the inside and the hidden facts which combine to form the whole, regardless of whether it is a piece of wood or bone. Marvelous are his ideas about the chemical reactions and his passionate love for all chemical occurrences which he applied to the reactions of the body long before his time. Paracelsus seeks to develop everything from its origin. In that he always observes three things: the heaven, the earth and the microcosm; it is similar with healing. Man can only be comprehended through a macrocosm; not through himself alone. Only the knowledge about this harmony perfects the physician.

This short condensation does not take a critical stand in the historical sense towards the statements of Paracelsus as measured against the knowledge of his time. It merely seeks to show how stimulating his writings are and the wealth of ideas which shines through everywhere, how intense his urge to find causal connections or at least to intimate them in his passionate way and bring them in accordance with the eternal laws in nature outside of the body and the same laws ruling inside the microcosm.

CHAPTER VIII

Different Authors' Cancer Therapies by Diet
— A Survey

K. H. BAUER wrote that "we must distinguish sharply between nutritional prophylaxis and cancer therapy by diet."[43] Dr. Bauer takes a strictly negative attitude to the question of dietary therapy in cancer. For this reason, he lists the dietary regimes of a number of authors: (1) Fischer-Wasels (1930-1935) recommended the avoidance of overeating, nutrition poor in sugar, water and salt, poor in vitamin B, cholesterol, alkaline, and a higher acidity to be reached by intake of acid foods and addition of acids. (See Dr. Kuhl.)

(2) Auler (1937-1941) recommended a non-sparing diet, rich in salt and spices, raw meat several times weekly, juices of vegetables and fruits and oils to replace animal fats.

(3) Freund and Kaminer, whose dietary experiments were highly regarded for a long time, suggested replacement of animal fats by vegetable oils to avoid growth of the sick bacterium coli and prevent the formation of normal fatty acids. Carbohydrates were to be reduced and the intestines were to be cleansed by means of physics and medication. Freund and Kaminer were the first to list permitted and prohibited foods (1912-1925).

(4) Kretz, Vienna (1939) leaned closely on the recommendations of Freund for the improvement of the general condition of the cancerous organism.

(5) Bruenings, Frankfurt a/Main (1930's) recommended a diet poor in carbohydrates and rich in proteins, aided by insulin; he believed in improvement by an acidifying effect.

---

[43] K. H. Bauer, *Das Krebsproblem* (The Cancer Problem), Springer Verlag, Berlin, 1949, p. 605.

(6) E. Salzborn, Vienna (1940) advocated a dietary regime for inoperable cancer patients which consisted of little protein and fat, few vitamins, minerals and foods with a reduced amount of carbohydrates because of fermentation and gas production.

(7) Ingebos (1942) recommended a regime based on the ideas of Mason in Loewen; the regime avoided fats and foods rich in fats, especially those rich in cholesterol, and also avoiding artificially colored foods and drinks. He prohibited salt and meat and fish—frozen, smoked or sterilized. Easily digestible foods were permitted: lean fish grilled or broiled, chopped lean meat, brains, and thymus which could be cooked. All vegetables should be served raw or cooked in water; vegetable soup and oatmeal, vegetable oils, fruit and potatoes were part of the regime; bread was permitted. Alcoholic beverages, pepper, mustard and paprika were forbidden, as was smoking.

Bauer presents a summary of answers to questionnaires submitted to 34 physicians by the *Monatschrift fuer Krebsbekaempfung*.[44] With the exception of Professor Denk of Vienna, all the physicians showed a negative attitude to dietary therapy in their answers. Some looked upon diet more as a means of preventing "causes of cancer" than a means of treating cancer.

In his book, *Cancer and Diet*, Dr. Frederick L. Hoffman reached the conclusion that cancer is not local in its origin; treatment should, therefore, not be limited to the local lesions. "A deranged metabolism is the result of dietary and nutritional disorders manifesting themselves in various ways, not difficult of ascertainment by modern methods of exact scientific determination, chiefly gastric and blood analysis, or other precise methods of indicating blood disorders.

"I am absolutely convinced that the underlying cause of cancer is to be found in an excessive intake of foods of a high organic or mineral content, or generally of an alkaline base instead of acid. . . . In brief, the teaching of modern-day nutritional science should be the urgency of moderation in all things—moderation in food intake, particularly as to highly-spiced foods, moderation in bodily fluids, including alcoholic beverages, coffee and tea, as well as moderation in the use of tobacco. Immoderation in any one particular direction favors the local development of malignant

---

[44] *Monatschrift fuer Krebsbekaempfung*, Vol. 9, 1936, p. 257

growths. . . . I consider my own duty discharged in presenting the facts as I have found them, which lead to the conclusion that overnutrition is common in the case of cancer patients to a remarkable and exceptional degree, and that overabundant food consumption unquestionably is the underlying cause of the root condition of cancer in modern life."[45]

In *Dietotherapy Clinical Application of Modern Nutrition,* carcinoma of the stomach is described as essentially a surgical problem. A post-operative diet is required only after subtotal or total gastrectomy. "Once the patient has survived the operation and the convalescence has followed, the diet is very liberal and practically *without restrictions.* Patients who have suffered partial resections of the stomach can manage practically the same diet as normal persons.[46]

Kurt Stern and Robert Willheim wrote, "In regard to the relation between food quantity and tumor growth, the prevailing majority of authors have expressed the opinion that food restriction is followed by a depression of neoplastic growth."[47]

Like F. L. Hoffman (1937), E. Friedberger (1926), A. Tannenbaum (1940-42), W. Caspar (1938) and others expressed the same opinion and advocate moderation in food. A real therapy is *nowhere to be found,* although some authors are not as pessimistic as others.

The different dietary propositions made at the International Congress for Totality Treatments of Tumors in 1952 were not put into practice, although many of the propositions had the correct approach.

It is not necessary here to pay attention to the many proposals for applying one or more vitamins, or enzymes or those mixed with minerals. It would be a primitive concept to propose that the administration of one or another enzyme, vitamin or mineral or their composition would change or counteract the enzymatic disturbance or intracellular nature.

Nearly 100 years ago, Otto Voelker wrote: "The degree to which a disease is open to therapeutic attack is inversely related

---

[45] Frederick L. Hoffman, L.L.D., *Cancer and Diet,* Williams and Wilkins Co., Baltimore, 1937.

[46] *Dietotherapy Clinical Application of Modern Nutrition,* edited by Michael G. Wohl, M.D., W. B. Saunders, Philadelphia, 1946, p. 573 and ff.

[47] Kurt Stern and Robert Willheim, *The Biochemistry of Malignant Tumors,* Reference Press, Brooklyn, 1943, p. 391.

to the number of remedies that we possess."[48] Nowhere is this more true than in cancer, for which treatments have been advanced by the thousands. The older ones included: crab or crab soup, no doubt an early application of the mistaken theory that "like cures like"; purgation; yeast treatment; different dietary regimes; hyperemia and its opposite; bloodletting; salves—first black and later, if this proved ineffectual, red ones; caustic pastes; hot iron-burnings; pipe clay; blood-cleansing teas; silver and gold; mercury; copper; phosphorus; arsenic—externally and internally; narcotics; compressions; colds—long before the recent venture into chemotherapy; acids; alkalis; diaphoresis; vegetable products of all sorts, including violet leaves and toads; auto-vaccine (Blumenthal); polysaccharide (Hatt); implanting of erysipelas streptococci, etc.

The modern cancer remedies include: surgery, X-ray treatment; radium; ionized minerals (gold, phosphorus, iodine, cobalt); combinations of vitamins; hormones; Revici's Iodoacetate; Krebiozin, and the newest proposal of "creation of cancer focci on the skin as cancer of one organ shields other organs to a considerable extent."[49]

As cancer author William H. Woglom writes, "If we have no cure of cancer today, surely it is not from lack of trying."[48]

To present a historical survey of all the therapeutic attempts to influence the cancer growth, or at least to alleviate pain, would be extremely difficult. A complete survey may run into thousands of enumerations, as old popular cancer remedies, based on natural observations, may be found in almost all countries of the world. Even in modern scientific therapy, almost all attempts have failed, whether in the fields of bacteriology, immunology or biochemistry. In summarizing the relations between tumors and enzymes, Kurt Stern and Robert Willheim said that "of the therapeutical uses of enzymes in tumor pathology it would be an extremely primitive concept if administration of one enzyme or the other were to be proposed as an effective means of counteracting an enzymatic disturbance of necessarily intracellular nature. As a matter of fact, no instance is known in general pathology, with the exception of gross intestinal deficiencies of enzymes, in which

---

[48] Quoted by William H. Woglom, *Approach to Tumor Chemotherapy*, 1947, p. 1.

[49] S. Peller, M.D. *Cancer in Man*, 1952, p. 488.

an enzyme therapy has proven useful (pepsin and trypsin)."[50] Professor Leupold had some results by changing the "blood-chemismus—the cholesterin-sugar-phosphatic system."[51]

Peller brought up a theory for cancer cure in his book by saying, "cancer of one organ shields other organs to a considerable extent. A cured cancer leaves an increased resistance to the development of another primary tumor in some other part of the body. Although the nature of this resistance is unknown, its utilization for cancer control is possible. . . . The primary tumor is a local manifestation of a general disposition to cancer."[52] Peller arrived at this notion from some observations in tuberculosis. It was concluded by several authors that tuberculosis of the skin (lupus) protects the other organs, especially the lungs, against the tuberculosis infection.

A few words may be added to the above-mentioned contradictions in cancer treatment: scientists have skirted the nucleus of the problem throughout the centuries as described in the history of medicine. As soon as one of Nature's secrets is uncovered, apprehension and skepticism appear.

The history of medicine is filled with tragic errors which allowed such a long time to elapse between the time of discovery of a basic principle and the actual medical application of the discovery for the good of mankind. To quote from a recent paper by Hammet, "Nowhere today is this delay more unhappily evident than in the field of cancer research. The accumulated data of Rous, Shope, Coley, Bittner, Strong, Andervont, Green, Greene, Williams, Taylor, Furth, Twombly, Cowdry, Diller, Bawden, Pirie, Stanley, Wyckoff, Kunitz, and others indicate beyond peradventure the path for getting at something of practical benefit to the cancer patient of the future other than surgery and radium.[53]

[50] Kurt Stern and Robert Willheim, The Biochemistry of Malignant Tumors.

[51] Prof. Ernst Leupold, The Significance of Blood Chemistry in Regard to Tumor Growth and Tumor Destruction, Georg Thieme Verlag, Stuttgart, p. 14.

[52] S. Peller, M.D., Cancer in Man, 1952, International Universities Press, New York, p. 488.

[53] Science, Vol. 103, No. 2685, 1946, p. 714.

CHAPTER IX

Early Cancer Symptoms

IN THE beginning, there is a general weakness with loss of pep and energy and complaints of easy fatigue or exhaustion, as may be seen in many different diseases. Between such early symptoms and the later diagnosed cancer there may be a period of years, weeks, and days; or else the cancer presents itself at the first consultation. It is of practical importance to note that some of the beginning cancers of the stomach are not indicated by clinical symptoms, but found by chance because of operations for other reasons. I have seen a number of cancer patients who had been examined in excellent cancer prevention clinics only a few months earlier, in whom nothing pathological or suspicious had been found. The public appeal for prevention and the attempt at early detection seem to be practically unachievable.

On the basis of the preceding explanation that cancer is a disease of the entire metabolism, concentrated essentially in the liver I do not believe that there will be a cancer-specific test for diagnosis. On the contrary, I have found similar, almost identical clinical symptoms in other degenerative diseases, such as tuberculosis, diabetes, arteriosclerosis, muscular dystrophy, liver cirrhosis and many others. Yet the metabolic disturbances in cancer cases, especially in more advanced cases, somehow seem to be different from metabolic disturbances in other degenerative diseases, although so far I do not have enough objective material to present them as sufficiently clear evidence.

According to my experience it seems important that the physician informs the patient either right at the beginning, or immediately after the first noticeable improvement, of the seriousness of the disease. Patients must learn what they have to do for the restoration of their vital organs. The treatment is difficult and drawn-out, and proper understanding is necessary for patients to adjust to it and carry it out. The restoration of the teeth is an absolute requirement for the treatment, to prevent infection and toxic disturbances from defects of the teeth and inflamed gums.

Prevention of Recurrence

After the restoration, I found that two components were necessary for prophylaxis: the maintenance of potassium and iodine in the body and the maintenance of the function of the liver and the *essential organs*. The potassium content in the serum can not be measured exactly but it is impossible to test it in the organs. The experience thus gained, however, enables us gradually to draw some conclusions, on the basis of which we can give the patients valuable directives for the future. For this reason, I repeat some of my findings as follows: Some patients maintain a lower potassium level in the serum for years; the majority even go a bit below the minimum, but continue to feel well and remain completely free of symptoms. When the potassium content goes 1.5 to 2 mg. below the minimum, and remains there for some time, patients must be warned to take up part of the medication and diet again to prevent a recurrence.

CHAPTER X

Cancer and Liver

A General Survey

"THE LIVER is the largest single organ in the body and is surpassed by none in the multiplicity and importance of its various physiologic activities. Accordingly, the state of the liver and the level of its functional efficiency are of great significance to the general bodily economy, both in health and in disease."[54]

Physiologically, it may be stated: the liver can remain damaged for a long time because the deterioration of the liver cannot be detected before the great functional reserves have been consumed. In addition, the liver has great capacity to regenerate, therefore, a partial destruction may be restored if the deterioration is not extensive and rapid.

The liver has manifold functions, and most of them are closely associated with the function of other organs. One is forced, therefore, to take several functional tests to measure the functional degree of the liver. The constant upward and downward trend of this large dynamic organ makes it necessary to repeat the tests before a more positive statement can be formed. The importance of the liver will be best described by comparison with the chlorophyll contained in the cells of leaves—maintaining metabolism and the life of the plant.

When several authors examined the function of the liver of 50 patients with various types of cancer of the gastro-intestinal tract, they found a pronounced hepatic dysfunction. [55] After removal of the tumors, the liver recovered to a certain degree, for some time. Thus, the changes showed that the deterioration can

---

[54] W. A. D. Anderson, *Pathology*, 1948, p 861.
[55] See Abels, Rekers, et al, Annal of Internal Medicine, 16, 221 (1942).

be reversed. May I anticipate that the treatment described here does the same: *The absorption of the tumor mass and glands and the restoration of the function of the liver.*

Jesse Greenstein stated that, "there seems to be little doubt that hepatic insufficiency is a concomitant phenomenon with cancer and, as the authors emphasize, such damaged livers impose an additional hazard to those normally accompanying operative procedures."[56]

In some biochemistry books on cancer, the liver deterioration in cancer is divided into three stages: The *first* stage represents the time of the development and the appearance of cancer. During that time the dysfunction of the liver is, as many authors assume, present but undetectable by means of tests or palpation. I believe, however, that the liver has lost K and K-group minerals so that the oxidizing enzymes can no longer be reoxidized in sufficient quantities to control all cell growth.

During the *second* stage, the tumor grows and some metastases appear in glands. One can palpate an enlarged liver (hypertrophy) and find some edema in the organs. At that time, we assume that the activity of the cancer has increased while the defense and the healing power of the body has decreased correspondingly.

In the *third* stage, in which the cancer has gained supremacy, rapid poisoning and destruction of essential organs set in with later dissolution of these organs, including the liver which can no longer maintain its substance and functions.

In the first stage, the tumor protein would seem to be supported by normal food; in the second stage, most probably, the protein is supported to a greater or lesser degree by the muscle tissue. At this time there is considerable hyperlipemia present, which remains until the reserves of the body's lipids are consumed.

In the third terminal stage, there is an acute, rapid loss of muscle and liver substance, since very little defense or resistance is left. How the tumor produces such a condition is unknown. Jesse Greenstein assumes the production by the tumor of a circulating toxin, which accelerates the catabolism of the body tissues.[57] Rudolf Keller thinks that the progressive loss of potassium and the minerals of the potassium group lower the electrical poten-

[56] Jesse Greenstein, *Biochemistry of Cancer*, 1954, p. 509.
[57] Ibid., p. 513.

tials and the defense of the cytoplasm in muscle and liver cells. The stimulation of the visceral nervous system by the loss of potassium and the increase in tumor poisons also seems to be a contributing factor to this deleterious effect. A high percentage —about 90 per cent—of our patients are terminal cases. These patients cannot wait for treatment to be developed. This was the reason that forced me to bring my treatment to its highest efficacy in every respect.

The first physician who drew attention to the combination of cancer and the liver or gallbladder system probably was Frerichs, in 1861. Later, many physicians agreed with him, such as Zenker, Fuetterer, Siegert, Karnot, Blond, etc. The existence of the relationship was denied by Krehl, Heller and others. The pathologists were also of different opinions: Aschoff and Backmeister decided that the disease of the liver and bile system were accidental findings. Lubarsch and others opposed this view.

Neither clinicians nor pathologists nor biologists were able to solve the problem *which was the first* or the causative factor. The great difficulty is that we cannot determine when the pathology of the liver or bile system starts.

The newer labeled examination with C^{14} glycine by Norbert E. and D. M. Greenberg[58] proved that the liver and plasma of tumor-bearing animals have an increased protein metabolism.

The same effect occurs also in pregnancy (measured by glycine C^{14} and P^{32} in livers of tumor-bearing animals) which reflects a quicker growth somewhere else in the body. This means that this condition is not specific for cancer and is not caused by specific toxins.

It is important to recognize that, in our body, all the innermost metabolic processes work together, are dependent upon one another, and will be deranged with each other in diseases. S. Spiegelman said in an article as well as at the Third International Congress of Biochemistry in 1955: (p. 185) "For over 60 years there have existed in the micro-biological literature a series of observations subsumed under the title of 'enzymatic adaptation,' in which a particular compound apparently evokes a well-defined change in the enzyme patterns of cells, grown in its presence. The last decade has witnessed a renewed interest in these analogous

---

[58] Reported in *Cancer*, 4: 383, 1951.

findings. There, genetic and enzymological aspects have been re-examined with the aid of more rigorous techniques and methodology than those that were available to the earlier workers. These newer procedures made it possible to show in a number of cases that the phenomenon of enzymatic adaptation possessed the following important features: a) the changed enzymatic activity was *not* due to the selection of pre-existent mutant types but rather to an included enzymatic modification against a constant genetic background; b) the observed change in enzymatic activity could be ascribed to the appearance of active apoenzyme rather than to the accumulation of co-factors or intermediates, unique to the metabolism of the inducing substrate. . . . It was necessary, therefore, to revise such statements as genes control potentiality of enzyme synthesis."

The problem of the liver was, and still is, partly misunderstood and partly neglected. The metabolism and its concentration in the liver should be put in the foreground, not the cancer as a symptom. There, the outcome of the cancer is determined as the clinical favorable results, failures and autopsies clearly demonstrate. There, the sentence will be passed—whether the tumors can be killed, dissolved, absorbed, eliminated and, finally, whether the body can be restored.

The progress of the disease depends upon the possibility of whether and to what extent the liver can be restored, of course, unless there are some complications and destructions in the vital organs.

The treatment of the liver is generally more symptomatic, but not with the described treatment.

"It has become increasingly evident that liver cirrhosis is intimately associated with primary liver cancer, and that environmental factors play an important part in the pathogenesis of both diseases," Berman stated. Kasper Blond said: "In the liver we have tried to show that cirrhosis of the liver is not a disease *sui generis*, but only a sign of a disorder of metabolism which causes a chain of events leading to many conditions which the medical generation of today considers to be diseases *sui generis*. The whole syndrome of metabolic disorders which we call oesophagitis, gastritis, duodenitis, gastric and duodenal ulcer, cholecystitis, cholangitis, pancreatitis, proctitis, and others are considered only stages of a dynamic process, starting with liver failure and portal hypertension, and resulting in cirrhosis of the liver tissue and in cancer. Cancer is a mutation of somatic tissues caused by chronic damage of the liver. The structural changes of the somatic tissues are the result, not the cause, of the metabolic disorders."[59]

Blond has studied this problem since 1928 to explain cancer physiology and pathology through bile production, absorption, secretion, and storage as a disorder of the cooperative organs. He came to the conclusion that we can solve most of the involved problems if we study the physiology of *man as a whole*, rather than cells, structures, or single organs. In that respect, he goes contrary to most cancer authors who emphasize "a direct study of the site of malignancy itself," as, for example, Jesse Greenstein.[60]

Blond did not try to develop a therapy on that basis but took his viewpoint from statistics and came to the conclusion that "98% of all cancers of the internal organs succumb not to the cancer but to the liver disorder."[61] He does not even make any suggestion to help the liver in the fight to defend or maintain the body. Blond's conception seems to be right and reasonable. His enumeration of the liver syndromes, however, seems to be too strongly pronounced. I find them much less accentuated even in the more advanced cases. Not all cancer cases have cirrhosis, although the majority show a "precirrhotic" stage of liver hypertrophy.

Dr. George Medes reported to the meeting of the American Chemical Society in 1955 that changes in the chemistry of the living cells all over the body have been determined in rats when liver-cancer strikes. He suggested that the discovery will shed new light on the way cancer forms in the body and the way it may be prevented. Dr. Medes concentrated on the synthesis and utilization of fats by living and growing tissues under various dietary conditions. Acetic acid, which is known to be formed from both fats and carbohydrates, has been used to represent foods. Earlier, Dr. Medes found that, while all tissues could use both of these substances for the production of fats, there was a difference in normal tissue and tumors. The normal liver of the rat utilized acetic acid to synthesize and oxidize it to carbon

---

[59] Kasper Blond, *The Liver and Cancer*, 1955, p. 136.
[60] Jesse Greenstein, *Biochemistry of Cancer*, p. 598.
[61] Kasper Blond, *The Liver and Cancer*, p. 197.

dioxide and water at several times the rate at which the tumor did, whereas the reverse occurred with glucose in normal and tumor-bearing rats.

In 1926, the Mayo Clinic reported the very low incidence in liver carcinoma of 0.083 per cent. That increased till 1949. The highest incidence was reported during 1948 to 1952. It is generally accepted that the rising incidence of primary carcinoma of the liver may be due to an increasing incidence of liver diseases and cirrhosis in general. These are regarded as causes of the neoplastic transformation. The latest statistics of the incidence of primary carcinoma of the liver show the predominance of this disease for certain racial groups and geographic areas.

In general, primary carcinoma of the liver is much more common in colored races than in the white race, while malignancies in general are less frequent in colored people. The percentage of liver carcinoma to other carcinomas is one to two per cent in Europe and America while Chinese have 33 per cent; Javanese, 36.1 per cent; Filipinos, 22.2 per cent; Japanese, 7.5 per cent; and South Africans in the Gold Mines, 86.6 per cent. Ewing and other authors found that primary hepatomas and 50 per cent of primary cholangiomas are associated with cirrhosis. The Damocles sword of cirrhosis hangs over all cancer patients who have far advanced malignancies in their abdominal organs. We know that all these organs send their blood through the portal veins into the liver where tumor cells settle very frequently as soon as the liver, working as a filter, has lost its defense power.

Teratomas of the liver are extremely rare. For liver function tests, see special textbooks. Abels, Rekers and others reported a high incidence of hepatic dysfunction in patients with cancer of the intestinal tract.

In his book, Spellberg says that "Primary cancer of the liver occurs so much more frequently in the cirrhotic liver as compared with the normal liver that cirrhosis has been referred to as a precancerous lesion."[62] And, he also says, "There is no dispute that an adequate diet is essential in the treatment of liver diseases."[63]

Several authors have observed that if the surgeon removes a tumor of one of the abdominal organs, the liver is the first organ

---

[62] Mitchell A. Spellberg, *Diseases of the Liver*, p. 427. Grune and Stratton, N. Y., 1954.
[63] Ibid., p. 129.

which recovers. This observation shows that the poisoning from the tumor seems to be the underlying cause of the liver disease (in later stages).

Experiments have revealed that in the second stage of cancer the sources for nitrogen will be taken, more or less, from the cancer-bearing body. During this condition the liver shows enlargement; the enlargement corresponds to the weight of the animal plus that of the tumor. Before death, however, the liver loses rapidly in size and weight, and the liver cells have to provide the body with its last reserves. Finally, it may be mentioned that liver perfusions have shown that in the liver cells many reductions of hormones and metabolic processes take place. The presence of androgens and activated vitamins and enzymes has proven that the liver can accomplish reoxidations and metabolic regenerations. Some authors think that most of the oxidizing enzymes are reactivated in the liver.

The functions of the liver cells are so vitally important for the body that they could be compared with the activity of the chlorophyll of the plants. The liver is regarded so unique biologically that recently it was called the "balance wheel of life."

CHAPTER XI

Survey of Treatment of Liver Pathology by Several Authors

DETWEILER WRITES regarding portal cirrhosis: "It is by no means uncommon for portal cirrhosis to exist unsuspected during life and only be found after death from accident, intercurrent infection, or other diseases. The early recognition of the disease, therefore, may be extremely difficult. Sometimes careful examination reveals loss of appetite, loss of weight, nausea, flatulence and occasional vomiting."[64]

In malignancy of the liver or in the intestinal tract, the symptoms are described: "The onset is very insidious and is manifested in weakness, loss of appetite, and failure in general health . . . there is usually progressive loss of weight and increasing secondary anemia (characteristic of any chronic or degenerative disease)."[65]

"Symptoms referable to the liver itself may be absent, but a sense of fullness and discomfort in the hepatic region is often noted. Jaundice, ascites and pain are absent in simple cases. Vague gastro-intestinal disturbances may occur."[66]

Three different systems closely connected with each other are in the liver:

1) The liver parenchyma,
2) the bile system and
3) the reticulo-endothelial system

---

[64] See *Textbook of Medicine*, Cecil, 1938, p. 791.
[65] Op. cit., p. 800.
[66] Op. cit., "Degenerative Diseases of the Liver," p. 803.

"The liver performs various detoxication processes, but it is not known exactly where and how these take place."[67] The same is true with reference to various enzyme systems, vitamins and minerals (copper, cobalt, manganese, iron, potassium, etc.). Enzymes and vitamins are combined, stored and reactivated mostly in the liver. Albumin is also formed in the liver, probably in the Kupffer cells, while globulin is formed in the lymphocytes, but is increased when the liver is impaired. The reason has not yet been found. The ratio of $\frac{albumin}{globulin}$ is therefore lowered in the liver diseases and used for one of the tests.

Neoplasia: About 1:200 malignant tumors arise primarily in the liver. Most malignancies are metastatic in origin and are derived from the intestinal organs.

Pathology-Liver

Fifty patients with various types of cancer of the general intestinal tract presented pronounced hepatic dysfunctions.[68] After removal of the tumors the liver recovered to a certain degree for some time, but the changes showed that the deterioration is reversible. May I anticipate here that the described treatment does the same: removal of the tumor-mass, glands, etc. and an overcoming of the dysfunction of the liver. According to Greenstein, "There seems to be little doubt that hepatic insufficiency is a concomitant phenomenon with cancer and, as the authors emphasize, such damaged livers impose an additional hazard to those normally accompanying operative procedures."[69]

During the *first stage*—development and appearance of the disease—the liver dysfunction is undetectable. During the *second stage*—tumor growth and some metastases in glands—one finds the liver mostly hypertrophic and, as we see in some cases, also hypertrophy or edema of other organs. In the *third stage*—an almost entire ruling (autonomy) of the cancer—with rapid poisoning, destruction and later dissolution of the organs, including the liver, which can no longer maintain its substance and functions.

[67] Jensen, *Modern Concepts in Medicine,* C. V. Mosby Co., 1953, p. 174.
[68] See Abels, Rekers, et. al, *Annual of Internal Medicine,* 16:221, 1942.
[69] Jesse Greenstein, *Biochemistry of Cancer,* p. 509.

In the *first* stage the tumor-protein would seem to be supported by the food—in the *second* stage most probably a part of the protein is supported by the muscle tissue and at that time there is considerable hyperlipemia present which stays there till the reserves of the body's lipids are consumed.

In the *third* (or terminal) stage there is an acute loss of muscle and liver substance and all resistance is lost. How the tumor produces such a condition is unknown. Greenstein assumes "the production by the tumor of a circulating toxin which accelerates the catabolism of the body tissues."[70] Rudolf Keller thought that the progressive loss of K-and K-group minerals are responsible for it by losing the electrical potentials and defense of muscle cytoplasma. The stimulation of the visceral nervous system by the loss of K and the tumor poisons seems also to be contributing to this deleterious effect.

The newer labeled examination with C^{14} glycine by Norberg and D. M. Greenberg proved that the liver and plasma of tumor-bearing animals have an increased protein metabolism.[71]

The same effect also occurs in pregnancy (measured by glycine C^{14} and P^{32} as in the liver of tumor-bearing animals) reflecting a quicker growth somewhere else in the body. That means that this process is not specific for cancer and is not caused by specific toxins.

The beneficial influence of large amounts of carbohydrates in the diet has been recognized. Besides the protective action of glycogen upon the liver cell, further benefit is derived from carbohydrate by virtue of its protein-sparing action. The protective value of carbohydrate appears to be twice that of protein when sufficient protein is already present in the diet to provide plenty and necessary amino acids for reparative purposes. An isocaloric amount of carbohydrate cannot be substituted for proteins without deterioration of the clinical and biochemical state. Fifty-eight grams may be spared by conversion to carbohydrate when 100 grams of protein are fed if the carbohydrate intake is enough to satisfy the immediate need for sugar. Nevertheless, the additional requirement of high "biologic value" protein in patients with liver disease are not known, the indications are that there is a great protein wastage. Anorexia, hypoproteinemia, and loss of weight

---

[70] Ibid., p. 513.

[71] See report by Norberg and Greenberg, *Cancer*, 4:383, 1951.

are positive evidence of protein depletion. Uncompensated liver cell protein catabolism also implies rapid loss of enzyme proteins of all types. Protein repletion may help, therefore, in restoring the necessary enzymes. There is little risk of protein surfeit even if the patient consumes protein beyond satiety. This reassurance is welcome since there is some reluctance in some quarters to overload the insufficient liver. Dock has demonstrated that the liver differs from the kidney in the capacity to handle protein excess. The hepatic artery circulation can take up the increased demand for oxygen when the protein content of the diet is increased to 74 per cent.

A dietary formula which patients accept even with marked anorexia consists of 350 to 500 grams of carbohydrate, 100 to 120 grams of protein, and 50 to 80 grams of fat. This composition of diet is recommended by Snell, Stare and Thorn, Patek, Patek and Post, Fleming and Snell; Ingelfinger and Holt follow this general formula with minor variations. Morrison prescribed a maximum protein regimen which comprises a daily diet of 2500 to 4000 calories with 200 to 300 grams of protein, 300 to 500 grams of carbohydrates and 50 to 100 grams of fat. Goodman and Garvin succeeded in administering a diet with a caloric value of 5000 calories derived from 150 to 250 grams of protein, 600 to 800 grams of carbohydrate and 150 to 200 grams of fat to 18 cases with acute hepatitis. Hourly feedings supplemented three regular meals. An almost "electric" response in the patients' physical and mental appearance was noted. Diets planned in excess of these amounts are not likely to be consumed in their entirety. It is a better policy to offer a diet which is acceptable regularly and consistently. The major problem is not to prescribe a diet of a particular composition but to insure the ingestion of a maximal amount of nutritious food. Missing a meal is a serious handicap in serious liver trouble. It is best replaced promptly by an intravenous infusion of glucose, several authors think.

Every effort is made to make food attractive. Fat and meat add to palatability. For this reason Hoagland recently questioned the wisdom of restricting fat. It appears that patients actually have little difficulty in digesting fats in spite of theoretical considerations. The fact should not be lost from sight that the protective effects of choline and methionine can be reversed by excess fat supplements. Ample fat, however, improves the efficiency of utilization of carbohydrate and protein in the diet. The objectives of improved appetite and increased caloric intake are readily achieved by a liberalized menu. A self-selected fare is a step forward in this direction. The dietitian and physician are invariably guided by matters of available food stocks and principles of diet; the patient knows his personal likes and dislikes better than anyone else. A single unappetizing item in a meal may completely abolish a capricious appetite. Appearance or odor may decide a patient against taking food.

Interest in the diet must not lag for a single meal; the anoretic patient is only too willing to skip the next feeding. Once a meal is consumed, there appears to be no difficulty in handling foodstuffs. Under constant goading, anoretic patients consume prodigious meals regularly, yet suffer no unusual distress. The dietary plan must be flexible enough, however, to permit variations depending on changes in the condition of the patient. For instance, with increasing ascites, cirrhotics find it difficult to swallow large meals. Small concentrated feeds are preferred. Regular-sized meals are resumed after paracentesis. In the average case of liver disease where food intake is a problem, the mid-day repast is usually the "best meal," and the evening meal the worst. It is advisable therefore to offer a light supper supplemented by a generous snack later in the evening. Abdominal distention tends to increase in the latter part of the afternoon and subside after supper. This may influence daily variations in appetite.

It is not a good policy to gorge the patient during one meal only to cope with a disinclination to eat several meals thereafter. Large helpings of fatty foods, although they temporarily improve the appetite, may only pay a limited dividend. Fats delay gastric emptying. Encroachment upon the next meal may prove a net loss in total daily caloric intake.

The protein, fat, and carbohydrate rations are discussed in detail below. The indications and contraindications for parenteral glucose, plasma, whole blood, purified human albumin, protein hydrolysates, synthetic amino acid mixtures and vitamins are reviewed. Diet, however, appeared to have no influence on liver tumors in rats produced by 2-acetylaminofluorene.[72] The manner in which diet produces its procarcinogenic or anticarcinogenic

---

[72] S. S. Lichtman, M.D. *Diseases of the Liver, Gallbladder and Bile Ducts,* Lea & Febiger, Philadelphia, 1953.

effect is unknown.[73] Chemical differences between mitochondria of normal liver and mouse liver hepatoma has been reported by Hogeboom and Schneider.

Some interesting observations in regard to the influence of diet on the development of spontaneous hepatomas in inbred CH₃ mice were made by Tannenbaum and Silverstone. These investigators have shown that increase of fat in the diet from two per cent to 20 per cent increased the rate of hepatoma formation from 37 per cent to 53 per cent. Low riboflavin intake resulted in a decrease of hepatoma formation. This can be attributed to the lowered caloric intake, which has been shown to inhibit growth of hepatomas in this species. It has likewise been shown that, contrary to the experiences in the induced hepatomas in rats, the spontaneous tumors in mice are not accelerated by a rice diet but, on the contrary, are accelerated by increased casein content. Methionine has likewise been shown to accelerate the development of these tumors in mice. The conclusion is drawn that the sulphur-containing amino acids, which are necessary for normal growth, are also necessary for growth and development of these neoplasms. Again a startling indication of the similarity between physiological growth and neoplasia!

Concerning lipotropic substances, Spellberg held that the object of the treatment is to remove the fat from the liver and to reinstitute the normal hepatic histology and physiology. With the tremendous amount of experimental work done on lipotropic agents, and their effectiveness in dietary fatty liver in animals, it is only natural that clinicians should turn to these substances in the treatment of fatty liver; however, the only type of fatty liver that choline (the most important of the lipotropic substances) can cure is the one due to choline deficiency. It is likely that at least some of the fatty livers in man are due to choline deficiency, but in the fatty livers of prolonged infection or those due to toxins, no deficiency of choline in the diet can be postulated, and therefore, no beneficial effect from choline can be expected.[74]

With regard to diet, Spellberg has said that the diet should be high in proteins of good quality, such as meat and fish. A protein intake of 150 gm. a day should be aimed at. The bulk of the calories should be provided by carbohydrates and, there-

[73] Ruth Lohmann, Kli. Wo., 1931, Nr. 39.
[74] Mitchell A. Spellberg, *Diseases of the Liver*, p. 309.

fore, this should be close to 350 gm. a day. The dietary fat should be kept to a minimum. Since a palatable natural diet high in protein cannot be devised fat free, at least 70 gm. of fat must be included. I cannot see how one can condone a high fat diet, especially in the case of fatty liver. What is the logic of supplying more of the substance that we are trying to remove from the liver? When some of this exogenous fat reaches the liver, it requires more lipotropic substances and makes the object of therapy more difficult. The diet should be low in salt if there is evidence of edema or ascites.[75]

"This is principally symptomatic but the diet is of great importance. It should consist entirely of milk and sugar or other carbohydrates. Animal proteins should be reduced to a minimum, as the liver has lost to a great extent, if not entirely, its detoxicating function. Intestinal antisepsis by means of bismuth, salol or calomel may be attempted but without much hope of success. The fluid intake must be maintained at two liters or more a day. The vomiting is best treated by giving fluids half hourly in small quantities but if persistent all foods by mouth should be stopped and intravenous, rectal or subcutaneous administration of glucose saline substituted."[76]

---

[75] Ibid.
[76] Jonathan Cambell Meakins, *The Practice of Medicine*, C. V. Mosby Co., St. Louis, 1944, p. 731.

CHAPTER XII

Development of Liver Medication in Chronic Degenerative Diseases

THE CLASSICAL nutrition was developed under the influence of the discoveries of Justus v. Liebig (1803-1873) and continued by several authors up to the time of v. Noorden, who regarded human nutrition more or less as material for oxidation and restoration. Prior to v. Noorden, the task of the physician was mostly the organization of calories according to the needs of the patient, to give him strength and power to resist chronic degenerative diseases for a longer period of time. In contrast to this more superficial procedure, the modern physician has the task to adapt quality and quantity of nutrition to other factors such as deficiencies in minerals, vitamins and hormones, selection of special proteins, fats, etc. The quantity of food is considered in most cases or adapted to the changing needs of the patients.

The nutrition of the healthy human being is no longer deemed basic for any dietary regime, as v. Liebig had regarded it. The modern concept of examining every item of the diet by itself before selecting it for a special regime produced only failures in my experience. The majority of nutrients are regarded as "pharmakon" according to the doctrine of Hippocrates; this means a medication prescribed for a special purpose in a special dosage. The dietary regime, therefore, does not attempt to compose special nutritional principles of general value. It examines and tests the effect of a properly dosaged diet on the reaction and course of the disease.

The fact that the liver therapy brought about the restoration of new red blood corpuscles (reticulocytes) made it a medication.

It seemed reasonable to assume that such a powerful substance, rich in activated enzymes, would also have similar strong pharmacological effects on other degenerative diseases.

Our experiments showed that patients who followed a dietary regime, rich in potassium, saltless, poor in protein and fat, responded much more strongly and positively to different types and doses of liver medication. On that basis we reduced the protein content of the regime more and more and finally came to the conclusion that we should discontinue all animal proteins in the beginning, as far as possible. We studied the response to different doses of liver medication and found the damaging influence of animal proteins. We found that additional small protein nutrients reduced urine secretion and sodium elimination, even if the urine test showed normal kidney function. We also observed that the detoxication process was retarded and the disappearance of allergic harmful reactions delayed.

Finally, we felt that it may be possible to draw conclusions from the effects of the treatment on visible processes in skin cancers to analogous reactions in the internal organs of the body. Experiences with diabetic patients revealed that additional protein nutrients burden liver and kidneys and make increased doses of insulin necessary. The end products of the general protein metabolism which is urea nitrogen, and uric acid which is from the cell metabolism, could be eliminated in greater amounts the less animal proteins were administered. Frequent occurrences of spasms in the diaphragm, the intestinal tract and even in the heart vessels pointed to overstimulation of the visceral nervous system by additional animal proteins under the conditions of degenerative diseases.

The nuclei of liver cells contain a greater amount of nucleic acids which have to be broken down to uric acid and purin bases. The favorable results obtained with a saltless diet and large doses of liver therapy in the form of raw liver, liver injections, and best with *liver juice** exceeded by far the results seen by the application of the normal nutrition plus the usual liver therapy.

Practical experience taught us that in malignancies it is advisable to apply immediately larger doses of *liver juice** and injections with the crudest liver extract like Lilly No. 370 3cc. combined with vitamin B_{12} 1cc equal 50 mcg. Vitamin B_{12} seems to

* See Appendix III, page 421

help the body make the correct use of amino acids, so that they will not be burned unnecessarily but used instead for constructive purposes. In cancer, it is one of the essential processes to restore the conditions under which foodstuffs can be used in the correct manner. In the last seven to ten years we treated a great number of patients, mostly difficult or terminal cases, with relatively favorable results.

The application of the liver therapy increased the effect of the therapy to a considerable degree. Some indications where the therapy was found favorable may be mentioned here:

    a) Intoxication during pregnancy.

    b) Tuberculosis of the lungs and other organs.

    c) Arthritis deformans in more advanced stages.

    d) Mental diseases and bodily asthenias.

    e) Spastic conditions, especially angina pectoris.

    f) Malignancies.

It may be added that leukemias and myelomas need greater doses of liver juice* and vitamin B_{12} too. In my opinion these two types do not really belong to the "cancers" (so called by Ewing) as their metabolisms are much "deeper" and more differently deranged than we see it in other cancer types.

In the case of all of these diseases, we have cause to assume that concomitant damage to the liver has occurred as a result of permanent intoxication or functional disorders of the neighboring organs (dropped stomach) or by *vagus-sympaticus* disturbances (in allergies). Casimir Funk pointed to the close connection between liver dysfunction, digestive disturbances and allergic diseases many years ago.

In the beginning of the treatment some patients vomit a great amount of bile and suffer from a kind of toxic diarrhea. They become excited, frantic and want to discontinue the treatment. These strong reactions are actually indications of the beginning of improvement, with increased bile production, greater activity of the liver and elimination of toxins and poisons. After a period of one or two days, patients feel greatly relieved, show better circulation, complexion and color, and have more appetite. Then it was found out that detoxication can be accelerated by the increase of coffee enemas and additional castor oil treatments (castor oil by mouth and castor oil enemas), and these violent reactions no long-

* See Appendix III. page 421

er occurred. We see again the fundamental importance of the liver for recovery; but we should not forget that the function of the liver depends upon the regulation of the visceral nervous system. Therefore, the discontinuance of all sedatives and most intensive elimination of toxins and poisons are indispensable: that means liver and pancreas apparatus taken as a whole and the visceral nervous system must be able to function freely.

Liver can be taken as nourishment even by those allergic patients who are highly hypersensitive to animal proteins; as therapy, however, liver nutrition is not sufficient, but must be supported by a more specific liver therapy. Where stronger liver stimulation appears necessary, as in cases of serious intoxication and degenerative diseases, extensive liver injections and liver juice* therapy are necessary. The combination of liver therapy and diet was necessary in serious cases of osteoarthritis, asthma, angina pectoris and malignancies. The combination of a saltless diet, poor in fat and proteins, with the liver therapy, regularly lowers the blood sugar considerably, so that the diet increased the effect of the liver enzymes, increased the effect of insulin, and decreased the adrenalin effect to a great extent. According to Ernst Leupold, the lowering of the blood sugar level is of great significance in cancer patients, and the decrease of the adrenalin effect is regarded so important, that in the last decade even both adrenals were removed by operation, which is too radical and prevents the restoration.[77]

The conclusion of Dr. Edward H. Ray was that "the benefits of the adrenalectomy are so meager and of such short duration that further use of this procedure should be discouraged.[78]

"After oophorectomy the adrenal glands are the most significant source of estrogens. Seventy-nine patients with advanced metastatic breast carcinoma underwent bilateral oophorectomy and adrenalectomy as a combination treatment-prophylaxis technique. There was no objective improvement in 38.7 per cent of the patients and subjective improvement in 57.3 per cent. Indications for this type of surgical management include objective

---

77 Prof, Ernst Leupold, *Die Bedeutung des Blutchemismus zur Tumorbildung und Tumor Abbau* (Significance of Blood Chemistry- in Tumor Production and Tumor Absorption, Georg Thieme Verlag, Stuttgart, 1954.

78 "Endocrine Therapy of Prostatic Carcinoma, from *The Journal of the AMA*, March 23, 1957, p. 1008.

demonstration of disseminated metastases. Jaundice from extensive metastases has been considered the only contraindication as far as the location of the metastatic lesions is concerned."[79]

SUMMARY

As a whole, the liver therapy may be looked upon as a kind of hormone-enzyme therapy, but in a very mild dosage and natural manner. It was found helpful in returning glycogen, K-group minerals and vitamins to the liver and other tissues and finally in preparing the conditions for the function of the oxidizing enzymes.

---

[79] Reported by Maurice Galante, M.D. and others, "Adrenalectomy for Metastatic Breast Carcinoma," *The Journal of the AMA,* March 23, 1957, p. 1011.

CHAPTER XIII

Scientists Term Radiation A Peril
to Future of Man*

A Cumulative Effect

SHOCK AND surprise were expressed by the committee on genetics in its finding that the American public was using up about one third of the safety limit in medical and dental X-rays. Its members called on the medical profession to reduce the use of X-rays to the lowest limit consistent with medical necessity.

This committee also urged a national system of personal records whereby every American would know his total amount of exposure. The effect of radiation is cumulative, it is said, no matter how long the period over which it is experienced.

The six committees studied the radiation problem in the fields of genetics, pathology, meteorology, oceanography and fisheries, agriculture and food supplies, and disposal and dispersal of radioactive wastes. . . .

Pathological effects: Dr. Shields Warren, Chairman—Recommendations will be made in the future. The committee concluded in agreement with geneticists that radiation, no matter how small the dose, shortens life in some degree. . . .

Dr. Weaver's genetics committee recommended as a general population safety limit that exposure to radiation should be held down to 10 roentgens for the first 30 years of a person's life. A roentgen is a unit for measuring the harmful gamma ray from medical and dental X-ray equipment, nuclear weapons explosions and from natural causes like cosmic rays and natural radium.

---

* Anthony Leviero, *New York Times,* June 13, 1956. Survey of a report held in the National Academy of Sciences, Washington, D. C. on the "Biological Effects of Atomic Radiation."

As a result of medical X-rays it is estimated that each person in this country receives on the average a total accumulated dose to the gonads or sex glands about three roentgens in 30 years. "Of course, some persons get none at all; others may get a good deal. . . ." Dr. Weaver declared it was "stupid genetically" to use X-ray for the fitting of shoes. He was referring to the X-ray devices that have become common in shoe stores and into which children often stare in awe, sometimes without regard to time at the shadows of the bones of their feet.

Dr. Weaver also condemned obstetricians who make X-ray pictures of pregnant mothers to show them how "beautifully formed" is the skeleton of their baby without realizing the "hazards" of the dose of three or four roentgens that is being administered.

In addition to six long summary reports of the committees, the scientists also issued "a report to the public" in the simplest language possible. Here the layman may read how radiation damage inevitably results from exposure, no matter how small the dose.

Radiation causes mutation or harmful changes in the genes or germ cells of the reproductive organs. Damage manifests itself in shortening of the life span, reduces ability to produce children, and sometimes, but not often, produces deformed or freakish children.

Even if the mutations is in one gene, there is some harmful effect that mutation will go on through every generation until the line that bears it becomes extinct.

The report explained how "every cell of a person's body contains a great collection, passed down from the parents, the parents' parents, and so on back, of diverse heredity units called genes."

The layman's report went on to explain:

"From the point of view of the total and eventual damage to the entire population, every mutation causes roughly the same amount of harm. This is because mutant genes can only disappear when the inheritance line in which they are carried dies out. In cases of severe and obvious damage this may happen in the first generation; in other cases it may require hundreds of generations.

"Thus, for the general population, and in the long run, a little radiation to a lot of people is as harmful as a lot of radiation to a few, since the total number of mutant genes can be the same in the two cases."

But damage to future generations due to radiation will be difficult to identify. The study of genetics damage has only just begun, with a report due on genetic effects observed in the populations of Hiroshima and Nagasaki, the Japanese cities destroyed by American atom bombs in World War II. . . .

The committee said the radiologists "may well receive doses in the course of their occupation ranging from very slight to about 1,000 roentgens."

In fixing a "reasonably safety" limit of 10 roentgens, the Weaver panel commented, "not harmless, mind you, but reasonable." Of this safety limit, the panel said, "we are now using on the average some three or four roentgens for medical X-rays."

"This is roughly the same as the unavoidable dose received from background radiation," the Weaver panel added. "It is really very surprising and disturbing to realize that this figure is so large, and clearly it is prudent to examine this situation carefully. It is folly to incur any X-ray exposure to the gonads which can be avoided without impairing medical service or progress."

While there exists no way of measuring a dose of radiation sustained by sex organs, the Weaver committee said that unless shielding was used some part of every dental or medical X-ray reached these organs. They said a dental X-ray would deliver about 0.005 roentgen to the gonads, and a general fluoroscopic examination two or more roentgens.

In the last 10 years science has introduced into the cancer therapy isotopes: radioactive iodine, cobalt, phosphorus, strontium, as well as proteins and hormones. In the beginning there was a lot of optimism about the new methods, but a great disillusion soon followed. (End of report.)

My own experiences show that the majority of patients who had 40 to 80 deep X-ray treatments and, in addition, 16 to 40 cobalt treatments could not recover at all. Some improved after a much longer period and others only partially.

The following appeared in an article on radiation in the *New York Times* on July 21, 1957:

SAFETY LIMIT IS SET

As a safety limit, the National Academy of Sciences has recommended, that the average person receive not more than ten roentgens of man-made radiation to the reproductive organs from conception to the age of 30.

The roentgen is a unit of measurement of radiation dose.

The report also lends new support to the repeated warnings of atomic officials and scientists that man faces a far greater danger from medical use of radiation than he does from the radio-active fall-out from atomic testings.

A similar warning came last month from Dr. Leroy E. Burney, Surgeon General of the United States Public Health Service, who said that in view of the increasing sources of radiation in the nuclear age, the time had come to reassess the safe levels of radiation from medical treatment.

In recent years there has been an increasing awareness in the medical profession of the potential danger of radiation from X-ray treatments, and steps have been instituted to limit the radiation dose.

ESTIMATE SEEN HIGH

The report states, that the estimate is probably accurate to within a factor or two. In other words, the thirty-year dose to the gonads could be as low as two Roentgens and as high as eight Roentgens. The belief among some radiation experts is that, if anything, the estimate is on the high side.

Because of the inevitable uncertainty of statistical analyses of limited data, scientists are recommending that a population sampling program be undertaken to determine more exactly how much X-ray radiation is received by the average person.

Such sampling program is to be recommended to the United Nations Scientific Committee on the Effects of Atomic Radiation by the International Commissions on Radiological Protection and Radiological Units and Measurements.

CHAPTER XIV

Mineral Metabolism in Degenerative Diseases

THE GENERAL approach to the treatment of patients with degenerative diseases should have as its purpose the overcoming of the
biochemical abnormalities which are more or less responsible for
the development of the disease. I am convinced that the problem
of chronic diseases is not one of biochemistry, chemistry or the
symptoms we observe in and on the body. Rather, it is produced
by deeper-lying forces which cause "deficiency of energies." Physicians observe biological symptoms and work only with them.
The real acting forces behind the visible chemical changes are
physical energies, expressed by Einstein as the "electro-magnetic
field." To a certain degree, this is closely connected with the
electrical potentials which are lowered in cancer, according to
almost all investigators (about 30) and also according to the
observations of Dr. Rudolf Keller.

The above-mentioned biochemical symptoms are expressed in
Hastings' "Terminology" as "intra-cellular" or "K-group minerals
in essential organs" and the "extra-cellular" or "Na-group minerals
in the fluids." Laboratory findings reveal that in chronic diseases,
sodium and calcium, both negatively charged, invade the weaker
positively charged organs; accordingly, K is lost from these
organs, opening the door to further negative metabolic transformations. *Here the disease starts, but not the symptoms.*

It is my opinion that K and Na also play an important role in
the cancer problem. These two minerals are the leaders of the
two electrically opposite groups. They are in close connection
with the development and maintenance of the human body as
well as with the origin and progress of the disease. The human

89

organism is, in embryonic life and early infancy, a sodium-animal, due to the relative preponderance of Na throughout the entire organism, but, in adult life, a potassium-animal. The potassium predominance must be maintained throughout life. To a certain degree it gives the basis for important developments in both directions—normal and abnormal. In this respect, the amount of minerals is necessary but the degree of their ionization is equally important, particularly in cancer.

We know now that what we have inherited is not a set of chemical substances, but a "pattern of dynamic energies," which directly distribute and ionize the minerals, hormones and enzymes, etc., for harmonic cooperation within living cells and tissues, where they belong and in which way they have to act and influence the growing tissue. Seen from this point of view, the chemical facts as they appear in the laboratory findings have the following line in our development: The unfertilized human egg cell is 1/10 mm in size, full of K-group or intracellular minerals (K, P, Mg, Mn, Cu, Fe, Au), electro-positive and has the corresponding enzymes, vitamins and protein-compounds, but the whole is inactive, waits and longs for animation. The sperm, which is 1/200 mm in size, contains the Na-group minerals and is electro-negative (Na, Cl. H_2O, I, Br. Al and the ionized part of Ca), together with the other group of enzymes and vitamins, but is active and brings on enlivenment. The fertilized egg becomes, through a process of discharging some compositions and absorbing a great deal of Na from the surrounding lymph fluid, distinctly negatively charged; a "Na-animal" is created and remains one throughout the entire pregnancy and up to six months after birth (Frank Golland). The tables on pp. 25, 26, 27 of Chapter 3 illustrate the different stages of development by taking the Na/K ratio as a guide.

In studying these figures, which are based on laboratory findings, one has to accept the strange fact that these Na-rich embryonal cells have, according to Speman, "organisator" power, which carry in themselves the dynamic patterns of the "preformed" future animal. The months of pregnancy and six months of extra-uterine life (Frank Golland) are only a "transitional stage" of a living being, which continues to pass over into normal life with an excess of K-group minerals in vital organs, until disease or old age makes it lose some of the K-minerals, together with the corresponding enzyme-functions, etc. Each cell carries in itself some potentialities of a normal living cell under normal internal and external environmental conditions, or else they fall back to their original embryonic state. R. R. Spencer and other investigators, with keen foresight, compare cancer cells not to the cells of old age but, rather, to embryonic ones. One important difference, however, is that cancer cells are not supplied with nerves and therefore lack nervous regulation. The experiments of Lohmann revealed that magnesium and manganese, both minerals of the K-group, inhibit the Pasteur effect there.

In *The Biochemistry of Malignant Tumors*, the Pasteur effect is described as follows: "The increased conversion of methylglyoxal to lactic acid which thus may be induced by the activated enzyme was believed to be responsible for the accumulation of lactic acid in neoplasm, and the rapid disappearance of methylglyoxal was thought to interfere with the re-synthesis of this compound to hexose."[80]

Inasmuch as our mineral metabolism is dependent upon the food produced by the soil, I would like to refer to an introduction to this subject by Charles E. Kellogg. "The soil is the living matter at the surface, and of the mineral matter beneath the surface, and of the atmosphere above and the solid rock beneath—essentially all living matter depends upon it, directly or indirectly, is, in fact, a part of those very processes that produce the soil upon which life depends.

"Plants and soils have grown up together, each partly a cause of the other—man has somewhat the same relationship to the soils. He may change them, either for better or for worse."[81]

HYPOKALEMIA

The leading mineral of the negative group, potassium, plays an important role in clinical symptomatology, for example, in *The Journal of the AMA*, we find the following summary:[82] It is known that K-deficiency may occur when the

---

[80] Kurt Stern and Robert Willheim, *The Biochemistry of Malignant Tumors*, p. 499.
[81] Charles E. Kellogg, *The Soils That Support Us*, The Macmillian Co., 1956.
[82] See *The Journal of the American Medical Association*, 143, 1950. p. 432.

(1) food shows diminished content of this mineral.
(2) in cases of vomiting, caused by many reasons, also by ob-struction in cancer.
(3) in leukemia, as leukocytes attract large amounts of K.
(4) in excessive diureses.
(5) adreno-cortical hormone favors re-absorption of Na and loss of K. If this hormone is over-active, the consequence is excessive loss of K.

HYPERKALEMIA

(1) usually does not occur as a result of oral administration as long as the kidneys are intact.
(2) in cancer, in advanced cases, one finds hyperkalemia not too rarely, caused by loss of K from tissues—*now* extracellular in the serum, on the *way to elimination.*
(3) in some cases of renal insufficiency, also in depression, in dehydration and in some forms of nephritis.

Based on other articles and my own experience, I would like to give the following summary of hypokalemia and hyperkalemia.

HYPOKALEMIA

(1) diabetes—more during insulin therapy.
(2) intravenous glucose and other injections, when free of K.
(3) Cushing's syndrome,
        Glaucoma
        Paralysis agitans
        Frequently in chronic arthritis, chronic sinusitis and other chronic diseases.
(4) following administration of Cortisone (Adrenal cortex)
(5) undernourished patient, also fasting
(6) loss of K in vomiting, diarrhea, gastric suction.
(7) familiar periodic paralysis.
(8) cancer—mostly in medium or far advanced cases.

HYPERKALEMIA

(1) loss of fluids—blood, in majority of cases dehydration.
(2) epilepsy—most cases.
(3) cancer patients more often in the period before they go over to the terminal stage (on the way to elimination).
(4) never in cancer patients during restoration time.
(5) Addison's disease.
(6) anuria—uremia (inability of liver and kidneys to excrete excess potassium in solution—lost from essential organs)
(7) acute and chronic asthma, and other degenerative allergies (also craurosis vulvae).

The content of potassium in the serum is, in many cases, misleading. The latest article of Burnell and Scribner also tends in this direction but starts to draw attention to the observation that "changes in the serum potassium concentration reflect changes in body need."[83] My experiences are mostly limited to cancer cases. The curves of these patients over years are very difficult to evaluate. (Not one examination, but the curve decides.) Single examinations can *not* be regarded as "an excellent guide to the potassium need of patients"—as the above-mentioned authors say. It does not give any definite indication of an increasing or decreasing amount of potassium present in the *tissues* of essential organs. There are only a few examinations made in serum and tissues at the same time. More coincident examinations of K made at the same time in serum and tissues and in different stages of the disease, are necessary for such decisions.

Potassium appears to play an indispensable and unique role in tissue protein synthesis, although the mechanism of its utilization is at present unknown. Potassium ions are indispensable in certain enzymatic reactions, and this may be a further reason for its urgent need. It appears that the heavy isotope K^{41} is definitely lower in tumors, as well as in tissues of tumor-bearing animals.[84]

Muscles, brain and liver normally have a much higher potassium content than a sodium content. It can be accepted as a

---

[83] See *The Journal of the American Medical Association,* Vol. 164, No. 9, June 29, 1957, p. 959.
[84] See A. Lasnitzki and S. K. Brewer, *Cancer Research,* 2.494, 1942.

general rule that as long as potassium is normally in the majority, sodium is in the minority. A similar relationship exists between magnesium and calcium, so that where magnesium is increased, calcium is diminished.

Kurt Stern and Robert Willheim wrote that "A tumor promoting property of potassium salts administered perorally or parenterally has been made very probable. The impeding action of calcium salts is much more problematic and the alleged anti-plastic quality of magnesium must be regarded as wholly unfounded."[85] In the older literature, controversial opinions were expressed regarding one of the most important mineral constituents of food, sodium chloride. Some authors suspected this salt as the most stimulating neoplastic growth agent and accordingly, recommended its restriction in the cancer diet.[86] Other clinical observations indicated that regimes extremely poor in salt, such as have been used for dietary treatment of tuberculosis,[87] exert a "rather unfavorable influence on human neoplasia."[88]

The effects of sodium chloride on tumors were studied in a number of animal experiments which were not conclusive. Whether cancer was stimulated by alkalosis or was hindered by acid formation has been long disputed. Finally, Ragnar Berg strongly rejected the viewpoint that diets producing alkalosis could be responsible for cancer development.[89] In evaluating most of these studies, one finds that all these attempts to change the hydrogen ion concentration in blood and tissues by special dietary combinations encounter great difficulties, since every author used some other food for that purpose. Some of the authors used thymus, an organ rich in protein and nucleic acids, but very poor in minerals; others used kidneys, livers and extracts prepared from different organs. According to the clinical observation that the incidence of malignant tumors in the duodenum and small intestines are extremely rare, they used for their experiments

---

[85] Kurt Stern and Robert Willheim, *The Biochemistry of Malignant Tumors*, p. 410.

[86] A. Lorand: *First International Cancer Congress*, Madrid, 2:48, 1933.

[87] Dr. Max Gerson, *Dietary Therapy of Lung Tuberculosis*, 1934.

[88] F. Blumenthal, *First International Cancer Congress*, Madrid 1:793, 1933, E. Hesse, *Deutsche Medizinische Wochenschrift*, 61:797, 1935.

[89] See *Zeitschrift fuer Volksernaehrung*, 9:277, 1934.

these organs in animals bearing transplanted tumors and in others to prevent any growth.

Blumenthal and Jacobs used a special extract of small intestines without much of a favorable result.[90] A slightly more favorable result was obtained by the feeding of the brain or extracts of this organ. These observations, made by A. H. Roffo, H. Vassiliades and C. Roussv during 1935-1937 are extremely interesting since the substance of these organs are rich in lipids which have generally been found to stimulate tumor growth. "The development of tar cancer in mice was found enhanced by the feeding of liver or pancreas to the animals,"[91] and the tumor-stimulating effect of liver feeding was confirmed in numerous studies of various tumor-bearing animals. An entirely different effect of liver feeding was observed by the production of liver tumors in rats by feeding butter yellow. This type of carcinogenesis could be prevented by a liver diet. It is interesting that feeding of liver could only prevent carcinogenic development of butter yellow, but it could not prevent the tumor production by benzpyrene or methylcholanthrene. The cause of these influences, which differ in various forms of neoplasms, was not given. Kurt Stern tentatively assumed that the effective unknown factors may be of an enzymatic nature and that vitamins and "these hypothetical agents may interfere with tumor development and tumor growth via metabolic mechanisms." I have expressed a similar opinion in several articles, and in this book explained the use of fresh calf's liver juice* in cancer therapy. These controversial observations and descriptions are chosen to demonstrate how controversial the biological literature in cancer is. For each positive effect one can find a negative one. Generalizations in cancer are most difficult to formulate. In my opinion, the area wherein they may be possible will be in the biological field of electrical potentials, ionization of minerals and reactivation of enzymes.

Greenstein has stated that "In tumors in rats, mice or man, the catalytic systems involved in aerobic oxidations are considerably reduced as compared with normal tissues and, indeed, in each species, are reduced to nearly the same extent. A high rate of glycolysis, an increased water content, and a low activity of

---

[90] See *Zeitschrift fucr Krebsforchung*, W.545, 1933.

[91] A. F. Watson, *American Journal of Cancer*, 19:389, 1933.

* See Appendix III. page 421

cytochrome are among the characteristics of practically all tumors in all species studied. Nearly all rapidly growing tumors in mice and rats produce identical systemic effects in the host animals, as shown by the marked reduction in liver catalase activity."[92]

Cancer is the most variable disease we have for which there are thousands of different names. The beginning can be most acute or very chronic, the course tedious or rapid, the complications innumerable, and it can be combined with many different deficiencies, with high or low blood pressure, with diabetes, arteriosclerosis and other diseases of old age. At the end, the intoxication increases and the liver deteriorates. Most of our life is built upon the activation and maintenance of the living processes. These are based on the mineral metabolism and function of the liver—which acts like chlorophyll in plants—accepting ions from the sun and transforming them as "life begets life." What Nature does in that wonderful, subtle form by transformations and combinations with these ions *we* cannot imitate biologically. Therefore, it seems to me advisable not to *attack the cancer directly* with X-Rays, radium or cobalt and damage at the same time the other parts of the body and its healing power. The more the whole body is detoxified, replenished and activated, the more the cancer is doomed.

The rare incidence of malignant tumors in countries where garlic is used in greater amounts (southern Italy, Greece, Montenegro, Yugoslavia) cannot be explained. I have seen two cancers of the breast disappear with the use of Fenugreek seeds tea in large amounts, combined with a saltless vegetarian diet. Two others were cured after the patients drank green leaf juice only for six to eight months.

The transformation of the minerals in the body and bringing them in sufficient numbers into the organs, where they belong, is a very difficult and complex task. A special relationship exists between sodium, chloride, and amino acids, which seem to parallel the amount of edema in the body. On the other hand, potassium belongs to a group which is associated with phosphoric acids and carbohydrates and is able to combine with these colloids. It is, therefore, more reasonable to speak of the potassium group and the sodium group as Rudolf Keller does.

---

[92] Jesse Greenstein, *Biochemistry of Cancer*, p. 589, 1954.

The effect of the diet is that the potassium group is enriched in the essential organs and the abnormal sodium content in these organs reduced to a minimum and eliminated into the extra-cellular fluids, where they belong.

The extracellular fluids which comprise the blood plasma, the tissue or interstitial fluid, lymph and fluid in serous cavities, amount to about 20 per cent of the body weight. The plasma water constitutes only about four and one-half per cent of the body weight. The fluids within the cells amount to 50 per cent of the weight of the body, or two and one-half times the extra-cellular fluids. The skeletal muscles contain about 50 per cent, the skin about 20 per cent, and the whole blood only about 10 per cent of the total body water. In general, the intracellular fluids have a high potassium content and a low concentration of sodium, whereas the extracellular fluids have large amounts of sodium and small amounts of potassium. The water content of various tissues in average percentage is taken from a table:[93]

	Percent
Muscle (striated)	75
Skin	70
Connective tissues	60
Blood:	
Plasma	90
Cells	65
Kidney	80
Liver	70
Nerve matter:	
Gray matter	85
White matter	70

The higher sodium chloride content in the urine of cancer patients during the first weeks of the saltless treatment proves that sodium chloride and water are retained in cancer patients. The majority of the patients did not show any type of definite edema on the skin. A few of them were even undernourished, seemingly dried out and emaciated, but still eliminated very large quantities of sodium chloride in their urine, especially at first. The retention was probably in the internal organs.

---

[93] Best and Taylor, *The Physiological Basis of Medical Practice*, Williams and Wilkins Co., Baltimore, 1950. p. 19.

If we contemplate the mineral metabolism as the basis for the construction of cells, we have to look into an invisible mineral circulation with a great storage power of the minerals of the potassium group and glycogen in the liver and equally for iodine and the minerals of the sodium group in the thyroid gland. If these mineral groups are partly displaced as we see in most acute as well as chronic diseases, we find simultaneously lower electrical potentials in the tissues and serum. Consequently, the storage power is smaller and the flow *from* the storage magazines is greater as the cells lose their normal attraction power with the lowered potentials. This smaller attraction power results in reduced storage of glycogen in liver and muscles and also in fewer minerals of the potassium group, while in the thyroid, the skin and other mainly negative tissues, the iodine and extracellular elements, show deficiencies or displacements.

The importance of potassium, iodine and blood sugar leads the physicians more and more to pursue these tests in almost all patients, as they give us valuable information not only about these mentioned substances but also about many other clinical processes. To have a better insight into the clinical processes of our patients, it is not sufficient to examine single substances, since we learn that a single substance does not travel alone from the blood to the tissue cells or inversely. To confirm this, one may stain a cell with many dyes; one single microscopic cell or part of it will not accept the stain of one dye only.

Behind the metabolism of minerals and matter there is a power of energy, an electrostatic and an electrodynamic one, and probably several other energies, which are the stimulating powers for all movements of matter. One should not think of matter in quantities or qualities only but also should take into account the quantities of energies which radiate from ionized minerals, and should stimulate and keep all important and vital functions of the cells active.

As H. Kaunitz and B. Schober have shown, the electrical potentials of liver and muscles went down by 30 millivolt or more after they injected diphtheria toxin or other poisons into the blood stream of a rabbit. After a few minutes one could observe with a microscope that some poisons entered the parenchyma cells which were repelled beforehand by the same cells. After one-half hour a quantity of sodium appeared in the liver parenchyma. This experiment, made in 1936, clearly shows that

1) intoxication is the first effect, which is followed by
2) loss of electrical potentials and
3) loss of potassium minerals.

This test demonstrates also the central position of the liver in all these processes. For centuries it was assumed by good clinicians that changes in the liver were the beginning of almost all diseases. As the liver gradually loses a part of its electrostatic maintenance power for reserves, it cannot support the entire body normally any longer from its reserves of glycogen, many minerals, vitamins and enzymes, especially during the night, but can store them during the daytime. K. H. Bauer wrote: "A great progress in the problem of cancer development is the recognition that it belongs to the *general* biology. The cells involved are changed into a different life existence. The fact that all kinds of tumors can be present in all living organisms is the confirmation of those findings. . . . Within all living beings the capacity exists to fall sick with cancer, which is a property of all tissues and organs."[94]

To bring the system to normal or near to normal for healing purposes, it needs animating energies besides the pure substances without which it is unable to act, cooperate and fulfill duties for metabolism and distribution. It is impossible to live without the energies which are moving all substances all over the body and are supporting all cells.

The attempts of old and new medical authors to abandon the most specific methods or the symptomatic treatments and to rely upon and to stress the "conception of totality" have many advantages. Putting the positive center of the liver and the negative center of the thyroid more in the foreground is necessary for this therapy.

There are some particular details in the mineral metabolism which characterize the new treatment. First, there is the artificial niacin besides the important potassium. Niacin showed very good clinical results when administered in large doses, six to eight times

---

[94] K. H. Bauer, *Das Krebsproblem*, p. 671.

50 mg. a day (it is the so-called pellagra preventive factor, also known as Vitamin B$_3$). The theoretical explanation was given later by Dr. W. Beiglboeck, who proved in animal experiments that it is a "potential restorer" and raises the depleted liver stores of glycogen. W. O. Fenn also thinks that it restores the depleted potassium stores in the liver. Niacin is not only a vitamin, indispensable for the protein metabolism, but also is, as Elvehjem and others showed, an efficient restorer of cell energies in a great number of diseases from the common cold to cancer.

Another characteristic feature of the treatment is the liberal use of iodine in the inorganic form of lugol-solution and the organic form of thyroid. Both are strong restorers of the electrical potentials and cell activity. The thyroid gland stores only 20 per cent of all the body's iodine content. The rest of the body's iodine is contained in the skeletal muscles, the liver and central nervous system, but it is also relatively highly concentrated in the pituitary gland and in the ovaries. The thyroid gland takes up about 80 times more iodine than does any other tissue. To help the body in the oxidation power, iodine must be radioactive (I^{130} and I^{131}). The I^{131} isotope has the longest half life (eight days).

In cancer patients we observe that the basal metabolism can be very high, up to 68 or down to minus 36. Corresponding is the iodine content of the blood serum above or below normal, and it can be very excessive in both directions, particularly in more advanced cases. With the therapy the high iodine content can be brought to normal or below normal in a relatively short time, from 10-20 days. That means that the body was losing great amounts of iodine at the beginning of the treatment and the therapy reversed this process. A very low iodine content may indicate that the body had already lost most of its iodine reserves and now absorbs iodine during the therapy in relatively great quantities. Not one examination, but the curve decides.

It is generally accepted that the organic iodine of the blood serum is a more reliable index than the metabolic rate, as the latter is not controlled exclusively by the thyroid. Iodine seems to play an important role in tumors themselves. In mouse and rat tumors the iodine concentration was found to exceed that of liver and muscle.

The iodine deposition in tumors is a debated question. It is reported *increased* by other authors, but only after the onset of regressive changes in the tumor.

An interesting report by Greenstein states that I^{131} in the blood of normal and tumor bearing mice is the same, but the *decreased* capacity of tumor-mice in concentration of administered I^{131} "is probably related to some change in the physiology of the thyroid glands themselves."[95] It would be shortsighted, even incorrect, to observe one of the mineral substances alone, or a group of them. *Innumerable metabolisms continue to act simultaneously, and many abnormal steps have to be made until a symptom appears.* The clinical signs are then uncharacteristic, such as fatigue, weakness, easy exhaustion, more excitability—all these can be due to many different deficiencies or causes. To stimulate the body with one or another vitamin, or a group of them, or a mixture of them with minerals, may help for a short while. It is a difficult decision to determine where to stimulate and where only to replenish the organs. This is a difficult task because the organs may have developed some pathological alterations in the meantime. Alarm symptoms or special infections may be exceptions but these are limited to a short period and require symptomatic treatment.

In most situations, especially in chronic and degenerative diseases, it is much safer and more favorable for the organism to be helped in its totality; this means the entire metabolism must be restored to normal or near-normal functions.

As far as the mineral metabolism is concerned, it seems to be the basis for the active development of a malignancy in a poisoned body. The mineral metabolism in itself is not enough to explain the number of factors involved in that biological situation. It seems to be the general basis on which many different deficiencies occur with serious consequences in the metabolic processes of protein, fats, and, to a lesser degree, in carbohydrates. Under such conditions the digestion and oxidation to the end products are progressively damaged. I will try to give an approximate picture about a conception of normal life and the deviation into cancer.

---

[95] Jesse Greenstein, *Biochemistry of Cancer*, p. 202.

Life means:	*Cancer means:*
1. Maintenance of the normal metabolism, its regulations and productions for hormones, enzymes, co-enzymes, etc., absorption and elimination power.	1. Slow intoxication and alteration of the whole body, especially the liver.
2. Maintaining the prevalence of the potassium group in vital organs and Na-group mainly outside in the fluids and some tissues.	2. Invasion of the Na-group, loss of K-group, followed by tissue edema.
3. Keeping the positive electrical potentials of the cells high as the basis for energy and function, simultaneously as a defense against invasion of the Na-group and the formation of edema.	3. Lower electrical potentials in vital organs, more edema, accumulation of poisons, loss of tension, tonus, reduced reactivation and oxidation power, dedifferentiation of some cells.
4. Maintenance of circulation, tension, tonus, storage capacity, reserves.	4. Cancer starts—general poisoning increases, vital functions and energies decrease —cancer increases.
5. Reactivation power of vital substances, especially enzymes.	5. Further destruction of the metabolism and liver parenchym — cancer rules — is acting, spreading.
6. Defense and healing power.	6. Loss of last defense—hepatic coma—death.

I would like to say a word about the problem of transmineralization in our body. I know how difficult it is for physicians to take a positive stand on that problem. Von Bergmann hoped that the time will come when we will learn to add the deficient substances therapeutically. I would like to formulate this hope differently, as I think the time will come when we will learn, according to the concept of totality, to add in the right composition, the substances which we find to be lacking. At the same

time the other substances and poisons which we found to be
antagonistic or counteracting have to be eliminated. The problem
of transmineralization is not yet recognized thoroughly enough
to show all the therapeutic difficulties which have to be overcome
to restore the disturbed harmony in the mineral metabolism, step
by step. From my own clinical experiments I have learned that
it is not only necessary to change the metabolism in one or another
substance, but it is also necessary to change the intake of proteins,
enzymes, vitamins, etc., simultaneously to activate all natural
healing forces which we need for our therapy.

CHAPTER XV

Distribution of Enzymes in Organs

MANY AUTHORS comment as K. H. Bauer says in his book: *The Cancer Problem* (page 116) translated, "one encounters again and again in the literature the conviction: the riddle of cancer can be solved by chemistry of enzymes . . ."[96] or by biochemistry as Dr. Radvin reported in the Senate Hearing 1957.

I think it will not be this way. It should be pointed out: the conditions in the cells have to be basically and functionally changed first; the whole metabolism in each cell is pathologically transformed in its protein and fat digestion and exchange. That change transforms automatically the enzyme-metabolisms which are adjustments to the preceding pathologies.

"Practically all reactions which occur in organisms can be attributed to the action of the enzymes."[97] The enzymes have an "extremely specific action," in order to make a reaction take place a certain resistance in the cell is to be overcome. That means: the molecules within the cells must be activated; a certain amount of activation energy has to be supplied by the body: for example—in the cells glycogen is broken down to carbon dioxide and water by a large number of enzymatic reactions. This is the most simple cell metabolic function and maintained for the longer period, while protein and fat metabolisms are in the same cells and at the same time quicker and farther reaching deranged.

Enzymes function as they are mostly organized in chain reactions—some are inextricably connected with the living organism, "they can not be extracted, with intact activity, from cells or

---

[96] K. H. Bauer, *Das Krebsproblem*, p. 116.

[97] James B. Sumner and Karl Myrbäck, *The Enzymes*, Academic Press, 1950, p. 1.

tissues." Therefore two types of enzymes were in existence (discernable):

1.) Enzymes that can be secreted and extracted.
2.) Enzymes which are inextricable (fixed in the cells).

Enzymes can be reactivated in the liver and have to be supplied to the cells.

The consequences for the cancer therapy are, that for the restoration of enzymatic functions the content of the cells has to be restored. That is impossible in cancer cells—possible and necessary in the other cells.

All investigators found that malignant tumors are characterized by a considerable electronegativity in the tissues and fluids. Starting from this premise, I looked over the accumulations of minerals in normal and abnormal tissues and their electropolarity. I found a center of high electronegativity in the thyroid, based upon the accumulation of an extracellular group. The classification in extracellular (negative) and intracellular (positive) substances is correct for *inorganic minerals* in electrical currents.[98] In biological experiments of living tissue, however, Hoeber discovered some striking deviations, confirmed by later authors, Matsuo, Wilbrand, and others.

The following table consists of the classical lyophile groups from Hofmeister and Spiro in the order of Hoeber's findings: [Contrary to the findings in inorganic electrochemistry K (potassium) is negative, traveling to the anode (Waelsch 1934) while Na. I. Br. is electropositive, traveling to the cathode (Keller 1930). In this book and other literature the minerals are characterized as positive according to the organs where they are deposited in the majority.]

TABLE 1

Electropositive	Borderline	Electronegative
Li, Na, Al, Fl	Ca.	Rb, Cs, K, NH₄
CNS, I, No₃ Br	Cl	Acetate, SO₄, PO₄, tartrate.

This table shows the antagonism of the extracellular group—positivating, to the intracellular group—negativating (both according to Hoeber).

---

[98] *Handbook of Nutrition*, American Medical Association, 1943, p. 97, Table 2.

As the first step, it was found that the minerals are deposited preponderantly either in the positive or negative sense in the organs of the body. As a consequence, one could differentiate the organs in prevalent positive or negative organs, as confirmed by measurements made by Kaunitz and Schober.

As a second step, it was revealed that many organic substances show a characteristic electric charge by being accumulated predominantly in more positive organs or in more negative fluids, connective tissue, thyroid, spleen, parietal cells, spermatozoas, growing malignancies.

As a further step, I tried to study the distribution of enzymes in different organs; there it appears to be a characteristic classification of one kind of enzymes in these and another kind of enzymes in other organs.

For some years, H. S. Burr and his collaborators published many significant facts concerning the electropolarity of malignant growth. The first important discovery was the observation that a bioelectrical alteration was found to precede the tumor development, and the second, that all malignant tumors are electronegative! The late G. W. Crile, and his collaborators, M. Telkes and A. F. Rowland, found a decreased electric polarization and an increased electric conductivity in malignant tumors which may be caused, in my opinion, by the greater sodium content in the growing part of the tumor (Goodman and others). Several investigators found, without exception, malignant tumor tissue negative by 10-20 millivolts with unpolarizable electrodes, whereas by using redox electrodes greater potentials were found which amounted to 100 millivolts and more, as unpolarizable electrode measures the ions and metal electrodes the electrons.

As one indicator for electropolarity, there was found, for instance, the distribution between blood corpuscles (intracellular, the electronegative substances) and serum (extracellular, positive substances). As another factor, there could be used the accumulation in organs such as the liver, nerve, brain, muscle, cortex of kidney or the acinus of pancreas, all preponderantly positive organs storing mostly negative intracellular matter whereas the cutis of the skin, medulla of the kidney, colloid of the thyroid and thymus, stomach and distal intestinal mucosa, bile capillaries and the connective tissues attract positive from extracellular matter, repelling normally the other. I have selected an author who did not use the word electricity in his biochemical works and does not propagate any hypothesis. The following tables are examples taken from Jesse P. Greenstein's tables.[99]

TABLE 1

	3 positive enzymes			2 negative enzymes	
	Arginase	Catalase	Cytochrom-oxidase	Alk. Phosphatase	Depolymerase thymonuclease
Positive structures					
Liver	246	8.00	8	4	14
Muscle skel.	4	.01	6	2	12
Brain	3	.00	10	12	4
Negative structures					
Spleen	6	.12	2	17	16
Skin	27	.01	..	5	10
Thymus	2	.00	..	2	3
Gastric mucosa	4	.00	1	17	6

If one knows two factors he has indications for the third one: For example, if one knows the electropolarity of the organ, where the minerals travel in the electric current and can find where they are accumulated, he can separate or describe them in antagonistic groups. Or if one knows the electropolarity of an organ and finds a certain mineral or enzyme accumulated there, he can designate their electropolarity simultaneously with the antagonism of the two groups. One group of minerals has a specific electropolarity biologically, simultaneously it has another *enzyme-system* (third factor).

One may learn from these figures that there is a distinct tendency of a certain type of enzyme to travel with the intracellular substances while the other type prefers the extracellular route. However, there are sufficient contradictory results to demonstrate that the electric factor alone is not a deciding factor, regulating all different kinds of exchanges in form of accumulation or repulsion.

In Table III of the same volume there is more favorable evidence for the electrical viewpoint. For instance, the catalase in the normal adult liver is 6.8. In the regenerating liver, which is also very positive, it is also 6.8. In the fetal liver, which is always found to be more negative, it is 0.4 and in hepatoma it is 0.0. With alkaline phosphatase, however, the order is reversed.

---

[99] Jesse Greenstein of the American Association for the Advancement of Science of August 4, 1944, p. 193.

This biologically positive enzyme-alkaline phosphatase, is usually one to four, for normal adult liver, 27 for fetal liver and 542 for hepatoma.[100]

The survey of Jesse P. Greenstein is not too unfavorable to the electrostatic theory. There the figures are again in the order of the more negative and more positive organs.[101] The malignant tumors behave always as negative structures. The example taken from this table is the cytochrome C (see Table 2, this chapter) which is found deficient in all malignant tissues like the identical minerals in the positive or negative organs; we may assume that it is moving about in the cells like the positive and negative minerals (see Table 1, this chapter). Such a *perfect* agreement between minerals and enzymes is probably the exception and not the rule.

TABLE II—Cytochrome C

Cytochrome C Activities of Rat Tissues (c)[102]

Positive Tissues		Negative Tissues	
Heart	2.34	Embryo early	.01
Kidney	1.36	Embryo late	.181
Skel. muscle	0.68	Tumor R 256	.02
Brain	0.35	Tumor R 39	.03
Liver	0.24	Tumor spontaneous	.01
Spleen	0.21		
(usually more on the negative side)			

For a comparison, here is a survey of the potassium of the organs of a rabbit, according to the analyses of W. O. Fenn (see Table 3, this chapter) who analyzed the organs first chemically and compared what he discovered with their contents in radioactive potassium. This table shows that the proportion of the activity of the organs for newly injected potassium is not identical with their contents in another stage, and it is also not perfectly identical with other analyses of the same animal in other stages or with the contents of other biologically negative or intracellular metals or organic compounds; but in all cases there is a close similarity of the distribution of many enzymes to the avidity for radioactive isotopes.

[100] *Op. cit.*, p. 198.
[101] Jesse Greenstein, *Biochemistry of Cancer*, p. 265, Table LXXVII.
[102] Quoted from *Symposium on Respiratory Enzymes*, Univ. of Wisconsin Press, 1949.

TABLE III—In positive organs

	Potassium	Radio Isotope
Muscle	119	1.5
Testis	101	1.5
Liver	87	2.4
Intestine	90	1.9
Heart	89	5.6
Lung	89	2.1
Brain	87	0.14
Kidney	60	1.5
Nerve	50	0.2
Bone	25.6	0.22
Skin	27	0.6
Plasma	5.50	0.15

In such tissues as the liver, lung, bone, and testis, the figures for intracellular matter alone do not give an accurate picture because these organs contain large amounts of the antagonistic groups. The bones, moreover, are a crystalline solid substance which contain large amounts out of proportion with the contents in protoplasmatic water-rich tissues. The high K-content of testis is also surprising.

SULFIDE

Now another example of a positive mineral traveling mostly to the negative organs.

TABLE IV

In Positive Organs		In Negative Organs	
Liver	0.41	Kidney	0.30
(bile system) neg		(cortex positive, medulla	
Brain	0.08	negative)	
Muscle	0.01	Spleen	0.18
Red cells	0.01	Lungs	0.17
Pancreas	0.47	Thyroid	0.15
(islands negative)		Stomach	0.24
		Intestines	0.81
		(muc. membrane negative;	
		muscle, nerves positive)	

The methods of determination of enzymes have not yet reached the accuracy of the modern determination of minerals. Even the figures for sulfide sulphur in the very accurate radioactive counter method give rather different results; for instance, in only four rats used in experiments by D. D. Dziewiakowski, twice the maximum was found in muscle and twice in skin, the minimum twice in liver, once in skin, once in hair.[103]

The concentration of the enzymes is varied at different times in different animals and cannot be compared with inorganic analytical results as analyzed by present methods. With regard to the great difficulties in arriving at a correct approach to an enzyme distribution in comparison with the mineral distribution, there is still a remarkable possibility of indication in the antagonism. One has to keep in mind that enzymatic action is fundamentally influenced by chemical factors other than electropolarity: the comparison with electropolarity may in one or another case also be a help in controlling enzyme analyses.

The electric factor of the movement of ferments is only one of many in various organs.

Transaminase Activities

Following are the values of Qt in different rat tissues of glutamic acid and pyruvic acid.[104]

heart	7
skel. muscle	13
brain	2
liver	46
kidney	3

M. G. Kritzmann reported questionable transaminase activity in malignant tissues and none in smooth muscle (chicken gizzard), lung, erythrocytes.[105] Also Euler, Gunther, and Forsmann, found low transamination values for malignancy.[106]

If this theoretical approach is useful, and if the distribution of the *organic* substances is predominantly influenced by their electric charge, then we may hope to find out in which organ these extracellular and intracellular substances are stored. When we find in which organs to locate the reserve stores of (a) minerals, (b) organic substances, (c) the kind of electropolarity, then it will be possible to localize the different enzymes, too.

---

[103] See The Journal of Biological Chemistry, 164:165, 1946.
[104] Phillip P. Cohen, Symposium on Respiratory Enzymes, 1942, p. 219.
[105] See Enzymologia, 5:44, 1938.
[106] See Zeitschrift fuer Krebsforschung, 49:46, 1939.

Conclusions

The most striking feature in this review of tables is that the liver parenchyma is the most positively charged organ containing very often most of the intracellular group, whereas the thyroid is the most negatively charged organ containing a marked accumulation of the extracellular group $\left(\dfrac{60 \text{ Na}}{40 \text{ K}}\right.$ in milliequivalents$\left.\right)$. It is remarkable that the enzymes are distributed according to these interpretations, in liver, muscle and heart on one side, and in thyroid, spleen and malignancies on the other side.

CHAPTER XVI

Mineral Accumulations in the Thyroid

IN CONNECTION with some problems of chronic diseases which respond to the administration of iodine but are not classified as iodine deficiencies, it seems advisable to learn whether minerals other than iodine in the so-called extracellular group (Na, Br, Ars, F, etc.) are disturbed in their metabolism and stored in the thyroid. As a fundamental first step, a determination of the Na-content of a normal thyroid gland and its relation to K, the leading mineral of the intracellular group, is assumed to be essential. If we know that Na is prevalent in any organ, and thus the proportion between K and Na in milliequivalents is smaller than one, we will also find in this organ the other minerals of the extracellular group Cl, Ca, H_2O, and others increased. If we find more K than Na, then, as H. Kaunitz, E. P. Fischer, and R. Keller have shown, there are also other minerals of the intracellular K-group accumulated in this organ. The analyses of lamb thyroids showed the following:[*]

TABLE I

	K mg %	Na mg %	K/Na in millimols
A	0.207	0.158	0.77
B	0.140	0.208	0.40
C	0.183	0.185	0.58
D	0.193	0.169	0.71

Accumulations of minerals in the thyroid compared with submaxillaris glands from rats:

[*] Examined in Laboratory of College of Physicians and Surgeons, New York.

	Sex	No.	Wet wt. grams	Na %	K %	K/Na ratio
A	M	4	5.135	0.136	0.318	1.38
B	F	3	1.815	0.121	0.308	1.50
C	F	4	2.621	0.121	0.334	1.63
D	F	4	1.805	0.097	0.316	1.92
E	M	4	2.500	0.121	0.343	1.67

This is only one example of the prevalence of K, the intra-cellular group, which is found in submaxillaris glands and most of the other organs of adult animals: muscles, heart, liver, kidney cortex, adrenals, brain, erythrocytes, etc., which all together comprise about 60 per cent of the body. The content of the Na-group is prevalent in about 29 per cent of the body and 11 per cent are on the borderline.

The above-quoted investigators have demonstrated that the K or intracellular group is electro-negative in biological surroundings and the Na or extracellular group is biologically positive. The K-group, therefore, travels to the positive cells and the Na-group to the negative cells and fluids. This is the reason why we expect a surplus of electropositive Na in the thyroid after electronegativity has been found in this organ. On the other hand, a predominance of either Na or K in the molecular K/Na ratio gives us an excellent indication of what other minerals we may expect to find in an organ, such as the thyroid gland.

The thyroid has, contrary to most of the other organs more sodium than potassium mols in milliequivalents per cent. The sodium content is greater because of the main content in the Na-rich colloid, while the epithelium cells contain considerable amounts of K in the positive granula and have many K-rich erythrocytes. The negativity is centered in the colloid, a paradox which can only be explained by an electrolytic process; similar findings are found in a number of plant and animal tissues. D. Gicklhorn described (1925) that alkaline root cells of *Sinapsis alba* make the surrounding soil acid, and N. Henning found a similar situation produced by parietal cells of the stomach. Living cells are apparently able to send out electrical potentials toward the outside into the dead space of the thyroid follicle or the open space of the stomach.

The electrostatic hypothesis claims that in living protoplasma the electrical charge cannot be guessed according to the charge in distilled water in the inorganic laboratory. It has to be determined experimentally and cannot be classified according to the ionic rule in aqueous solution but is mostly dependent upon the lyophile (colloid with strong, weak, or lacking lyophile-solvable capacity) series of Hofmeister and Spiro (first published in 1895). This series includes the positive half of both acids and alkalis, represented by lithium and sodium, calcium, iodine as one group, and the electronegative half of the series, characterized by potassium, phosphate, citrate, sulphate as the other group. These two groups in plants and animals were known, by biochemists, more than one hundred years ago. The two antagonistic groups have also been called extracellular and intracellular, a misleading designation. The thyroid is an electronegative center or cathode of the body, very small, and therefore with a small amperage, but with a high voltage in the colloid. Table I of this chapter shows that the Na is deposited and accumulated in the thyroid. Therefore, we have to consider that the so-called extracellular Na must, in this instance, be intracellular. It should be emphasized that the whole positive half of the lyophile series (CNS, I, Br, Na, Ca, Cl, As , F , Al) is accumulated in the thyroid. It is found electronegative as a redox potential in the colloid, its main mass, by DeRobertis and Gonzales (1946) and by all earlier investigators. The thiocyanate (CNS) was always found biologically more positive than the iodine. The clinical significance is that thiocyanates and other compounds of similar constitution plus thiouracil (not yet examined), sulfa drugs, and salicylates have a tendency to replace iodine. Therefore, iodine appears to be a very mobile and vulnerable substance in the thyroid as demonstrated by its easy replaceability (in biology).

The second element in the positive half of the lyophile series is the iodine. There is no doubt that the iodine is attracted with particular force by the normal thyroid, but less so in hypo- as well as hyperthyroidism. In both, the iodine content is decreased in the thyroid, in hyperthyroidism even up to 1/10th of the normal. The difference is that *blood* iodine is markedly elevated in most cases of hyperthyroidism while it is decreased in hypothyroidism. Another element, which is very near to the positive head of the series is ionized calcium. Calcium was always found greatly accumulated in the thyroid by biochemic essay and by microchemical incineration. According to the textbook on biochemistry by Oppenheimer, Aron and Gralka, nearly 40 mgm.

per cent was present in 100 grams which means rather more in mols than the normal thyroid stores I plus Na. Then follows bromine, which Tanino has found in thyroids of corpses of hospital patients to be accumulated in twentyfold amount of iodine, if the patients had received *bromides* during their disease. The bromine content of the thyroid is a maximum in comparison to other organs with one exception: the wall of the aorta. The loss of iodine and its various effects on the entire nervous system should be seriously considered whenever bromide therapy is used clinically.

There remain fluorine and arsenic, which have their maximum accumulation in the thyroid on account of their biological electropositivity. This maximum refers to the protoplasmic organ or parenchymal cells, not to the solid crystallized structures such as hairs, bones and nails. The bones, for example, have a thousand times more calcium than the thyroid, but among 34 other kinds of protoplasmic structures, *calcium* is found at its maximum in the *thyroid* and activated or ionized there.

According to the anlyses of the alkali metals, found deposited in the thyroid, we may conclude that the thyroid as a whole is relatively electronegative and that the colloid in its follicles (60 per cent in normal thyroid) has a rather high negative voltage. The contents of the other elements or radicals, according to the above-quoted earlier publications, confirm this thesis or, at least, do not contradict it.

If the thyroid is the strongest electronegative center of the body, according to others and our own findings, we have to discuss some consequences for the clinic. The other organs which seem to come very near to the great negativity of the thyroid are the bile capillaries and the pancreas "Langerhans" islands.

The liver proper is supposed to be the chief positive center of the organism in relation to electrostatic theory. Not on account of the electronegativity of the bile capillaries, but from merely practical experience, I have given bile preparations for many years to weak or cachectic patients with chronic debilitating diseases. Later, I may try to apply the bile medication to this theory as it produced in the majority of the cases a beneficial effect, whatever the reason for it was. In cancer there may be a gradual loss because of less ability to be reabsorbed.

The other organs which are also predominantly negatively

charged—the spleen, the skin and the connective tissue—contain proportionately more iodine, sodium, bromine, etc., and the other members of the lyophile series are important for therapeutics in this respect. The next neighbor to iodine in the lyophile series is bromine, which is only 10 or 15 millivolts less biologically positive than iodine.

What happens, for example, to the thyroid, if bromides are administered? F. Tanino tried to answer this question. He analyzed the thyroids of corpses of hospital patients (time and dosage are not reported) after the administration of bromides. Most of the old people were quite emaciated, had lost the iodine of the thyroid for the greater part and had accumulated bromide instead. I list here a few figures of Table II of Tanino which gives the results of thyroids, moist glands, with medium colloid content.

TABLE II

Sex	Age	Disease	mg % Br	mg % I	Br/I(normally 1/45)
Female	22	Tuberculosis	18.4	2.6	7.0
Male	77	Myocardia	53.4	3.9	13.8
Male	58	Pneumonia	23.7	1.4	16.6
Male	42	Nephroscleroisis	39.3	1.4	27.3

In thyroid, bromine is normally 1 mgm. per cent or a little more (Labat). The normal thyroid contains in moist glands 0.03 to 0.06 per cent iodine.[107]

The figures show a tremendous loss of iodine, in some cases reduced to a minimum from an average of 45 mgm. per cent to 1.4 mgm. per cent. These significant clinical findings, important for clinical bromine therapy, are generally overlooked. As for an explanation, it may be stated that the mass action law of Goldberg and Waage (1852) has a strong effect in the exchange of bromine for iodine. The normal blood serum has the relation of 1/1000 of bromine to iodine, about one mgm. and not gamas like iodine. As early as 1913, Labat had discovered that normal animals accumulate the largest store of bromine in the thyroid.

The study of Tanino's figures, which show in all other cases the same tendencies more or less, raises some new problems. If we remember that bromine medication may produce a characteristic eczema and almost the same rash is observed by other neighbors of the lyophile series, we ask ourselves whether the

---

[107] Sollmann, *Pharmacology*, p. 973.

skin affliction, called bromine or thiocyanate eczema,[108] may not be partly a result of iodine deficiency. Or we may consider whether the somnolence or rather an iodine deficiency is present. As a matter of fact the other neighbors in the Hofmeister-Spiro series produce a similar tendency to sleep. After we had found that the thyroid is a store of Na, Br, I, and other minerals of the electropositive and lyophile series which travel in the biological milieu to the cathode, we were interested in the examinations of A. E. Rappaport, who examined many body organs in their alkalinity or acidity expressed in pH. He examined the corpses of hospital patients 30 hours after their death and still found strong differences in acidity. The highest alkalinity in the thyroid was usually one and a half units of pH higher than the brain (equivalent to 78 millivolts). We have to remember that the brain is one of the counterparts of the thyroid chemically as well as electrically and that it has recorded the minimum in iodine and other substances of the positive half of the lyophile series while the thyroid has the maximum content. The cerebrum, so strongly influenced by traces of iodine, has only a minimum of iodine in its own substance (Von Fellenberg).

The pH of thyroid and brain is, according to Rappaport:

Thyroid	Brain
8.4	7.2
7.9	6.5
8.3	7.1
7.7	7.0
8.5	7.5
7.8	7.3
7.9	7.2

In this table, four pneumonia patients had 7.2 in the thyroid and 5.9 in the brain.

Conclusion: The striking alkalinity of the thyroid gland is proved in this way.

Each cell has its own metabolism and special function but all cells depend upon and are supported by the whole metabolism. For its proper intake and output each cell needs the eliminating and digestive power of the general metabolism. Everything is equally important for single and total life processes.

---

[108] *Op. cit.,* p. 987.

CHAPTER XVII

The Healing of Cancer

As EXPLAINED previously, cancer is not a specific illness but a general, chronic, degenerative disease. To a certain extent, it may be due to the inheritance of a predisposing factor such as a weak liver but more frequently it is caused by outside influences which have come about by our way of life. A noted cancer biologist, Professor Little, expressed this thought as follows: "Cancer develops where there is a general breakdown of the whole body."

Most scientists reject this and similar theories and continue to adhere to the conservative doctrine that cancer is a localized disease, at least in the beginning. They consider it a specific syndrome,[109] despite the fact that they do not know the underlying cause. Later when it spreads over the body, it is called a generalized disease, but it is only secondary. Accordingly, the recognized treatments are *local* treatments—surgery, X-ray, radium, or chemical treatments by application of mustard gas, ionized phosphorus, iodine, cobalt,[110] copper, or the administration of sex hormones. The chemical and hormone treatments are supplementary treatments only. Contrary to the opinions of the majority of the scientists, a number of pathologists feel that they can no longer maintain the doctrine of a local development of cancer. They, therefore, turn to a more general theory. To give a few examples of these new approaches, let us cite Professor Siegmund (translated):[111] "The theory of cancer is a question of the

---

[109] See *Cancer Alerts. A Reference and Source Book for Physicians.* Abstracts prepared by the New York Academy of Medicine, 1957.

[110] See JAMA, Vol. 165, No. 3, May 18, 1957.

[111] See *Ganzheitsbehandlung der Geschwulsterkrankungen.* 1953, pp. 212, 272.

defense of the mesenchym (connective tissue) especially a defense work of the whole organism against damages penetrated from outside or developed from inside. In the end, the therapy is a so-called parenteral digestion. Nutrition is originally an external factor but the organism acquires a disposition growing into premorbidity through constant intake of denaturalized food." Professor Pischinger places the activation of the mesenchym more precisely into the foreground:[112] "The mesenchym consists mostly of connective tissue cells which are distributed all over the body, especially between all organs and tissues. It contains some different types of cells. This tissue was long ignored until a few scientists discovered the importance of this so-called 'filling tissue,' now characterized more precisely as the 'reticular system,' containing the mesenchymal defense and parenteral digestive apparatus. From the pathology we learn that almost every tumor is surrounded by such tissue, and the same tissue also embraces all new cancer establishments. This connective tissue is almost inactive and paralyzed in cancer, incapable of helping or protecting the body any longer in defense or healing."

A number of scientists have tried various methods to stimulate the reticular system as well as the reticulo-endothelial system, which seem to control and regulate the growth of cells. Failure of these systems may cause the uncontrolled growth, which is a characteristic part of cancer.

I have found that this important system cannot function sufficiently and satisfactorily because the entire body is poisoned and has lost part of the ionized minerals of the K-group and simultaneously some of the electrical potentials, etc. Many scientists regard these systems as part of the healing apparatus.[113]

Professor G. von Bergmann described this method of cancer development by writing (translated): "Cancer metabolism takes place once the body is no longer capable of producing an active 'inflammation metabolism' . . . the cancerous organism is anergic in respect to inflammation."[114] The experiments of his assistants, Ruth Lohmann and Peschel demonstrated, as reflected in the following tables, that cancer cells can be killed in fluid from a

---

[112] Op. cit., 1953, pp. 106, 117.

[113] See Ganzheitsbehandlung der Geschwulsterkrankungen (Totality Treatment of Tumor Diseases) edited by Prof. Werner Zabel. Stuttgart, 1953.

[114] See von Bergmann's Functionelle Pathologie, Julius Springer, Berlin, 1932, p. 173.

normal inflammation metabolism, not in blood serum. This indicates the fact a normal body can kill cancer by producing an inflammation.

TABLE I[115]

I	Out of Serum		Out of Inflammation Fluid		II	Out of Serum		Out of Inflammation Fluid	
	QO_2	$Q \nearrow O_2 \searrow H$	QO_2	$Q \nearrow O_2 \searrow H$		QO_2	$Q \nearrow O_2 \searrow H$	QO_2	$Q \nearrow O_2 \searrow H$
0 hours	10, 8	23, 4	11, 2	21, 8	0 hours	11, 3	17, 6	12, 0	21, 1
6 hours	10, 2	21, 8	6, 9	13, 3	12 hours	8, 8	16, 6	0	0
10 hours	9, 7	18, 9	2, 8	2, 9					
14 hours	9, 6	17, 5	0	0					

TABLE II[116]

	Normal Serum	Inflammation Fluid
Oxygen pressure	117 mm Hg	6 mm Hg
Sugar content	100 mg %	6 mg %
Lactic acid content	10 mg %	125 mg %
Bicarbonate content	25.10^{-3} molar	$8, 9.10^{-3}$ molar
pH	7, 48	6, 29

The papers of Friedrich Kaufman on non-bacterial inflammation revealed that these inflammations are followed by mesenchymal inflammatory reactions of genuine nature, with capillary activity, cell activation and loss of white blood cells. In the same animals, changes in the liver were found at the same time, on the epithelian parenchym, in connection with the liver cells themselves as well as by inflammatory reactions on the mesenchymal tissue.

A few of my own experiments with cantharidin plasters have confirmed the fact that cancer patients could not produce an inflammatory reaction after irritation by cantharidin chemical. The only exception was a case of beginning skin carcinoma, which produced about a third of the normal reaction; but the blister fluid could no longer kill cancer cells. After several months or longer of detoxication, diet and medication, patients showing favorable response were able to produce a normal inflammation metabolism, capable of killing cancer cells. In this country, I was

[115] *Op. cit.*, p. 174.
[116] *Op. cit.*, p. 171.

not in a position where I could carry out enough experiments to constitute a scientific proof of the fact that general detoxication and restoration of the metabolism are basic parts of the healing of cancer.

G. von Bergmann widens the conception of inflammation as an allergic reaction by writing: "The sicknesses which are in our doctrine of diseases separated according to the different organs have common biological reactions with cellular procedures surpassing the defense of the reticulo-endothelial apparatus. Included in the allergic reacting organs are: the diseases of the stomach as well as the colon, the great glandular parenchymatous organs of the liver, pancreas, meninges, endocard, pericard, synovia of the joints—finally the muscles, not the least being the heart muscle, in particular the vessels, the arterioles, venules as well as the capillaries—all of them reacting with invisible biological structural changes of the cells and tissues and in the 'humural condition.' "[117]

The theory of the functional part of the diseases von Bergmann calls "pathology of the function," which can lead in both directions either to the advantage or disadvantage of the organism.

Now we come to the core of the problem as to whether we can influence these biological or allergic reactions, and how far and in what manner one can direct them.

The cancerous body presents in general an "anergic reaction" as far as the cancer mass and its metabolic poisons are concerned. Therefore, in more advanced cases, light infections may be fatal. All attempts to stimulate the system by virulent skin infections or combinations of their toxins to an allergic response against the cancer consistently failed.

Later the unspecific allergic reactions became clinically more important symptoms regarding the progress of the doctrine of the inflammation. First von Pirquet and later Schick studied the internal inflammatory conditions more intensely.

It was found that the *cantharidin blister fluid* can be used as a measurement indicating the degree of inflammatory preparedness (called allergy) of the total body, its variability during the course of the infections and other noninfectious diseases, and, I would like to add, for the confirmation of the healing in chronic

---

[117] *Op. cit.*, p. 166.

diseases and cancer although not enough experiments have been carried out to date.

The decisive step forward came when the Berlin pathologist, Professor Roessle, published his experiments. He showed that guinea pigs reacted with different types of white blood cells disappearing from the irritating capillaries by the same stimulus but *after* different kinds of previous treatments were applied to the animals in using injections of various protein solutions. On such a basis, more and more authors came to the conclusion that the body and *its present state* of inflammatory preparedness decide the degree and type of inflammatory-reaction, not the degree or type of the applied stimulus. Likewise, Virchow's cellular pathology is no longer valid in this respect, but the predominant functions of the cells and their changes are effective.

The same discovery was made in the field of tuberculosis by K. E. Ranke when he stated that not the virulence nor the amount of tuberculosis bacilli determine whether there will be an exudative or productive type of lung tuberculosis, but rather the character of the reaction of the organism against the stimulus is decisive. The reciprocal effect between reagens and reactor can be so great that any common virulent streptococcus stock, for example, can be changed to a weaker type such as streptococcus viridans which occurs in sepsis lenta (older observations).

To see the advantages of the allergic inflammation we have to look into the anatomical and biological findings of this function. This subject is described at length in my tuberculosis book,[118] which also includes an explanation of the Arthus phenomenon in limiting the spot and saving the body.

We learn from pathological and experimental findings that in cancer there is no sufficient blockade around the tumor. The way is free for new settlements to spread and thus poison the body and keep it under its destructive rule. The degree of the barrier and the capacity of the elimination organs, particularly the liver, determine the progress of poisoning and breakdown of the body, while the defense apparatus becomes more and more inactive.

---

[118] Gerson, Max, M.D.: *Dietary Therapy of Lung Tuberculosis*, pp. 158, 165, 166, pursuant to the tests of Roessle with respect to the reaction proceedings in the allergic tissues.

The fact that we regard the body in its entirety should not lead us to assume that the tumor, the glands and the metastases can be influenced at one time or even cured all together. The concept of totality should not let us forget that each sick organ, even each node and gland, has its own pathological anatomical conditions, on which the method of healing essentially depends. Osteolytic and osteoplastic processes can exist in the same organ or even in the same vertebra nearby and it appears that each single spot, node, tumor or destructive process has some biological laws; despite this, it remains the task of the treatment to subordinate all the pathological and healthy organs, tissues, and cells for the benefit of the whole. This is the natural way for the metabolism to be supported by the autonomous nervous system with the reticulo and reticulo-endothelial system. The close cooperation of the liver is essential.

Because of the continuous failures in the extensive experimental research, most of the authors are unsuccessful in solving the cancer problem. In my opinion, primarily because comprehension of the detoxication has always been overlooked in clinics, we are not sufficiently trained in that direction. In addition we have to take into account that we have very little or transient or symptomatic results in other chronic diseases. After such experiences, it is very difficult for the physician to accept the idea that a cancer patient can be completely restored. G. von Bergmann wrote: "A systematic *therapeutic* development of this theory may not be possible, . . ."[119] This means that he, as most other authors, never expected that it might be possible to restore metabolism in a cancerous organism to an extent sufficient for healing purposes.

I repeat: The cancerous body is anergic, which means that it cannot prevent cancerous growth nor respond and defend itself against it. The treatment, therefore, has the task of restoring these normal functions so that the defense apparatus, liver with reticulo and reticulo-endothelial system can function and that finally, the conditions are restored for production, activation and reactivation of oxidizing enzymes.

We have very often seen, in the more advanced cancer cases, that there are only a few lymphocytes (on the average 3-10 in

---

[119] von Bergmann, *Functionelle Pathologie*, p. 173.

the so-called "differential count"). This shows that the body is no longer capable of producing the necessary amount of lympho-cytes for its normal need or for its healing power. We see not only in cancer, but also in other chronic diseases, that the body has lost the activity of the valuable and necessary mother-tissue of lymphocytes. If we follow the suggestions of some authors, we may assume that the reticular and the reticulo-endothelial systems both are the terminals of the visceral nervous system. These authors also think that the functions of our internal organs depend, to a greater degree, on the functions of that autonomous system. Professor Pischinger reminds us in his article that these tissues also play a central role in the "budget of the oxygen," thus helping to bring oxygen into the cells. From Professor Schade's work we know that the connective tissue is interposed between the capillary and the epithelial cell, or any other cell, in the body. If we assume that the visceral nervous system, the reticulo-endothelial system, the interposed connective tissue and, on the other hand, the reactivation also of the oxidizing enzymes is more or less damaged in the cancer body, we may understand that some abnormal cells are forced to go over from the use of oxygen to the use of fermentation, which changes the life conditions of these cells and their growth and penetrates the surrounding tissue to the greatest degree.

In all experiments except for one which could not be con-firmed, it was found that cancer cells cannot be stimulated or forced to change their abnormal functions back to normal ones. There is no other way but to kill these cells to dissolve and absorb them. I believe the surest way to achieve this end is to restore to the body its ability to produce non-bacterial inflam-matory reactions. The idea of producing bacterial inflammations in a cancerous body was correct in principle. However, it is not enough to introduce a temporary inflammation into the body. The body itself must be able to do it and do it continuously, because many cancer cells remain hidden in some areas where even the blood stream cannot reach them. In order to maintain this healing process, it is, of course, necessary to apply the treat-ment long enough to restore all vital organs to normal function (liver, reticular system, nervous system, etc.) to reproduce the same reactive processes as used by the body itself, for healing purposes.

From observation of the skin, I could learn what types of proteins and fats are favorable, at what time the reserves of the tissues must be refilled, and what is necessary to produce the best healing reactions and, finally, how to keep them at the level necessary for healing purposes. For these tests, therefore, we had to select cases which had skin cancer, or, better still, such cases which had internal cancers and skin eruptions of acute or chronic nature, or cancers with additional skin metastases or additional skin cancers. It may be generally concluded that cream, fatty cheese, all animal fats, some oils, egg yolks, strawberries, and all fat varieties of meats indicated their harmfulness on the skin, probably because they were only partially digested, whereas lean meats, fresh butter and some different types of oil were not harmful.

In all cases where the metabolism was above plus 25 per cent, almost all proteins and fats were unfavorable. In cases where the metabolism was minus 10 per cent and lower, all fats and oils were harmful, whereas lean meat and egg whites were so to a lesser degree. In quite advanced cases there was no time for such examinations as the treatment had to be applied immediately and most intensely. In a few such cases the content of cholesterol in the blood was greatly increased, while trypsin and lipase were almost lacking. The milder cases had less cholesterol and at least some trypsin and lipase content. Almost all cancer cases showed an acceleration of the healing processes when thyroid and lugol solution drops were increased, while hormone therapy was generally harmful in the beginning. Where there was hardening of the arteries, thyroid and lugol were especially favorable. Also in such cases where we could not verify the improvement on the reactions of the skin, longer, intensive and more frequent treatments with iodine (thyroid plus lugol) and potassium compound were required.

It is our assumption that every defense and healing power of the body depends on the capacity of the body to produce a so-called "allergic inflammation."[120] Every healing is introduced by a kind of inflammation as we learn in surgery. It is also true in medicine. All different types of foreign bodies, such as bacteria and injuries, have the capacity to bring about such a healing

---

120 *Ibid.*

inflammation in a healthy body. It presents an afflux of blood with redness and swelling. The redness is caused by the opening of the capillaries and some special cells. The fluid of the swelling is not identical with edema fluid; it is a product of hyperemia and inflammation; it is an extravasate through finely damaged capillaries. The different kinds of fluid in edema and inflammation are not yet fully known. Otto Warburg demonstrated that the cancer cell has good living conditions in blood serum and in the inflammation fluid these conditions are lacking, for this fluid is composed in such a way that the cancer cell will not find enough sugar in it for glycolysis. Warburg showed that when the sugar level sinks to 20 mg. per cent, the lactic acid production falls to half and that the low level is lowered still further in the inflammation. In chronic or degenerative diseases such as tuberculosis, arthritis, arteriosclerosis, etc., the body has lost the capacity to bring about such an "inflammation reaction."

In cancer some authors[121] say where the body has been sick before, cancer could develop. G. von Bergmann explains the impossibility to prevent or cure cancer: "Cancer sets in where the body is incapable to produce an active inflammatory metabolism." (p. 173.) Strong denies (1940) that "up to the present there is not yet one cancer attacking defense mechanism revealed." Dr. J. L. Alibert and several students (1808) were inoculated with cancerous material from a female breast tumor. It produced violent inflammatory reactions. Then Emil Weiss of the Peoples Hospital, Department of Pathology, Chicago, inoculated an extract of human cancer into patients affected with cancer. The aim of that clinical trial was to find what therapeutic effect such treatments have. After injections, chill and temperature lasted for two hours and more. The results were a marked increase in appetite, more strength, and a slight increase in weight. The lymph nodes diminished and became much harder. No cure was obtained—only temporary improvement.

Dr. Fehleisen (1883, Berlin Charité) inoculated real erysipelas infection into cancerous areas. This resulted in many failures and a few remarkable successes. G. von Bergmann thinks that every experienced clinician knows of a few carcinomas cured by intervening inflammatory processes.

---

[121] See *Ganzheitsbehandlung der Geschwulsterkrankungen.*

Dr. William B. Coley, New York (1891), devoted his life to this dramatic treatment with erysipelas inoculations, later with pyogenic mixtures such as streptococcus, staphylococcus and pyocyaneus, still later adding bacillus prodigiosus. Coley's results and those of others remained quite uncertain and sparing. The great majority of the medical profession remained very skeptical about this method of cancer treatment.

The idea of helping the cancerous organism through a strong inflammation is old but was correct from the beginning. The problem is to find the surest and most effective way to do this.

Cancer patients have different types of allergic reactions. Some patients with Hodgkin's disease responded with alcohol-induced pain due to malignancy.[122] The pain was regarded as an allergic reaction brought about by a carcinoma, as it was not present before the disease. The patient had apparently enough power for an allergic reaction but not enough for an "allergic inflammation"—not intensive and active enough for an "allergic inflammation" which is the decisive part of the body's "weapon of healing power." Consequently, it appears that there must be a characteristic difference between allergic reactions and allergic inflammations, since both are not quite separated in their limitation and causation. At the beginning of the cancer we can assume that with the allergic reaction there is still a part of an allergic inflammation present and effective, too weak, of course, for healing power, but to a certain degree sufficient to restrict the tumor and to keep it temporarily localized. It is reported in the same article that the patient with allergic reaction to alcohol (20 ml.) had only a slight discomfort caused by the allergic reaction to alcohol when the roentgenogram showed that the tumor was larger and better defined. Later, the "anergia" increased when the tumor grew faster, and there was no longer pain after drinking the quadruple amount of gin (80 ml.). Such observation indicates most probably that the increase of intoxication decreases gradually the allergic reaction to nil. These and other observations are significant signs of the reduction of allergic reactions by progressing intoxication imminent in a cancerous body. *It therefore appears that the body's capacity to produce*

---

[122] See J.A.M.A., May 18, 1957, Vol. 164, No. 3, p. 333.

an allergic inflammation (healing power) depends on a most complete detoxication and an equilibrium in the metabolism to near normal.

The healing apparatus seems to have retained part of its embryonic capacity and healing purpose for a type of regeneration,[123] when it falls back into the embryonic state temporarily and is activated above the degree of its normal function.

The completely detoxified body is then able to produce an allergic inflammation if the healing apparatus (liver, visceral nervous system and reticulo-mesenchymal system) can be activated sufficiently. Everything that can help to bring it about and strengthen the necessary allergic inflammation may be used for that purpose after the general detoxication has taken place. Bacterial preparations (Coley and others) or Pyrifer, or any similar preparations are effective, as far as they can stimulate the visceral nervous system in connection with the liver and the mesenchymal defense and healing apparatus. We have to bear in mind that there are very different reactions according to the state and energy-capacity of the healing apparatus. It may be advisable to stimulate, in addition to my treatment, the liberated visceral nervous system and the reticulo-endothelial apparatus with a measured bacterial reagens. However, I have had no experience with it. We do not know what stimulus acts first and what tissue should be activated. G. von Bergmann (p. 171) quotes the description of the course of the inflammation from an article by Kempner (translated): "At any stimulus an exudation and immigration of white blood cells sets in. The chemical composition of the exudate is the same as that of the serum (in the beginning). As soon as the exudate and the inflammatory cells are present, there starts an own life separated from normal tissue within the inflammation area, in the center of which is the metabolism of the inflammatory cells. The velocity of the inflammatory reactions depends upon the presence of inflammation cells. These cells have an oxidative and digestive metabolism and by means of this metabolism cause an acidosis of the inflamed tissue and reduction of the inflamed space of oxygen and energy-producing substance (sugar). Acid formation and deficit of energy-producing sub-

---

[123] George W. Crile, *A Bipolar Theory of Living Processes.* MacMillan Co., 1926, p. 166.

stance bring about damage or destruction of inflamed tissue, a kind of swelling, degeneration and necrosis."[124]

After the inflammation has killed the tumor mass, (see Tables I and II, this chapter) necrosis sets in. In necrosis of circumscribed localized areas the important function is the digestive power of leukocytic enzymes of fibrin and debris in inflamed areas, for indigested fibrin acts as a foreign body and leads to fibrosis. "The term necrosis is used to describe the changes which the dead tissue and cells undergo after their death. The term necrobiosis is used in reference to the physiologic death and replacement of certain cells which are constantly occurring, e.g., blood cells and in epidermis."[125]

My own observations have shown that far advanced cancer patients have lost their allergic migraine reaction and other kinds of allergic reactions. During the healing time the migraine symptoms recur partially but disappear when the patient is cured entirely, as the combined dietary regime is enough to cure allergic migraine symptoms in most cases without combination with cancer; I also made similar observations with other allergic manifestations. In all these instances it was found that the degree of allergic reactions varies inversely with the degree and period of shorter or longer lasting intoxications. Cancer patients with allergic syndromes are forced to maintain part of the diet without salt and with low animal fats and proteins for many years.

I do not believe that there is fundamentally more than one healing apparatus in the body. Strong said (1940): "Up to the present there is not yet one cancer attacking defense-mechanism revealed."

The treatment is, of course, unspecific. To reject any dietary regime because of insufficient physiological proof is not sound.[126]

On the skin where we had been able to study the healing of lupus (see my Tuberculosis book, p. 200) we could also observe the following in cancer: After the body is detoxified, inflammation with redness and slight swelling of the involved spot starts. A few days later the reduction of the edema and infiltration sets in. The abnormal spot and the secondary infections will be dissolved by the digestive enzymes and finally absorbed into the blood

---

[124] von Bergmann, *Functionelle Pathologie*, p. 171.
[125] W. A. D. Andersen, *Pathology*, p. 95.
[126] K. H. Bauer, *Das Krebsproblem*, pp. 605-607.

stream. Under the microscope, we see the creation of new capillaries which penetrate into the infiltrate and the necrotic mass and build the so-called granulation tissue.

They secrete all different hormones and probably also enzymes, similar to the placenta tissue in cooperation with the oxidation processes (it is the function of leukocytes, lymphocytes, histiocytes). The healing process starts with hyperemia and then the different stages of reabsorption follow. The blood pictures show at that time an increase in leukocytes and lymphocytes and a small increase in monocytes. During the healing time a small increase in lipase was confirmed, a necessary development for the digestion of the fatty cell fragments. At the beginning of the dietary regime, we saw and learned that some nutrients hinder the healing process, whereas others further it. These observations were used as indicators to point out what substances damage or which other ones are necessary for the healing process in that period.

Despite the observation that we can see the healing processes in skin cancer under the microscope, the fact remains that we do not know exactly the organ or organs which have to be stimulated and we do not know what part of the treatment activates them.

We do know that a healing apparatus is present and functions in a healthy body—and we learned, in addition, by means of this treatment that it can be reactivated if the body can be sufficiently detoxified (in degenerative diseases and cancer).

We have the distinct impression that the internal organs present similar or equal situations under treatment which the skin cancer reflects. The X-rays prove it on the bones, lungs and other organs.

Deep reaching cancerous ulcerations need several corresponding inflammations (so-called "flare-ups") until the larger area is covered with more granulation tissue or new skin.

These "flare-ups" come at intervals and with some women just before their menstruation.

My idea is that the detoxication obtained by frequent enemas, by the dietary regime and some medication pave the way for the first allergic healing inflammation; the body must be maintained detoxified and in a metabolic equilibrium even with a partially functioning liver for the following "flare-ups."

We should not forget that after the killing of the tumor mass and its dissolution, the absorption, until recovery is a constant heavy burden on the elimination apparatus, in particular on the liver and kidneys. If we do not help the patient intensively day and night to eliminate these additional poisonous substances, as I have seen it at the beginning of this treatment, there is a serious danger that the patient may fall into a hepatic coma.

In the first two weeks of this treatment we observe that the patient awakes from the half comatous mood, caused partly by a previous high sedation therapy and partly by the toxins from the growing tumor masses accumulated and now activated in the body. In the first ten days the urine shows much elimination of NaCl, up to eight grams per day, rarely ten grams. Acetone plus two to three, disappears in about one week, often together with a trace of albumin and hyaline casts.

The red blood picture recovers steadily in four to six weeks; the white differential count shows that its production apparatus has to carry the burden.

Within a few days all white cells have toxic granules, the lymphocytes increase slowly, the number of leukocytes remains increased for a few weeks also the percentage of neutrophiles. We learned that the stronger the detoxication, the quicker and more surprising are the results, as long as we are able to keep the metabolism free of poison and equalized in many respects despite the fact that we have to handle other heavily damaged or even partly destroyed organs.

In this way it is possible to bring the cancer-mass or masses out of their partial seclusions or hiding places back into the exchange of the general metabolism, into its support and regulation. However, the detoxication is only a part of the healing process though an important part. Simultaneously, the metabolism has to be balanced at least to a certain degree. The sick organs are unable to do so themselves for a long period, especially in advanced cases.

The body needs essentially: the important minerals (K., I., P.), the oxidizing enzymes and coenzymes, and the hormones.

All of them must become activated in the body and must be re-activated there, otherwise they are lost. Equally important is the restoration of the pH (minerals in the cells) so that the enzymes can function again step by step.

All the explanations in this book about the healing of cancer as well as other presentations would be not much more than words, if we were not able to demonstrate the corresponding clinical facts of real healings. But after these facts are achieved, these conceptions are explanations for our clinical observations.

Our modern civilization has brought about such widespread changes in our nutrition that some cancer authors speak about a so-called pre-cancerous condition. I feel it must be expressed more generally as a pre-*morbid* pathology. For our task it is important to know that we have no longer a *natural* nutrition; therefore, the therapy is more difficult. The pre-stages probably could be recognized by examination of K, I, urea-N and uric acid, and could be more easily restored. The cancerous tissues, however, must be killed, since after their microsomata and mitochondria took in certain biochemical changes in minerals and electrical potentials and probably also particles of a new protein substance into their cell formation, they cannot be retransformed to normal.

Finally, healing of cancer means the restoration of the entire metabolism with its enteral and parenteral digestion together with its defense and healing functions.

Extirpation of cancer growths does not mean a cure of the disease. The improvement which frequently follows an operation may show that the liberation of the body from such poison-producing mass is a great help for the system, and points to the direction that the partial detoxication of the body benefits the cancer-bearing system at least to a certain degree, and temporarily. The improvement seems to be only in the beginning, after the operation and in localized cases only, but this is not sufficient for the production of an allergic inflammation. In the literature, the allergic or healing inflammation is referred to as "changes in the environmental conditions." This is an incorrect conception.

CHAPTER XVIII

Role of Allergy in the Healing Process of Cancer

It seems certain that the healing power in cancer has to be introduced by an allergic reaction. To understand this healing power, one must have a brief explanation of the problem of allergy itself. Dr. von Pirquet had explained allergy as a change in tissue reactions. This means a hypersensitivity developed in the body caused by an infection or after injection of a protein (allergen). Anergy is the contrary; it refers to a diminished or lack of reaction against an antigen. H. H. Dale expressed the allergic reaction and consequent function as follows: "A change in the dispersity of protoplasma colloids occurs if the praecipitin fixed in the cell protoplasma encounters the antigen onto which it has a specific affinity. A change in the dispersity of the protoplasma colloids sets in, which induces an enzymatic dissolution and the production of histamine-like substance or histamine itself."[127] The reacting organs at the allergic attack are particularly the unstriped muscles and the capillary endothel, both of which stay under the regulation of the automatic nervous system and endocrine apparatus.[128]

When the tumor masses are in process of dissolution, there is a greater amount of highly active protein-*intermediary substances* such as histamine, histidine, etc., which can activate different pathological reactions all over the body. These counteract the

---

[127] See *Bulletin*, Johns Hopkins Hospital, 31, 1310, 1920.
[128] See Arthur F. Coca, *Familial Nonreaginic Food Allergy*, 2nd edition, 1945, Charles C Thomas, Springfield, Illinois.

healing power. To neutralize and eliminate them is the task of the therapy.

Small quantities of indole, skatole and phenol are absorbed into the bloodstream, undergo detoxication in the liver by conjugation with sulphuric acid and potassium or with glycuronic acid.

What really happens in the body in allergic reactions or stronger in anaphylactic shocks is that normal enzymatic processes are reduced.[129] This idea is based on the following findings: Abderhalden and Wertheimer found reduced amount of tissue, gas-exchange and less oxidation; Loehr found diminished digestion of aromatic proteins; Hashimoto and Pick found pathological proteolytic processes particularly in the liver cells. Since these reactions occur in different organs and tissues, A. F. Coca calls them "species specific shockorgans" or "shocktissues."

The kind of allergen stimulant does not determine the type of reaction (variant) as every patient has his own and his individual type of reaction with which he responds to each stimulation therapy. These are mostly gradual differences. (p. 103, my Tbc. book)

It is nowhere clearly explained why normal allergies are suppressed when tuberculosis is active and why they reappear when the tuberculosis process improves. Normal allergic or even anaphylactic reactions appear when the poisons have obtained a kind of peak and the body is able to neutralize, digest and eliminate them. Pneumonia healed in former times after the body had produced a detoxication crisis with abundant perspiration, diarrhea and sometimes vomiting. Then healing set in. The visible syndromes are the accompanying bodily signs of that kind of detoxication or cleansing reaction—with local and general symptoms which can also be regarded as the start of a healing process. The therapy has to imitate the detoxication. After that elimination, patients with asthma, migraine or gout feel greatly relieved.

As for nutrition, it is necessary to keep away all substances from the sick body which can produce allergic and other biologically stronger reactions such as caused by fats, animal proteins, vitamins (except vitamin C and niacin) and hormones, because

---

[129] Lichtwitz, *Klin. Chemie*, 1930, p. 16.

they counteract the normal allergic healing reaction which is so necessary in the beginning to kill the tumor tissue.

This perception shows four consequences clearly:

1) The strongest detoxication (not only mechanically by enemas) is in cancer the *conditio sine qua non* for the start of the healing. A poisoned body is anergic and cannot react to the favorable side. *The detoxified body can.*

2) The maintenance of the detoxication is absolutely necessary and the greatest therapeutical help for the liver.

3) The liver, the main transformation and elimination organ, must be able to induce the procedure, to maintain it, even if it has to undergo some proteolytic processes, which particularly hit the liver cells, according to E. F. Pick.[130]

4) The healing is limited or even impossible in cases where and when the liver is no longer able to render and maintain this vital service of constant detoxication and temporary allergic reaction to the body.

J. Jensen stated, "It must be emphasized that the whole subject of allergy is vast and complex and that it still has many problems which are as yet unsolved."[131] The confusion becomes even greater when we see the majority of the cancer authors push the allergy problem aside as unessential or do not mention it at all.

A. F. Coca reported that "all of 297 persons with malignant growths of the breast presented symptoms of idioblaptic allergy; two persons accidentally included in the group were found to be free from idioblaptic constitution and both of these had had non-malignant growths of the breast."[132]

In his chapter on "Diagnosis of Allergy," Jensen concluded, "The answer depends upon their definition of allergy."[133] Every author makes his own definition.

The allergy problem is touched upon here only to make the healing of cancer understandable. To eliminate confusion, I suggest the following:

An allergic reaction may be thought to be a *diminished*

---

[130] Arch. f. exper. Path. 70, 89, 1914.
[131] J. Jensen, *Modern Concepts in Medicine*, C. V. Mosby, 1953, p. 367.
[132] Arthur F. Coca, *Familial Nonreaginic Food Allergy*, p. 185.
[133] Jensen, *Modern Concepts in Medicine*, p. 363.

enzymatic reaction (Lichtwitz), an allergic inflammation to be
an increased enzymatic reaction (von Bergmann). Both are enzymatic by nature and both are caused by the function of the same
apparatus, (capillary endothel—or reticulo-endothelial system—
small arteries, visceral nervous system and enzymes activated
and supported by the liver). Therefore, the name "allergy" is
justified in describing these different reaction complexes. In
reality, the degree only is different as well as the place of response.
Biologically, it can be regarded as an unspecific, healing-inducing
inflammation. It is a structural response to an immune process
beyond the limits of physiological function. Whether or not the
body can accomplish the healing process remains still questionable. Further development during the treatment will show if the
body can be restored sufficiently to accomplish it.

The task of the therapy is to prevent all impeding infectious
or poisonous reactions (including those caused by drug allergies
and allergies to food when not digested to the end products).
These will hinder the allergic healing inflammation.

CHAPTER XIX

Introduction to the Diet

Diet, in the sense of Hippocrates, is a complete regime regulated by the family physician according to medical indications. Nutrition should be regarded as a remedy, prescribed as to kind and quantity or items to be forbidden. Nutritional prescriptions are a part of the total *therapy* only and must be completed by other prescriptions. The knowledge of such additional therapy is indispensable for the practice. A few directives as to the effectiveness on the various organs of response should be described in advance.

When I started the first treatment, weeks and months produced an increased sensitivity toward various natural stimuli caused by nutrition and medication. This increased sensitivity had some beneficial effects, but also some damaging ones. On the one hand, it helped to attack the tumor and metastases very quickly, but on the other, it made it difficult to feed the patients, as various allergies developed, for instance, against liver injections, liver juice*, orange juice, minute amounts of lemon, and different fruits and medications. Among the medications the most striking were opiates, codeine, novocaine (all types), penicillin and other antibiotics. It became necessary to find means of excluding all allergic reactions as far as possible. We succeeded in excluding the nutritional allergies by adding large doses of potassium and simultaneously applying a strictly saltless diet, increasing the doses of lugol solution and thyroid and increasing detoxication by means of additional coffee enemas and more frequent castor oil treatments. Patients remained sensitive to X-rays, so that even fluoroscopic examinations were damaging and had to be omitted as far as possible. They also remained sensitive to prolonged exposure to sunshine. Hypersensitivity to

* See Appendix III. page 421

novocaine also persisted, so that dentists were advised not to use more than a third of the normal dose of 2 cc (0.6-0.7 cc). Anesthesia with this reduced dosage proved even more effective than that formerly achieved with the normal amount. Patients also retained a hypersensitivity to physical and mental exertion, so that a maximum of rest was necessary during the first months. Even after four or six weeks of treatment the more advanced patients were generally unable to do marketing and prepare the diet and juices by themselves. If there is a condition of perspiration, weakness and depression, the entire body should be rubbed two or three times a day with a soft brush wrapped in a washcloth and soaked in the following solution: one-half glass of water to which is added two tablespoons of rubbing alcohol and two tablespoons of wine vinegar.

The general function of the dietary regime, as developed by me originally for the treatment of tuberculosis, was regarded in many different ways by various authors who had spent years of work with it. One called it anti-phlogistic, another, dehydrating, a third, increasing the favorable inflammatory process, a fourth, acid-forming, a fifth, alkalizing, and yet another, increasing the healing processes in the system by unspecific stimulation therapy. The truth of the matter is that most of the above opinions are correct—they are partial effects which, taken all together, may be expressed as aid in the sense that it is activating the healing process in the whole system.

In biology the study of the functions of one substance in an organ is very difficult and disappointing.

Szent-Györgyi says "the more we study and know the single reactions of the muscles, the less we understand its function—and the function is a part of the whole body." In experiments on foodstuffs, scientists also examine single items in different sicknesses. The results are often very contradictory.

Dr. Alexander Brunschwig of New York Memorial Hospital was puzzled about the immunity phenomenon in cancer, as most surgeons are. The existence of some bodily defense against cancer "can hardly be denied." But "at best" this defense is "relatively feeble." What is more proper than to strengthen the defense, which, in a higher degree, means the healing power?

It is well known that my approach of studying the *whole* metabolism in its reaction is contrary to the prevailing viewpoint of the medical profession, which adheres generally to the thought that something specific, such as one medication, or a specific serum, or a combination of different sera, will have to solve the cancer problem. It has become more evident of late that the application of surgery and X-rays is encountering more skepticism by some surgeons and the public.

Until very recently, it appeared that whatever did not fit or agree with the prevailing practice or doctrine was "not scientific" and was pushed aside.[134] None of the so-called "food-fanatics" probably assumes that one or the other item, used once, for a week, or for a year, will prepare the underlying conditions for cancer. This book explains that *chronic* intoxication and degeneration of the liver-pancreas apparatus and the whole metabolism may cause the underlying conditions for cancer. All other superficial presentations are misconceptions and mislead the reader. The introduction to the above-mentioned article reads as follows:

Sugar, white flour, preserves, spices, cheese, canned goods, cooked foods and tomatoes all cause cancer, we hear. Grapes, on the other hand, can ward off cancer and even cure it. These are some of the misconceptions about cancer which various food-fanatics and crackpots have held throughout the ages.

"None of them, of course, is true. Science has not found that any dietary item can lessen one's chances of getting cancer or recovering from cancer. Aluminum cooking utensils were once thought by some to cause cancer. Many people still believe that chemical fertilizers, used instead of the old-fashioned organic kind, make people more susceptible to cancer. Another myth which has grown only in comparatively recent years is that water fluoridation causes cancer."[135]

What "other" scientists and their followers assume is something entirely different. Their opinion repeated in short is, that many different damaging food items, taken together, or in combination with other damaging factors, such as artificial fertilizer, aluminum kitchen utensils, and dead food such as frozen food or food

---

[134] The introduction to the article *Environmental Cancer* in *Cancer News* (1956, Vol. X, No. 3, p. 3) can be regarded as the mirror of thought of the majority of leading authors in the medical profession. In that article all seems to be based on "science" and "science experiments" and "scientific knowledge." In reality, however, this "all" is talking around the core of the issue and evading the real problem.

[135] *Ibid.*

changed by chemical additions for preservation, and in addition other deficiencies in food, caused by refining processes or poisons caused by canning, etc., all taken together, can seriously influence and continue to influence our body and its vital organs. Nobody can reconstruct such conditions in animal experiments, but many observations in the history of peoples demonstrate their downfall by influences of civilization in a broad sense. Such accumulations (not one or another item) of poisons prepare the conditions for cancer diseases. In many cases, even the lifespan of a physician's practice is not sufficient to observe in many people the accumulation of all damages, as it may take sixty to seventy years or longer to observe the outbreak of the disease in healthy people with a strong body, a resistant liver and good reabsorption power.

It goes without saying that vegetarians also get cancer. Some of them conclude—how can such a treatment help against cancer when even vegetarians may become afflicted?

(1) they do not know what conditions are necessary to maintain the normal metabolism—

(2) that our modern agriculture decreased potassium and iodine in our nutrition, precisely the minerals essential for prevention of cancer—

(3) that some people with weak organs are not sufficiently protected by diet *alone*—

(4) the therapy comprises much *more* than a vegetarian diet and has been successful in some vegetarians also.

As far as I know, experiments with the whole metabolism in that respect are not being carried out anywhere in the world. All the experiments performed in that direction in the past twenty or thirty years show mostly the above-mentioned influence of single items on the whole metabolism. The results of these experiments are partly contradictory and partly conflict with other ideas. This is understandable, as animals and humans vary considerably in their metabolic equilibrium.

The amount of damage done by chemical fertilizers, spraying, and insecticides which lead to a chronic poisoning of the soil can be estimated when we realize how many poisons go into the fruit and vegetables we eat, into the cattle, the eggs and butter we consume and the milk which we and our children drink. We also have to realize the enormous amount of food one patient needs in a single year. Here is a record of the average quantity of intake of some patients in the course of one year; a very great part of which is converted into juices.

> 1800 pounds of carrots
> 1300 pounds of apples
> 350-450 pounds of calf's liver (juice)*
> 145 heads of red cabbage
> 400 heads of lettuce
> 125 pounds of green peppers, etc., etc.

I am more than ever convinced that biochemistry and metabolic science will be victorious in healing degenerative diseases, including cancer if the *whole* body or the *whole metabolism* will be attacked and not the symptoms.

---

* See Appendix III, page 421

CHAPTER XX

Introduction to Nutrition and Diet

To BEGIN with, I would like to describe a few observations and experiments which demonstrate the importance of proper nutrition to general health and prove faulty nutrition as being an underlying cause of disease.

Several authors on nutrition think that, in modern times, cattle are better fed than people. Without knowing it, many vegetarians today are "starving." The protein content of most vegetables and fruits went down in the last ten to twenty years and we would have to make great efforts to bring it back to normal or even near normal. Here is an example: Corn has been allowed to fall in its protein content from 9.5 to 8.5 per cent in the last ten years. A few examinations of various vegetables have shown that by the use of artificial fertilizer and DDT spraying, the K-content as well as the protein content went down considerably while the sodium content increased. On the other hand, agricultural experts have raised the protein content of clover and alfalfa on a pilot farm in Vista, California; the protein percentage of alfalfa was raised from 12½ per cent to 32 per cent—equal almost to meat.

The diminution of proteins in fruits and vegetables necessitated the addition of animal proteins to the diet, as the patients weakened after four to six weeks, especially those with cancer in the intestinal tract, those in the advanced age groups and those who were very far reduced in their body substance, especially the muscular system.

I do not intend to discuss all problematic questions of the dietary regime, such as, for instance, the intake of sufficient protein to cover the increased loss of that substance. In practice, I have seen that most of the advanced or terminal cases refuse a higher intake of protein, especially cooked meats, fish, eggs, etc. Many of them have a special desire for raw food, but refuse even finely chopped raw meat or fresh raw egg stirred in orange juice. I observed that almost all patients with a higher protein intake could *not* be saved. In some cases I observed a much quicker growth of the cancer or metastases.

It seems that cattle fodder is supervised more carefully than human nutrition. There are interesting experiments made on rats, which show the following: When rats are feeding from organically grown soil, they have perfectly healthy organs through many generations. Other groups of rats, living on ordinary food in the United States and Britain developed, within one generation, all the degenerative diseases and pathology known in human beings.[136]

Rats feeding on large quantities of organically grown substances have been found to have better fur, to be more peaceful among themselves and less aggressive towards other animals. Other experiments showed that rats susceptible to cancer showed a decline in incidence of cancer when given proper nutrition from the time of their birth.

Dr. Pottenger's experiments on cats showed that cats fed common food, without raw substances and raw milk, became nervous, sick and even homosexual. Several weeks' treatment with raw milk and raw vegetables returned them to normalcy!

Dr. Biskind[137] made a special study on DDT wherever it is used and presented in detail the damages on the human body. "We have found as much as 13 parts per million in butter on the New York market and Department of Agriculture reports indicate that very much higher values are not at all improbable. In addition, I have seen several instances in which exposures to DDT sharply increased the insulin requirements of diabetes." (This refers to the impairment of liver and pancreas.)

Among other clinical symptoms of poisonings, he reported: "one patient had signs of severe liver involvement—was completely improved when all DDT-containing foods were removed."

---

[136] See *Prevention Magazine*, April, 1957.

[137] (Hearings before the House Committee to investigate the Use of Chemicals in Food Products) H. Res. 323.—Reprint 2-52, Lee Foundation for Nutritional Research, Milwaukee 3, Wisconsin.

Dr. Biskind's and D. F. M. Pottenger, Jr.'s observations showed that in the years from 1945 to 1950, blood cholesterol in his patients "was increased," actually caused by newer insecticides.

In experiments of the Federal Food and Drug Administration with insecticides "five days after feeding showed the insecticides in the gizzard, the liver and the kidney, the tissues of the heart and brain and sciatic nerve fibre."

With larger doses, F.D.A. scientists have also shown that it is possible to store many times the amount in the body-fat that would be acutely fatal intravenously in a single dose. Since DDT mobilizes from the body fat into the blood stream, the intravenous dose is the logical comparative one. Cumulative intoxication from extremely small amounts in food can thus be as dangerous as direct exposure to much larger amounts.

"The soil is the meeting place of the living matter at the surface and of the mineral matter beneath the surface, and of the atmosphere above and the solid rock underneath. Essentially all living matter depends upon it, directly or indirectly—is, in fact, a part of those very processes that produce the soil upon which life depends. Plants and soils have grown up together, each partly a cause of the other. Man has somewhat the same relationship to the soils. He finds some are better suited to his needs than others. He may change them either for better or for worse."[138]

Soil science has a contribution to make toward the future, but certainly not by itself. Since science itself has become so specialized, it is difficult to see science as a whole and its relationship to politics, art, business, and agriculture. More and more, modern education seems to make people specialists—members of a group or clique—and leads them away from the masses, from real democracy. The kind of science that is super-specialized cannot lead people to better relationships with each other and the land, nor can so-called "pure" science, which is too cold or too snobbish to face the real problems. Some see a danger that farmers as well as other people may turn their problems over to some special group, some special bureaucracy, rather than to think out the problems for themselves and make their decisions by the democratic method.

---

[138] Charles E. Kellog. The McMillan Company, 1956.

There exist abundant supplies of nearly all natural resources in the United States and especially of soil. Enough injury to the soil has taken place to indicate a pressing need for adjustments of agricultural people to the soil upon which they live. Since there are many soils these relationships are too complicated to be resolved by a few simple slogans or programs.

The modern technique of canned food goes back to the application of heat by the attempts of Apperts who tried to gain the award, established by Napoleon in 1795, for the best plan for "food conservation for his army." In 1804, he published his work. In 1810, Peter Durand received the first English patent for the metal can. In 1841 the first factory for canned food was founded in Norway. Later in 1845 the first factory in Dessau, Germany, was established. In 1873, Robert Koch introduced the autoclave. In 1859, factories for canned food were set up in the United States. In 1879, the first cans for sardines were made in Stavanger, Norway. In 1937, the production of canned vegetables in the United States amounted to 189,919,000 crates; there also were 63,744,000 crates of fruits and 12,300,000 crates of fish. The technique of frozen food was introduced by C. von Linde (1931). The technique of conservation is ancient. It begins with the use of salt for meat and fish and vegetables, and the use of sugar for fruit. It became more developed in our modern biochemistry.[139]

The canned food industry has grown into an important factor in our modern civilization. Thus, the nutrition and feeding of families has been put on a mass production basis. The cans stay in the foreground and the mistakes in that respect, no matter how insignificant they may appear, became an ever-increasing calamity in our present day society.

W. C. Kinney, of Vista, California, recently produced on his organic farm apricots on composted, mineralized soil that contain the following analysis:

Moisture	86.15%	
Ash	.70%	
Protein	1.41%	
K_2O	4150	ppm
Na	748	ppm
CaO	291	ppm

---

[139] Werner Kollath, *ibid.*, pp. 70-71.

MgO	69.2	ppm
P_2O_5	1340.0	ppm
S	15.2	ppm
Fe	20.8	ppm
Mn	6.9	ppm
B	.28	ppm
Cu	.69	ppm

The increased protein content also has many disadvantages.[140] Economic pressure, in terms of lower actual cash returns for the farmer's crops, has brought a new element into the planning and thinking of some of our top agronomists. The grower's pay for his year's work is being considerably reduced through the toll taken by pests and disease. So the emphasis is being shifted, at least in some quarters, to the development of resistant plants and to *biological controls* instead of poisons.

Along with this trend there is just beginning to be a realization of the fact that increasing numbers of consumers are willing to pay top prices for really high quality foods. In this regard, the most advanced research shows that "high protein content" by itself is not necessarily the answer. Work with the amino acids has shown, among other things, that high protein brought about by excessive nitrogen fertilizing can actually *lessen* rather than increase the nutritional value of grains and vegetables. At the same time, scentifically managed *organic fertilizing* can give better results, in terms of food values, even with a relatively *lower protein* content.

In the *New York World-Telegram & Sun*, May 8, 1957, an article reported that "Rockland County's strawberry crop is ruined, the rest of the county's $2,000,000 fruit crop is threatened and virtually every bee in the county has been killed by the Department of Agriculture's massive aerial spray of DDT, the state agriculture agent of the county charged today."

In my opinion, it was not the one spraying that caused such disastrous damage, as the previous 12 years of increased spraying with increased poisons produced an accumulated toxic and pathological condition in soil, animals and human beings. I called it: "our External Metabolism" (see page 15, line 1).

[140] E. E. Pfeiffer, M.D., "Balanced Nutrition of Soils and Plants," *Natural Food & Farming*, May 1957, p. 6.

The article concluded as follows: "DDT is, and is recognized and admitted by the defendants to be, a delayed-action, cumulative poison such as will inevitably cause irreparable injury and death to all living things, including human beings, animals, birds, insects and the predators and parasites of harmful insects, if ingested, inhaled or brought into contact therewith in sufficient quantities or over a sufficient period.

"Some human beings, including some of the plaintiffs, have already absorbed . . . and now irremediably retain in their bodies an accumulated amount of DDT which is toxic and pathological, so that the threatened spraying upon their persons will endanger their health and lives, and the threatened spraying on their gardens and other cultivated lands will make it unsafe for them, this year, or even thereafter, to eat the produce therefrom."

NUTRITION (DETERIORATION)

The preparation of the juices is described in the prescription booklet. There, the physician will find an outline of the diet as it is used at the present time and also a description of the preparation of vegetables. The prescription booklet* also contains an outline of the medication without indicating the exact doses. Instead of that, one cancer case is presented in full detail, from beginning to end. I believe that the physician will thus have

TABLE 1

	Potassium	Sodium	
Apples	125	15	
Potatoes	440	19	In 100 grams fresh substance
Turnips	332	59	Ash content of the edible por-
Cabbage	243	20	tion of some common foods
Lima beans, dried	1743	245	(modified from Lusk)
Oatmeal	380	81	

a much clearer idea of how the medical treatment can be applied in the best manner. The details of the agriculture of foods and vegetables cannot be given *in extenso* in this volume. Space will only permit a few brief chapters to deal with the problems of artificial fertilizers, organic gardening methods, the poisons of spraying and all other factors damaging to foods and vegetables in their preparation and distribution.

---
* (Chapter 33.)

For the choice of fruits and vegetables, it was most important to know the potassium content as well as the sodium content.[141] The table shows that the potato has the lowest sodium content, of 19 milligrams in 100 grams of fresh substance, while the potassium content is 440 milligrams, or 32 times as much. The content of the apple is fifteen to 125, or about eight and one-half times as much.

The accuracy of this table is quite uncertain, as the vegetables, fruit and milk show quite different figures at different times. The more our agriculture turns away from natural methods, the more the contents of fruits and vegetables are changed: the sodium content rises, the potassium content diminishes.

In the near future, hospitals and cancer clinics and clinics for chronic degenerative diseases will be more or less forced to use fruits and vegetables grown by organic gardening methods, or we physicians will see that our results and therapeutic successes of the treatments will be fewer and fewer.

The poisoned soil will not only help to increase degenerative diseases, but it will also reduce the healing power of the body when brought under special conditions where it functioned favorably previously.

---

[141] See the *Physiological Basis of Medical Practice*, 5th edition, by Chas. H. Best and Norman Burke Taylor, p. 770 (The Williams and Wilkins Co., 1950).

CHAPTER XXI

The Saltless Diet

THE ROLE of salt in human nutrition has been a disputed subject for a long time. Some authors regard salt merely as a condiment or stimulant which is harmless in small quantities, possibly harmful in larger quantities, but definitely dispensable in normal nutrition, to the extent that it is not a natural content of food. Others believe that salt is indispensable in human nutrition and that the sodium chloride found in foods is not enough to meet the requirements of the normal human being.

The exponents of both views have given reasons in support of their respective viewpoints.

Wolff-Eisner asserts that salt is comparable to a vitamin, and that its complete exclusion could not be tolerated any longer than the exclusion of food itself. (It might be argued here that "complete" exclusion is impossible anyway, inasmuch as varying quantities of NaCl are found in food naturally.)

Wolff-Eisner adds, however, ". . . that cooking salt is the only salt which does not occur in sufficient quantities in normal nutrition and that it, therefore, must be added artificially." There are different views as to the quantity of salt which, according to this theory, must be added to cover man's salt requirements.

The average European consumes ten to fifteen grams of salt per day and in the United States the average consumption is ten to twelve grams per day, whereas the values are quite different in Asia and Africa. All physiologists agree that these values far exceed the salt requirements. In other words, they agree that people consume salt mostly because it makes food more tasty, not because the body requires it.

Bunge conducted several experiments in 1901 on the need

153

for salt. He found a small demand for salt in animals which eat a lot of meat, whereas he discovered the demand much greater in those living on vegetation. He believed that the same relationship was to be found among human beings. He found that the population of cities, in which larger quantities of meat were eaten, consumed one-third of the quantity of salt used by the mainly vegetarian rural population. Similarly, he found little demand for salt among the meat-eating nomads. On the other hand, the salt demand among agricultural negroes was so great that, in some tribes, salt actually had barter value.

From his own experiments, Bunge gathered that the body eliminates large quantities of salt if it consumes much potassium, such as found in large quantities in vegetarian nutrition. (His classical experiment in 1901, however, is not indisputable in theory, although its conclusions are correct.)

Abderhalden shared Bunge's views as to the reasons for the increased demand for salt among vegetarian tribes: The higher potassium content of nutrition leads to increased elimination of sodium and, therefore, causes an increased demand for salt.

Bunge considered the addition of four to five grams of salt daily necessary for the maintenance of the "salt balance" (per Voit); Hermannsdorfer disputed this in his doctorate dissertation, stating that while man consumes up to 15 grams of salt per day, he could undoubtedly manage on one or two grams of salt. In fasting experiments on himself, to test the elimination of salt, Hermannsdorfer generally took two grams of salt.

These views are considered one-sided in some respects despite their having common usage. My experiments on thousands of patients, as well as on myself, reveal that the demand for salt is something to which our nerves of taste have become accustomed since youth. Just as one might say that all people have a need for alcoholic beverages and that even animals—especially the human-like apes—can become chronic alcoholics, and, concluding from this fact that alcohol is a necessary component of human nutrition, it would be just as incorrect to base a claim of the indispensability of salt on its universally practiced use.

There are certain tribes which do not use salt. Homer has mentioned them, and Sallust talked of the Numidians who did not use salt. But apart from that, even if all the people in the world had eaten salt since time immemorial, this still would not prove that it was to their advantage. After all, there had always been chronic diseases whose etiology we cannot ascertain even today; thus, we cannot judge to what extent they may have been caused by an unreasonable way of life.

Just for the sake of curiosity, we might point to the fact that, even today, there are tribes who live without salt. Professor Vrgoc reported that tuberculosis was unusually prevalent among the settled Kirghizians, whereas it occurred only rarely among the nomadic ones.[142] The nomads use no salt, whereas the Kirghizian peasants do use salt, which is freely available in the Steppes, as an addition to nutrition, in the manner of the Russian peasants. (Note: the role of *Kumys*—strong alcohol—will not be dealt with here.) The Kirghizians reported to Vrgoc that they had noticed a deterioration of their senses of sight and smell since partaking of bread and salt. Nomads who use salt lose the ability to scent wolves. Vrgoc also reported that fishing and hunting tribes of Siberia show a marked dislike of salt. On his expeditions to the North Pole, Nansen used the Eskimos' dislike of salt to get rid of uninvited guests by offering them strongly salted food. Stanley and Livingstone, too, reported on finding tribes to whom salt was unknown and who showed certain toxic symptoms after taking it for the first time. (Also see Albert Schweitzer's report.)

We observed healthy nurses after several months of unsalted nutrition and found that their first reaction to normal home-cooking was diarrhea and nausea. This shows what far-reaching effects the habitual consumption of salt may have on the organism. After going six months without salt, a nurse who had believed that she could not do without it reacted to this spice as a young boy reacts to his first cigarette.

The evaluation of alcohol, tobacco and salt as parts of human nutrition is closely connected with national and even religious and political motives which are not always related to medical considerations. It would, therefore, be wise to omit the ethnographic aspect from a discussion of the meaning of salt in human nutrition. We should also avoid the mistake of quoting examples from the animal world to prove that the intake of salt is "natural"

---

[142] Quoted in *Dtsch. Aerztezeitung.* 176/129.

or necessary. We have refused to use the argument of "natural nutrition"; this term must be rejected when used—apparently—to the disadvantage of the diet. Whether a form of nutrition is natural or not has nothing to do with the question of whether or not it is of therapeutic value in diseases. This is the only decisive question in practice.

Nevertheless, for the sake of completeness, a few brief remarks regarding the desire for salt in animals are in order.

In areas of great expanse, such as in Central India and in the Dekkan, there is an enormous wealth of game and no availability of salt. Presumably, the same situation exists elsewhere. It is of special importance to note that apes in particular show no need for salt; mixed human nutrition is offered to them only in captivity, when they accept it as readily as they learn to drink alcohol, smoke tobacco and eat roast meat.

According to Dr. Gustav Riedlin, thorough experiments in the use of salt were conducted by Hahnemann, the founder of homeopathy, and his students. In these experiments, Hahnemann and his students consumed considerably greater quantities of salt for weeks and months than they were normally accustomed to consume in food. The harmful effects are described in the book (pp. 9-15).[143]

Arguments against a "saltless" diet ("saltless" means without addition of salt to food) were enumerated by Wolff-Eisner[144] approximately as follows:

In a nutrition rich in vegetables, the body requires the addition of salt, as this does not occur in sufficient quantities in the food "as the only salt." As the potassium carbonate of vegetables combines in the organism with chloride and sodium to form sodium chloride and sodium carbonate, it causes the elimination of chloride and sodium. This means that sodium as well as chloride must be given to the body to make up this loss—hence the addition of salt!

In this work, Wolff-Eisner quotes the well-known experiments of Bunge, who asserted that regular partaking of potatoes, which contain 31-42 times more potassium than sodium, is possible only if NaCl is added to this food.

---

[143] Gustav Riedlin, *Das Kochsalz* (*Salt*), Ed. Paul Lorenz, Freiburg, 1924.
[144] It should be noted here that not only salt, but also fruity acids participate in such changes of the metabolism.

In the same work, strangely enough, it is mentioned that a) apples contain even 100 times more potassium than sodium, yet one may consume large quantities of apples—one may even have exclusive apple days—without the addition of NaCl. b) According to general opinion, the hydrochloric acid of the stomach is dependent on the body's salt intake. Therefore, if the intake of salt is missing, the formation of hydrochloric acid must decrease, which would affect appetite, digestion, etc. for "lack of salt inhibits production of hydrochloric acid." c) Finally, Wolff-Eisner remarks that the sweat of tubercular patients contains up to one per cent salt, so that perspiration deprives the body of salt.[145] d) Furthermore, it is said that the kidneys regulate the body's ionic state; in fever and in the majority of infectious diseases, the salt content of the urine is diminished, even if the patients are given salt. (Consequently, it is argued, there is no need to regulate the intake of salt, if the kidneys are healthy, as the kidneys regulate the elimination of salt anyway. Since, according to Roth-Koevesti, even diseased kidneys are capable of eliminating five grams of salt in a liter of urine, the intake of five grams of salt is unobjectionable for such kidneys.)

Inasmuch as some of these arguments are also voiced by our patients, who see particular nutritive value in salt and appreciate the stimulative effect of salt upon appetite and thirst, physicians are sometimes forced to take them into consideration.

As far as Wolff-Eisner's first argument is concerned, it must only be said that that which appears objectionable to him is particularly desired by me, i.e., the increased elimination of NaCl. For if, Wolff-Eisner's presentation, which is based on Bunge's view, is correct, i.e., if the elimination of NaCl from the body's salt resources is furthered by vegetarian nutrition, it is precisely that which my diet wants to achieve. The more salt is eliminated by it, the more effective the diet is in some respects. It appears to us that it would be equally inexpedient to replace the decreased sodium and chloride, which we desire, by the feeding of salt, as it would be inexpedient to make up increased elimination of sugar in the urine of diabetics by increasing sugar intake.

"No human dietaries, howsoever prescribed, even without added salt, are so low in sodium that they cannot support life."[146]

---

[145] *Med. Welt*, 1929, p. 1821.
[146] See Alfred T. Shohl, *Mineral Metabolism*, p. 121.

The argument for the necessity of the addition of salt to potatoes was mentioned above, as well as the fact that apples—containing 100 times more potassium than sodium—are not salted, except by special gourmets. (This shows the importance of the role of habit and taste. Peasants would laugh at people who add salt to apples, yet they add salt to potatoes themselves.)

It is known that there is a connection between the hydrochloric acid of the stomach and the intake of salt. However, the dependence of this hydrochloric acid upon salt intake has not been proven, and is contrary to my experience.[147] According to Rosemann, the stomach juices of normal humans contain 400-500 mg. of hydrochloric acid. Its pH lies between 0.97 and 0.80. If we consider the regulation for the production of stomach juice, it shows how the entire organism, especially the liver, participates in its formation, just as it participates in all other bodily occurrences, irrespective of the organ in which the particular process takes place.

HOW WHITE MAN'S DIET
AFFECTS NATIVES OF AFRICA[148]

"I have to point out a happening in the modern civilization of the Hospital, something which happened this year.

"We had to perform the first appendicitis operation on a native of this region. How it turned out that this so frequent sickness of white people did not occur in the colored of this country cannot be convincingly explained. Probably its still exceptional occurrence is traceable to a change in the nutrition. Many natives, especially those who are living in larger communities do not now live the same way as formerly—they lived almost exclusively on fruits and vegetables, bananas, cassava, ignam, taro, sweet potatoes and other fruits. They now begin to live on condensed milk, canned butter, meat-and-fish preserves and bread.

"The date of the appearance of cancer, another disease of civilization, cannot be traced in our region with the same certainty as that of appendicitis. We cannot state decisively that formerly

---

[147] See Eimer, *Deutsch. Med. Wo.*, 1930, No. 24.

[148] From Professor Albert Schweitzer's "Briefe aus dem Lambarenespital" (Letters from the Lambarene Hospital) in Africa, 1954.

there was no cancer at all, because the microscopic examinations of all tested tumors, revealing their real nature, has only been in existence here for a few years. Based upon my own experience, going back to 1913, I can say, if cancer occurred at all it was very rare but that it became more frequent since. However, it is not spread as much as it is among the white race of Europe and America.

"It is obvious to connect the fact of increase of cancer with the increased use of salt by the natives. In former years there was only available the little salt extracted from the ocean, which came up to the hinterland. There was a very limited traffic only. The salt had to be transferred by dealers of the tribe living at the coast to those tribes living next to them up-stream. In this way it reached one tribe after another and moved further and further to the interior, where the dealers handed over only the portion which was left over from distribution among their own tribe and the chiefs charged heavy customs for the passage through their region. With this procedure it scarcely could get farther than 120 miles inland. According to information of old people here, whom I still knew at the beginning of my activity, formerly there was no salt whatsoever in the interior.

"This changed in 1874 when the whites came to this land and handled the traffic up-stream. The European salt was shipped in small sacks of a few pounds. Still at the time of my arrival in Lambarene, salt was so precious that it prevailed as the most valuable and the most generous type of remuneration. Who ever had to make a trip on the river or travel along the paths of the virgin woods did not take along money but salt (also tobacco leaves imported from America), thus trading bananas and cassavas for his oarsmen and carriers. By and by the consumption of salt increased. Today it is used much less among the colored than among the whites. The patients we feed in our hospital receive a few grams a month and are satisfied with this small amount.

"So it is possible that the formerly very seldom and still infrequent occurrence of cancer in this country is connected with the former very little consumption of salt and the still rare use of it. Curiously enough we did not have any cancer cases in our hospital.

"It should be mentioned that the infectious diseases among

the whites gradually appeared. It remains questionable if tuberculosis was spread formerly as much as now, even if it occurred at all times. According to my observations it became more frequent after the First World War."

The experiments of Kremer[149] have also shown conclusively that the value of stomach acids in patients on the diet remained normal for several months, although salt intake was limited to salt contained in natural food. The appetite of patients does not suffer by lack of salt; as a rule it even improves, particularly in serious diseases, after the start of the treatment.

The elimination of a little salt in the sweat of some patients is of no importance whatever in therapy, for the therapy brings about a fast decrease and early complete cessation of perspiration. Straus correctly attributes this, as well as the decreased mucus secretion, to the water-withdrawing effect of the saltless diet. He concludes from this that the deprivation of salt also has favorable therapeutic effects upon such diseases (such as Bronchogenic, vaginal discharge and pus secretions, etc.).

The last argument, that healthy kidneys regulate the ionic state of the organism anyway, and that it is therefore unnecessary to limit salt intake, is phrased much too generally and does not take into account important factors apart from kidney function, which affect the elimination of NaCl (hormones, tonus in the visceral nervous system, circulatory regulations).

The fact that diseased kidneys are still capable of eliminating five grams of NaCl per liter of urine has no particular meaning for our problem regarding the quantity of salt intake. Nevertheless, the chloride ion deserves a special position among the substances to be concentrated by the kidneys. While the kidneys are capable of increasing concentration of uric substance 40-80 times, uric acid 25-50 times, sugar (in diabetes) 30-50 times over their concentrations in the plasma, chloride concentration can be increased only two to five times[150] For the past 40 years, practical experience was gathered about the effects of salt limitation upon diseases of kidneys. It was shown just here that *radical* limitation of salt intake, in the sense of Straus' "strict form" (with less than 2.5 g of NaCl per day) or the "third degree" of Noorden (with 1.5-3 g of NaCl per day) which corresponds to the usual saltless

---

[149] *Med. Welt*, No. 11/1930.
[150] Lichtwitz, *Klin. Chemie*, 1930, p. 501.

nutrition, decreases the burden on the diseased kidneys. "As soon as the diseased kidneys are not over-irritated and over-burdened by the excessive intake of chlorides in nutrition, they recover in an amazingly short time and . . . eliminate more NaCl on a saltless diet than on the previously salt-rich diet!"[151]

Noorden also pointed out that such saltless nutrition cannot cure kidney disease; the removal of a constant irritation can only improve healing conditions. Something similar applies to the effect of our diet. The elimination of salt does *not* serve to cure various diseases, but it is an important supporting factor of the diet. A damaging irritation is removed by the elimination of salt. Furthermore, if the elimination of salt by normally functioning kidneys is limited by fever, as Wolff-Eisner points out, and remains limited in spite of further salt intake, this should not lead to the conclusion that the body regulates salt distribution so well that physicians should leave this function to the body. This only shows that the organism cannot digest the given quantities of salt in fever states. Therefore, a temporary radical limitation of salt nutrition (fasting, refusal of nutrition) is also correct in acute diseases (infectious diseases). And, if diseased kidneys can eliminate five grams of salt, this does not mean that five grams of salt should be given. On the contrary, it would appear to be more obvious to conclude that, by sparing the kidneys and other organs, one should try to achieve in all diseases similar results as in kidney-therapy and, lately, also in heart diseases, cancer, etc.

Claude Bernard was probably one of the first to investigate the question of origin of hydrochloric acid in stomach juice. He injected potassium ferrocyanide and lactate of iron into the veins. The substances gave a Prussian blue reaction in the presence of free acid. The mucosa of the stomach turned blue after the injection but not the parietal cells of the fundic glands.

The ultimate source of the chloride is undoubtedly the sodium chloride of the blood. Chlorides are ionized Cl in the parietal cells, secreted into the stomach's free space; there they combine with free H ions and built free H Cl which is not secreted as such. The venous blood leaving the gastric mucosa shows a fall in chloride and a rise in bicarbonate of Na.

In conclusion, it should be stressed that the entire mineral

---

[151] Noorden-Salomon, *Handbuch der Ernaehrung*, 1920, p. 913.

metabolism of the animal organism has not been sufficiently explored so far. Therefore, we cannot as yet make any definite statements about the roles of chloride and sodium—both individually—as well as in their combination in NaCl and in other combinations. We must be content by establishing certain relationships and conditions in a healthy or a sick body.

CHAPTER XXII

Salt in Cancer Diet

DR. HOFFMAN refers to the epoch-making research of Waterman which throws much light on "The electrical behavior of cells exposed to salt changes in their environment. In the polarization of the cells under such conditions Waterman has found a criterion for the discovery of the earliest changes and the very onset of abnormal processes in the tissue, at a time when in all other respects the organs appear still perfectly normal."

According to Meyer, "when unbalanced, the salts become a source of trouble for cell metabolism." And that, therefore, "it thus becomes obvious that the kind of food consumed and the regular functioning and correlation of all these organs determine in part the quantity and the ratio to one another of the salts present in the serum.[152]

Mineral imbalance then becomes a question of profound importance in all discussions of the causative nature of cancerous processes. I quote further from Meyer in connection with this question as follows:

"Giving food credit for that much of a *contributory influence* toward the development of cancer, always remembering the small percentage of actual cancer cases among those predisposed, is, of course, vastly different from saying that already existing cancer could be benefited by special diet, a suggestion upon which we look, in common with the great majority of the medical profession, as having no standing in medical experience and no justification of being made the basis for cancer medication."

"With this conclusion, however, I (Frederick Hoffman) am

---

[152] O. E. Meyer Göttingen, 1923.

by no means in agreement. On the contrary I am of the opinion that the diet of cancer patients has a profound effect on cancerous processes which can be increased or decreased according to the food intake and its regulated chemical composition."[153]

Therapeutically we find the following: the saltless diet and detoxication reduce Na, Cl, H_2O in the whole system. This is the removal of cell edema simultaneously with the reduction of the negative electrical potentials. Thus the way is paved for the activated negatively charged K group minerals and positively charged iodine components. These changes seem to force the cancer cells to a higher metabolic rate. In my opinion, the mineral metabolism united, of course, with a number of other revived processes bring about the decisive role for the death of the cancer cells. Cancer cells can ferment only; therefore they are unable to adapt to the new intensive changes—they break down and die. This part of the metabolism must be properly composed and constantly reactivated by the function of the liver. Thus, we may assume that almost all vital functions, functions of the restored mineral metabolism, the detoxication, etc., necessary for healing power, are anchored in the liver.

Some authors regarded salt as stimulating neoplastic growth and recommended its restriction in the cancer diet.[154] A contrary opinion was expressed by F. Blumenthal and E. Hesse in 1935, who saw that regimes extremely poor in salt have a rather unfavorable influence on human neoplasias.

Other authors found that a protein-poor and K-rich regime produced favorable conditions for tumor development, by inducing an alkalosis. They emphasized: "No cancer without alkalosis." The well-known food chemist, Ragnar Berg,[155] objected strongly to that viewpoint: a diet producing alkalosis may be responsible for the development of cancer. All of these opinions still remain in the category of theories.

The available facts on the role of sodium and potassium in cancer are not clear. The findings of the authors and their conclusions are, on the whole, very disappointing. My opinion is that cancer is not a specific disease, has no uniform symptoms

---

[153] Frederick L. Hoffman, L.L.D., *Cancer and Diet*, The Williams & Wilkins Co., Baltimore, 1937, p. 347.

[154] See op. cit., p. 410.

[155] Zeitschrift fuer Volksernaehrung, 9:119, 1934.

and is not equally developed to a certain degree. Cancer is an extraordinary symptom only. The underlying cause is to be found in the poisoning of the liver. That is most probably the reason why the biological findings are inconclusive and so contradicting. Cancer is a disease of the liver lately called a "balance wheel of life"—where most metabolic functions are more or less concentrated. From here the other organs can be pathologically influenced and damaged or poisoned. Among the great number of observations, there are some which seem to be correct but they are not confirmed by laboratory experiments. Waterman found: "the sodium content of blood serum is unchanged in cancer patients." Benedict and Theis concluded that the "blood serum in cancer patients contains the normal amount of sodium." Pitts and Johnson examined the sodium content of blood serum and of blister fluid in cancerous and noncancerous patients and discovered that "the sodium content of these fluids was the same in cancer patients and in normal patients." Dr. Fry described in the *British Cancer Review* of 1926 the fact that in the blood of tumor-bearing rats the amount of sodium is 25 per cent above normal when the tumor is growing actively, and 60 per cent above normal when the tumor is receding. Marwood went so far as to say salt is the root cause of cancer.

TASK OF THE SALTLESS DIET IN CANCER

The main task of the saltless diet is to eliminate the retained Na, Cl, H_2O, together with toxins and poisons from the tissues all over the body.

All poisons and other substances difficult to eliminate are stimulants for the sick tissues, especially liver and kidneys. That condition seems to be the reason why sodium chloride excretion increases in tuberculosis, cancer and other chronic diseases after two to three days on a saltless diet, and this condition stays at that higher level for about eight to ten or fourteen days, corresponding to a favorable development in the course of the disease. After that is accomplished, it stays near the normal level with the saltless diet, but shows a higher Na-Cl excretion, together with more fluid from time to time for two to three days, and later for one day. Such so-called "flare-ups" go along sometimes with nausea, diairhea and nervous disturbances, caused probably by greater bile secretion and stimulation of the visceral nervous system. After each "flare-up" the patient feels easier and mentally improved.

Indications for Saltless Diet

(a)   Edema and abnormal deposition of sodium and chloride in the subcutaneous tissue (nephropathias).

(b)   Cardio-renal insufficiency.

(c)   K-loss and Na-retention, in chronic diseases, especially in tuberculosis, cancer, etc.

(d)   Detoxication, the degree of which must be in proportion to the degree of the disease-and which must be maintained during the period of restoration.

CHAPTER XXIII

Insecticides

WE HAVE learned in recent years that spraying with modern insecticides is doing more and more damage to our food and to our bodies. I cannot emphasize too often that our food production represents our external metabolism. Whoever is interested in this field may read the *Hearings Before the House Select Committee to Investigate the Use of Chemicals in Food Products, House of Representatives Eighty-First Congress, Second Session.*[156] There is clearly described in the hearing of Dr. Biskind what he observed in this field and what he recommended ought to be done.

The following is a brief survey of this hearing: "The introduction for uncontrolled general use by the public of the insecticide DDT, or chlorophenothane, and the series of even more deadly substances that followed, has no previous counterpart in history. Beyond question, no other substance known to man was ever before developed so rapidly and spread indiscriminately over so large a portion of the earth in so short a time. This is the more surprising as, at the time DDT was released for public use, a large amount of data was already available in the medical literature showing that this agent was extremely toxic for many different species of animals, that it was cumulatively stored in the body fat and that it appeared in the milk. At this time a few cases of DDT poisoning in human beings had also been reported. These observations were almost completely ignored or misinterpreted.

"In the subsequent mass use of DDT and related compounds a vast amount of additional information on the toxicity of these materials, both in animals and in man, has become available.

---

[156] Created Pursuant to H. Res. 323 (Reprint #2-52 Lee Foundation for Nutritional Research, Milwaukee 3, Wisconsin).

Somehow a fantastic myth of human invulnerability has grown up with reference to the use of these substances. Because their effects are cumulative and may be insidious and because they resemble those of so many other conditions, physicians for the most part have been unaware of the danger. Elsewhere, the evidence has been treated with disbelief, ignored, misinterpreted, distorted, suppressed or subjected to some of the fanciest double-talk ever perpetrated.

"Early last year I published a series of observations on DDT poisoning in man. Since shortly after the last war a large number of cases had been observed by physicians all over the country in which a group of symptoms occurred, the most prominent feature of which was gastroenteritis, persistently recurrent nervous symptoms, and extreme muscular weakness. The condition was of unknown origin and, following an outbreak in Los Angeles in 1947, was thereafter widely attributed to a "virus X." As with all other physicians, a large number of my patients had this condition.

"I, like others, found it extremely puzzling; it resembled no infectious process I was acquainted with, and it had features strongly suggesting some kind of intoxication. I had known that DDT was far more toxic than current mythology admitted, but it was only when I came across an item in the literature indicating the vast amount of DDT already in use in our agricultural economy that the possibility that this agent was involved occurred to me. I immediately consulted available textbooks and found that the signs and symptoms of known DDT poisoning were sufficiently similar to the cases I had seen to warrant further investigation. In fact, in 1945 two British authors had described with great accuracy part of the disorder following exposure to DDT in three human subjects.

"The syndrome consists of a group of or all of the following: Acute gastroenteritis occurs, with nausea, vomiting, abdominal pain, and diarrhea. A running nose, cough, and persistent sore throat are common, often followed by a persistent or recurrent feeling of constriction or a lump in the throat: occasionally the sensation of constriction extends into the chest and to the back and shoulders and may be associated with severe pain in either arm and may easily be confused with a heart or gall-bladder attack. Pain in the joints, general muscle weakness, and exhausting fatigue are usual; the latter are often so severe in the acute stage as to be described by some patients as paralysis. Sometimes the initial attack is ushered in by dizziness and fainting. Insomnia, intractable headache, and giddiness are not uncommon. Disturbed sensations of various kinds occur in most cases; areas of skin become exquisitely hypersensitive and after a few days this disappears, only to recur elsewhere, or irregular numbness, tingling sensations, itching or crawling sensations, or a feeling of localized heat may take place. Erratic twitching of voluntary muscles is common. Usually there is diminution of ability to feel vibration in the extremities. Loss of weight is not uncommon.

"Disturbances of equilibrium may occur. There may be attacks of rapid pulse and palpitation associated with contraction of blood vessels in the skin, sweating of the palms and a sense of impending loss of consciousness, followed by slow pulse, flushing of the skin, relaxation and cessation of palmar perspiration.

"The subjective reactions tend to recur in 'waves,' as numerous patients have described them. Some have actually been able to clock the reaction with considerable precision from day to day. The reactions appear most likely to occur during periods of low blood sugar. Additionally, consumption of alcoholic beverages or acute emotional stress may provoke a severe exacerbation.

"Often, patients with this disorder complain of a "hollow feeling" in the epigastrium which bears no constant chronologic relation to the ingestion of food, and in fact may take place immediately after a full meal. Attempts to eat further may provoke sharp repugnance for food and occasionally may lead to an attack of hiccups or nausea. In other patients, actual overeating indistinguishable from the compulsive types seen in certain psychogenic disturbances may result.

"Hardly a single sensory nerve appears to be immune to involvement in this disorder: disorders of vision, smell, taste and hearing may occur. Pain of varying intensity and duration may involve any area of the skin and may localize in a joint or even in a tooth. Severe peripheral neuritis involving intense, protracted pain in one or more of the extremities is frequent. Pain in the groin, usually bilateral, is a frequent complaint. In the acute stages, mild convulsions involving mainly the legs, may occur.

"After subsidence of the acute attack, irregular spasm throughout the gastrointestinal tract often persists for weeks or months,

associated with increased fatiguability, which only gradually re-
gresses. Fever occurs occasionally during the initial stages but
is not the rule. Except for a tendency for anemia, and in some
cases a relative increase in certain white blood cells, no constant
changes are observable in the blood. Many of the patients have
an acute bout of apprehension associated with the foregoing
symptom complex and rarely is this relieved by reassurance as
to the absence of physical findings sufficient to account for the
severity of the disturbance.

"Most striking about the syndrome is the persistence of some
of the symptoms, the tendency to repeated recurrence of others
over a period of many months—some patients fail to show complete recovery even after a year—and the lack of detectable lesions
sufficient to account for the severity of the subjective reaction.

"The high incidence, the usual absence of a febrile reaction,
the persistence and erratic recurrence of the symptoms, the lack
of observable inflammatory lesions, and the resistance even to
palliative therapy, as I have already indicated, suggested an intoxication rather than an infection. The epidemic first appeared at
about the time DDT came into widespread use by the civilian
population. The signs and symptoms described in the pharma-
cologic and toxilogic literature as characteristic of DDT poisoning
turned out to be identical with those appearing in patients with
the affliction described.

"By far the most disturbing of all the manifestations are the
subjective reactions and the *extreme muscular weakness*. In the
severe, acute cases, patient after patient has used identical words,
'I felt like I was going to die.'

"I found similar descriptions in reading about the so-called
'Iceland disease,' the most characteristic symptom of which is
extreme muscular weakness, which begins in the legs, then
spreads to both arms and hands; patients even have difficulty
in swallowing. (*Newsweek*, May 1957)

"The sensation can perhaps best be described as one of un-
bearable emotional turbulence. There are at various times excitement, hyper-irritability, anxiety, confusion, inability to concentrate, inattentiveness, forgetfulness, depression, and especially
extreme apprehensiveness. These episodes can easily be confused
with anxiety attacks having a psychiatric basis. The combination
of apprehensiveness, confusion, and depression has led to suicidal

impulses in a number of my patients. Several insisted after a week or two of a more or less continuous disturbance that they did not want to live if the reaction persisted. This reaction was the more difficult to bear because its source was unknown and, when the cause became apparent, explanation as to the etiology was usually of great help in tiding the patient over this difficult period. One such patient who had been heavily exposed to DDT was treated psychiatrically for his suicidal depression for months without success. This depression vanished within a few weeks when exposure to DDT was reduced to a minimum by removing it from the immediate environment and restricting the foods most heavily contaminated. Parenthetically, one cannot help but wonder how often exposure to the DDT group of compounds has been implicated in otherwise inexplicable suicides. Certainly in a person already mentally disturbed the additional stress of DDT poisoning could be disastrous. In addition, the mental effects of DDT may easily lead to accidents.

"A characteristic history is that of a person—and in a number of cases, an entire family simultaneously involved—who, previously well and able to make satisfactory emotional adjustment to his environment, suddenly is affected with the syndrome described and remains partially disabled for many months. Usually, the condition remains undiagnosed and frequently these patients make the rounds of doctor after doctor and institution after institution seeking at least a diagnosis, if not relief. The extent to which this can go is illustrated in the case of an exterminator who had used both DDT and chlordane.

"At the time I first saw this patient he had spent two and one-half years visiting various physicians and institutions seeking relief from his disabling symptoms, which consisted of pain and sense of constriction in the throat and chest, irregular headaches, and pain in his head, neck, and shoulders, muscular twitching all over his body, insomnia, inability to concentrate, forgetfulness and inattentiveness, disturbing sensations in various parts of the skin, repeated gastroenteritis and recurrent extreme muscular weakness. In the process of seeking a diagnosis he asked doctor after doctor whether the insecticides were responsible for his ailment and was repeatedly assured they could not be. He was subjected to virtually every test known to medical science and even had his skull opened for injection of air into his cerebral ventricles for X-ray purposes to make sure he had no brain tumor. None of the many tests and examinations could account for his symptoms. Finally one of the psychiatrists to whom he was referred recognized the ailment as having a toxic basis.

"When I saw the patient he had an enlarged liver, signs of nutritional impairment, reduced ability to feel vibration in his legs and a reduction in his pulse pressure. Under ordinary circumstances none of these signs, nor all together, could account for all his symptoms. When he was advised to give up his job and seek less toxic employment, to remove all traces of DDT and chlordane from his environment, was given nutritional therapy to alleviate the liver damage and put on a diet low in insecticide residues, he showed prompt improvement within a week. Four months later he was almost free of symptoms. He was then unknowingly exposed to DDT in a restaurant kitchen which had just previously been aerosoled with DDT. Within half an hour the entire syndrome returned and required more than a week to subside.

"Again, two months later he was inadvertently exposed to chlordane from an old kit he had previously used. This time there was a very severe exacerbation which required nearly two months for subsidence. Fortunately, this patient now is almost completely well for the first time since 1947."

The symptom of an enlarged liver is quite non-characteristic as we see it in many acute and infectious diseases, as well as in degenerative diseases, including cancer. I had not yet had the opportunity to study all different poisons present in a cancer body where they produce the destructive work most strikingly expressed in the liver, the visceral nervous system and the circulatory apparatus, particularly the capillaries. These are just the organs needed for healing purposes.

Especially interesting is an observation made in England. When wheat was milled about one-third of the DDT residue was found in the flour thus showing that the insecticide had quickly penetrated the grain husks. Rats fed with the bread made from this flour, like hens fed with the unmilled grain, showed wide and rapid distribution of the insecticide in their bodies.

We are especially interested here in the problem that, in association with liver damage, there often is an increased fragibility of the walls of the small blood vessels and the capillaries.

Later they may have a tendency to rupture easily. Dr. F. M. Pottenger in California has repeatedly observed a rise in blood cholesterol in human beings, more frequently than he ever saw before. He has seen that syndrome in about one-third of his patients and assumed that it may be caused by DDT poisoning of the liver. Even if most of these observations are the personal work of Dr. Biskind, they are partly confirmed by a few other clinical workers in this field.

What has been done to date to prevent these unfavorable consequences, is not very encouraging. An article in the *New York Times,* February 1, 1952, stated that the Beechnut Packing Company spent about $668,000 in the past six years to keep residues of new pesticides out of baby food and peanut butter. I hope that in the following years more substantial and critical work will be done in this direction.

CHAPTER XXIV

The Significance of the Content of the Soil to Human Disease

THE FAMILIAR expression "mother earth" is justified. When we take from and rob the earth we disturb the natural equilibrium and harmony, producing sickness of the soil, sickness of the plants and fruits (the common nutrition), and finally sickness of both animals and human beings.

As a physician who has spent much of his life investigating the nutritional aspects of disease, I have often had occasion to observe a definite connection between dietary deficiencies and diseases, and between dietary deficiencies and a sick or poor quality soil.

The relationship between soil and plants on the one hand and animal and human nutrition on the other is to me a fascinating subject. This relationship is a natural cycle in which one may distinguish two great parts:

I. The first part, which may be called "external metabolism," is comprised of the following:

   (a) Plants and their fruits.

   (b) Composition of the soil in which they grow—thus being the real basis of all nutrition.

   (c) Transportation, storage and preparation of these foodstuffs.

II. The second part, known as "internal metabolism," consists of all the biochemical transformations that take place when such foodstuffs enter the animal body and support the nutrition and growth of its cells and tissues.

When foodstuffs are ingested, their metabolism is influenced directly by the biochemical changes of the individual body and indirectly by the condition of the soil from which they came. The type of metabolic change thus directly affects the nutrition and growth of the body tissues. There is an external and an internal metabolism upon which all life depends; both are closely and inextricably connected with each other; furthermore, the reserves of both are not inexhaustible. There are, of course, some exceptions, about five to ten per cent of the population who have an extraordinarily well-functioning reabsorption and good storage capacity apparatus.

This is to emphasize the great importance of metabolism to human health, i.e., the soil as the basis of life which is generally neglected to a great extent.

I think it was correct for the Department of Agriculture to have given its 1938 yearbook the short but expressive title "Soils and Men," and that of the 1939 yearbook, "Food and Life." We may compare the work of the soil to a mother feeding her baby.

TABLE 1—Average composition of soil solutions from cropped, fallowed, and air-dry stored soils after 8 years

	Displaced solution from—		
Ingredient	Cropped soil a. P. p. m.*	Fallowed soil b. P. p. m.*	Original Stored soil c. P. p. m.*
Carbonic acid	85	53	73
Sulphuric acid	472	394	238
Nitric acid	181	1,560	1,043
Phosphoric acid	1.8	1.7	5.3
Chlorine	......	43	263
Calcium	203	559	381
Magnesium	86	134	107
Sodium	42	64	116
Potassium	27	63	75
Silica	......	......	48
Total solids	1,097.8	2,871.7	2,349.3

* P. p. m.—Parts per mille.

C. A. Browne stated that "the plant is the great intermediary by which certain elements of the rocks, after their conversion into soil, are assimilated and made available for the vital processes of animals and man. The simple inorganic constituents of the atmosphere and soil are selected and built up by the plants into protein, sugar, starch, fat, organic salts and other substances of marvelous complexity."[157]

Table 1 will give the reader a good picture of the great losses in mineral nutrients sustained by soils as a result of cropping and leaching. The amount of minerals dissolved each year from the soils of the drainage basis of four American rivers has been estimated by Clarke to average 79.6 tons annually per square mile.

This table shows: the soil needs activity, the natural cycle of growth, rest and return of waste to maintain its productivity—its life. We must not only take, but also give back nitric acid and potassium.

TABLE II—Effects of continuous cropping on the yield, ash content, and composition of the mineral matter of oats and buckwheat

Straw of Oats[1]

Year	Yield of dry matter Gram	Ash content Percent	Ingredients in total ash			
			Potash Percent	Lime Percent	Magnesia Percent	Phosphoric acid Percent
1869	946	8.08	37.38	3.95	2.41	2.62
1873	613	7.45	39.36	4.52	2.66	2.70
1875	538	6.95	18.38	6.02	3.37	2.78
1877	380	7.04	15.29	8.07	9.78	3.39
1879	380	7.99	11.69	8.60	4.31	4.01

Green Buckwheat[2] (Whole Plant)

1872	355	7.50	35.26	37.72	12.35	6.95
1874	270	7.56	27.90	41.88	13.32	5.24
1876	222	9.02	27.22	42.42	13.94	6.15
1878	293	8.39	34.67	40.33	11.62	6.07

[1] Averages of crops on 4 different soils for 5 different years.
[2] Averages of crops on 4 different soils for 4 different years.

The first part of this table makes it clear that the straw of oats shows a reduction of potash to less than a third in ten years, while the whole plant of buckwheat scarcely shows any difference in six years, since leaves and blossoms cannot thrive without sufficient potassium.

Otherwise, with K deficiency we open the door to acute and chronic diseases. The maintenance of K-prevalence (60 per cent in the most essential organs) is very important in plants, in animals and men.

---

[157] See C. A. Browne's article, "Some Relationships of Soil to Plant and Animal Nutrition."

TABLE III—Analysis of the ashes of the vines and tubers of 3 varieties of potatoes grown in the same year, on the same soil, under similar conditions of fertilization, cultivation, weather, and harvest

Variety	Total mineral content Percent	Composition of ash		
		Potash Percent	Lime Percent	Magnesia Percent	Phosphoric acid Percent
Odenwalder Blue vines	10.93	6.68	50.96	7.59	2.92
Industry Blue vines	9.69	3.71	49.63	10.11	2.78
Gisevius Blue vines	11.08	11.55	29.96	10.55	2.70
Odenwalder Blue tubers	4.39	50.34	1.14	4.78	6.83
Industry Blue tubers	4.39	50.11	3.64	6.15	7.29
Gisevius Blue tubers	4.32	52.08	1.39	5.32	9.96

TABLE IV—Influence of successive years and cuttings upon the potash, lime, magnesia, and phosphoric acid content of the ash of Frankish lucerne

Year	Cutting	Mineral content			
		Ash Percent	Potash Percent	Lime Percent	Magnesia Percent	Phosphoric acid Percent
	First	10.52	21.10	16.82	3.99	5.42
1928	Second	10.28	15.08	21.11	3.89	5.93
	Third	10.84	16.42	23.71	3.88	4.52
	First	11.43	42.43	15.66	4.46	5.34
1929	Second	11.46	28.71	22.51	3.84	5.76
	Third	9.95	18.19	24.92	4.22	4.32

That deficiencies in minerals of the soil produce some corresponding sicknesses on plants was worked out with great endeavor. Liebig's "law of the minimum" that "the deficiency of one nutrient in the soil will retard the assimilation of other nutrients by plants," could not be maintained, as later experiments revealed.

One of the most interesting parts of modern research in soil, plant and animal nutrition is that some trace elements—copper, manganese, cobalt, iron, iodine, boron, and zinc—are necessary in parts per million, i.e., very tiny amounts—yet without these trace elements, plants and animals suffer from serious diseases. Iodine is unique among these trace elements as its deficiency has no direct effect on the plant itself; experiments show the same growth and the same yield on 3 or 4 generations with or without iodine, but the following generations showed a significant decrease in crop. (These experiments were done by Prof. Falk and myself.) We did not find any explanation in the observations of others about the detrimental effect on man and domestic animals.

TABLE V—Composition of South African soils associated with lamziekte and styfziekte diseases of cattle

Mineral Constituent	Lamziekte soils, Armoedsvlakte, Vryburg		Styfziekte soils		
	Dolomitic areas (1) Percent	Leached areas (2) Percent	Lidgerrton, Natal heavy loam (3) Percent	Athole, Ermelo medium gray loam (4) Percent	Normal
Lime	12.07	0.16	0.08	0.05	0.9
Magnesia	21.34	.12	.43	.05	
Total potash	.11	.42	.73	.03	
Total phosphoric acid	.12	.03	.09	.06	0.7
Available potash	.016	.011	.02	.004	
Available phosphoric acid	.001	.005	.001	.001	

The dependence of our body upon the soil is demonstrated in the following two iodine tables. These show that fresh fruits and vegetables—living tissue enzymes—retain iodine in the thyroid in the summer; contrariwise, in and after winter, there is a greater loss of iodine through the urine.

Iodine in Urine Excreted by People with Goitre

Month	mg.	%
January	45.74	78.2
February	50.25	85.0
March	52.88	90.4
April	53.12	90.8
May	44.69	76.4
June	29.83	51.0
July	27.61	47.2 less excreted
August	28.19	48.2
September	34.46	58.9
October	32.18	55.0
November	35.50	60.7
December	37.49	64.1

Iodine in Thyroid Glands of Rats During a Year

Month	Iodine content of fresh substance %
January	203.6
February	181.2
March	215.8
April	230.7
May	304.2
June	342.9
July	498.2 more retained
August	426.8
September	400.2
October	375.0
November	280.3
December	230.7

TABLE VI—Iodine is naturally enriched in the following plants: (Dept. of Agric. Misc. Pub. No. 369)

Iodine (parts per billion)

Plant or part of plant	Maximum	Minimum	Average	Remarks
Asparagus, edible portion	3,780	12	1,168	
Carrots, roots	2,400	2	309	
Lettuce, edible portion	6,740	71	1,137	
Spinach	48,650	19	9,382	
Spinach (Germany)	48,650	15,600	26,417	Iodine fertilization.
Turnip, whole plant (Pa.)	2,080	740	1,434	No fertilization
Turnip, whole plant (Pa.)	94,960	19,540	42,304	Fertilized with KI.

TABLE VII — The minor-element content of some important crops in Fluorine: This table is added to show the fluorine content of fruits and vegetables, thus proving that additional fluoridation of water is unnecessary—and can be harmful. Nature uses fluorine in minimum doses in the skin to cover and protect fruits like cherries, peaches, apples, apricots, potatoes, beets, etc.—also in the enamel of our teeth.

Plant or part of plant	Location	Mg./kg.
Alfalfa, above-ground portion	France	56.5
Apple, pulp	"	2.1
Apple, skin	"	27.8
Apricot, edible portion	"	25.0
Asparagus, young shoot	"	79.4
Banana, edible portion	"	3.8
Beans, garden; edible pods and seeds	Austria	.6
Beets, leaves	France	134
Buckwheat	"	25.3
Cabbage, head	"	10.8
Carrots, root	"	3.4
Cauliflower, edible portion	"	25.7
Cherries, pulp and skin	"	37.0
Cress	"	12.0
Figs	"	19.8
Grapes, edible portion	"	8.1
Kidney beans, mature seed	"	21.0
Kidney beans, green seed	"	2.1
Lentil	"	18.0
Lettuce	Austria	1.2
Mustard, black; seeds	France	15.8
Mustard, black; leaves	"	68.0
Onions, bulb	Austria	3.0
Peach, pulp	France	39.3
Pear, pulp	"	1.7
Potatoes, tuber	"	3.0
Radish, root	"	20.0
Rice, polished	"	9.4
Spinach, leaves	"	30.0
" "	Austria	1.7
" "	"	1.3
Strawberries	France	14.0

Tomato, fruit	"	40.6
Tomato, edible portion	Austria	None
Turnip	France	20.2
Walnuts, edible portion	"	7.8

The birth of hairless pigs has been caused experimentally by feeding brood sows diets low in iodine and has been prevented by supplying iodine compounds, seen immediately in the following generations; but, iron in mice takes effect in the fifth or sixth generation only. This shows at the same time that some of the deficiencies are transferred to the following or later generations by nature —through the fertilization apparatus: the egg or spermatozoon— as there is no other way.

Familiar examples of the results of a deficiency of trace minerals are:

(a) *Sand drawn of tobacco,* due to magnesium deficiency if the soil contains less than 0.2% MgO.

(b) *Chlorosis of tomatoes* on Florida soils, which can be cured by manganese additions.

(c) *The wilting of leaves in tobacco* is caused by copper deficiency.

(d) *Failure of cattle to develop normally* is often due to deficiency of iron, copper or possibly cobalt in plants. (Iron directly connected to chlorophyll.)

(e) *The abnormal accumulated occurrence of animal and human goitre* in parts of Switzerland, Wisconsin, Minnesota and Washington is due to iodine deficiency.

(f) "Lame-sickness" of cattle in South Africa is due to deficiency of Ca. K. P. in leached areas.

(g) "Bush sickness" of sheep in New Zealand is due to lack of cobalt.

(h) Hairless pigs due to iodine deficiency.

(i) In human beings some acute and chronic diseases are due to the following deficiencies:

Bad teeth, to K and Ca
Rickets, to Ca and P
Anemias, to copper and iron
Myedema and goitre, to iodine
Starvation edema, nephritic edema, cardiac edema, cardiorenal syndrome, old age (thyroid deficiency), etc., all more or less due to deficiency of several minerals
Skin and bone tuberculosis, to K. P. Ca, etc.

Overliming is productive of chlorosis and with plants susceptible to iron—chlorosis—lime should be sparingly used.

Soil losses are generally brought about through cropping or
erosion—mostly the losses are of N. P. K., less of Ca and magnesium. (See Table 1.) One such group of figures for a silty clay
loam at Ithaca, N. Y., shows the average amount removed under
a standard rotation (corn, oats, wheat, clover, timothy) to be
as follows:

	Pounds per acre
Nitrogen	60
Phosphorus	25
Potassium	50
Calcium	30
Magnesium	20

All various mineral and trace soil losses can best be restored
by stable and human manure, except phosphorus. Once the
original supply of P has been depleted, it must be replaced by
chemical fertilizers in connection with manure for even the high
P-content of guano, up to 12 per cent and even 20 to 25 per cent,
is not sufficient. Thus, several authors assume that the East Coast
may be a desert after 150 to 200 years if we do not help to prevent
such continuing conditions as prevail today.

There are two familiar types of erosion—water and wind erosion. When man steps in and cultivates the land, he creates conditions that may result in an enormous acceleration of erosion.
This is the most disastrous of the evil things that can happen to
the soil. Forests must be considered the best defense against erosion and on steep slopes certain protection is necessary.

Factors influencing the mineral composition of crops, according to C. A. Browne, are:[158]

1. Difference in soil (organic—bacterial)
                      (inorganic—pH)
2. Differences in cropping (time)
3. Variety of crop—*rotation*
4. Period of growth of crop—successive cuttings
5. Climate—sunshine—oxygen
6. Water supply
7. Kind of fertilizer—even ploughing under legumes
   (lupines)

---

[158] *Ibid.*

(We added: Cultural practices, environmental conditions and
earthworms interpolating an intermediate metabolism.)

Natural manure exerts the best influence on crops: the Peru-
vian planter can raise 1,760 pounds of cotton per acre, using
guano, compared with an average of less than 300 pounds in
Louisiana and 390 in Egypt. Therefore, export of guano is no
longer permitted in Peru.

While I was a consultant to the Prussian Ministry of Health
in Germany during 1930-33, I had occasion to advise Dr. Hirtsiefer, State Secretary of Health, about the deplorable condition
of the soil around certain large cities, especially Essen, Dortmund
and Dusseldorf. I suggested the use of human manure, mostly
wasted by canalization in place of chemical fertilizers. This was
carried out along with the planting of vegetable gardens around
these big cities. Composts, i.e., a mixture of dried manure from
humans and animals plus straw and leaves, were used to cover
these gardens in October and November and were allowed to
remain through the winter. The soil was then ploughed in the
spring; planting was done from four to six weeks later. Depending
upon the original condition of the soil, it took several years or
more to develop a fertile topsoil by this method. According to
Dr. Hirtsiefer, the results were highly satisfactory, in that vegetables were obtained which were greatly superior in both quantity and quality to those previously obtained by the use of commercial chemical fertilizers. It is interesting that no human disease
was transmitted by this type of fertilizing, due, most probably,
first to the compost being exposed to sun, air, freezing and snow
throughout the winter, and second to the fact that most patho-
genic bacteria will not survive long in a healthy soil which normally contains much antibiotic material.

This is the method of the natural cycle used for over a thousand years by the farmers of the ancient Teutonic or Allemanic
Empire, now known as Western Europe.

For more than 30 years Professor Czapek of Prague collected
an enormous amount of information about the mineral content of
the lowly potato. He found that whenever artificial fertilizer was
used on potatoes, there generally was a great increase in the
potato crop but that at the same time there was more sodium

chloride and H_2O and less starch and K, P, etc.; therefore, there was a greater vulnerability to many diseases in which excess NaCl and H_2O play a prominent causative and dangerous part. For example, excessive swelling in various degenerative diseases is felt by leading medical authorities everywhere to be closely connected with the excessive intake of NaCl and H_2O. This tendency in humans may more or less be accentuated by potato tubers and other fruits produced by a sick soil. Many chronic diseases start with edema; in acute diseases, where there is more tendency to edema, the degree of disease is relative to the degree of edema.

In *Readers Digest*, Dr. Thomas Barrett referred to the earthworm and soil.[159] A French peasant told Dr. Barrett, "*Le Bon Dieu* knows how to build good earth and he has given the secret to the earthworms." Dr. Barrett believes that the earthworm contributes a great deal toward the building of fertile soil because of the structural changes it makes in the soil, i.e., a loosening of the topsoil. It is my theory that perhaps the earthworm's metabolism also transforms vegetable and animal waste into rich humus—thus they change the earth's minerals into soluable plant food. Their endless tiny tunnels enable rain water and oxygen to penetrate the soil. The earthworm does not require much oxygen as it has a predominantly fermentative or anaerobic metabolism. After being transformed by earthworms, working around the clock, the soil has been found to be five times richer in nitrogen, seven times more plentiful in phosphate, eleven times richer in potash. (Connecticut Experimental Station report.)

Results: "Vines yielded top-quality grapes. A single carrot, diced and cooked, filled three standard cans. Some of his peaches weighed a pound."

On a commercial fox ranch in the Harz Mountains the owner made a striking animal experiment. He used vegetables and fruits raised by organic gardening to cure foxes with lung tuberculosis after reading in a journal of my method of treating lung tuberculosis. He cured six out of seven foxes with the dietetic regime, containing among other things a great deal of K plus living tissue enzymes; he observed that the furs became extraordinarily good. He then advertised to buy sick foxes from other farms for very

---

[159] *Readers Digest*, May 1948, p. 129.

little, and established a large business as the low cost tuberculosis foxes regained their health and produced high quality fox furs.

We must conclude from these observations that unless the soil is cared for properly, the depleted soil with its abnormal external metabolism will bring about more and more abnormalities of our internal metabolism, resulting in serious degenerative diseases in animals and human beings. The soil needs activity—the natural cycle of growth; it needs rest; it needs protection from erosion; and finally, it needs less and less artificial fertilizer, but more and more of the use of organic waste material in the correct way, to maintain the soil's productivity and life. Food produced in that way—we have to eat as living substances, partly fresh and partly freshly prepared, for life begets life. Organic gardening food seems to be the answer to the cancer problem.

CHAPTER XXV

Cancer Diet and its Preparation*

THE DIET is completely different from normal nutrition. It is limited to fresh juices of fruits, leaves and vegetables; large quantities of raw fruit and vegetables are given in their natural form, or finely grated, salads of fresh leaves, fruits and vegetables, vegetables stewed in their own juice, compotes, stewed fruit, potatoes and oatmeal, the Soup of Hippocrates and a saltless rye bread. All must be prepared fresh and without addition of salt. After six to twelve weeks, animal proteins are added in the form of pot cheese (saltless and creamless), yoghurt made from skimmed milk, and buttermilk.

This diet forms the basis of the medical treatment. It is based on the principle that sodium must be excluded as far as possible and the tissues must be enriched with potassium to the highest possible degree.

This diet is digested more easily and quickly than normal nutrition; it burdens the metabolism as little as possible and stimulates the elimination of poisonous substances as well as abnormal intermedial substances of the metabolism. The amount of calories is smaller and the body digests each meal faster; therefore, larger portions and more frequent meals must be served. Patients should eat and drink as much as possible. Some may even demand extra food for the night.

Forbidden:

Tobacco, salt, sharp spices (fresh or dried herbs are permitted), tea, coffee, cocoa, chocolate, alcohol, refined sugar, refined flour, candies, ice cream, cream, cake, nuts, mushrooms, soy beans

---

* Partially repeated from prescription booklet.

and soy products, pickles, cucumbers, pineapples, all berries (except red currants), water to drink (stomach capacity is needed for the juices).

All canned foods, preserves, sulphured peas, lentils and beans, frozen foods, smoked or salted vegetables, dehydrated or powdered foods, bottled juices.

All fats, oils, salt substitutes (especially sodium bicarbonate—whether in food, toothpaste or gargle), hair dyes (in the course of the healing periods, we observed many factors which not only retarded healing processes but produced new growths, and we learned from these observations how many factors in our modern civilization which we had regarded harmless damage our bodies).

Temporarily Forbidden (Especially for the first months):

Milk, cheese, butter, fish, meat, eggs.

Equipment:

Not to be used: Pressure cookers or steam cookers, pots or any tools of aluminum.

To be used: Stainless steel, glass, enamel, earthenware, cast iron, tinware.

For the preparation of juices, two machines are needed: A separate grinder and a separate press, preferably of stainless steel. Do not use one-piece apparatus such as liquifiers, centrifuges, juice mixers or juice masters, etc.

Directions For Necessary Foods:

Fruit (no cans), apples, grapes, cherries, mangoes, peaches, oranges, apricots, grapefruit, bananas, tangerines, pears, plums, melons, papayas, persimmons, etc.

Pears and plums are more easily digestible when stewed. Stewed fruit may also be used. Dried fruit may be used if unsulphured, such as apricots, peaches, raisins, prunes or mixed fruit—wash, soak and stew.

Forbidden:

All berries, pineapple, nuts, avocados, and cucumbers.

Juices:

Always freshly prepared (it is *impossible* to prepare all juices for the day in the morning).

Start with less and increase the quantity gradually.

Daily portions (prescribed by the physician) in eight ounce glasses:

———glasses of orange juice
———glasses of apple and carrot juice
———glasses of green leaf juice
———glasses of grape juice
———glasses of grapefruit juice
———glasses of tomato juice
———glasses of apple juice
Add to each glass————————————————

Do Not Drink Water Because The Full Capacity Of The Stomach Is Needed For Juices And Soup.

Preparation of vegetables:

All vegetables must be cooked slowly, over a low flame, without addition of water. The slow cooking process is very important, in order to preserve the natural flavor of the vegetables and keep them easily digestible. Valuable components are lost in fast cooking by excessive heat, because the cells burst, the minerals go out of their colloidal composition and become more difficult to be absorbed. An asbestos mat may be used to prevent burning. A little of the soup mentioned above may also be used, or tomatoes, or apple slices may be placed at the bottom of the pan to give up more fluid. In some cases, this also improves flavor. Only spinach water is too bitter, contains too much oxalic acid and must be discarded. Tomatoes, leeks and onions should be stewed in their own juices, as they contain an abundance of fluid by themselves. Red beets should be cooked like potatoes, in their peel, in water. All vegetables must be carefully washed and cleaned. Peeling or scraping is forbidden, because important mineral salts and vitamins are deposited directly under the skin. The pot (not aluminum) must close tightly, to prevent escape of steam. Lids must be heavy and fit well into the pots.

Raw fruit or raw vegetables, when finely grated or shredded, must be used fresh, as quickly as possible. Raw, still living tissues, may not be stored after any kind of preparation. The same applies in particular to the juices. Cooked foods (soup and fruit) may be kept in the refrigerator for 48 hours.

Absolutely Required:

Fruit and vegetable juices, fresh calve's liver juice and raw food. At least the quantities ordered by the physician should be eaten and drunk, even though that may present some difficulties to patients during the reaction period. During these reaction periods the patients themselves ask for raw, uncooked foods, more apple juice, raw and grated apples without peel, mixed with finely mashed bananas, which may be whipped with a fork into a light puree. Because of the great sensitivity of the patients or the hypersensitivity of the intestinal tract, even the raw juices must be mixed with a thin, filtered, oatmeal. Depending upon the severity of the case, fruit juice and diluted oatmeal should be mixed half and half; later, only two tablespoons of the liquid oatmeal should be added, until the reaction period is overcome. Raw, grated apples should be taken in large quantities. If they are to be consumed raw, it is advisable to peel them in order not to burden digestion and to reduce gas formation. Apples should be taken in every form: raw, finely grated, baked, apple sauce or as compote with raisins. Carrots should be used raw, finely grated, best with the same amount of raw grated apple, also cooked, lightly baked, sprinkled with honey or bread crumbs. Potatoes should be baked, i.e., placed in the oven in their skins, until they are soft, or mashed, or as potato salad, mixed with celery salad with a dressing of vinegar or lemon juice.

Peppermint Tea—preparation:

Add one tablespoon of dried peppermint leaves to two cups (one pint) of boiling water. Let it boil for five minutes and strain. Add brown sugar or honey and/or a little lemon juice, to taste.

Enemas:

Inasmuch as the detoxication of the body is of the greatest importance, especially in the beginning, it is absolutely necessary to administer frequent enemas, day and night (on the average, we give coffee enemas every four hours, day and night, and even more frequently against severe pain, nausea, general nervous tension and depression). Enemas also help against spasms, precordial pain and difficulties resulting from the sudden withdrawal of all intoxicating sedation. On the average, every other day, we give two tablespoons of castor oil by mouth, followed by a cup of black coffee, and, five hours later, a castor oil enema, in addition to the coffee enemas, without interrupting their frequency. Difficult as this may be to believe, experience has proved that frequent enemas completely eliminate the need for sedation. Some patients take enemas every two hours, or even more frequently, during the first days of the treatment. More advanced cases are severely intoxicated and the absorption of the tumor masses, glands, etc., intoxicates them even more; many years ago I lost several patients by coma hepaticum, since I did not know, and therefore neglected, the vital importance of frequent and regularly continued elimination of poisonous substances, with the help of juices, enemas, etc.

To make enemas most effective, the patient should lie on his right side, with both legs drawn close to the abdomen, and breathe deeply, in order to suck the greatest amount of fluid into all parts of the colon. The fluid should be retained 10 to 15 minutes. Our experiments have shown that after 10 to 12 minutes almost all caffeine is absorbed from the fluid. It goes through the hemorrhoidal veins directly into the portal veins and into the liver. Patients have to know that the coffee enemas are not given for the function of the intestines but for the stimulation of the liver.

According to the experiments of Professor O. E. Meyer and Professor Heubner of the University of Goettingen, Germany, it is not certain whether the caffeine stimulates the liver cells directly or indirectly through the visceral nervous system. In any case, the effect is an increased production of bile, an opening of the bile ducts and greater flow of bile. At the start of the treatment and during "flareups," the bile contains poisons, produces spasms in the duodenum and small intestines, and causes some overflow into the stomach, with resultant feeling of nausea or even vomiting of bile. In these cases, great amounts of peppermint tea are necessary to wash out bile from the stomach. Thereafter, patients feel much easier and more comfortable.

A cup of coffee taken by mouth has an entirely different effect. It contains 0.1 gram to 1½ grams of caffeine. It heightens the reflex response (Schmiedeberg), lowers the blood pressure, increases heart rate, perspiration, causes insomnia and heart palpitation, the local irritation stimulates peristalsis (stomach motility). For this reason it eliminates the castor oil faster from the stomach.

Therefore coffee by mouth had to be limited to one cup taken by mouth after the castor oil.

CHAPTER XXVI

The Practice of the Therapy

IF WE propose a new therapeutic approach to the scientific world, we must ask ourselves two questions: First—Are we justified in presenting that approach to the scientific world and to suffering humanity? Second—Is it ripe for discussion and serious criticism? Are there enough facts which make it worthwhile and will it be of value to present the practical aspects and show directions for future research work promising continued progress?

The practice of the therapy consists mainly of the following components:

1) Fast and far-reaching detoxication of the whole body is the basis of the treatment.
2) Help the restoration of the various metabolic functions inside and outside of the digestive tract (enteral and parenteral digestion).
3) Enable the digestion of cancer masses and cells through the purified blood stream—their absorption and elimination.
4) Restoration of the cancer destructions and recovery of the essential organs, especially the liver.
5) If the liver and the digestive tract are not entirely restorable, continuation of the diet is necessary partly or completely to prevent recurrences as far as possible.

In the beginning, the most important part of the therapy is an intensive detoxication of the entire body. In practice it seems necessary to apply frequent coffee enemas, four to six times in 24 hours, in more advanced cases every four hours day and night or even more in the first two weeks. (High colonics cannot be administered, because too much of the sodium from the mucous membrane in the colon is washed out.) At the same time a castor

oil treatment is applied every other day, consisting of two tablespoons of castor oil with a cup of black coffee with brown sugar by
mouth, and five hours later a castor oil enema.

ENEMAS:
We distinguish between four types of enemas for regular use:
1) *Camomile Tea Enema* with 30 caffeine drops from a ten
   percent solution. Use one quart of water of body temperature, add half a glass of camomile extract and the prescribed caffeine drops. To make the camomile extract, take
   four tablespoons of dried camomile flowers or leaves, or a
   mixture of both, to one quart of water. Let it boil for five
   minutes and then simmer for ten minutes. Strain and
   keep in a one-quart milk bottle, well covered, in the refrigerator. This type of enema is used only in mild cases or
   during the restoration period.
2) *Coffee Enema*. For the preparation take three tablespoons
   of ground coffee to one quart of water. Let it boil for three
   minutes and then simmer for 20 minutes or more. Strain
   and use at body temperature. The daily amount can be
   prepared at one time.
3) *Castor Oil Treatment*. For the castor oil treatment, the following is necessary: At 10 a.m., take two large tablespoons
   of castor oil with a cup of black coffee, sweetened with
   brown sugar. Five hours later a castor oil enema, as follows: Mix one quart warm water with toilet soap (no
   flakes). Add three to four tablespoons of castor oil and stir
   until it becomes an emulsion. Add 30 caffeine drops and
   1/2 teaspoon of defatted ox bile powder. One quart of
   enema coffee may be used instead of one quart of water
   with 30 caffeine drops.
4) This one is not a real enema, but rather a therapeutic
   process. In cancerous diseases of the colon, we use half a
   quart of the usual green leaf juice, as prepared for drinking, at body temperature. Let it flow in very slowly and
   keep as long as possible, since it is best when it is entirely
   absorbed by the colon. Where there is a colostomy, we use
   a catheter and let it flow into the diseased part, very slowly. In diseases of the vagina or cervix, or urine bladder, we
   let smaller quantities flow into these parts to help rid the

body of odorous necrotic tissue discharges. Little bleedings are no contra-indication. This procedure is actually requested by patients as it brings them much relief from pain, discomfort and offensive odor.

Furthermore, it is necessary for the patient to drink freshly prepared vegetable juice every hour. This consists of four glasses of the Juice of apples and carrots in equal parts) and also four glasses of green leaf juice. All these juices contain plenty of active oxidation enzymes enriched by a 10 per cent solution of minerals of the potassium group (potassium gluconate, potassium acetate, and potassium phosphate, monobasic). The oxidation enzymes of these juices, once pressed out of the cells and activated, are easily destroyed by oxygen from the air as well as from changes in light and temperature. They may lose 60 per cent of their active oxidation power within half an hour. Therefore, they must be consumed immediately after pressing.

From the beginning, I felt that the tumor had to be killed while some scientists were satisfied to arrest the growths for as long a time as possible. In one of my articles I enumerated eleven points of difference between normal and cancer cells. The most important points are: cancer cells have more Na (ionised), live on fermentation (not on the normal oxidation), are negatively charged electrically, do not have the normal exchange with blood and serum, and grow and spread uncontrolled. Studying these I felt there must be a way to prevent the fermentation, that is, to eliminate the basic facts upon which fermentation is built and can function. The fermentation is vital for the life of the cancer cell. That is the object upon which we could base further tests and explorations. How could it be done? The most Na-free diet has to be applied to extract Na from cancer cells through the blood and lymph stream. Instead of Na, potassium and the oxidizing enzymes have to be brought in with the help of an allergic inflammation. This reactivated power of the detoxified body had to be perfected to the highest degree as the cancer cells with their highly negative electrical potentials have the power to repulse forcefully whatever is counteracting their life process, maintained by fermentation.

The details have been explained elsewhere. We will concentrate on the parenteral digestion-the most important part for the practice of the cancer treatment.

In the last six years, during which a further deterioration of fruits and vegetables was noticed, two to three glasses of fresh calf's liver juice were added. The fresh calf's liver juice contains the highest amount of oxidizing enzymes, most of the minerals of the potassium group, especially a high content of iron, copper and cobalt, as well as hormones and vitamins in the best activated composition. The liver juice is prepared from equal parts of fresh (not frozen) young calf's liver and carrots. Do *not* add any medication to liver juice in order not to change the pH.

To describe the preparation of food and juices, the different reactions and the various complications, especially in the more advanced cases, I would have to go into too much detail.

In more advanced cases it takes a long time, about one to one and a half years, to restore the liver as near as possible to normal. For the first few weeks or months, the liver has to be considered as weak and unable to resume its normal functions, especially that of detoxication and of reactivation of the oxidizing enzymes (R. Schoenheimer). For that reason it is necessary to help the liver in that regard with the continuation of coffee enemas and castor oil treatments in a slowly diminishing degree, according to the advanced condition of the disease. We have to bear in mind that there still are some unripe cancer tissues in the body, or hidden cells in glands or lymph vessels or necrotic tissues, after the large tumor masses have been absorbed and are no longer palpable or seen clinically outside. These immature cells do not respond as fast as the ripe cancer cells, for, according to my clinical observations, there is a common rule which follows: the more malignant the cells (the more apart from normal cells) the quicker they respond. Immature cells are seemingly not yet developed enough in the abnormal direction to respond so fast. This is the reason why benign tumors, scars, adhesions, etc., also do not respond as rapidly as the ripe, fully developed cancer cells. The restoration of the destroyed parts is a similar procedure as the formation of granulation tissue in chronic ulcers or cavities of lung tuberculosis. This new tissue shrinks finally and brings about scar formation which remains for a while but can be partly absorbed later. Von Bergmann[161] believed that a cancer patient could not produce a healing inflammation; he saw in that fact the reason why cancer is incurable and would remain so, since just cancer metabolism

---

[161] Von Bergmann, *Pathologische Physiologie in der Klinik.*

sets in where the body is incapable of producing such metabolic reaction as is necessary for healing inflammation. We see, on the contrary, that a cancer patient is able to produce an inflammation with active hyperemia, little temperature and slight red swelling, after an intensive general detoxication had taken place and had continued for a while in more advanced cases. The same cancer patient earlier presented more degenerative signs of edema, cyanosis and induration in all different forms and combinations, but after his circulation was restored with the detoxication the cyanosis disappeared and the edema was no longer present. Fischer-Wasels was one of the first authors who tried to find the hidden link behind the cancer problem as a kind of a *general intoxication.* But his assistant assumed that the intoxication had been caused by a specific substance which he thought he had detected much later. That substance, however, could not be confirmed by other researchers. In that way, the first attempt in the right direction was lightly pushed aside, as it turned out to be something not specific. Unfortunately, physicians are trained in that manner—a cause of a disease and medication must be something "specific."

We should keep in mind that a precancerous development does not mean the pre-stage of any kind of skin cancer, but it does mean a gradual intoxication with a loss of the normal content of the potassium group and the iodine from the tissues of vital organs. That chronic loss opens the door for the invasion of sodium, chloride and water into the cells, producing a kind of edema. In my opinion it must be assumed, as a rule, that sodium and iodine favor undifferentiated, quicker growth, seen in embryos and cancer; while potassium and iodine assure a more differentiated slower growth with normal cell division. Here sodium and potassium are the exponents of two mineral groups with opposite electrical potentials, keeping the body in a controlled equilibrium, of course, with the help of the visceral nervous system, hormones, vitamins, enzymes, etc. All of these are mostly deranged very slowly by chronic intoxication with the ensuing edema.

Gudenath's tadpole experiment has suggested that iodine is necessary for higher differentiation and increased oxidation and could be used for that reason against cancer development, but not alone.

In former periods when there was not enough detoxication in

my treatment, after the tumor was killed, the patient did not die of cancer but of a serious intoxication with "coma hepaticum" caused by absorption of necrotic cancer tissue, as several autopsies have shown. The solution is that all these former failures can no longer occur if there is an intensive detoxication maintained long enough and a potassium plus iodine predominance kept present. Finally, it is the task of the therapy to reactivate the functions of the whole body which means all its healing factors too: the visceral nervous system, the reticular system, the recticulo-endothelial system and the liver as the most important organ for elimination and restoration. Only a detoxified body has both power of resistance and healing.

To prove that my favorable results are obtained in the above mentioned way, the following three experiments are in progress:

1) Examination made of potassium content in serum and tissue particles which show that the healing is based partly on the restoration of potassium predominance in tissues.

2) Liver punctures do not show for a long time the damage of the liver microscopically, but show biochemical changes in mineral and enzyme content.

3) A cancerous rat is connected surgically with a healthy one to prove that the healthy metabolism of the normal rat is able to cure the cancerous growth of the companion.

SUMMARY FOR THE PRACTICE OF THE THERAPY.

These brief instructions on the diet (without going into necessary medication) provide directives for the medical care. Physicians must become thoroughly familiar with the handling and application of these "dietary tools."

This therapy requires intensive knowledge on the part of the physician in this new and thus far neglected special field. The clinical appearance of cancer is foggy and unclear in the beginning; the nucleus is hidden and hard to focus; it is my opinion that the liver only shows precise and decisive symptoms after it has used up all reserves and is near a break-down. Although leading specialists endeavor to describe decisive symptoms of cancer in the various organs,[162] I feel that early cancer detection will remain a difficult problem for quite some time.

It should be remembered that a successful therapy requires harmony of the physical and psychological functions, in order to achieve a restoration of the body in its entirety.

After more than 25 years of cancer work I can draw the following conclusions:

1) Cancer is not a local but a general disease, caused chiefly by the poisoning of foodstuffs prepared by modern farming and food industry. Medicine must be able to adapt its therapeutic methods to the damages of the processes of our modern civilization.

2) A method is elaborated to detoxify the body, kill the tumor masses and to absorb and eliminate them. (Restoration of the healing power.)

3) A way has been found to restore the liver if not too far destroyed and repair the destruction caused by the tumor masses.

4) To prove the return of the allergic reaction (healing power) cantharidin plasters are applied on the skin at weekly or longer intervals.

---

[162] See Abstract of New York Academy of Medicine and reprint of the New York City Cancer Committee in the book, *Cancer Alerts*, 1957.

CHAPTER XXVII

Reactions - Flare Ups

A NUMBER of patients have remarked, within the first two weeks of the treatment, that they cannot "stand" the diet and wish to discontinue it. They based their opinion on the following occurrences: Nausea, headaches, in some cases vomiting, spasms in the intestines, more gas accumulation than usual, no appetite, inability to drink the juices, and difficulties with coffee enemas. All of the above are symptoms of what we call "the reaction period." These reactions appear with the present treatment after from three to six days, and in more difficult cases after eight to ten days; they recur almost every ten to fourteen days, and later once a month. There is no connection with menstruation in women. However, in some cases, I observed the return of menstruation which had already ceased for years. The return occurred after three to four months of the treatment, with intense spastic pain on both sides of the lower abdomen. As far as the regular "reaction periods" are concerned, one may observe that the patients vomit some bile with an offensive odor. I assume that this bile, flowing out of the common duct, causes some spasms in the duodenum or the upper small intestines, and flows over into the stomach, producing nausea, bad breath, coated tongue and reluctance to food, and even to juices. At such times patients need large quantities of peppermint tea, served with some brown sugar and a bit of lemon. They drink one to two quarts of this liquid a day; some patients consumed as much as four quarts in 24 hours. These masses of tea wash out the accumulation of bile from the stomach and duodenum, relieve the patients of the spasms, and permit them to resume the intake of juices and administration of coffee enemas. The juices must be mixed with gruel; patients refuse to take cooked food, but accept raw grated apples, mashed bananas, applesauce. Such a "flare up" may last from one to three days. After a "flare up," patients feel greatly relieved, normal circulation resumes, the yellowish color with an occasional tinge of jaundice, which sometimes is noticed on the sclera of the eyes at these periods, disappears, and patients are able to eat and drink again. With the present treatment, and more frequent enemas, we reduced the "flare up" period for the most part to 24 hours, and in rare cases, to two days. The first "flare up" is the most violent one and is usually accompanied by severe headaches, weakness of the entire body, bad mood, and feeling of depression. Patients remain in bed.

Subsequent "flare ups" lose in violence and duration and can be made more easily bearable by more coffee enemas. Some patients increase the number of their coffee enemas by themselves, some taking as many as eight or ten or twelve in 24 hours, as they feel great relief after each coffee enema. Some of the patients suffer outbreaks of perspiration or offensive odor during these periods; these persist a little longer than other symptoms. The aromatic acids eliminated during these reactions are so intense they may form chemical compounds with the paint of the walls and ceilings of the patients' rooms, and these compounds cannot be removed by soap and water or other cleaning methods. The room often had to be repainted after the patient's departure.

At the beginning of the treatment some patients assume that these are allergic reactions and refer to them as such in their reports to physicians. Some claim that they never could stand orange juice; others say they could never take even a small piece of apple, and still others claim they could never stand tomatoes or peaches, prior to the treatment. One patient reported that she had been unable to take even a half grain of thyroid in 20 years, as her metabolism was always minus 20 and less. All physicians tried to give her thyroid and lugol solution, starting with the smallest doses and in weak solution. With this treatment, she was able, almost from the beginning, to take up to five grains of thyroid and 18 drops of lugol solution, half strength, per day.

Laboratory analysis shows a trace of albumin and a greater amount of sodium in the urine during the reaction periods. The blood count shows a relatively higher number of leukocytes (up

to 12,000-18,000) and an increase in lymphocytes if the lymphocyte count was abnormally low before, or a slight decrease in
lymphocytes if the lymphocyte count was abnormally high before.

The detoxication during the reaction periods gives the patients
a great psychological relief; generally after a few days they lose
their fears and depressions, and demand getting out of bed. Their
feeling of well being is supported by conversations with other
patients, who report similar favorable effects after these "flare
ups." Clinically, these "flare ups" are favorable reactions and
should be regarded as part of the healing process.

CHAPTER XXVIII

Short Practical Explanation
of the Medication

THE MEDICATION has to bring into the body two minerals—iodine and potassium. Iodine, or I, is an item of the positive minerals traveling to the negative pole or negative tissues, while potassium, or K, is the leading mineral of the negative group traveling to the positive pole or positive tissues. To help the cells function, the minerals must be activated or ionized, then they work partly as "perpetuum mobile."

Iodine is applied in two forms—as thyroid in organic composition, and as lugol in inorganic combination. Thyroid is administered in relatively high doses—one gr. five times daily—during the first three to four weeks, then five times one-half gr. daily, and later three times daily one-half gr. When the B.M.R. and P.B.I. remain normal for a period of three to four months, thyroid medication should be discontinued.

Lugol solution (always use half strength)—given during the first weeks in larger doses three drops six times daily—has been proved to be a favorable iodine combination for this therapeutic purpose. Lugol solution contains five per cent iodine, ten per cent potassium iodide in water. According to Holler and Singer,[163] iodine invades cancer tumors when inflamed, *not* otherwise. Therefore it was important to describe v. Bergmann's explanation that "allergic inflammation fluid" dissolves cancer tissue.

My own observations confirmed that favorable inflammatory reactions in skin cancers and melano sarcomas start before healing sets in and again later in "flare ups," gradually diminishing

---

[163] Sollmann, *Pharmacology*, 1942, p. 958.

in intensity and reappearing in longer intervals. (The findings of both authors are thus confirmed by my clinical observations.) It is assumed that iodine is necessary in the control of normal cell differentiation. Experiments on cancer cultures demonstrated that smaller iodine doses made the cancer cells grow more rapidly. A larger dose—such as is used at the beginning—is favorable in inhibiting any excessive growth. Some patients—about 20 per cent —also need some additional thyroid doses later. These are mainly those who have a higher percentage of lymphocytes or show adipositas with a low Basal Metabolism Rate.

A later article published by Del Conte and Maria Stux (*Acta Endocrinol.* November, 1955 20. 246-256) shows "definitely that iodine inhibits production of thyrotropin by the hypophysis," . . . It is evident, therefore, that "the inhibiting action exerted by iodine on the thyroid is mainly due to pituitary inhibition."[164]

The majority of newer studies using radioactive iodine have come to the conclusion that iodine acts directly on the thyroid cell and not by interference with the action of the thyrotropin.[165]

The clinical conclusion that thyroid helps to eliminate Na, Cl and H_2O is old but in cancer therapy it is important to know that it paves the way for refilling with K minerals while the *intra*cellular removal of Na, Cl and H_2O in different tissues and cells is correspondingly accomplished. (See my Tuberculosis book)

The absorption of edema brings a great deal of additional toxins and poisons into circulation. It is noticeable during this time and the following periods of "flare ups" that the patient suffers from nausea, distended abdomen and spasms. Detoxication and elimination have to be set in motion quickly and efficiently.

Potassium appears to play an indispensable and unique role in tissue protein synthesis, although the mechanism of its utilization is at present unknown. Potassium ions are indispensable in certain enzymatic reactions, and this may be one reason for its urgent need in the medication. It appears that the heavy isotope K^{41} (see Lasnitzki)[166] is definitely lower in tumors, as well as in tissues of tumor-bearing animals.

Muscles, brain and liver have normally a much higher potas-

---

[164] See *Year Book of Medicine*, 1956-57, p. 643.
[165] Sidney C. Werner and others, *J. Clin. Endocrinol*, 15, 715. June, 1955.
[166] Lasnitzki and L. K. Brewer, *Cancer Research* 2.494. 1942.

sium content than a sodium content. It can be accepted as a general rule that as long as potassium is not diminished (normal), sodium is diminished. A similar relationship exists between magnesium and calcium, so that where magnesium is increased, calcium is diminished and vice versa.

Potassium composition (ten per cent) is administered immediately; four teaspoonfuls ten times daily in all juices, except liver juice, mostly for three to four weeks, according to the previous degree of the disease. Then the amount of potassium is reduced to half. In some cases it became necessary to *repeat* the first medication and the dietary regime after some time to activate the treatment again.

The *decision* to apply large K-doses in a compatible composition immediately was finally made after about six years of indecisive clinical experiments, until I saw regularly better and more extensive *clinical* progress. The laboratory reports about K were fluctuating and not in conformity with the clinical picture. The literature presented a different viewpoint; there, almost all tables except the articles of Moravek[167] showed an undiminished K-content in cancer tissues. He found diminished K in the beginning and later uncertain ups and downs. The situation was cleared when Lasnitzki found the ionized K^{41} "diminished in cancers." The leading cancer specialists still rely on the laboratory work in their decision. For example, one says: "Jedenfalls ist von irgendeiner gesetzmaessigen Abweichung der Tumoren in ihren anorganischen Stoffen bis jetzt keine Rede."[168] The translation of which is: "Anyway, there is no regular deviation of the inorganic substances found in tumors."

Dr. Joseph Ross of Los Angeles Medical Center used tracer atoms of radioactive potassiums. He and Dr. Belton Burrows of Boston found that patients with chronic illnesses showed a marked decrease of potassium, one of the substances important in muscle contraction and strength. They came to the conclusion that the extent of dilution of the radioactive atoms with normal body potassium can indicate the total potassium content of the body. Such measurements enable physicians to recognize potassium

---

[167] V. Moravek Acta Radiol. et canc, boh. slov. 2.70. 1939, Zeitschr. f. Krebsforschung, 1952, 35.492.509

[168] K. H. Bauer, p. 114.

deficiency in a patient and indicate the amount of potassium that should be administered to make up the deficiency.

According to my clinical experience, it is very difficult to bring the potassium deficiency in a body back to or near to normal.

The addition of the lacking potassium does not make up a deficiency even in a relatively healthy body. In seriously ill bodies, many months, sometimes even one to two years, are needed to restore normal potassium content in the vital organs. We do not as yet know enough about the extent of potassium restoration in the various organs, without a separate examination of each organ, because the blood potassium level does not provide decisive information thereon. A few of my examinations were not sufficient to supply more certain indications in that respect.

In a recent article, Barnell and Scribener[169] came to the conclusion that serum potassium concentration can be used as an excellent guide to potassium need. My experiences in advanced cancer cases and some in chronic diseases contradict these findings. The serum is only a passage channel for support and exchange. Low K-figures may show best healing, because the depleted tissues reabsorb K, while high figures may be found in failures, because the tissues lose K.

For practical purposes, it is advisable to apply the potassium medication until the blood serum level is in normal range. Higher fluctuations are frequent at the beginning of the treatment; some lighter fluctuations continue even in the later periods. We see them even in normal persons, more even during menstruation and during pregnancy. Even a common cold can effect deviations for short periods. The interpretation of the potassium blood level can be quite misleading. In the beginning, we often see a potassium level above the normal range, which does not show that there is an abnormal amount of potassium in the body; on the contrary, it indicates that the body is losing greater amounts of potassium constantly. The reverse can be seen during the restoration period, when the potassium level is below the normal range, which may indicate that the body is reabsorbing greater amounts from the blood serum, affecting the equilibrium to the extent that it goes below the normal level.

---

[169] "About Serum Potassium Concentration as a Guide to Potassium Need." *J.A.M.A.*, Vol. 164, No. 9, 6/29/57, p. 959.

The combination of the blood level with the clinical observations teaches us that the restoration of the potassium content in the organs is a difficult and long drawn-out process.

Niacin (or nicotinic acid, the pellagra medication) is one of the B_2 vitamins and should be given from the beginning in sufficient amounts; it should be given without too much interruption and should not be diminished too fast. Niacin helps to bring back sufficient glycogen into the liver cells. It helps, furthermore, in the protein metabolism and acts to open the small arteries and capillaries; therefore, it must be discontinued in the event of bleeding. It also raises the electrical potentials in the cells. It improves the characteristic pellagra phenomena, especially: glossitis, stomatitis, vaginitis, urethritis and proctitis, the dermal erythema and some mental changes, as well as porphyrinuria.

Niacin is administered for a long time: 50 mg. six times daily, rarely more; after four to six months the dosage should be reduced.

Patients are easily frightened in the beginning when niacin causes a diffuse redness and heat all over the body or, more often, on the head and arms; this reaction is harmless and lasts only a few minutes. To avoid such reactions it is advisable to dissolve the tablet on the tongue *after* a meal or a glass of juice.

In regard to the other vitamins it may be stated that in general, one vitamin or one mineral should not be applied to relieve a vitamin or mineral deficiency. We know particularly from the work of Werner Kollath and other authors that the application of one vitamin or one mineral can be, in turn, responsible for unfavorable functional changes in the intestinal tract or nervous system. Niacin is an *exception* in cancer. On the other hand, it is observed that niacin while curing pellagra can manifest a thiamine deficiency. Kollath demonstrated in *chronic* degeneration cases caused by vitamin and mineral deficiencies that a single vitamin or single mineral can easily bring about an acute sickness.

We should not overlook the fact that in some slightly acute cases an artificial vitamin is helpful, but in cancer it is different. We have to face a very sick, poisoned body. In such a milieu, cancer cells can work, and grow freely and undisturbed. The noncancerous tissue (normal tissue) in a cancer body does not react as other healthy tissue, according to my observation.

Vitamin B12 was discovered about eight years ago by Dr.

Tom Spies in Birmingham, Alabama during the course of his work on undernourishment. He found that the vitamin works especially against different types of anemia to the extent that they are caused by malnutrition. Even degenerative changes on the spinal cord can be brought back to near normal with greater doses of B12. The nucleus of the vitamin is a cobalt substance, which is present in most fruits and vegetables in minimal amounts. The daily requirement is unknown. It is assumed that B12 helps to combine aminoacids to build protein substances. A sick body and especially a cancer-bearing body is unable to combine aminoacids to build proteins properly, but burns them to form the end products instead. Animal experiments show that vitamin B12 is very potent in the restoration of all different tissues, be they damaged by age, chronic illness, operations, degenerative diseases, intoxications or by other means. This may be the reason why we find it part of all different vitamin combinations on the market today.

Several times I observed that vitamins in good combinations with or without minerals produced a *regrowth* of cancer or new spreadings in a few days. The patient felt better for a shorter or longer period through what may be regarded as the stimulation of the entire metabolism. However, the cancer regrew, caused by what some other authors explained as the greater attraction power of the cancerous tissue.

To these observations also belong cases of young boys and girls suffering from osteosarcomas who at first showed remarkable results but ten to fourteen days after the administration of calcium compound the cancers started a rapid regrowth and were beyond cure. I had the impression that calcium-composition worked in the cancer body like Na; according to Rudolf Keller, calcium belongs to the Na-group, but stays on the borderline. I don't know any other reasonable explanation for it.

In the development of that therapy 15 years ago, I had several other setbacks: the worst was the loss of 25 patients out of 31 who were just a few months symptom-free and to whom I had administered the opposite sex hormones to give them strength— in accordance with the initial findings of Dr. Charles Huggins. The first five patients felt so much better within a few weeks, and this misled me. This disaster threw me into a deep depression. I almost lost the strength to continue this cancer work, as the worst blow of all was the loss of my young hopeful friend J.G.[170] who was treated by more than fifteen cancer authorities and given up with a prognosis for a few weeks. However, after a recovery within eight months, I agreed to let him have some sex hormones. Six weeks later the brain tumor regrew, histologically, an astrocytoma. He was returned to the former treatment and died.

The therapeutic work for restoration of the liver was difficult and took the longest time to be built up. Even today it is the most difficult problem for the therapy. We apply the following:

a) Liver juice*
b) Liver injections
c) Lubile-defatted bile from young animals
d) Pancreatin tablets.

a) Liver Juice* preparation and its importance are described in other chapters, tables follow. It is the most powerful weapon we have against cancer, bringing into the liver and body all essential minerals, enzymes and other substances to replenish *after* the detoxication of the sick liver, which is incapable for some time of building and activating these substances. (Cellular Therapy)

b) It should be mentioned here that the liver injection returns some vitamins into the body, enzymes and minerals which are valuable in helping replenish this organ, and in addition that it contains some hormones, including that of the adrenal cortex as well as sexual hormones and many others in natural form but in minute quantity which were never found to be harmful.

c) The more intensive detoxication treatment made the use of lubile less necessary. Today it is used mostly for castor oil enemas and, in some cases, when the liver remains hard for a long time or where the entire bile apparatus is damaged to a greater extent by adhesions and scars.

d) Hypodermic trypsin injections (made from pancreas) were advocated against cancer in 1905 by J. Beard and in 1906 by Shaw-Mackenzie, but they proved disappointing. The administration of digestive enzymes in digestive disorders has not fulfilled early expectations. Despite this fact, I found pancreatin

---

[170] Described in the book: *Death Be Not Proud*, by John Gunther. The case will be dealt with fully in Vol. 2. Case explained in Appendix II, page 416 and 4173.
* See Appendix III. page 421

in many cases a valuable help in the therapy. A few patients cannot stand pancreatin; the majority are satisfied to have less digestive trouble with gas spasms and less difficulty in regaining weight and strength. We use the tablets after the detoxication; each contains five grains and is uncoated. The patient takes two or three tablets two or three times after meals, and later less.

It should always be borne in mind that cancer is a degenerative disease. The regeneration is only possible through the metabolism. Its restoration is hard work, but it is essential and the last refuge for these advanced cases.

Retrospectively, I think the results were arrived at because I did *not* follow most of the scientific literature nor the laboratory findings, as far as they did not accord with the clinical confirmations. "Der Erfolg am Krankenbett ist entscheidend," Professor Kussmaul said. (The result at the sick-bed is decisive.) I do not want to make the mistake Winston Churchill expressed so clearly: "Men occasionally stumble over the Truth, but most pick themselves up and hurry off as if nothing had happened."

CHAPTER XXIX

Rehabilitation of the Cancer Patient

THE TASK of rehabilitation is to restore the patient to a life comparable to that which he led prior to the appearance of symptoms of cancer and the subsequent damages. To reach such a degree of rehabilitation is possible only in beginning or medium-advanced cases. Partial rehabilitation only is possible in further-advanced cases, and no rehabilitation (for practical activity) is possible in some of the terminal cases. After a patient is more or less free of symptoms, he goes home and is confronted by some of the following problems:

(a) *Medical*
1) The organization of the treatment at home.
2) Lack of help.
3) Inability and inexperience in cooking, especially of this type of diet.
4) After weeks of perfect rest at the clinic, with all conveniences and prepared foods and juices, he finds himself without help or a doctor's advice at home.
5) Difficulty in shopping and provision of necessary fresh foodstuffs.
6) Difficulties in procuring proper medication from regular drug stores (frequent offers of unsuited items or substitutes by pharmacists—such as calcium gluconate instead of potassium gluconate, which helps the cancer to regrow!).
7) Re-examination—observation.

(b) *Economic*
1) Depletion of funds because of many expenses connected with previous treatments and operations.

2) Long duration of the treatment.
3) A lengthy absence from work necessary for strict cooperation.
4) More expensive preparation of the dietary food as compared to ordinary home cooking.
5) Tendency to put patients into hospitals or nursing homes,
covered by insurance plans, to avoid disturbance of family
life and expenses.

(c) *Psychological*

1) Unfavorable environmental influences.
2) Opposing views of friends and some physicians.
3) Long period required for the restoration of the entire body.
4) Changes in the way of life for the present and the near
future.

The chief concern is the patient's will to live and to be cured.

A small number of patients, about ten to twelve per cent of
the total, do not realize the seriousness of the disease; such realization is necessary if one is to follow such a strict treatment.
These patients are quickly satisfied when they see good results
in others and feel themselves relieved of pain in a matter of days.
A similar percentage reject the treatment; some do not like to
give up their eating habits while others will not accept food
without salt; another group has different problems.

A few had come to feel hopeless and pessimistic during the
long period of previous treatments so that they could not regain
enough energy for future life. One woman, who was with her
mother, had the best results the first week; then the husband
came, and they quarreled all night. The patient was dismissed;
the mother took her to her home but could not accomplish
anything. Needless to say, similar individual cases can be found
in all long, drawn-out degenerative diseases.

The mental condition of the patient and psychological cooperation of the family and the environment play important roles
in the restoration of the body. Every patient needs faith, love,
hope and encouragement. To accomplish this difficult task, the
patient has to see progress on himself and favorable results
on others.

CHAPTER XXX

Most Frequent Mistakes of Patients in the Application of the Treatment

AFTER ABOUT four to six weeks in the clinic most of the patients feel stronger and have lost most of their original anxiety and depression. They think they can relax their adherence to rules and schedules. They frequently find no one to help them sufficiently with the preparation of the juices, diet, application of enemas, etc.

In general, people go to hospitals for operations or serious illness; the family considers them recovered upon their return. This is different with cancer. Cancer is a degenerative disease, not an acute one, and the treatment can be effective only if carried out strictly in accordance with the rules for one and a half to two years. We repeat here that it is not a symptom that is treated, nor a specific disease, but the reactions and functions of the entire body which have to be transformed and restored.

As an illustration of the difficulties encountered, I quote the following from a patient's letter: "I feel like I have gone downhill since arriving home due to the strenuous past week—can't see how it could have been avoided. I have stayed on the diet—just have not managed to get in all the juices until the past two days." As an explanation of the foregoing, it should be mentioned that the patient had ten operations in eight years prior to arriving at the clinic. Naturally she was seriously weakened but gained strength in four weeks; this led her to the assumption that she could now take care of all the shopping, preparation and treatment by herself, without help.

Furthermore, at the time of their leaving home, patients often had been given up by relatives, physicians and friends, none of whom had been able to offer any further advice. Upon their return, they suddenly find that everyone has contrary opinions to offer, criticizing components and preparation of the diet and suggestions "to make it easier." One patient, when friends and relatives began offering contradictory advice and suggestions, asked them whether these opinions ever helped a patient who had already been given up. This question put interfering persons in their place. Also physicians often use the phrase: "Diet has nothing to do with cancer," despite the fact that they had given up a patient before, and now see the improvement.

Another frequent mistake patients make is to feel, that "a little bit" of one or the other forbidden foods cannot do them much harm. This is an entirely mistaken notion; besides, these "little bits" tend to become larger and more frequent: they do not fail to produce harmful results.

Again, we often find that patients are helped by persons who have to leave the house to go to work at a certain time and, therefore, prepare most of the day's juice supply in advance and the evening supply upon their return home. This renders the juices largely ineffective, for the following reasons:

1) Juices consist of living matter with active ferments, fast neutralizing oxidizing enzymes, which are most necessary for the sick body.

2) The body needs an equilibrium of active oxidizing enzymes, supplied throughout the day. These cannot be maintained active except by freshly pressed juices, given at hourly intervals.

A number of items on the market cannot be used for purposes of the diet, especially vegetables and fruits processed with chemicals for longer preservation, sold in plastic bags (carrots, spinach, lettuce, beets, cherries, etc.); fruits and vegetables with color added—some red potatoes, yams, sweet potatoes, and oranges and dried fruit which have been sulphured or otherwise preserved.

Aluminum utensils, pressure cookers, orange squeezers into which the half orange is inserted with the skin; if the skin is also pressed out, it will emit harmful fatty acids and aromatic substances contained in its surface.

Two machines are required, a separate grinder and a separate press, for the correct preparation of juices, especially of liver juice. Centrifugal machines, in which air has insufficient access to the grinding process, cannot be used. When the grinding wheel rotates against a resistance with insufficient access of air, positive electricity is produced and induces negative electricity on the surrounding wall. The exchange of the positive and negative electricity kills the oxidizing enzymes and renders the juice deficient. These are findings of experiences over many years in which patients who used a one-unit machine had no success.

Cooked vegetables must be prepared in an appetizing manner. It must be borne in mind that a complete change in the accustomed taste is involved; therefore, vegetables must be prepared with much care and imagination. It is not possible just to omit water, salt, fat, condiments, etc. Vegetables can be made tasty by means of fresh and dried herbs and different fruits.

It is not easy to keep strictly to the treatment if a convalescent patient does not have enough help. In all cases a life is at stake. After a remarkable improvement and a renewal of faith and hope, some patients discontinue the treatment because of mistaken advice and family aversion. This way, the notion is spread that the treatment is helpful only at the start. Anyway, a good number of patients follow their prescriptions, are cured and are living a normal life after five and more years.

CHECK LIST FOR A CANCER PATIENT ON THE GERSON THERAPY

The answer to each question should be "yes"; any deviation usually slows or stops healing. "It is advisable not to start the treatment, if for any reason strict adherence to it is not possible."

- Is a press-type juicer being used? (grinding and pressing separated) One-unit juicers produce failures (p. 217).
- Is the whole veal liver for juice* fresh, unfrozen, under 4 lbs.?
- Is cooking and enema water free of fluoride, chlorine, water softeners, and other chemicals? (Some bottled water is fluoridated.)
- Has all salt, tobacco, alcohol, and black tea been eliminated?

* See Appendix III. page 421

- Have all except permitted seasonings been eliminated? (p. 241)
  Have drugs been eliminated (except aspirin, pp. 247, 397, 401)
- Is toothpaste or treatment with fluoride, bicarbonate of soda, salt, etc. eliminated? Some health store toothpastes are good.
- Are all aerosol sprays, air fresheners, insecticides, paint fumes, and similar materials eliminated from the home? (p. 399)
- Are deodorants, hair dye, permanents, lipstick eliminated?
  Have the forbidden proteins, Fats, oils, and other foods been excluded from the diet? (Pp. 235-6, 238-9)
- Have the other forbidden items on p. 238 been excluded?
- Are the dietary regime and the medication and the enema regime all being combined in the amounts stated on pp. 235-248?
- Has aluminum cookware been eliminated?
- Is exposure to sunshine and TV minimized? p. 139
- Have vegetables and fruit for the diet and juices been organically grown? Nutrient content of organic produce is often several times that of non-organic produce. Pp. 175-85. Insecticides can stop healing, pp. 167-73.
- Do the patient and assistants understand reactions, flare-ups and the importance of detoxification? Do they understand that during reactions, flare-ups, or any pain or discomfort, coffee enemas should possibly be given more frequently? also the importance of continuing the castor oil treatments? (Pp. 235-6, 247-8, 190-1, 193-4, 198, 201-3, 407, 417-8)
- Does the person helping the patient understand how to alter the diet during reactions and flare-ups? (p. 187-91, 201-2)
- Is sufficient help provided for the patient? The patient must rest and conserve energy to promote healing.
- Is the food varied and appetizing? (Pp. 241-4. 139-43, 187-91)
- Are the juice cloths properly cleaned and boiled? (p. 241)
- Is it understood that sometimes a return to a strict, intensive program is necessary-same as the first 3-4 weeks? (Pp. 207, 236)
- Are changes in the therapy being made according to p. 235 and 236 and according to the condition of the patient?
- Is a food mill being used to make the soup? (2 qt. Foley Food Mill from housewares stores)
- Are tart apples (McIntosh, Pippin, Granny Smith, Winesap, etc.) used for juices when possible rather than "Delicious" apples?

CHAPTER XXXI

Some Failures
Medication: Not Specific

THE GREAT majority of my patients are far advanced cases who have little or no appetite and are barely able to take the necessary amount of juices and digest them. For that purpose gastric juice has to be applied in the form of acidol pepsin: two capsules three times daily before meals. In addition, they need the digestive enzymes of the pancreas as the poisoned organs stop or diminish the secretion: trypsin, lipase and diastase. All these are secreted by the pancreas; therefore, pancreatin is administered in some cases: three tablets three to five times a day, not during the first two weeks, and later less if needed. These enzymes are also needed for the so-called parenteral digestion of tumors and cancer: the natural activated enzymes are better, of course. The healing of cancer in the latter part of the treatment can be considered as a parenteral digestion. After I recognized the healing of cancer to be a parenteral digestion, the entire therapeutic endeavor was subordinated to this purpose. This means that after the cancer mass is killed, the dead piece must be dissolved; I have a collection of such eliminated dead pieces from rectum, cervix, bladder, vagina, esophagus, tonsils, intestines, or wherever they find a way out of the body.

The most drastic set-back occurred when I added to the therapy the opposite sex hormones, so highly recommended at that time by Professor Charles Huggins. These hormones were first applied in five cases which could not recover fast enough. In the first three to four months, I observed a pronounced improvement. Therefore, I administered these hormones to an additional 25 patients. All of these patients already were free of cancer symptoms but they still felt weak. Most of these cases had received previous X-ray treatment of long duration.

The outcome of this hormone treatment was disastrous. I lost 25 of my best cases. After a remarkable improvement within three to five months, they died within three to four weeks. Only five of them could be saved.

I feel that the specific sex hormones, even small doses, stimulate the liver and consume the painstakingly re-accumulated reserves of the liver.

Instead of applying the damaging specific sex hormones I found it very helpful to add Royal Jelly capsules, 50 mg., two capsules about half an hour before breakfast.

Other failures resulted from a substitution of so-called caridin for lugol and thyroid, as well as from the application of some other hormones and vitamins, ovarian substance, vitamin E., A., D., etc. and from difficulties in finding the proper combination and dosage of the potassium compound, for which about 300 experiments had to be made. Finally, I administered calcium and phosphate compositions in a number of cases where the X-rays showed far advanced decalcification and in three cases of hemophilia, complicated by osteosarcoma tumors. The bleedings had been stopped with this medication but the tumors started to grow immensely.Several of these cases were lost.

Summarized briefly, I found that on the basis of my treatment the above-mentioned substances—hormones, some vitamins, calcium phosphate compositions (called Mineralogen) and caridin— had a carcinogenic effect. Further experiments showed that cod liver oil and other oils and fats, including egg yolks and cream also had a carcinogenic capacity—in these advanced cases—but the entire therapy is not specific.

During 1948-49, I observed that the results of the treatment at times were less favorable than they should have been. As I was interested for a long time in knowing the mineral content of various fruits and vegetables I made some tests of the contents of apples, carrots, potatoes and tomatoes. To my great surprise, I found that all of them had lost more or less some of their normal potassium content and at the same time were richer in sodium.

Studying the material more closely, I learned the importance of the soil for our health and wrote chapter 24: "The Significance of the Content of the Soil for Health and Disease." In this article

I concluded that the soil and all foodstuffs produced by it, must be called *our external metabolism,* forming the basis of our internal metabolism which feeds and supports the function of our digestive organs and through their activity also the parenteral digestion and all upon which that depends.

I would like to repeat that after recognition of the fact that cancer tumors and cells must be digested, therapy has to be arranged in a manner that all endeavor has to be subordinated to the principle of restoring the digestive tract and the parenteral digestion to normal and if possible to stimulate it to a "hyperfunction during the healing period." That seems to be what a body does under normal healing conditions. (Rokitansky, Vienna, predecessor of Virchow.)

Although the medical profession applies all the accepted and experimental treatments first, their results did not essentially diminish the death rate in the last 28 years, as the article[171] of George Crile, Jr., M.D., F.A.C.A., Cleveland, Ohio, Cleveland Clinic, shows. "If the time between the appearance of the first sign or symptom and the beginning of the treatment were the main factor in influencing the outcome of the disease, the present program of early and wide excision should show promise of controlling the death rate. Unfortunately, statistics since 1930 show no decrease in the death rate.

"Failure of cancer control programs to diminish the death rate indicates that surgery and radiation, no matter how skilfully applied, do not often prevent or permanently control metastasis from highly malignant invasive cancers. A number of recent studies of cancer of the breast indicated that mortality is a constant process little affected by treatment."

In closing I would like to emphasize again that this book is written for the purpose of presenting 50 cases, almost all of them far advanced, so-called terminal cases. In a second volume there will be published fewer chapters, but many more such cases. Every case which had been given up by cancer experts shows how far-reaching the results of this treatment are. These facts render any statistics unnecessary.

---

[171] Reprint from *Surgery, Gynaecology and Obstetrics,* September 1956, Vol. 103, 342-352. Also *Yearbook of Pathology and Clinical Pathology,* 1956-1957, p. 69.

The nucleus of the therapy is to keep in mind the problem as a whole and not to lose sight of the details of the pathological reactions.

CHAPTER XXXII

Tables

FOODS — TABLE*

Name	Protein	Fat	Carbohydrate	Ratio** K Mg Ca P NaCl	Ratio K/NaCl
Apples	0.3	0.4	14.9	50-1	40-1
Apricots, fresh	1.0	1.0	12.9	10-1	9-1
Artichokes, fresh	2.9	0.4	11.9	1.8-1	0-7
Aspargues	2.2	0.2	3.9	6.5-1	4.5-1
Bananas	1.2	0.2	23.0	2.6-1	2.3-1
Stringbeans, green	2.4	0.2	7.7	7.4-1	5-1
Beets	1.6	0.1	9.6	3-1	2.5-1
Beet leaves	2.0	0.3	5.6	9-1	5-1
Broccoli	3.3	0.2	5.5	4.4-1	2.75-1
Brussels sprouts	4.4	0.5	8.9	4-1	3-1
White cabbage	1.4	0.2	5.3	5.7-1	3-1
Carrots	1.2	0.3	9.3	4-1	3-1
Cauliflower	2.4	0.2	4.9	6-1	4.4-1
Celery stalks	1.3	0.2	3.7	1.6-1	1.1-1
Swiss Chard	2.6	0.4	4.8	5-1	3-1
Cherries	1.1	0.5	17.8	140-1	120-1
Corn	10.0	4.0	74.0	10.5-1	5-1
Cucumber	0.7	0.1	2.7	4.2-1	4-1
Currents, fresh	1.6	0.4	12.7	33-1	26-1
Dates	2.2	0.6	75.4	2.3-1	2-1
Egg plant	1.1	0.2	5.5	5-1	4.4-1
Endive	1.6	0.2	4.0	3.8-1	3-1
Figs, dried	4.6	1.2	68.4	7.5-1	6-1
Figs, fresh	1.4	0.4	19.6	39-1	29-1
Grapefruit	0.5	0.2	10.1	100-1	90-1
Grapes	1.4	1.4	14.9	150-1	125-1
Kale	3.9	0.6	7.2	4-1	2-1
Kohlrabi	2.1	3.0	. .	5-1	3.7-1
Leek	1.5	. .	8.5	9.5-1	7-1
Lemonjuice	0.9	0.6	8.7	17-1	14-1
Lettuce, head	1.2	0.2	2.9	4-1	3-1
Orangejuice	0.9	0.2	11.2	22-1	18-1
Molasses	. .	. .	60.0	3-1	2.3-1
Cow's milk	3.5	3.9	4.9	2.3-1	1-1
Oat flakes	14.2	4.0	68.2	9-1	4-1
Onions	1.4	0.2	10.3	9-1	6-1
Parsley root	1.5	0.5	18.2	19-1	14-1
Peaches	0.5	. .	12.0	27-1	25-1
Pears	0.7	0.4	16.0	51-1	43-1
Peas, dried	23.0	1.5	60.0	13-1	8-1
Plums, fresh	0.7	0.2	13.0	110-1	99-1
Prunes, dried	2.3	0.5	71.0	15-1	12-1
Potatoes	2.0	. .	20.0	8-1	7-1
Radishes	1.2	0.1	4.2	3.1-1	2.4-1
Raisins	2.3	0.5	72.0	7.4-1	6-1
Rhubarb	0.5	0.1	4.0	7-1	6-1
Spinach	2.5	0.5	3.4	4.6-1	4-1
Squash E.P.	1.2	0.3	7.5	17-1	15-1
Sweet Potato	1.8	0.7	28.0	4.7-1	3.7-1
Tomatoes	1.0	0.25	4.0	6.3-1	6-1
Turnips	1.1	0.2	7.0	3.8-1	3-1
Turnip tops	2.9	0.4	5.4	4.7-1	2.3-1
Water cress	1.1	0.3	3.7	2.9-1	2-1
Water melon	0.5	0.2	7.0	7-1	6-1

* Reprinted from Journal of the American Dietetic Association. Vol. 25, No. 4. April 1949.
** Potassium group.

FRUITS AND VEGETABLES

	K	S	Ca	Mg	P	
Apple, entire fruit						
Gloucester, stony loam, N.H.	0.83	0.09	0.04	0.04	0.68	
Apple, entire fruit						
Maximum	1.41	0.09	0.11	0.059	0.142	
Minimum	.49	0.034	0.023	0.018	0.020	
Mean	.78	0.06	0.04	0.029	0.067	
Apple, edible portion						
Maximum	0.90	. . .	0.177	. . .	0.113	
Minimum	0.62	. . .	0.021	. . .	0.055	
Mean	0.74	. . .	0.077	. . .	0.071	
Carrots, roots						
Gloucester, stony loam, N.H.	5.92	0.15	0.376	0.187	0.35	no fertilizer, Nitrogen,
Bridgehampton, very fine, sandy loam, N.J.	3.37	. . .	0.32	0.17	0.32	Phosphate, Potash fertilizer used.
Maximum	5.95	0.18	0.56	0.25	0.65	
Minimum	0.48	0.13	0.24	0.12	0.14	
Mean	2.10	0.16	0.40	0.17	0.33	
Cauliflower, edible portion						
Maximum	3.71	1.13	0.71	0.29	0.88	
Minimum	3.45	1.01	0.13	0.24	0.51	
Mean	3.58	1.07	0.35	0.26	0.76	
Lettuce, head						
Maximum	7.91	0.31	1.38	0.44	1.05	
Minimum	2.69	0.25	0.33	0.04	0.19	
Mean	5.98	0.28	0.77	0.24	0.56	
Oats, grain matured						
Maximum	1.71	0.09	0.51	0.41	0.40	
Minimum	0.78	0.07	0.21	0.13	0.16	
Mean	1.15	0.08	0.35	0.25	0.23	
Peas, edible portion, all sizes, fresh						
Maximum	1.89	0.15	0.43	0.22	0.78	
Minimum	0.79	0.09	0.10	0.15	0.23	
Mean	1.41	0.13	0.19	0.18	0.57	

Sodium and Potassium Content of Public Water Supplies

Place	Sodium mg./100 cc	Potassium mg./100 cc
Boston, Mass.	0.3	0.2
Chicago, Ill.	0.3	0.1
Corpus Christi, Texas	15	0.6
Los Angeles, Calif.		
Aqueduct source	6	0.6
Metropolitan source	17	0.5
River source	5	0.5
New York, N. Y.	0.3	0.2
Philadelphia, Pa.	2	0.4
Pittsburgh, Pa.	6	0.5
Portland, Ore.	0.1	0.1
Richmond, Va.	0.7	0.2
Rochester, Minn.	0.7	0.2
Rochester, N. Y.	0.3	0.2
San Antonio, Texas	1	0.1
San Francisco, Calif.	1	0.3
Santa Barbara, Calif.	10	0.3
Tampa, Fla.	0.5	0.1
Tulsa, Okla.	0.3	0.4

* Taken from *Journal of the American Dietetic Association*, Volume 25, April 1949. Sodium and Potassium in Foods and Waters. Determination by the Flame Photometer. Charles E. Bills, Francis G. McDonald, William Niedermeier, and Melvin C. Schwartz. Research Laboratory, Mead Johnson and Company, Evansville, Indiana. (From Table 2).

Sodium and Potassium Content of Foods. Analysis made on Edible Portions of Unprocessed Foods except as otherwise designated.

FOOD	SODIUM Na mg./100 gm.	POTASSIUM K mg./100 gm.	
All-Bran cereal	1,400	1,200	
Almond, roasted in oil, salted	160	710	(too fat)
Anchovy Paste	9,800	200	
Apple sauce, canned	0.3	55	(loss of K)
Apricot, dried	11	1,700	
raw, with skin	0.6	440	
Asparagus tips, fresh	2	240	
Avocado	3	340	
Baking powder, Alum type	10,000	150	(generally used)
Phosphate type	9,000	170	
Tartrate type	7,300	5,000	
Banana	0.5	420	
Barley, pearled	3	160	
Beans, baked, Heinz, Navy			
with pork and tomato sauce, canned	480	210	
with tomato sauce, canned	400	140	
dry, Navy	1	1,300	
green, in pods, canned	410	120	
green, fresh	0.9	300	
frozen	2	110	

FOOD	SODIUM Na mg./100 gm.	POTASSIUM K mg./100 gm.	
Lima beans, canned	310	210	
fresh	1	680	
frozen	310	580	
Beef, corned	1,300	60	
dried	4,300	200	
lean, koshered, raw	1,600	290	
lean, raw	51	360	
Beets, raw	110	350	
Bread, low-sodium-14 commercial "saltfree" breads:			
maximum	76	200	
minimum	4	72	
average	28	120	
Broccoli, fresh	16	400	
frozen	13	250	
Brussels sprouts, fresh	11	450	
frozen	9	300	
Buttermilk, cultured	130	140	
Cabbage	5	230	
Candy Bars, (a)	170	300	
(b)	220	150	
marshmallow	41	6	
milk chocolate	86	420	(cream)
Cantaloupe	12	230	
Caraway seed	17	1,400	
Carrots, canned	280	110	
scraped and trimmed	31	410	(see difference)
Catchup, tomato	1,300	800	
Catfish (fiddler) Ohio River	60	330	
Cauliflower, buds, fresh	24	400	
buds, frozen	22	290	
Celery, salt	28,000	380	
seed	140	1,400	
Stalks, less leaves	110	300	
Cereals, dry			
All Bran	1,400	1,200	(do not use)
Corn flakes	660	160	
Farina, cream of wheat, quick cooking, enriched	90	84	
Pablum	620	380	
Rolled oats	2	340	(use all different types)
Ry-Krisp	1,500	600	
Wheat flakes	1,300	320	
Chard, large leaves	210	720	
small leaves	84	380	(use these)
Cheese			
American Swiss	710	100	
Cheddar	700	92	
Cottage	290	72	(salted) see potcheese saltless.
Cherries			
Sour, frozen in syrup	2	78	
Dark, raw	1	260	(best)

FOOD	SODIUM Na mg./100 gm.	POTASSIUM K mg./100 gm.	
Chicken, raw, breast meat	78	320	
leg meat	110	250	(cooked K lower)
Cod, raw	60	360	
frozen fillets	400	400	
liver oil	0.1	0	
salted, dried	8,100	160	
Coffee, regular dry	2	1,600	
Corn, flakes	660	160	
Popcorn, popped, oiled and salted	2,000	240	
Crackers, Graham	710	330	
Rye, Ry-krisp	1,500	600	
Crisco (vegetable shortening)	4	0	
Currants, Zante, dried (Zante raisins)	22	730	
Dandelion greens	76	430	
Date, semi-dry, California	1	790	
Dill, seed	13	1,000	
Eggplant, less skin	0.9	190	
Endive Greens	18	400	
Figs, dried	34	780	
raw	2	190	
Flour, Buckwheat	1	680	
Garlic, less skin	6	510	
Gelatin, Dessert, flavored, Jell-O	330	210	
Grapes, Concord, less seeds and skin	3	84	
Emperor, less seeds with skin	4	180	
Grapefruit, fresh	0.5	200	
Halibut, raw	56	540	
steak, frozen	460	500	(do not use)
Honey	7	10	
Horse-radish, prepared	96	290	
Ice cream	100	90	
Kale, leaves and midribs	110	410	
Kumquat, pulp and rind, less seeds	7	230	
Lemons, candied	50	12	
fresh	9	360	
Lentils, dry	3	1,200	
Lettuce, head	12	140	
leaf	7	230	
Lime, pulp and juice	1	100	
Liver, raw			
Calf	110	380	(important because of oxidizing enzymes)
Goose	140	230	
Maple syrup	14	130	
Marmalade, orange	13	19	
Matzoth, American style (salted)	470	120	
Passover (unleavened bread)	1	140	
Mayonnaise	590	25	
Meat extract, flavored	11,000	6,000	(refrain)

	SODIUM Na	POTASSIUM K	
FOOD	mg./100 gm.	mg./100 gm.	
Milk, cow's			
buttermilk, cultured	130	140	
whole dry	410	1,100	
liquid	50	140	
Milk, human, from 4 mothers,			
49 to 77 days post-partum	11	51	
Milk, human, from 10 mothers			(nature arranged
3 to 10 days post-partum	37	68	for growing baby,
			more K, less Na)
Mushrooms, canned	400	150	(not to be used)
raw	5	520	
Mustard, greens	48	450	
prepared paste	1,300	130	
Nectarine, less skin	2	320	
Oats, rolled (oatmeal), dry	2	340	
Okra, fresh	1	220	
Oleomargarine	1,100	58	(for comparison only)
Olives, green, pickled	2,400	55	
Onions, less tops and dry skins	1	130	
Oranges, Temple, pulp and juice	3	220	
Parsley, fresh	28	880	
Parsnip, scraped and trimmed, fresh	7	740	
Peaches, dried	12	1,100	
frozen in syrup	3	120	
raw, less skin	0.5	160	
Pears, Bartlett, canned in syrup	8	52	
raw, less skin and core	2	100	
Peas, dry, split	42	880	
fresh	1	370	
frozen	100	160	
Peppers, green, empty pods	0.6	170	
Persimmon, wild	0.6	310	
Pickle, dill	1,400	200	
Pineapple, canned in syrup	1	120	
raw	0.3	210	(too many aromatic
			acids)
Plums, raw	0.6	170	
Potatoes, chips	340	880	
sweet, canned	48	200	
raw, less skin	4	530	
WHITE, CANNED	350	240	
raw, less skin	0.8	410	(best)
Pretzel	1,700	130	
Prunes, dried	6	600	
raw, with skin	0.7	210	
Pumpkin, raw, less rind and seeds	0.6	480	
Quince, raw, less skin and core	0.7	290	
Raisins, seedless	21	720	
Zante	22	730	

FOOD	SODIUM Na mg./100 gm.	POTASSIUM K mg./100 gm.
Rhubarb, frozen in syrup	2	160
raw	1	70
Rice, brown	9	150
flakes	720	180
wild (Ziazania)	7	220
Sage	20	670
Salt—theoretical value for pure NaCl	39,342	0
Shortening, vegetable	4	0
Soda, baking—theoretical value for pure NaHCO$_3$	27,373	0
Soft Drinks	18	0.6
Soup, beef, canned, diluted as served	410	100
tomato, canned, diluted as served	380	110
vegetable, diluted as served	380	120
Spinach, canned	320	260
frozen	60	380
raw	82	780
Squash, raw, Acorn, less rind and seeds	0.4	260
Hubbard, less rind and seeds	0.3	240
White summer, less rind, with seeds	0.2	150
Yellow summer, less rind, with seeds	0.6	200
Squash, cooked, frozen	6	120
Sugar, light brown	24	230
white	0.3	0.5
Tangerines, pulp and juice	2	110
Tapioka, dry	5	19
Tomatoes, canned	18	130
catchup	1,300	800
juice, canned	230	230
raw, with skin	3	230
Turnips, raw, leaves	10	440
white, less skin and tops	37	230
yellow (rutabaga) less skin and tops	5	260
Watermelon, pink part of fruit	0.3	110
Wheat Bran, crude	15	980
Flakes, cereal	1,300	320
Wild rice (Ziania), dry	7	220
Yeast, compressed	4	360
Zwieback	250	150

In analyses of Swiss chard, it was observed that the immature leaves contained 84 mg. sodium per 100 gm. and the mature leaves 210 mg., this being the highest sodium concentration seen in any of the unprocessed plant products.

Throughout the survey it was noted that *variations in sodium content were much wider than in potassium content.* This was true not only for different products, but for different samples of the same product. To some extent, this was the result of human interference, but it was also evident in purely natural products. It was most evident, percentage-wise, in plant products of low sodium content. For example, three bananas showed 0.2, 0.6, and 0.8 mg. sodium per 100 gm., and similar differences were noted in other products on which several analyses were made.

Sodium chloride is employed for many purposes besides seasoning, preserving, pickling and koshering. As brine it is used (a) in the flotation process of sorting green peas from hardened peas and heavy extraneous matter, (b) for preventing enzymatic discoloring of freshly sliced apples and pears which are to be canned, (c) as a heat transfer and blanching agent in freezing foods, and (d) for regenerating base-exchange water softeners (the sodium appears in the softened water as bicarbonate, and water thus treated is used in canning to prevent toughening of vegetables).

Sodium propionate is used to inhibit mold in bread, cake, and cheese. Sodium acid phosphate is used as an acidulating agent. The secondary phosphate is used for emulsifying process cheese, for stabilizing evaporated milk, and as the quickening agent in quick-cooking farina. Sodium acid sulphite is employed for sulphuring fruits prior to drying. These few examples may serve to explain the almost ubiquitous occurrence in processed foods of sodium in amounts greater than are present in the corresponding natural products.

From American Meat Institute
New York Office

Unit — 100 Grams	RAW CALVES LIVER		RAW LAMBS LIVER	
Water	70.8%		70.8%	
Calories	141		136	
Protein	19	gr.	21	gr.
Fat	4.9	gr.	3.9	gr.
Carbohydrate — Total	4	gr.	2.9	gr.
Ash	1.3	gr.	1.4	gr.
Calcium	6	mg.	8	mg.
Phosphorous	343	mg.	364	mg.
Iron	10.6	mg.	12.6	mg.
Vitamin "A" Value — I.U.	22,500		50,500	
Thiamin	.21	mg.	.40	mg.
Riboflavin	3.12	mg.	3.28	mg.
Niacin	16.1	mg.	16.9	mg.
Ascorbic Acid ("C")	36	mg.	33	mg.

ANALYSIS OF RICHARDS LIVER SUBSTANCE (Liver Powder)

The composition of mammalian liver fluctuates a bit with the source of animal, season of the year, etc., so some variations may be expected. Richards Liver Powder has the following approximate composition:

Protein	70%
Carbohydrate	12 to 15%
Fat; less than	0.5%
Ash	4.4%
Moisture	5-6%

Vitamins:

Thiamine	7.1	micrograms per gram
Riboflavin	120.	" " "
Pyridoxine	5.1	" " "
Ca. Pantothenate	255.	" " "
Nicotinic Acid	305.	" " "
Inositol	935.	" " "
Folic Acid	40.	" " "
Biotin	4,040.	millimicrograms per gram
Ascorbic Acid	1.9	milligrams per gram
Choline	10.	" " "
B-12	Approximately 1.5 microgram per gram	

Amino acid composition of liver protein (calculated to 16% nitrogen):

Arginine	6.6	Phenylalanine	6.1	Leucine	8.4
Histidine	3.1	Cystine	1.3	Valine	6.2
Lysine	6.7	Methionine	3.2	Glycine	8.5
Tyrosine	4.6	Threonine	4.8	Serine	7.3
Tyrptophane	1.8	Isoleucine	5.6	Glutamic Acid	12.2
				Aspartic Acid	6.9

Mineral content (taken from Winton, "Structure and Composition of Food," Vol. III):

Potassium	1.3 - 1.4%
Sodium	0.37 - 0.40%
Calcium	0.022 - 0.036%
Magnesium	0.085 - 0.094%
Iron	0.010 - 0.022%
Copper	0.008 - 0.016%
Phosphorus	1.6 - 1.7%

Report of Semiquantative Spectrographic Analysis of Samples of Crude Liver Extract

ARMOUR CRUDE LIVER EXTRACT

Boron	0.00019%	0.0000015%	nil	0.00017%	nil
Silicon	0.00089	0.000085	0.00010%	0.00046	0.000022%
Iron	0.00080	0.0000055	0.00027	0.00086	0.000030
Sodium	0.033	nil	nil	0.22	nil
Magnesium	0.0068	0.000030	0.0020	0.0063	0.00024
Manganese	0.00014	nil	nil	0.000060	nil
Lead	0.00089	nil	nil	0.000077	nil
Aluminum	0.00084	0.111134	nil	0.000042	nil
Calcium	0.0086	0.000096	0.00019	0.011	0.000055
Copper	0.00028	0.0000067	0.00010	0.000087	0.000023
Zinc	0.00079	nil	0.0023	nil	0.0011
Nickel	0.00037	nil	nil	nil	nil
Cobalt	0.000024	nil	nil	0.00019	nil
Potassium	0.024	nil	nil	0.060	nil
Chromium	0.000056	nil	nil	0.000022	nil
Phosphorus	nil	nil	nil	nil	nil

LEDERLE'S CRUDE LIVER EXTRACT

Boron	0.0017	nil	0.00047
Silicon	0.0082	0.0063	0.0039
Iron	0.00025	0.029	0.000033
Sodium	0.29%	1.1%	0.44%
Magnesium	0.013	0.00073	0.0048
Manganese	0.00021	0.00024	0.000021
Lead	nil	0.0015	nil
Aluminum	0.00027	0.00022	0.000055
Calcium	0.036	0.017	0.19
Copper	0.00025	0.00011	0.000030
Tin	nil	0.012	nil
Nickel	0.0011	nil	nil
Cobalt	0.00025	nil	nil
Potassium	0.025	0.022	0.066
Phosphorus	0.083	nil	nil

Composition of Liver, 100 Grams, Edible Portion

Food and Description	Water	Food—energy	Protein	Fat	Carbohydrate Total	Carbohydrate Fiber	Ash	Cal-cium	Phos-phorus	Iron	Vit. A value	Thia-mine	Ribo-flavin	Niacin	Ascor-bic acid
	Pct.	Cal.	Gm.	Gm.	Gm.	Gm.	Gm.	Mg.	Mg.	Mg.	I.U.	Mg.	Mg.	Mg.	Mg.
Liver — Calf, raw	70.8	141	19.0	4.9	4.0	0	1.3	6	343	10.6	22,500	.21	3.12	16.1	36
Sheep or Lamb, raw	70.8	136	21.0	3.9	2.9	0	1.4	8	364	12.6	50,500	.40	3.28	16.9	33

From: Science, May 3, 1957, Volume 125, Number 3253
Instrumentation for Bioengineering
Variation in Normal Sodium, Potassium, and
Calcium Levels in Wistar Albino Rats

"In the last decade there has been a marked increase in the use of flame spectrophotometry for physiological studies of electrolyte changes in tissue fluids. As a rule, small numbers of control animals have been used since most studies are predicated on the belief that electrolyte concentrations in the blood normally remain stable within fairly narrow limits. For some time it has been appreciated that the functions of many organs undergo diurnal variation, but only recently has attention been focused on the fact that marked changes in serum constituents also occur."

TABLE I-Morning-evening and (day-to-day comparison of serum ion levels (milliequivilents per liter in male SF = Wistar rats. All dates are 1955; "CV" represents coefficient of variation.

Expt. No.	Date bled	Time	N	Body Wt. (g ± σ)	Sodium X	σ	CV	Calcium X	σ	CV	Potassium X	σ	CV
1	6 May	11 a.m.	11	281 ± 31	153.3	1.8	1.2	5.43	0.30	5.5	6.50	0.50	7.7
2	6 May	11 p.m.	11	294 ± 28	156.4	1.4	0.9	5.23	0.18	3.4	5.83	0.50	8.5
3	17 May	11 a.m.	12	195 ± 12	157.3	1.9	1.2	5.14	0.17	3.3	6.02	0.44	7.3
4	17 May	11 p.m.	10	189 ± 14	159.6	2.2	1.4	5.21	0.18	3.4	5.48	0.26	4.7
5 (Total)		11 a.m.	23	236 ± 10	155.4	2.7	1.7	5.28	0.28	5.3	6.32	0.58	9.2
6 (Total)		11 p.m.	21	239 ± 12	157.9	2.4	1.5	5.22	0.18	3.4	5.66	0.43	7.6

TABLE II-Statistical analysis of serum ion data; P, probability; d.f., degrees of freedom; t=Fisher's test

The numbers in column 1 refer to the experiment numbers in column 1 of table 1.

Comparison	Sodium t	d.f.	P	Calcium t	d.f.	P	Potassium t	d.f.	P
Experiments 1 and 2	4.32	20	< 0.01*	1.80	19	≈ 0.10	3.06	20	< 0.01*
Experiments 3 and 4	2.51	20	≈ 0.02*	0.89	20	≈ 0.40	3.31	19	< 0.01*
Experiments 5 and 6	3.14	42	< 0.01*	0.83	41	≈ 0.40	4.20	41	< 0.01*
Experiments 1 and 3	5.03	21	< 0.01*	2.74	21	< 0.01*	2.61	21	≈ 0.02*
Experiments 2 and 4	3.77	19	< 0.01*	0.24	18	< 0.50	2.00	18	≈ 0.05*

"The net effect of these investigations points to the need for considering diurnal and day-to-day variations in serum ions when dealing with electrolyte changes in animals. Rigid standardization of the time of sampling is mandatory in experiments when small numbers of animals are used to establish 'normal' ion levels and when the interpretation of electrolyte shifts is predicated on the assumption that such levels represent a stable base line."

* See Appendix III, page 421

Name: Reverend, R.C.

DAILY SCHEDULE FOR TOTAL TREATMENT OF CASE NO. 5, page 272

(for hourly schedule, see page 236)

DATE	DURA-TION[1]	JUICES 8 OZ. EACH VEG./FRUIT	LIVER	DIET, DAILY	ACIDOL PEPSIN	POTASSIUM COMPOUND SOLUTION	THYROID	LUGOL ½ Strength	NIACIN 50 mg.	PAN-CREATIN	INJECTION 50mcg B-12 + 3cc LIVER	R.J. Royal Jelly[5]	COFFEE[6] ENEMAS	CASTOR OIL TREATMENT	TESTS
3/8	2 wks.[1]	1 orange 5 apple-carrot 4 green leaf	2[2]	regular	3x2 caps.	10x4 tsp.	5x1 gr.	6x3 drops	6x1 tabl.	4x3 tabl.	one daily	- - -	every 4 hrs.	every 2nd day	cbc
3/23	3 wks.	same	2	regular	3x2 caps.	10x2 tsp.	3x½ gr.	6x1 drops	6x1 tabl.	4x3 tabl.	same	- - -	same	same	K in serum BMR
4/14	1 wk.	same	2	regular	3x2 caps.	10x2 tsp.	3x½ gr.	3x1 drops	6x1 tabl.	4x2 tabl.	same	- - -	3 daily	2 a week	Urea N, uric acid in serum
4/21	4 wks.	same	2	add daily ½ lb. potcheese[3], 1 glass buttermilk or yogurt	3x2 caps.	8x2 tsp.	2x½ gr.	6x1 drops	6x1 tabl.	3x1 tabl.	same	- - -	same	same	K in serum BMR
5/22	4 wks.	same	2	same	3x2 caps.	8x2 tsp.	3x½ gr.	6x1 drops	6x1 tabl.	4x3 tabl.	same	- - -	same	same	K in serum cbc
6/22	5 wks.	same	2	buttermilk, yogurt, potcheese	3x2 caps.	10x2 tsp.	3x½ gr.	6x1 drops	6x1 tabl.	4x3 tabl.	same	- - -	same	same	Urea N, uric acid in serum
7/23	3 wks.	same	2	potcheese, 1 glass skimmed milk instead of buttermilk	3x2 caps.	10x2 tsp.	3x½ gr.	4x1 drops	6x1 tabl.	4x3 tabl.	every other day	- - -	2 daily	1 weekly	Urea N, uric acid in serum
8/13	6 wks.	same	2	same, much raw food	3x2 caps.	8x2 tsp.	- - -	6x1 drops	4x1 tabl.	3x3 tabl.	2 weekly	- - -	3 daily	- - -	Uric acid K in serum
9/24	6 wks.	same	2	same	3x2 caps.	8x2 tsp.	- - -	6x1 drops	4x1 tabl.	- - -	2 weekly	- - -	2 daily	- - -	same
11/25	6 wks.	same	3	same, juice of 6½ lemons[4] in orange & apple-carrot juices	3x2 caps.	6x2 tsp.	- - -	4x1 drops	3x1 tabl.	- - -	2 weekly	- - -	2 daily	- - -	Urine cbc
12/14	6 wks.	same	3	no more lemons[4]	3x2 caps.	8x2 tsp.	3x½ gr.	6x1 drops	5x1 tabl.	- - -	2 weekly	2 caps daily	2 daily	- - -	K in serum
1/25	9 wks.	1 orange 4 apple-carrot 4 green leaf	3	same as last time	3x2 caps.	6x2 tsp.	2x½ gr.	3x1 drops	6x1 tabl.	- - -	2 weekly	2 caps daily	2 daily	- - -	K in serum cbc
3/29	7 wks.	same	3	same	3x2 caps.	7x2 tsp.	- - -	3x1 drops	6x1 tabl.	3x3 tabl.	1 weekly	2 caps daily	1 daily	- - -	BMR cbc
5/20	- - -	same	3	add ½ oz. fresh sweet butter, lean fish once weekly	3x2 caps.	6x2 tsp.	- - -	5x1 drops	4x1 tabl.	3x3 tabl.	1 weekly	2 caps daily	1 daily	- - -	Urea N, uric acid in serum

1 Duration of the initial program is sometimes extended to 3 or 4 weeks, depending on the case (pp. 205, 207). In some cases the patient must later return to this initial treatment (p. 207).
2 In many cases the patient will benefit greatly by increasing the number of liver juices* to 3 or more daily (pp. 196, 411).
3 Non-fat (uncreamed), unsalted cottage cheese may be used instead of potcheese.
4 The juice of 6½ lemons was an addition to the therapy to fight the effects of a virus infection (p. 275).
5 The royal jelly was an experimental material, it is helpful but not essential.
6 Coffee enemas may sometimes be required at 2 hour intervals (pp. 193, 236, 408. 417. 416). If enemas are administered this frequently, physician must observe for signs of electrolyte imbalance.

* See Appendix III, page 421

ANNOTATED HOURLY SCHEDULE

Patients and assistants should read and understand pages 187-248 and Appendix II before beginning treatment.

CAUTION: The following schedule reflects normal diet and dosages for the initial weeks of treatment. As suggested by the following notes, it is essential that the diet and dosages be regularly adjusted by a physician trained in the Gerson Therapy.

Name: _____ Start Date: _____
Change Date: _____

	(1), (9)	(1)		(2)	(3)	(4)	(5)	(6)	(7)	(8)	(9)	(10)	(10)	(11)
TIME	JUICES 8oz. ea.‡	DIET	LIN-SEED OIL Tbsp. p. 246	ACI-DOL PEPS IN caps.	POTASSIUM COM-POUND SOLUTION tsp. in juice	LUGOL 1/2 Str. drops in juice	THY-ROID 1 gr. tabl.	NIA-CIN 50mg tabl.	PAN-CRE-ATIN tabl.	ROY-AL JELLY 50 mg caps.	INJEC-TION 100 mcg B-12 combined w/liver	COFFEE ENEMAS	CASTOR OIL TREAT-MENT	TESTS
8:00	O	Break-fast		2	4	3	1	1	3		ONCE DAILY	EVERY FOUR HOURS OR MORE AS NEEDED	EVERY OTHER DAY	COM-PLETE BLOOD COUNT; SERUM ELEC-TROLYTES; URIN-ALYSIS; T_3, T_4
9:00	G				4									
10:00	AC				4	3	1	1						
11:00	C				NO MEDICATION									
12:00	G				4									
1:00	AC	Lunch	1	2	4	3	1	1	3					
2:00	G				4									
3:00	C				NO MEDICATION									
4:00	C				NO MEDICATION									
5:00	AC				4	3	1	1	3					
5:30	AC				4	3								
6:00	G				4			1						
7:00	AC	Dinner	1	2	4	3	1	1	3					

‡ JUICE key: O=Orange G=Green AC=Apple-Carrot C=Carrot

(1) **The diet and juices** are described on pp. 187-190, and 237-245. The diet must be modified during reactions and flare-ups (pp. 190, 201-203). Cultured dairy proteins (yoghurt & pot cheese) should be added at (not before) the sixth to eighth week according to the physician's judgement (pp. 80, 145, 146, 235). Exception: use churned, not cultured buttermilk. Because low nutrient levels and pesticide content of commercial produce may prevent healing, ORGANICALLY GROWN produce is extremely important (pp. 146-151, 167-185, 220, 410).

(2) **Acidol Pepsin** (Acidoll) is available from Key Co., 734 N. Harrison, St. Louis, MO 63122. Dosage: 2 before each meal (pp. 219, 235, 246, 407, 411)

(3) **Potassium** (10% solution, see pg. 246) - Dosage (first 3-4 weeks): 4 tsp. in each of 10 orange-, carrot/apple-, and green-juices (10x4 daily). Thereafter, the physician will normally reduce the dosage to 10x2 for 20 weeks, then 8x2 for 12 weeks, and 6x2 for the duration of treatment. However, more frequent adjustments by the physician are common (pp. 207-208, 235, 246, 393,409,410).

(4) **Lugol's solution** (half-strength) - dosage (first 3-4 weeks ONLY): 3 drops in each of 6 orange- and carrot/apple-juices (6x3 daily). Thereafter, the physician will normally reduce the dosage to 6x1 for 8 weeks, and 3x1 for the duration of treatment. DO NOT add to liver- or green-juice (pp.32, 205, 235, 246,409).

(5) **Thyroid** - Dosage (first 3-4 weeks only): 5x1 grain daily. In the example case on page 235, the dosage was reduced to 3x½ grain for 8 weeks, then 3x½ grain for 14 weeks. More frequent adjustments by the physician are common (pp. 205, 206, 235, 246, 409). Tachycardia (pulse over 120) may indicate overdosage. Discontinue temporarily during menses.

(6) **Niacin** - Dosage: 50mg at least 6 times daily for 6 months. In advanced cases Gerson used 50mg every hour around the clock {Rev. Gastroenterol. 12(6) 419-425, Nov-Dec, 1945]. Reactions (hot, red skin) are temporary and harmless. Minor bleedings are no cause for concern, but discontinue during menses or in case of hemorrhage (pp. 99, 209, 235, 246).

(7) **Pancreatin** - Dosage: 3 tablets 4 times daily, or according to patient's needs. A few patients do not tolerate pancreatin well, but most benefit from it (pp. 211-212,235, 246, 411).

(8) **Royal Jelly** (not required) - dosage: l00mg in capsules or honey, ½ hour before breakfast. Do not take with hot food. Available from some health food stores (pp. 200, 235).

(9) **Liver extract(crude) and B12** - Dosage: 3cc liver and .1mg B12 combined in a single syringe, injected into gluteus medius, daily for 4-6 months or more. The physician will normally reduce frequency gradually over the course of therapy. NOTE: **Liver juice** is an extremely important part of the liver medication - Dosage: 3 glasses daily (minimum) for full course of treatment, 18-24 months (pp. 80-82, 196, 210-211, 235, 240, 246, 393, 407, 409, 411, 412).*

(10) **Coffee enemas** (pg. 247) - Dosage (first 6 weeks, minimum): While lying on right side, retain for 12-15 minutes - EVERY FOUR HOURS. For limited periods of time, against severe pain, coffee enemas may be used as frequently as every two hours. However, physician must monitor serum electrolytes frequently. **Castor oil** - Dosage: 2 tbsp. by mouth, and five hours later a castor oil and soap enema (pg. 247) - EVERY OTHER DAY. Later, as necessary or as prescribed, (pp. 81, 166, 190-195, 198, 201-203, 206, 235, 393, 406-410, 416-418).

(11) **Blood chemistry, Complete Blood Count, T3, T4, Urinalysis** - All tests should be taken before beginning treatment and at 4-6 week intervals for at least the first 6 months. Test results may be affected by healing reactions and flare-ups, (pp. 235, 415).

(9) **All other medications** - DO NOT abruptly discontinue ANY medications you are taking prior to using the Gerson Therapy. In certain cases, Gerson-trained physicians will advise gradual discontinuance.

---

* **See Appendix III. page 421**

CHAPTER XXXIII

Combined Dietary Regime

The treatment requires guidance from a physician as there are often complications of "flare-ups" and activation of chronic infections or other bodily weaknesses which need special medical attention.

To know this prescription booklet thoroughly, read it over again and again.

NECESSARY FOOD:

This diet is quite different from the usual nutrition. It consists mainly of:
Fruit
Juices of Fruit, vegetables and leaves
Vegetables, salads
Special soup
Potatoes
Oatmeal, bread, etc.

All Freshly Prepared and Saltless
* * *

The dietary regime is the basis of the treatment. The main task is to detoxify the entire system to restore the functions of the liver and the metabolism: digestive changes of food from intake to output.

Neither dietary regime alone nor medication alone is effective. The combination is essential for success.

This food is easily and quickly digested; the body needs larger portions and more frequent servings. Eat and drink as much as you can, even during the night when awake.

FORBIDDEN FOODS & SUBSTANCES

bottled	refined
canned	salted
frozen	smoked
preserved	sulphured

alcohol	flour (white)
avocados	Fluoride in toothpaste, gargle[1]
berries	hair dying and permanents
beverages (commercial)	ice cream
bicarbonate of soda in food,	mushrooms
toothpaste, gargle	nicotine
candy	nuts
cake	oil
chocolate	pineapples
cocoa	salt & salt substitutes
coffee, incl. instant	spices (pepper, paprika)
cream	soy beans and products
cucumbers	sugar (white)
epsom salts	tea
fat	water, drinking

TEMPORARILY FORBIDDEN (UNTIL FURTHER NOTICE)

butter	fish
cheese	meat
eggs	milk

UTENSILS
USE: Stainless steel, glass, enamel, earthenware, cast iron and tin.

DO NOT USE: Microwave ovens, pressure cookers or any aluminum pots or utensils.

Notes (4th Edition): 1. Fluoridated water is prohibited for internal use.

UTENSILS FOR THE PREPARATION OF JUICES
USE: A separate grinder and a separate press.

DO NOT USE: One-unit machines such as liquifiers, centrifuges, juice mixers or masters, etc.

DIRECTIONS FOR NECESSARY FOOD
FRUIT (NO CANS)
Fresh fruit in large quantities should be used:

Apples	Mangoes
Apricots	Melons
Bananas	Oranges
Cherries	Peaches
Currants	Pears
Grapes	Plums
Grapefruit	Tangerines, etc.

- *Pears and plums are more easily digested when stewed.*
- *STEWED FRUITS may also be used.*
- *Unsulphured dried fruit may be used, such as raisins, peaches, dates, figs, apricots, prunes or mixed fruit — wash, soak and stew.*

FORBIDDEN[2] (see list)
- *All berries and pineapple; their aromatic acids cause unfavorable reactions.*
- *Avocados, nuts — too much fatty acid.*
- *Cucumbers*

JUICES (daily)
ALWAYS FRESHLY PREPARED (8oz. glass)
DAILY PORTION (not canned)
A:_____ Glasses of orange juice
B:_____ Glasses of apple and carrot juice
C:_____ Glasses of green leaf juice
D:_____ Glasses of grape juice
E:_____ Glasses of grapefruit juice
F:_____ Glasses of apple juice

Add to each glass: _____

_____

- *DO NOT DRINK WATER (because the full drinking capacity is needed for juices and soup).*
- *No LUGOL in green leaf juice.*

---

2. Recent clinical observations and laboratory animal experiments suggest that an amino acid, canavanine, in ALFALFA SEEDS AND SPROUTS may cause flare-ups or rheumatoid diseases (SLE, RA) in both monkeys and humans. BOTH ARE FORBIDDEN

FRESH CALF'S LIVER JUICE FOR ONE GLASS*

Cut 1/2 lb. fresh unwashed, NOT FROZEN, young calf's liver into 1" strips, (weight of entire liver 2½ to 4 lbs.) Add ¾ lb. of whole fresh carrots (not those in plastic bags[3]) and one small apple.

Take alternate portions of liver and carrots and grind twice[4], mix well.

FOR PRESSING — put 2 white paper napkins[5], each folded in half, crosswise on moistened cloth. Place 2 tablespoons of mixture in center of napkin. Fold 4 sides of napkin over mixture, then fold cloth in the same way and press. Repeat process until all is pressed, each time taking new paper napkins. Drink IMMEDIATELY and take some orange juice after. Use nylon cloth 12" square.

If you cannot get fresh liver daily[6], buy double the amount. Use half at once and save the other half unwashed in a tightly covered glass jar in refrigerator, above freezing — 36°F. (DO NOT FREEZE) for the next day.

• No medication in liver juice.

_____ Glasses a day.

PREPARATION OF JUICES
• CITRUS JUICES: Squeeze only with a reamer type juicer of glass, plastic, porcelain or an electric machine.
• DO NOT use any juicer into which the half orange is inserted with the skin. (If the skin is also pressed out, it will emit harmful fatty acids and aromatic substances contained in its surface.)
• DO NOT USE aluminum juicer.

APPLE AND CARROT JUICE: Use apples and carrots in equal portions.
• Wash apples, do NOT peel. Cut and remove core with seeds.
• Wash carrots, do NOT scrape.
• USE SEPARATE GRINDER AND SEPARATE PRESS.
• Do NOT use liquifiers, centrifuges, juice mixers or masters, etc.

If the patient goes to work again, apple and carrot juice only may be taken and kept in a thermos no longer than 2 to 3 hours (not in refrigerator).

---

3. USE ORGANICALLY GROWN PRODUCE. Food grade plastics have improved, but items pre-packaged in small quantities often contain preservatives to prolong "fresh" appearance.
4. It is not necessary to grind twice if grinder has fine grid which produces very well ground (almost liquefied) pulp.
5. Use food grade "microwave approved" white paper towel.
6. Liver should be bagged, airtight, and immersed in ICE water IMMEDIATELY after slaughter. Once chilled (30-60 minutes) liver should be kept in a tray of ice in a refrigerator (NOT in freezer—DO NOT FREEZE). With this procedure, liver may be viable as tong as 96 hours.

* See Appendix III. page 421

GREEN LEAF JUICE[7]: Procure as many of the various kinds of leaves as possible mentioned below (no others).

Lettuce	Endives
Red cabbage leaves (2 or 3 leaves)	Romaine
Beet tops (young inner leaves)	Green Pepper (¼ of small one)
Swiss chard	Watercress (¼ bunch)
Escarole	

- ADD 1 MEDIUM APPLE for each glass when grinding.
- Grind TWICE[4], press, drink IMMEDIATELY.

PRESSING PROCESS: Take 1 or 2 coarsely woven cloths, nylon -12" square, place cupful of pulp into center of moistened cloth, fold in thirds in both directions and press. Rinse cloth after each juice preparation and boil in soap water every night, rinse thoroughly. It is most important to clean machines well. If juice retains taste of cloth, take a new cloth. Left-overs of all pressings can be used only for compost or as animal food (chickens, cats, dogs, etc.).

PREPARATION OF VEGETABLES

VEGETABLES: (All freshly prepared and saltless). Use all vegetables except mushrooms, leaves of carrots, or radishes and mustard green.

Vegetables must be cooked without water slowly on low flame until well done. To prevent burning, place on asbestos mat[8] or two under the saucepan. You may add some stock of the special soup. Spinach water is too bitter for use and should be drained off. Onions, leeks, and tomatoes have enough liquid of their own to keep them moist while cooking. (Beets should be cooked like potatoes in their jackets with water). Wash and scrub vegetables thoroughly, but DO NOT peel or scrape them. The saucepan must be tightly covered to prevent steam from escaping. Covers must be heavy or close fitting (you may place wax paper under lid). Patients must have freshly cooked foods only.

No carrots, fruits or vegetables should be bought in plastic bags[3], neither potatoes nor oranges with color added should be used.

Sprayed insecticides (poisons) cannot be removed by washing, as they are absorbed into the plants, having been taken up by the roots from the soil.

---

7. DO NOT add Lugol's Solution to green leaf juice.
8. Asbestos has been found to be a toxic substance. Mats of other materials - such as steel - are suggested.

To vary flavors you may also use very small quantities of the following (NO OTHERS): Allspice, anise, bayleaves, coriander, dill, fennel, mace, marjoram, rosemary, sage, saffron, tarragon, thyme, sorrel, summer savory:
Chives, onions, garlic and parsley can be used in larger amounts and can often be helpful to improve the taste. **Spices must be used sparingly as they may counteract the healing reaction.**

SALADS:
Very important are the following raw vegetables
(finely grated if necessary or chopped, mixed or separate):

Apples and Carrots	Tomatoes	Radishes	Chives
Lettuce	Escarole	Scallions	Green Peppers
Chicory	Cauliflower	Endives	
Watercress	Romaine	Knob Celery	

Dressing: (Optional) Mix 2 tablespoons lemon juice or wine vinegar. 2 table-spoons water, 1 tablespoon brown sugar, a little diced onion, grated horseradish (not bottled).

AGAIN - NO OIL, FATS

SPECIAL SOUP:

About _____ glasses a day.
For 1 person use a 2-quart pot, use the following vegetables[9],
then cover with water:

1 medium celery knob, if not in season,	2 medium onions
substitute 3-4 stalks of branch celery	*little* parsley only
(pascal celery is preferable)	1 1/2 lbs. tomatoes or more
1 medium parsley root	1lb. potatoes
2 small leeks (substitute 2 small onions)	

Do NOT peel any of these vegetables; just wash and scrub them well and cut them coarsely: cook them slowly for 3 hours, then put through food mill in small portions; scarcely any fibres should be left. Vary the amount of water used for cooking according to taste and desired consistency. Let soup cool off before storing. Keep well covered in refrigerator NO LONGER than 2 days; warm up as much as needed each time.

---

9. Garlic may be used at liberty for cooking, or squeezed fresh into hot soup.

POTATOES:
Baked potatoes _____ a day. May be eaten with soup, applesauce,
or yogurt (If prescribed).
- For a change you may also use potatoes boiled in their jackets,
  or mashed (with a little soup)
- Sweet potatoes are permitted once a week (no color added).

Potato salad: Use boiled potatoes (see above), peel. slice and while hot, add
dressing (see page 242).

OATMEAL:
In the morning for breakfast.
- A large portion of oatmeal daily: old fashioned oats —
  Scotch, Irish or plain Quaker Oats.
- ½ cup oatmeal to 1 cup water.
- Cook slowly in water until done — about 5 minutes.

Take oatmeal with: (No milk)

Raw grated apples	Bananas
Brown sugar or honey	Apple sauce
Blackstrap molasses	Raisins
Stewed prunes	Peaches, etc.
Apricots	

BREAD, FLOUR, ETC.:
Use saltless rye bread _____ lb., about _____ slices a day.

You may occasionally use:
- Brown or wild rice
- Potato flour, Tapioca
- Corn starch, barley, lentils
- Bread crumbs (grate unsalted dried pumpernickel left-overs).

SUGAR AND SWEETENING:
Use raw sugar, brown sugar[10], maple sugar, and syrup, light honey,
unsulphured molasses, at least _____ tablespoons a day.
Maple Sugar Candy (100% pure) may be used.

PEPPERMINT TEA:
This should be used when food is not well tolerated, in case of indigestion, or during reaction period (flare-ups), nausea or gas.

To prepare: Take 2 teaspoons of dried peppermint leaves to 2 cups of boiling
water, boil 5 minutes and strain. Add brown sugar and lemon juice if desired.

---

10. Brown sugar should be as little refined as possible.
"Brown sugar" is often white sugar with molasses added.

SAMPLE MENU
Adapt menu to your personal prescription

BREAKFAST
1 glass juice
Large portion oatmeal
Bread, dark rye, toasted or plain,
with prescribed honey or stewed fruit (no preserves)

LUNCHEON
Salad (raw food)
Pot cheese and buttermilk (if prescribed)
1 glass warm soup
1 glass juice
Large baked potato
Vegetables, cooked
Dessert: fruit, stewed or raw

DINNER
Salad (raw food)
Pot cheese and buttermilk (if prescribed)
1 glass warm soup
1 glass juice
Large baked potato
2 vegetables, cooked
Dessert: raw or stewed fruit

JUICES AND MEDICATION
Fill in chart and adapt it according to later changes (draw your own chart).
In the beginning some patients may find it difficult to consume all the prescribed food and juices.
After good detoxication-in about one to two weeks-the metabolism should improve and the appetite increase.
In that way the treatment has to be adapted to the degree of the disease, to the "flare-ups" and other complications and interferences.

DAILY MEDICATION CHART[11], (see page 236)

TIME OF JUICES	TEASPOONS POTASSIUM	DROPS LUGOL	TABLETS NIACIN	TABLETS THYROID
8:30 Breakfast				
9:00				
10:00				
11:00				
11:30 Liver Juice*	NO MEDICATION			
12:30 Luncheon				
3:00 Liver Juice*	NO MEDICATION			
4:30 Liver Juice*	NO MEDICATION			
5:00				
5:30				
6:00				
6:30 Dinner				

The dietary regime is the basis of the treatment: it excludes most sodium-containing foods, while it helps to refill the tissues with the important potassium lost before.

This food is easily and quickly digested, the body needs larger portions and more frequent servings. Eat and drink as much as you can, even during the night when awake. Neither the dietary regime alone nor medication alone is effective-the combination is essential for success.

11. The above schedule reflects the workday hours of Gerson's Nanuet clinic. Patients were instructed to adopt an hourly schedule on returning home. A more conservative clinical schedule was created by physicians of the Gerson Therapy Center of Mexico (see page 236).
* See Appendix III, page 421

- THYROID (Armour) _____ grains, 1 tablet _____ times a day.

- LUGOL SOLUTION(half strength) _____ drop
_____ times a day, in juice, not in green juice.

- 10% SOLUTION OF POTASSIUM[12]
Potas.; gluconate, acetate, phosphate aa. (monobasic)
_____ teaspoons _____ times a day, in juice.
Potassium and Lugol can be added to the same juice.

- LIVER INJECTIONS[13], intramuscularly
Crude Liver Extract, Lilly, #352 _____ cc
_____ times _____ combined
with Vit.B12 _____ cc(1cc-50mcgr.)

- FRESH CALF'S LIVER JUICE[14]*
1 glass _____ times a day.

- NIACIN _____ mgm
1 tablet _____ times a day, to be dissolved on
the tongue AFTER some juice or food.

- ACIDOL PEPSIN[15] (Winthrop) _____
capsules _____ times a day before meals.

- LUBILE[16] _____ capsules _____ times a day after the
first half glass of soup; also for enema.

- 10% SOLUTION OF CAFFEINE POTASSIUM CITRATE
Caffeine benzoate: 5.0, Potassium citrate: 5.0, Aq. Dest. ad: 100.0

- LINSEED OIL[17] cold pressed (food grade), 1 tablespoon each morning
and evening. After 4 weeks reduce to 1 tablespoon daily.

- PANCREATIN Lilly No. 1001, 5 grs.
_____ tablets _____ times a day.

_____

Signature of Physician

_____

12. 100 grams (equal parts of each salt) dissolved in approx. 1 quart water.
13. Lilly #352 discontinued. Both Lilly and Rugby have acceptable material.
14. NO MEDICATIONS in this juice. Ask butcher for "bob veal liver".*
15. For current supplier, see page 236, #2.
16. No longer available. See page 211.
17. Added 2nd edition, see pp. 397-398.
* See Appendix III, page 421

CAUTION - VERY IMPORTANT!

NO OTHER medication (except aspirin[18]) should be taken without consulting your physician.

After detoxification by this treatment the body becomes hypersensitive and the usual anesthetic dose may be dangerous. Therefore your dentist should be advised to use 0.7 cc Novocaine instead of the usual 2cc with or without adrenalin.

No other anesthetics or drugs, including those used for dental purposes, should be taken without previous consultation with your doctor. Heavy or shock reactions may result.

RESTORATION OF THE LIVER

This treatment should be followed strictly, both in the clinic and later at home, for at least 18 months, according to the progressive restoration of the liver and the other organs.

The liver is the main organ for the regeneration of the body's metabolism: transformation of food from intake to output.

It is advisable not to start the treatment, if for any reason strict adherence to it is not possible.

ENEMAS - NO HIGH COLONICS

1. Coffee enema:

Take 3 tablespoons of ground (drip) coffee (not Instant) to 1 quart of water, let it boil 3 minutes and then simmer 15 minutes more. Strain and use at body temperature. The daily amount can be prepared at one time (a coffee concentrate can be made, then diluted to required strength).

2. Castor Oil Treatment:

To do the Castor Oil Treatment, the following is required:

At 5 AM, take a small piece of fruit and follow it with 2 tablespoonfuls of castor oil, orally. Drink 1/2 to 2/3 cups of regular black coffee (not enema coffee) with a teaspoonful of natural brown sugar (i.e. 'Sucanat'). Then take the regularly scheduled 6 AM coffee enema.

At 10 AM (5 hours after the oral castor oil) take a castor oil enema, as follows: In the enema bucket, place 5 tablespoonfuls of castor oil, add 1/4 teaspoonful of ox bile powder and mix thoroughly. In a separate 1 quart container, mix the regular strength enema coffee. Take a piece of regular soap (as you might use to wash your hands or face, NOT detergent such as 'Dove') and rub the soap into the coffee for a few moments. Then add this soapy coffee to the castor oil in the enema bucket, stirring vigorously. You may use an electric mixer. Still, the oil tends to float back to the top - therefore a helper has to stir this

---

18. See pp. 197 & 401.

coffee/castor oil mixture while it is going into the rectum. Don't attempt to hold this enema; but it is alright if you can. The castor oil enema takes the place of one of the regularly scheduled coffee enemas.

The very early morning hour for taking the castor oil is important in order for the oil to clear the stomach by the time meals and juices arrive. If taken later, the patient runs the risk of being nauseated all day and not able to consume the juices and meals. The coffee with a little sugar helps to activate the stomach so that the patient is not nauseated with the oil remaining in the stomach. Only in cases of diabetes or hypoglycemia, omit the sugar. *Ox bile is NOT to be used orally.*

3. Camomile tea enema:
Take one level cup of dried Camomile flowers: simmer in one pint of water for 30 minutes in covered saucepan. Strain and keep in covered glass bottle not longer than 3 days. Take one quart of water at body temperature, add half a glass of camomile extract and 30 caffeine drops.

TAKE ALL ENEMAS LYING DOWN ON THE RIGHT SIDE WITH THE KNEES PULLED UP TOWARDS THE CHIN.

TO START YOUR TREATMENT the following should be procured:
- Necessary medication (see prescription)
- Enema bag or bucket (see enemas)
- Juice extracting machine and press (see preparation of juices)
- Food mill (see special soup)

To know this prescription booklet thoroughly, read it over again and again. This prescription booklet is required for every visit.

SPECIAL NOTES TO PHYSICIAN (Revised for the 4th Edition)
The Gerson Therapy is an immune enhancing, combined medical regime resting on salt & water management, therapeutic nutrition, detoxication, and regulation of the rate of metabolism. Because the Gerson Therapy relies on the stability of normal tissues, organs, bone marrow, blood vessels, and G.I. tract, its positive effects may be compromised by:

1. Extensive pretreatment with chemotherapy
2. Long term steroid usage, eg: prednisone
3. Removal of pituitary, adrenals, pancreas, more than 2/3 of stomach, colon (with ileostomy)
4. Multiple tappings of lungs or abdomen
5. Extreme liver damage (pg. 199)
6. Transplanted organs which require immune suppressing cyclophosphamide management

PART II

EDITOR'S NOTE - FEBRUARY 3, 1986

The Gerson Institute was incorporated June 27, 1978, twenty years after the publication of *A Cancer Therapy: Results of Fifty Cases*.

Since that time, staff of the Gerson Institute have attempted to follow up as many as possible of the 50 cases in this book. Because all of the following cases were treated more than 30 years ago, hopes were not high of finding many, if any, of these patients. 34 would be beyond the average life expectancy if they were found to be living. But, a number of patients and families of patients have been located. Ten of these patients are known by us to be living in good health at this time: cases 1, 5, 7, 11, 12, 13, 14, 18, 35, & 38. Four, cases 23, 28, 41, and 42, are known to have lived healthfully to old age, dying of natural causes. Others may, in fact, be alive and well, but are lost to follow up.

A number of well documented cases, patients cured by Gerson but not described in his book, have become known to us. We have also located patients who were successfully treated with the Gerson Therapy by physicians other than Gerson.

Because the Gerson Institute exists to encourage incorporation of the Gerson Therapy into contemporary medicine as a primary management for cancer and chronic degenerative conditions, the editors will appreciate contact from any patients treated by Gerson, or other physicians employing his therapy.

In 1986, the relationship between diet, nutrition, and cancer is no longer questioned. However, the role of therapeutic nutrition in the treatment of cancer has not been explored by the majority of current cancer authorities. The contributions of Gerson alone are insufficient to excite the interest of the research community.

If you are a physician using the Gerson Therapy to treat cancer or other diseases, please contact the Gerson Institute. As part of its non-profit charter, the Institute provides professional counsel to physicians who elect to use the Gerson Therapy. Cases which have adequate documentation are essential to our efforts to persuade a skeptical but curious medical profession.

The Gerson Institute
1572 Second Avenue, San Diego, CA 92101
Telephone: (619) 685-5359
www.gerson.org

CASE No. 1*

Mrs. D.S.-B., age—44, married, two children.

Diagnosis: Exceptionally large tumor mass of the pituitary gland. Surrounding bones partly destroyed.

Mount Sinai Hospital Report—June 1943

Patient noticed progressive loss of vision in both eyes during 1941-1942. Had diplopia which lasted two months. Diminution in the temporal field of right eye progressed to complete hemianopsia by March 1943. In April 1943 she noted that vision in the remaining half of right visual field was diminishing. Examination in June revealed blindness in temporal field of left eye. There was amenorrhea since November 1942. Patient lost 15 pounds between 1942 and 1943.

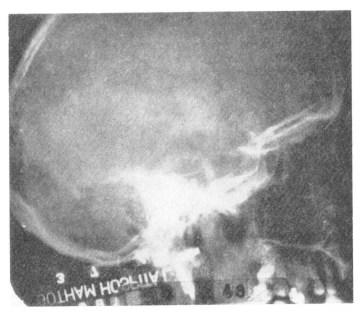

Case 1, No. 1 — 3/7/46

On admission to hospital, positive findings included moderate pallor of both optic discs, impairment of visual acuity in both eyes, bitemporal

---

* This case with illustrations was published in *Medizinische Klinik*, Munich, Germany, No. 4, January 29, 1954.

hemianopsia with an additional lower nasal quadrant anopsia (incomplete) with the right eye. X-rays showed marked enlargement of the sella turcica with the erosion of the walls of the clinoid processus.

Patient was given series of X-ray treatments with some slight improvement of visual acuity but no change in the visual fields. She was discharged to the referring physician. She was advised to have pituitary gland tumor mass removed, but refused.

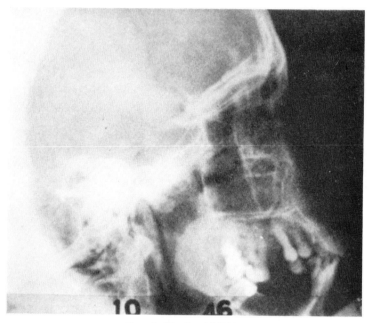

Case 1, No. 2 — 10/1/46

First Diagnosis: Chromophobe Adenoma of the Pituitary.

Condition of patient on arrival at my department, Gotham Hospital, N. Y.–March 1944.

First seen. Diagnosis: Exceptionally large tumor mass of the pituitary gland, sella turcica to great extent enlarged. Surrounding bones partially destroyed. Right eye, blind. Left eye almost destroyed due to partial destruction of left optic nerve.

Gotham Hospital

Patient was brought to us in an ambulance. She was unconscious. Treatment was started immediately.** One of Mrs. S-B.'s relatives was able to bring plenty of fruit and vegetable juices. Teaspoon by teaspoon, day and night she was induced to take these juices. At the same time, she got many enemas with the result that she regained full consciousness after one week. At the end of two months, patient was feeling fine and able to do her own

---

** In all cases, treatment was started immediately.

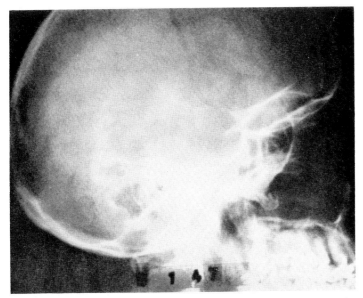

Case 1, No. 3 — 6/1/47

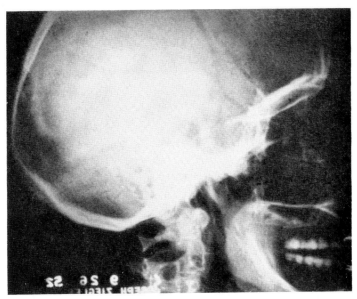

Case 1, No. 4 — 9/26/52

housework. At the end of eight months, she was able to resume duties as secretary to her husband. She is still functioning in that capacity. Although she has only half of the left retina functioning, she can read and write without disturbance.

Note: The enlargement of the sella turcica was and remained to such an extent that our outstanding radiologist declared that he and others had never or seldom seen anything like it.

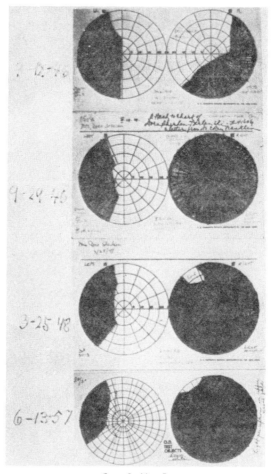

Case 1, No. 5
3/12/46 - 9/29/46 - 3/25/48 - 6/13/57

Report of Eye Specialist, June 15, 1957

Vision: OD—No useful vision, probable light perception in upper nasal quadrant.
OS—20/20.
Corneal sensitivity normal.

Conjugate excursions full.

No muscle anomalies.

OD—No light reaction (direct elicited).

There is a consensual reaction from right to left. I can elicit no consensual reaction from left to right.

Direct light reaction prompt.

Intra-ocular tension—.18 in each eye.

Slit lamp examination—Normal, except there is a web-like structure in the OD which is vestigial and has no significance.

Interior—Right papilla shows advanced optic atrophy with narrowing of all optic vessels.

Left papilla—moderate temporal waxen pallor (this is typical of what is seen in pituitary adenoma).

Fields: OD—Only questionable light perception in upper nasal quadrant.

OS—Modified temporal cut (this temporal cut is much smaller than one I did eight or ten years ago).

Patient is in good health and working power.

Any physician who is interested may see the original X-rays and hospital reports on request of any specific case in this section.

CASE No. 2

Mr. C. H., age—48, married, two children.

Clinical Diagnosis: Schwannoma of the left cerebello-pontine angle. French Hospital, New York.

Biopsy report and operation:

"The usual approach to the cerebello-pontine angle was made through a small opening in the left posterior occipital region.

"A firm hard tumor mass was encountered in the region of internal acoustic foramen. It was not the usual type of acoustic neuroma, and looked more like spindle cell sarcoma. Most of the tissue was removed. Marked bone destruction was encountered.

"Pathological report of specimen was diagnosed as Schwannoma of the left cerbello-pontine angle."

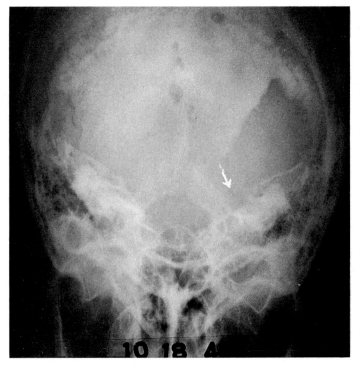

Case 2, No. 1 — 10/18/49

Previous History:

It started around the end of November, 1948, with difficulty and weakness in both legs. During the following months it became worse and affected the tongue. It was difficult for the patient to move the tongue and to speak. The left hand also became weaker and he could not move the fingers, the hand nor the wrist joint. Some days he could speak in the morning all right but during the day it got worse. He never drank nor smoked. Neurologic examination revealed nystagmus in both eyes, tongue deviated to the right. The tendon and skin reflexes were irregular. The symptoms became worse at the beginning of 1949; an operation was performed on April 6, 1949. I saw him once March 23, 1949, but my treatment started on May 23, 1949, after the operation had been performed. At that time he showed involvement of the 5th, 7th, and 8th cranial nerves with cerebellar dysfunction. Left arm and leg were spastic and atactic out of control, the left mouth corner hung down. As the tumor could not be removed entirely, his wife was given a hopeless prognosis after the operation.

At the end of June, the patient started to walk with a cane despite poor equilibrium. At the end of July, 1949, the left arm was movable; the feeling was partly restored but the control was poor. The sensitivity in the

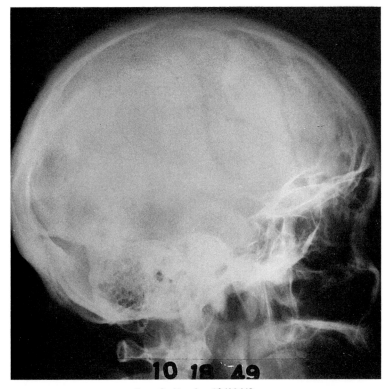

Case 2, No. 2 — 10/18/49

left half of the face returned slowly. At the end of October, 1949, the left arm and hand were more movable and stronger. Motility of the tongue and left facialis was greatly restored. In November, 1950, the patient started to work in the garage. Vision in right eye normal; patient could read and write normally. Left eye deviated medially; to avoid double vision it was covered by a dark glass. In the last months of 1950 the bulging out brain mass in the area of the operation scar was no longer palpable. Half a year later that part was even drawn in.

During the following years patient worked as watchmaker and even repaired cars, radios and other things. Left arm and leg remained a little weaker, the leg spastic and atactic. Last seen July, 1957.

X-Ray findings: Partial destruction of the anterior upper part of the left os petrosum. Sella turcica enlarged altogether, anterior and posterior wall thinned, posterior wall partly destroyed. Anterior and lower wall now again stand out, posterior wall unchanged. The process of pyramid shows no essential changes.

Last X-Ray findings: Anterior upper part of left os petrosum almost restored.

The nasal accessory sinuses are pneumatic.

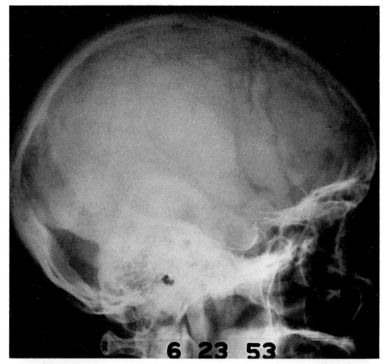

Case 2, No. 3 — 6/23/53

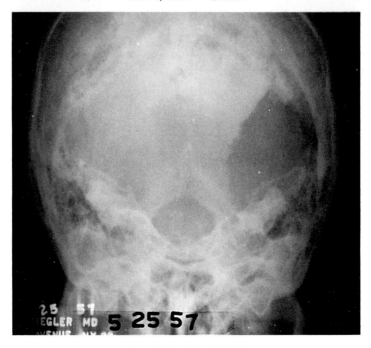

Case 2, No. 4 — 5/25/57

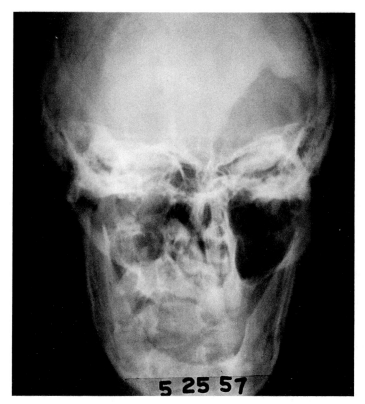

Case 2, No. 5 — 5/25/57

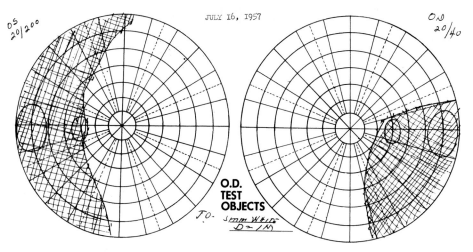

Case 2, No. 6 — 7/16/57

Report of Eye Specialist: (Former vision fields not available.)

> July 5th, 1957: Complete paralysis lateral rectus OS - 7th also ...
> Ulcer of left cornea, for which advise lid closure.
> Vision: OD-20/40
> OS-20/200
> Pupillary reactions present - Papillae good color but left papilla
> is a little hazy.

CASE No. 3

Miss M.K.,age-17½.

Clinical Diagnosis: Neurofibromata with rapid growth, many metastases
                    of sarcoma type, also brain tumor with hemiparesis,
                    left side.

Biopsy and operations:

> 1. Operation February 1941, removal of tumor on the lower part of nose.
> 2. Operation March 1943, removal of recurrent tissue mass.
> 3. Operation 1945, again removal of recurrent tissue.
> 4. Operation June 1949, two tumors removed, one from forehead, one
>   from top of head.
> 5. Operation February 1950, a large tumor the size of a potato removed
> together with the middle lobe of the right lung. Mother was told prognosis
> was hopeless as the surrounding area of the pericard was covered with new
> nodes.

Report of Indiana University Medical Center:

Patient was first admitted to the James Whitcomb Riley Hospital, March
6, 1943, complaining of a swelling of the upper lip which had become progressively larger since she was two years old. Past and family histories were
essentially negative.

Physical examination showed a soft tumor mass involving the upper lip.
There was a scar from a previous attempt at removal of the mass,
Psychometric examination showed I.Q. to be 112, The tumor was removed

March 9, 1943, and at surgery was found to be quite extensive with some pressure atrophy of the underlying bone. The histopathological diagnosis was plexiform neurofibroma of the lip. No other lesions of the Von Reckling-hausen type were found. Her post-operative course was satisfactory and she was discharged from the hospital March 18, 1943.

She was followed in out-patient clinic at six-month intervals with no evidence of recurrence of tumor until February, 1945. The mass continued to enlarge and she was readmitted to the hospital June 25, 1945. The tumor was excised as completely as possible June 29, 1945.

The histopathological report stated that the neurofibroma showed features suggestive of *rapid growth and possible development of sarcoma.* Patient was discharged from the hospital July 8, 1945, with instructions to return to clinic in one month, but she failed to keep the appointment.

Report of lung operation, Boehne Tuberculosis Hospital, Evansville, Ind.:

Small amount of straw-colored clear fluid is present in the thoracic cavity. Tumor is readily visualized, situated subpleurally and related to spine which lies medial and posterior to tumor mass. It measures approximately 10 x 6 cm and presenting surface is soft and yields sero-sanguinous fluid on puncture with #22 needle and syringe.

Pleura is divided and inferior portion of tumor is dissected free, using sharp and dull knife ends. Then division of pleura is completed across rounded surface of yellowish slightly firm tumor, and inferior medial thickened pseudopol-like portion of tumor seems to vanish into tumor substance as its color becomes yellowish with appearance of degeneration at its superior extent. Inferior end is lost beneath vertebral pleura beyond tumor. Remainder of tumor is shelled out from under pleura after apparent attachment, in form of thickened nerve trunk taking origin from spine, is severed as far as possible toward origin, and remaining end cauterized. At point of origin, this nerve trunk seems to be unsually firm, becoming softer and merging into tumor as it increases in size.

Microscopic Pathology: Some areas have a loose hyalinized appearance; other areas show slightly elongated fusiform or spindle shaped cells with sometimes a fibrillar matrix. There is some variability as to size, shape and staining reaction of some of these cells and also as to number. A number of the nuclei become almost giant size and take a dark basic stain. In one particular area, there are a number of ganglion cells.

Pathologic Diagnosis: Specimen A: Cystic ganglion neurofibroma with phagocytosis of blood pigment arising from a thoracic nerve trunk and showing an early malignant change.

"We were inclined to believe from our findings and her history of other tumors that she might have a recurrence elsewhere at some future time."

"Twelve tumor specialists told mother that I would *never get well* and that there was *nothing they could do!*"

Condition when first seen June 20, 1950: There were 12 smaller tumors all over the body; one at the middle part of the left upper jaw bone,
> one at the right upper lateral eye bone (orbita) pressing
> on the eye lid,
> one at the right temporal part of the head,

one at the left upper arm,
two at the right lower arm,
two on the left hip bone, — abdominal wall, etc.

Hearing at right ear was reduced, and right eye partly closed, due to ingrown cataract.

Within one month most of the tumors were no longer palpable; after two months, all tumors disappeared. During the following month most of the enlarged scars were greatly reduced. As the liver tests remained abnormal, patient was advised to continue the treatment to the greatest extent. After marriage, she was off the diet for two years entirely against medical advice. All remained well for about two years when she first noticed (December, 1955) that the right arm became shaky and made her unable to write. Later on she became dizzy and was unable to go downstairs. She fell several times when walking at home or on the street. During the following months her vision was reduced, especially in the right eye. She felt tightness and pressure in the skull. The eye specialist found far advanced symptoms of a brain tumor and on May 15, 1956, recommended an immediate operation for decompression to avoid blindness. She returned to my cancer clinic on May 19, 1956, with her mother. On May 22, 1956, the eye specialist found that the case was a serious one and deserved the utmost immediate care (decompression) to avoid blindness. With the agreement of the mother we decided against the operation but instead decided to apply the most intensive treatment for an extensive time. On June 22, 1956, the same eye specialist found "a phenomenal improvement." Correspondingly the whole body, the patient's walking, writing and other actions improved; she continued to do so and still does, according to her and her mother's letters.

At the end of May, 1957, patient's mother called; the patient had suddenly become unconscious and had shown strong epileptic fits. Two local physicians had diagnosed the condition as regrowth of the tumor. My explanation was that it may most probably be an intoxication or infection. I advised to give the patient coffee enemas every two hours and to force as much juices and peppermint tea into her as possible, day and night. In two days the patient was entirely restored; as cause of the accident her mother found out that the kitchen maid had not cleaned the grinder after the preparation of liver juice over the weekend so that the remnants from the calf's liver remained in the grinder for two and a half days, fermented there and caused the terrible poisoning on Monday.

The last report which was received at the end of July noted the further improvement of the patient.

Report of Eye Specialist, May 22, 1956

Vision: OD—20/100
OS—20/40-1
Anisocoria: Pupil OD larger than OS
Corneal anesthesia OD
Corneal reflex OS probably normal
Rolling component nystagmus in all conjugate gazes, also there is a varying component nystagmus from the primary position (seen with ophthalmoscope).

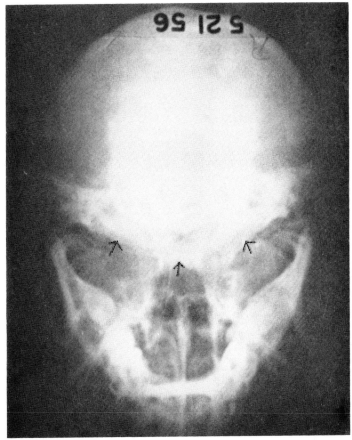

Case 3, No. 1 — 5/21/56

Effort conjugations show an occasional disassociated movement — this is suggestive of brain stem involvement. The components of nystagmus are much more rapid in the left than to the right. The component to the right is more of a rolling motion to the right.

Interior: OD—Immature cataract — media otherwise clear 1½ to 2 diopters of papilledema

OS —*Three* diopters of papilledema

In my opinion this papilledema is characteristic of increased intracranial pressure. It is plerocephalic.

A careful and personal attempt was made to do fields and functional testing, but the patient's cooperation was in no way sufficient to make plotting reliable.

Findings: 1. Plerocephalic papilledema (due to increased cranial pressure)
2. Anisocoria
3. Intermittent diplopia

4. Occasional disassociated movements

5. Corneal anesthesia OD

Diagnosis: Expanding brain lesion most likely metastatic to cerebellum and brain stem.

It is my feeling that this is a serious case and deserves the utmost and immediate care.

Report of Eye Specialist, June 22, 1956

Vision: OD—20/100 (Cataract)
OS —20/25

The nystagmus is present on a less marked basis. I can detect no evidence of disassociated movements today.

Aniscoria present — corneal sensitivity normal in OS.

Corneal sensitivity much more in evidence — OD.

There are objective signs of diminished papilledema —

OD—1 diopter of elevation

OS —2 diopters of elevation

The remarkable change is the fact that there are no hemorrhages in OS as previously seen.

There is still an occasional diploplia which I'm inclined to feel is due to the refractive difference in her eyes.

This increase of vision in her left eye from 20/40-1 to 20/25-1 is phenomenal.

On the whole, much improved.

Report of Eye Specialist, October 26, 1956

Patient seen October 19, 1956:

Vision: OD—20/200
OS —20/20-2
Corneal reflexes normal.
OD Left cornea less sensitive than right.

Anisocoria: OD—3mm
OS —4mm

Interior: ophthalmoscopic:
OD—3 diopters of papilledema
OS —3 diopters of papilledema
I can detect no hemorrhages.

Intermittent diplopia —

Discussion: Visual acuity in OS has apparently increased; however, the papilledema has *increased* since last examination.

o   o   o

As to increased papilledema:

I observed it also in other cases *temporarily*, indicating hyperemia in the scars and whatever is left of the tumor, repeated flare-ups, so-called allergic healing inflammations.

Report of X-ray Specialist, June 21, 1950

Examination of the dorsal spine reveais no evidence of bony or joint pathology.

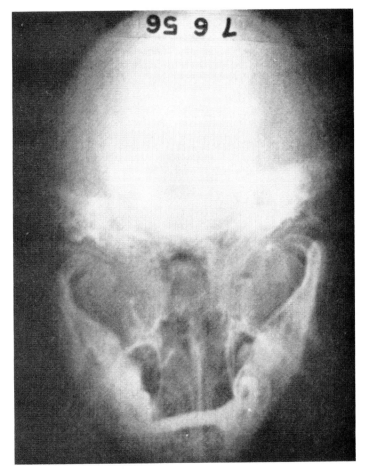

Case 3, No. 2 — 7/6/56

Report of X-ray Specialist, December 20, 1950

Examination of the skull reveals no evidence of bony pathology.

Report of X-ray Specialist, December 7, 1955

X-ray Examination of Chest, P.A. and Lateral Views.
A small streak-like shadow is seen above the diaphragm.
These findings point to old pleural thickenings.
A small calcareous deposit is seen in the left upper lobe.
There is an operative defect of the right 6th rib.
No other pathological conditions are revealed.

Report of X-ray Specialist, May 22, 1956

X-ray Examination of the Skull, P.A., Lateral View and Base.

The fossae digitatae throughout the cranium are considerably deep.

There is a defect at the apex of the petrous bone involving also the adjacent portion of the great wing of the sphenoid bone pointing to a metastasis.

CASE No. 4

Mr. P. V., age—16 years.

Clinical Diagnosis: (After operation.) Spongioblastoma, left part thalamus.

Biopsy report and operation findings:

Initial complaints, headaches and double vision intermittently for two and a half years. Numbness of the left side of the face for three and a half months. Objective findings on physical examination.

1. Healed scar of right frontal craniotomy, and healed scar over bioccipital hole.
2. Bilateral homonymous hemianopsia.
3. Pale optic discs.
4. Double vision on upward and downward gaze.
5. Hyperesthesia, and paresthesia over the left face, left anterior trunk, left leg and foot.
6. Right homonymous hemianopsia without macular sparing.

Laboratory work: Urine analysis negative.

Spinal fluid: Clear and colorless. Protein 30 mg.%. Pandy 0.

Wasserman negative.

Blood Kahn negative.

Diagnostic procedures:

1. Feb. 20, 1950. "It must be concluded that this E. E. G. gives no significant change which could be referable to the thalamic lesion, even in testing responses to photic stimulation with nostrazol."
2. March 20, 1950. This E. E. G. shows remarkably little abnormality, considering the content and location of the lesion in the thalamus.
3. X-ray of the skull: March 17, 1950. Left fronto-tempero-

parietal craniotomy with a free bone flap, not displaced. There is a small collection of fluid underneath the flap. There has been removal of a good deal of the anterior part of the left temporal lobe. Posteriorly and medically calcification can still be seen, indicating the presence of residual tumor.

4. Encephalogram: Feb. 2, 1950. There is an expanding lesion in the middle, and posterior portions of the left thalamus. There is not a great deal of difference between the pneumographic picture now and that of 1947, from Zurich.

Operation, Feb. 28, 1950.

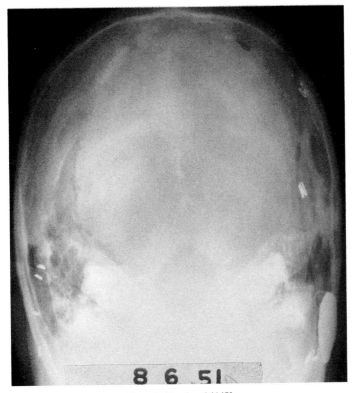

Case 4, No. 1 — 8/6/51

Left osteoplastic craniotomy and removal of tumor. Summary: this neoplasm is highly cellular. It seems to be a glioma. It is calcified in its central portion. It was anterior to the pons, and above the tentorium as well as in the thalamus. Further X-ray therapy might be advisable. The patient became aphasic on the 3rd post-operative day, but even at that time was mentally alert and seemed to understand verbal command and to be oriented. On the same day, evidence of a left third nerve paralysis became apparent, a left complete 5th had been present from the last post-operative day, this included motor function. Speech recovery was gradual but continual and continuing at the time of discharge. Initial speech began as a conglomeration of French, German, Hungarian, and classical Latin. French speech returned first, after that Hungarian and then English. The wound healed without evident complication. At the time of discharge, the patient showed a complete left 5th, including both sensory and motor components and all sensory divisions. His left 3rd weakness had improved, the left pupil was still larger than the right, and a slight reaction was sluggish and so were the corresponding eye movements. The hyperesthesia and paresthesia noted above in admission examination had completely disappeared from the left anterior trunk, left leg and foot. Reading was difficult for the patient but possible and he wrote well. Recent memory was poor and concentration limited.

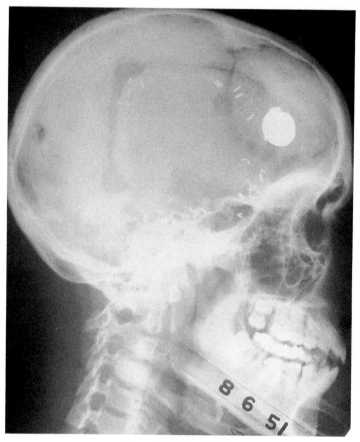

Case 4, No. 2 — 8/6/51

Condition when first seen, June 17, 1951. In the last two weeks patient observed that the right half of upper and lower lid became paralyzed. Since three to four weeks, his gait was worse, the balance became very difficult, he could not write, as he did not feel the pencil in his hand.

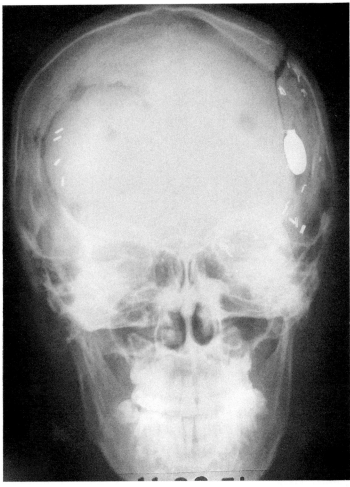

Case 4, No. 3 — 11/23/51

Since the last operation, the left eye has closeu. He could open it, but liked to close it, in order to avoid double vision. He felt weaker than any time before, but gained 10 pounds since January, 1951. After the operation, there started a flow of saliva on the left side, and when the numbness of the right part of the lid occurred, it flew out, also, on the right side. It was uncontrollable for him. Right arm and right leg were very much reduced in motility. He observed that after the first operation, his sense of smell was lost; it returned after the second operation somewhat on the left side. He complained that he had a very bad smell inside of himself, while "the others" cannot smell anything outside.

The patient looked pale and depressed, spoke abruptly, not clearly pronounced. In the following weeks, right leg and arm became somewhat spastic, with increased tendon reflexes.

The X-ray studies revealed: extensive operative defects of the skull-bilateral. Large area of finely stippled calcifications in the lower posterior and medial portion of the parietal lobe or thalamus opticus.

After the first operative findings and the second operative findings from two authorities in neurosurgery, the parents were given a fatal prognosis in a relatively short time. Patient was reexamined April 21, 1955, in Montreal; he was in good condition, deeply interested in music, had a great musical library of records, mostly classical. He spoke more with a remarkable skill of the right halves of the upper and lower lip. His tongue was still drawn a little bit to the right, his feeling all over the body was mostly restored, but the motility of the right arm and leg was only partly restored. He reported that he could see much better than a long time ago.

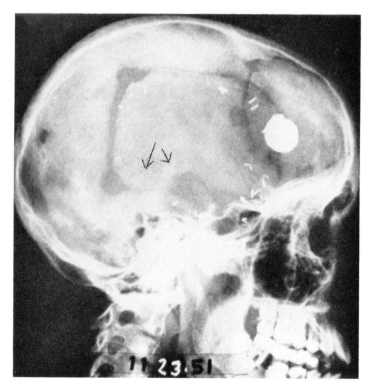

Case 4, No. 4 — 11/23/51

X-ray Report

I have re-X-rayed the skull of P. V., as you instructed (11-23-51). I have also compared present films with the films taken in the Montreal Neurological Institute on March 17, 1950, i.e., shortly after his operation. As far as I can see, no gross changes have occurred since March, 1950.

The absence of any displacement of the calcification would speak against further growth of the tumor.

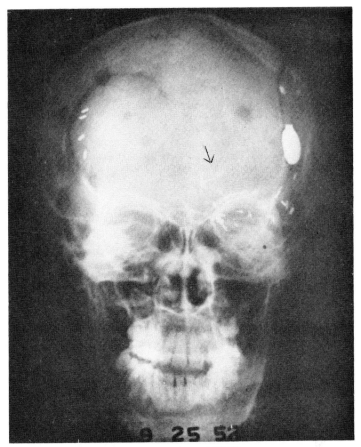

Case 4, No. 5 — 9/25/52

The patient remained unfit for practical life, he was a burden for the family. The ailing mother could no longer prepare the diet without help. For this reason the treatment was discontinued.

Such cases with a chronically deteriorated liver can be saved only and kept alive with the continuation of the treatment, which can be eased only to a certain degree. A number of similar cases, operated on the brain and treated with X-rays showed equally disappointing conditions. The damages on the floor of the third brain ventricle, where the neurovegetative centers are situated, belong to this category.

Last Report, July 27, 1957

After this case was submitted to the publisher, I was informed that the boy died suddenly on June 8, 1957, and that the therapy had been discontinued for two years against my advice.

CASE No. 5

(See Table, page 235.)

Rev. R. W. C., age 35 years, married, two children.

Clinical Diagnosis: Cerebellar Pontine Angle Tumor.

Previous History

In March, 1955, patient observed that his hearing on the telephone was diminished. A few months before he felt a condition of soreness and acidity in the left half of his mouth.

Patient had sinus trouble since boyhood; since 1940 the trouble was more pronounced in frontal sinuses. Tonsillectomy August, 1940; appendectomy July, 1940.

Patient had psycho-analytical therapy in several clinics, and osteopathic treatments for temporal stiffness in neck and aches in lower spine, which was more outspoken when under tension. A year ago there was a tendency to a tic in lower left eyelid and a tingling sensation on left half of tongue; speech remained free, while in the last months a numbness developed in lower left corner of mouth. Periodically there was some dizziness and loss of equilibrium, then a walking automatically to the right. There was a buzzing in left ear, in which there was loss of hearing.

During that period, hearing of the other ear increased as well as sensitivity on the other half of face.

Report of Head of Neurosurgical Department, University of Pennsylvania

"On February 17, 1956, I saw your patient Rev. R. W. C. This is a 35-year-old white, married, male Baptist Minister who has had decreased hearing in the left ear, paresthesias in the left side of the face, occasional unsteadiness of gait, all of which have been present for about a year. In addition, he had had a major nervous breakdown while in college, and he has tended to be a high-strung, tense individual.

On examination I found that he had slight weakness of the facial nerve on the left side and he also had some slight loss of sensation of the left cornea and left side of the face. There was also very definite clinical evidence of loss of hearing on the left side. The balance of the neurological examination was normal.

In this patient we are dealing with a lesion involving the fifth, seventh and eighth nerves on the left side. The differential diagnosis, of course, lies between an inflammatory lesion and a *cerebellar pontine angle tumor*. I have planned to review the X-rays and if the suspicion of an acoustic neuroma is sustained by this examination, it may be necessary to admit him to the hospital sometime in the next month for electro-encephalography, vestibular tests, and consideration of a sub-occipital craniotomy.

This was a most interesting patient."

P.S. "Since dictating the above, I have reviewed the X-rays and seem to feel that this is an acoustic neuroma, and have advised the patient to enter the hospital within the next three or four weeks. He stated that he would discuss the problem with you and would let me know as to his decision."

Condition when first seen: March 8, 1956

Left corner of mouth cannot be lifted up, left soft palate and uvula drawn to right, gait unsteady, when eyes closed patient cannot turn left.

Skin and tendon reflexes essentially normal, except both knee-reflexes weak — sensibility reduced on left side at face, neck and lower abdomen, no ataxia, not spastic.

Audiogram: left ear negative,
           right ear in normal range.

At the end of September, 1956, he was less depressed, *walked* much better with closed eyes; there was unsteadiness only when he was tired. The left corner of the mouth and soft palate were in normal position.

May, 1957, worked for 6 months, first part-time, later did all work except house visits.

Psychic much freer and showed more self-confidence.

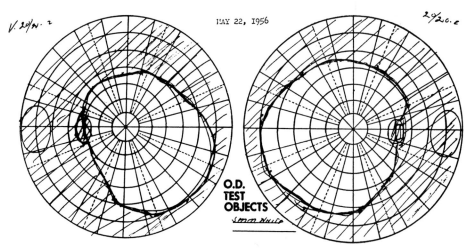

Case 5, No. 1 — 5/22/56

Reports of X-ray Specialist, March 9, 1956

X-ray examination of the Skull, P. A., Lateral Views and Base. No definite bony changes are seen. But it must be mentioned that the region of the Clivus Blumenbachi appears somewhat thinned.

July 24, 1956.

Lateral View of Skull.

There is about the same condition as seen on March 9, 1956.

Reports of Eye Specialist, May 22, 1956

Vision: OD—20/20-2
        OS —20/20-2

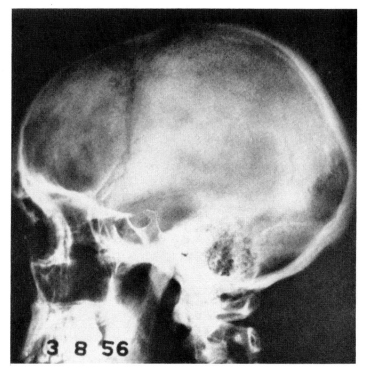

Case 5, No. 1 — 3/8/56

Anisocoria: Pupil OD larger than OS
Corneal sensitivity: OD—apparently normal sensitivity.
OS: I'm not able to elicit any corneal reflex — apparently completely
    anesthetic.
Conjugate movements all normally full except limited upward gaze —
    fine component nystagmus in all conjugate gazes. It is interesting
    to note that the right lateral gaze elicits an increased varying
    component (this is to be expected in cerebello pontine angle
    tumors).
Pupils dilated for a careful interior study:
    OD—Normally outlined — venules moderately engorged.
    OS —Nasal margin slightly hazy — venules engorged.
Impression: Cerebello pontine angle tumor.
Fields: enclosed.

June 21, 1956:
Vision: OD—20/20
        OS —20/20
Pupils equal — no anisocoria apparent today.
OD—Corneal reflex normal.
OS —Diminished corneal sensitivity, but the sensitivity has definitely
    improved.
No limitation of upward gaze detected today.

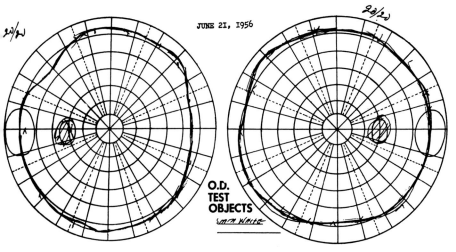

JUNE 21, 1956

O.D.
TEST
OBJECTS
5mm White

Case 5, No. 2 — 6/21/56

Nystagmus on extreme lateral gaze.
I can see no change objectively in nystagmus.
The fundi generally, and the vasculature are apparently within the
limits of normal.
Fields enclosed.

November 2, 1956:
Mild palpebral conjunctivitis, probably a temporary thing, resulting
from recent virus infection.
Pupils equal.
OD—Corneal reflex normal.
OS —Slightly diminished reflex.
    Conjugate excursions full.
    No muscle involvement.
Interior: Normal.
    Diminished symptoms.

January 25, 1957:
No diplopia detected.
Cannot detect any anisocoria.
Slightly diminished corneal reflex OS.
Interior normal.
No muscle anomalies, either concomitant or paralytic.
Conjugate excursions full.
Field test (confrontation test shows no field changes).

March 29, 1957:
Vision: OD—20/20
        OS —20/20
Pupils equal, regular in outline and react consensually and directly.
OD—Corneal reflex normal.
OS —There is probably a slightly diminished sensitivity in the left cornea.

Conjugate excursions full . . . On extreme lateral gazes, a fine intermittent nystagmus develops.

The papillae, vasculature and fundi generally are normal.

Fields were plotted and found to be within normal limits.

May 17, 1957:

Fields normal.

Symptoms attenuated.

P.S. When I first saw this patient, the papillae were distinct, but at
that time I thought the venules were abnormally distended — today, I'm not impressed by this, and it is my opinion that the
entire vasculature picture is objectively normal.

August 1, 1957:

Vision: 20/20—OD
            20/20—OS

The eye findings are identical to those of May 17, at last eye study.
Vasculature is grossly normal.

The fields were accomplished. Copy enclosed.

The fields, if any change is present since last study, appear to be a little
improved.

December, 1957:

Patient in normal condition and has been working full time for more
than one year.

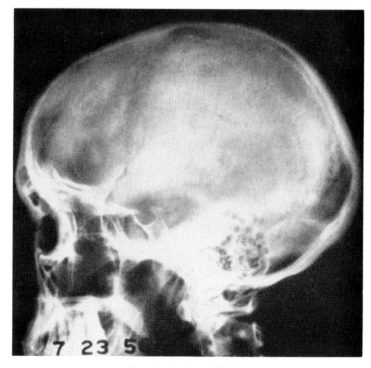

Case 5, No. 2 — 7/23/56

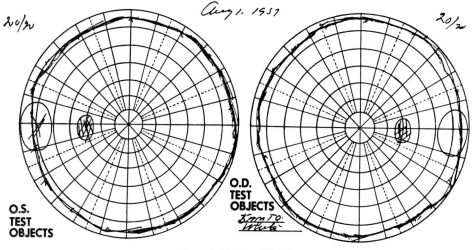

Case 5, No. 3 — 8/1/57

CASE No. 6

Mr. G. C. S., age—47.

Clinical Diagnosis: Pituitary Tumor.

Previous History

Report from Queens General Hospital revealed the following: "Patient admitted to the hospital July 6, 1953, with chief complaint of severe headaches and greater loss of vision in the last one and a half months. More progressive loss of vision over 4 to 5 years, known as luetic since the age of 21 — treated. Admission diagnosis was chiasmal lesion."

"Visual fields showed greatly diminished vision in both eyes, greater in the left. The cerebro angiogram showed probable presence of a mass of the frontal or fronto-parietal area, probably a meningioma, which may explain the loss of vision and the psychotic episodes of the past. Patient was discharged to return later for surgery, July 20, 1953."

Wasserman Blood 4 plus. Blood sugar 78 mg.%.

X-ray of the skull: A curvilinear radiolucent defect is noted in the left frontal region which appears to be a residual of previous surgery. The optic foramina are symmetrical and of normal size bilaterally. No evidence of erosion or encroachment on either optic foramina. The sella turcica is not enlarged or deepened. The anterior clinoid appears normal. The posterior clinoids and the dorsum sellae appear somewhat thinned and demineralized. This may possibly be of clinical significance although it cannot be stated that there is any unequivocal destruction. The floor of the sella appears normal.

Angiography: The anterior cerebral artery appears to be displaced upwards, laterally and posteriorly, more marked on the right side than on the left, suggesting a continguous space-occupying lesion anteriorly situated.

Electroencephalogram showed a normal record.

Chest X-ray negative.

Final Diagnosis: Brain tumor. Patient refused operation after discussion with brother, who is M.D.

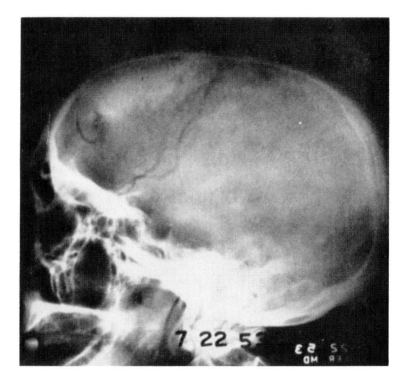

Condition when first seen July 22, 1953. Patient was almost blind; he could hardly find his way in his own room, and had to feel his way around. He complained about continuous deep headaches and dizziness; his equilibrium was disturbed when he stood up and tried to walk, and he staggered and was unsteady. Patient had heavy dull pain in front and back of skull, and in addition, sharp shooting pain in right supraorbital area, lasting some minutes. Tendon and skin reflexes showed no special significance.

X-ray examination by specialist July 23, 1953, showed the following: The upper portion of the dorsum sellae was very thin and decalcified. The posterior clinoid processes were small and irregular. The anterior clinoid processes appeared to be normal.

The findings had to arouse the suspicion of a tumor in the region of the dorsum sellae.

The upper medial border of the right orbita was rather thin as compared with the left side.

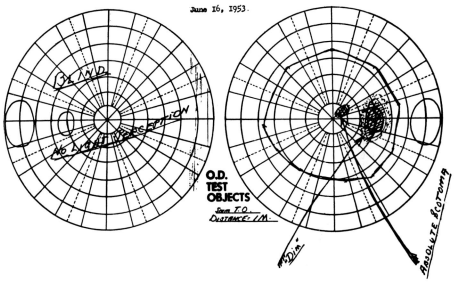

June 16, 1953.

O.D.
TEST
OBJECTS
5mm T.O.
Distance: 1 M.

Case 6, No. 1 — 6/16/53

No pathological conditions of the optic foramina were seen.

In the following days headaches and pain decreased, but there was a twitching in the right facialis area, sometimes strong and painful.

At the end of September, 1953, patient was free of pain, headaches, dizziness; gait was free and sure, right facialis became normal after 2 weeks and remained normal. In December, 1953, he went back to work, could see with the left eye much better than he could in a long time; however, he could not see so well in the center. The vision of the right eye was normal as far as reading and writing were concerned. Wasserman reaction (blood) taken May 26, 1954, was negative, without antiluetic therapy.

Reports of Eye and X-ray Specialists, February 6, 1954

X-ray Examination of the Skull. P. A. and Lateral Views (Contr. Films).

There is a slight increase in calcification at the dorsum sellae and the posterior clinoid processes.

Otherwise there is the same condition as before.

At the end of 1954, patient passed examination as insurance agent and

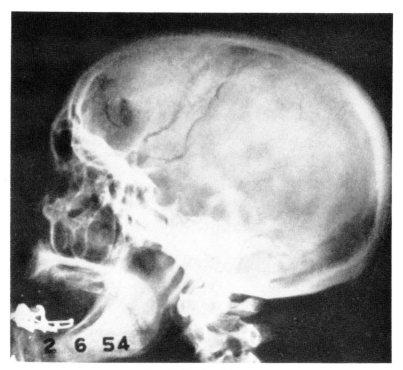

Case 6, No. 2 — 2/6/54

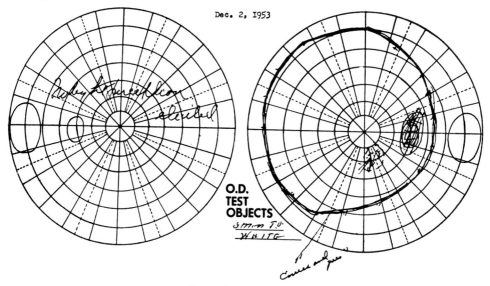

Case 6, No. 2 — 12/2/53

started studies for bar examination. Because of that intensive work, he gave up diet and treatment gradually more and more. In March, 1955, the condition in left eye showed a recurrence and patient could hardly differentiate fingers; the right eye remained good. In May, 1955, the right eye became worse and showed new deterioration. Reexamination on June 6, 1955, showed the following vision field and eye examination:

June 16, 1955:
Vision: OD—20/30
   OS —No light perception elicited — present glasses.
Pupillary status: OD—Direct reaction to light and convergence limited.
       No consensual from OD to OS elicited.
     OS —No direct or consensual reaction elicited.
       No consensual from OS to OD.
Corneal sensitivity: normal — no nystagmus — no paralytic or concomitant muscle anomalies.
Intra-ocular tension: normal.
Ophthalmoscopic study: OD—Media clear except a few floaters in anterior vitreous.
         Vasculature study shows a moderate narrowing of the entire retinal arteriolar tree. Pallor of papilla more marked on temporal side.
The atrophy is objectively primary — typical of pituitary adenoma (?)
OS—Media clear except a few floaters in anterior vitreous. Marked narrowing of retinal arteriolar tree. Optic atrophy — primary in character.
Field study: Lack of light perception prevents field study in left eye.
OD—Field has the following characteristics:
  1. Narrowing of field.
  2. Enlarged blind spot with "Dim" about its periphery Para-central scotoma in superior temporal quadrant.
Interpretation: The field is not typical of a pituitary adenoma; however, in my more than twenty years of experience I have found this bizarre type of field present in such cases as this.
At the end of July, 1955, patient recovered again and felt fairly well restored except for the vision in the left eye. The re-examination of the eyes and vision field December 2, 1955, showed the following:

December 2, 1955:
Vision—OD—20/25
   OS —No change since last visit.
     Light perception questionable — present glasses.
OD—Limited reactions to light and convergence stimulation.
   No consensual from OD to OS.
OS —No consensual or direct reaction to convergence or light stimulation.
   Corneal sensitivity normal, no nystagmus, no concomitant or paralytic muscle anomalies.
Intra ocular tension normal.
Interior study:
  OD—Few floaters in anterior vitreous, moderate temporal pallor of discs.

OS –Few opacities in vitreous – advanced optic atrophy.
Very marked narrowing of vasculature.
The field (OD) is improved.

In November, 1955, he was very satisfied with his bodily and mental condition and had no special complaints.

August 3, 1957:
Vision: OD–20/70-1
OS –No light perception.
Eyes white and quiet – A C normal.
Anisocoria: OD larger than OS
Pupils irregular.
Light and convergence reactions present in OD.
No direct or consensual reactions elicited in OS.
Unable to definitely demonstrate consensual reaction from OD to OS.
Interior: OD–Rather marked pallor and vessels moderately narrowed.
OS –Waxen pallor OD advanced atrophy objectively.
OS –Waxen pallor od advanced atrophy objectively.
Vasculature markedly narrowed.
Intra ocular tension–OD–18
OS –18
Studying and working. Discontinued treatment Christmas 1956.

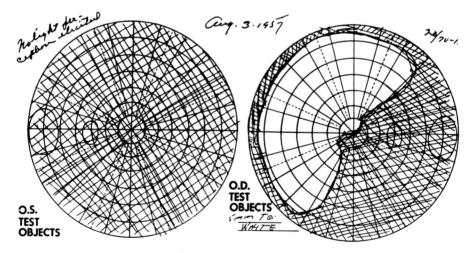

Case 6, No. 3 – 8/3/57

CASE No. 7

Girl A. H., age—15.

Clinical Diagnosis: (Post-operative): Cervical and Upper Thoracic Intramedullary Glioma.

Previous History

Patient was admitted to Beth Israel Hospital, Newark, September, 1945, at which time she gave a history of difficulty in walking, paresthesia and numbness of the right fourth and fifth fingers, coldness and numbness of right hand and lower arm with continual perspiration over the rest of the body. The coldness and numbness spread gradually to both hands and arms. Menstruation had ceased and severe weakness was present. Patient complained of severe pain, localized from the back to the neck, to the head and forehead; she was afebrile.

A diagnosis of spinal cord tumor was made and on October 15, 1945, an extensive laminectomy was performed with removal of laminae from dorsal one to dorsal three. Consequently, the laminectomy was extended upwards in two stages until the spines and laminae of cervical four to cervical seven were also removed. Hospital report reads: "Here too the dura was tense and on opening it the cord in this region had a glistening reddish-grey appearance as if it was completely infiltrated with gliomatous tissue.

"The cord bulged through the opening in the dura. Exploration laterally and anteriorly was carried out to be sure we were not dealing with an anteriorly placed extramedullary tumor. A fine needle then was inserted into the midline of the cord but no cystic fluid could be obtained. Inasmuch as the patient had fairly good motor power in the lower extremities, it was not deemed advisable to incise the cord for biopsy.

"The dura was left open for decompressive purposes and closure was completed using interrupted #1 catgut in layers for muscle and fascia."

Following administration of one X-ray treatment, patient was near a collapse and this treatment was discontinued.

Condition at time first seen, October 27, 1945: Patient gave history of extreme weakness and of three to four severe attacks of muscle spasm in both lower arms and shoulders following the operation. These symptoms were present in addition to the above described ones. Physical examination revealed essentially the following: marked weakness in the right whole arm and hand associated with a moderate degree of cyanosis and numbness in the right little finger, right Babinski, missing right upper abdominal reflexes, deep tendon reflexes increased bilaterally, enlarged pupils, marked ataxia in finger to finger and finger to nose movements, imbalance and uncertainty present.

Neurological examinations were confirmed by neurologist who was in accord with the operative report.

My treatment started immediately. The patient gradually improved but in the following year she had three serious so-called "flare-ups." During one of these, in October, 1946, neurological examination revealed a lack of sensation in the right hand, an increase in both patellar reflexes, marked clonus in both ankles, marked positive Babinski bilaterally; it was decided that the patient had taken a turn for the worse, despite the possible expected beneficial effects of original decompression.

From this point on she improved steadily. Neurological reexamination in May, 1948, by the same consultant revaled "a definite improvement." The only residual signs present were a slight hyperactivity of the knee jerks and a positive Babinski on the right. After four years treatment with the dietary regime the patient typed, danced, skated with little or no evidence of any previous serious neurological disease.

BLOOD COUNT REPORTS

	4/2/46	1/27/47	4/25/47	6/6/47	2/9/48
Hemoglobin	90%	92%	70%	70%	80%
Red Blood Count	4,320,000	4,550,000	5,720,000	4,010,000	4,140,000
White Blood Count	9,750	5,700	9,350	6,200	9,450
Differential:					
Polys	52%	71%	60%	55%	58%
Lymphocytes	28%	25%	36%	39%	36%
Monocytes	10%		1%	4%	3%
Eos.		1%			
Basoph.		1%		2%	
Stabs.		2%	3%		3%
Bands.	10%				

Basal Metabolic Rate:

January 27, 1947	April 25, 1947	June 16, 1947	February 9, 1948
plus 16%	−4%	−4%	plus 1%

Patient stayed on the diet till middle of 1949; for three years, all was well. In July, 1952, she started to complain about pain in the middle of her head and dizziness with some sudden black-outs. These black-outs lasted one to two seconds and appeared three to four times a day. The right leg started to become weaker; when she walked, the leg became stiff and the right arm spastic. Later, the fingers of the right hand lost the strength so that she could not keep a book or a piece of paper in the right hand. She had to eat at that time with the left hand. At the end of July a diagnosis of brain tumor was made, localized in the middle part of the left basic center. Treatment was immediately applied and patient recovered from pain and weakness in the following months. Beginning December, 1952, she was free of pain, free of dizziness, right leg became stronger, and she could walk up and down stairs but the right arm showed stiffness and slight ataxia. She was last seen June 28, 1956. In the last two years she went off the diet more or less; stiffness in the right arm and fingers increased and reduced the use of the right arm and hand to a high degree.

She has had some rehabilitation treatment and has been helped by a chiropractor. Patient remained free of pain and discomfort; there was no dizziness and no other disturbances. Vision was normal and hearing was, according to her own feeling, on the left side rather above normal (hyper-sensitive). Last report, 7-27-57. Patient reported that she will take mechanical treatments to improve stiffness and weakness in right arm and leg. She asked for my opinion and I had to inform her that I saw less favorable results from mechanical and rehabilitation treatments and more favorable results by the continuance of a moderate diet. Both results are not satisfactory but that is the best I can say, according to my experience.

This patient as some others, (about 15%) show that in some special cases the duration of the treatment cannot be determined. The restoration of the entire body functions, especially the liver, is decisive and later the maintenance of this restoration is important. Otherwise the best accomplishments remain partial results only or temporary healings. These observations render reexaminations of the metabolism unavoidable.

CASE No. 8

Mr. C- H. Ch., age—50, married, four children.

Clinical Diagnosis (postoperative): Cervical cord angioma.

Biopsy, operation and previous history:

"A 47-year-old Chinese male first noted impaired temperature sensation and some numbness over the left lower extremity. For 2 months he has noted pain in the region between the shoulders, on the right more than on the left. For about 1½ months he has had obstinate constipation, and for a week difficulty in voiding. For about a month there was also some weakness in left lower extremity beginning to involve the right leg a few days prior to admission.

"On examination there was slight unsteadiness in gait, a bit of weakness in the right lower extremity, deep reflexes greater on the right. There is a loss of temperature sensation on the left from about C7 down and diminished from about T3 down, at which point there appeared to be a sensory level. Tenderness was noted over the first thoracic spine. The spinal fluid was xantochromic and showed a partial block, the total protein was 50 mgms%.

"At operation a vascular malformation was found extending from C5 to T1. A pantopaque myelogram was done. One of the observers considered that it showed a vascular malformation.

Operation: 12-4-47:

"Cervical laminectomy for vascular malformation (angioma). Under local anesthesia, through an incision extending from C4 to T2 the spines and laminae of C6, C7 and T1 (?) were removed. When the dura was opened between guide sutures many abnormal tortuous arteries were exposed on the surface of the cord. The dura was closed and the wound sutured in the usual manner.

"Above patient admitted to Mount Sinai Hospital November 25, 1947, with history of impaired temperature sensation and some numbness over the left lower extremity. For two months he has noted pain in the region between the shoulders."

Previous history after operation: He had 19 deep X-ray treatments. After that treatment, both arms and legs were paralyzed, the whole body down from the neck. In my absence, he was treated by Dr. M. with my treatment beginning May, 1949. The swelling at both hands and arms improved; he could also feel hot and cold on both arms and along the body. He had appetite, was hungry, and could eat better. His mental capacity was always good.

Condition when first seen, Sept. 8, 1949. Patient complained about being paralyzed all over except for his neck and head. There was no active motility on both arms and hands as well as on the muscles of the body; both legs were stiff and showed only some involuntary jerking. He presented some spasms in both biceps, and wrist and finger joints particularly on the left hand. Temperature was slightly increased to 100 degrees, and a little above. Patient sat in a wheelchair; he was unable to control urine and stools, and could not feed himself. October, 1949. The patient was more energetic and less tired. Temperature was now—mostly normal. As to the motility, he improved his use of the right hand to a certain degree and fingers 1 to 3 of that hand. Also the left arm moved better, but there was no improvement in either leg; however, the whole body, arm and legs present no longer any swollen area. January, 1950: The condition of the patient improved somewhat more. The spasticity and involuntary cramps on both legs were greatly reduced; patient could sit straight on the bed, turn his body to the left side, and started to perspire, which he could not do since the operation. He could take the left arm backwards and stretch it out forward. The legs remained inactive. June, 1951: Patient could feel when the urine was coming, and wet the bed only once at night; stools were not yet controlled, but conformed to two to three times every twenty-four hours. December, 1952: Patient regained some activity. He could hold a glass as well as the telephone receiver with the left hand. Patient had a relatively fair control over his urination, but hadn't active control over elimination of stools; this is, however, regulated, timely, in the morning and in the night.

After the operation, his basal metabolism rate went down to minus 20 and even to minus 23, and it took a long time to bring it up again.

His last report was received on my request July 23, 1957. The interesting part is a good description of his present condition, how far the recovery has progressed, it may be given exceptionally.

Answering your request of July 23, I can truthfully say that I am ever grateful to you for your treatments and thankful for your concern over my health.

Your treatments have effectively restored almost to normalcy the functioning of internal organs. The digestive system has improved to such an extent that I can eat like a normal person without any bad effects. Of course, due to the lack of exercises, bowel movements are mechanically facilitated. Shortness of breath only appears under pressure of hot and humid weather. Anemia is gone and no more headache. I look like a normal person and friends are surprised at my rapid recovery. The only discouraging factor is that the nervous system doesn't indicate any betterment: no feeling in the lower part of the body; left hand can scarcely hold spoon or fork to feed myself; and the right hand is weak and has symptoms of spasm.

CASE No. 9

Mrs. A. B., age—30, married, two children.

Clinical Diagnosis: Chorionepithelioma, metastases in abdomen and lungs.

Biopsy Report, Maimonides Hospital, Brooklyn, N. Y.

"Fragments of endometrium showing syncytial elements. Status post-currettement revealing trophoblastic elements as in chorionepithelioma."

Previous History

December 16, 1952, menstruation occurred last. Six weeks later, there was bleeding. In the afternoon, she had a miscarriage. On January 25, 1953, the physician removed from vagina the remaining abortus substances. After a week of bed-rest, bleeding stopped; there was no scraping. Three days later, bleeding recurred. Ten days more of bed-rest were prescribed. In bed she had no bleeding, but bleeding set in immediately when she got up. On February 17, 1953, she was admitted to Maimonides Hospital, Brooklyn. Intravenous glucose, currettement was administered February 23, 1953. Two days later she was discharged. At home there was again bleeding. Aschheim-Zondek test positive, diagnosis, chorionepithelioma. March 4, 1953, she was admitted to Bellevue Hospital. Aschheim-Zondek was plus plus. On April 9, 1953, a total hysterectomy was performed. On April 20, she returned home. Urine examination on April 25, was positive. There was pain in right lower abdominal quadrant. Constipation was severe. Anemia developed; liver injection and iron pills were administered. Blood pressure was very low. When urinating, there was a pain in bladder, and occasionally a dull pain across the back. X-rays of lungs taken April 19 were negative. Electrocardiogram was normal, BMR plus 6. A creamy white discharge from vagina developed. She saw several prominent gynecologists; all regarded her as hopeless. One recommended 40 deep X-ray treatments. However, she could stand only one.

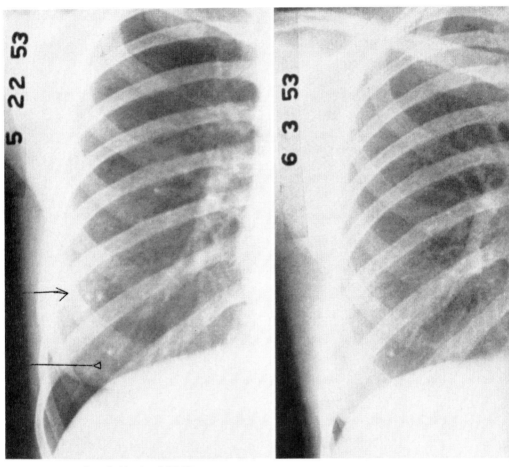

Case 9, No. 1 — 5/22/53   Case 9, No. 2 — 6/3/53

First seen May 4, 1953. Patient had terrific pain, localized mostly in the lower abdomen and lower back. Was confined to bed, lying there with bent and adducted legs on her abdomen. It was almost impossible to examine her, as every little touch was painful. There was a long, small mass palpable in right lower abdominal quadrant, size 4x1″ and two smaller masses, very painful on touch. The liver was enlarged, surface free as far as palpable. The spleen was not enlarged. The lungs showed nothing abnormal.

On May 19, Aschheim-Zondek in urine was negative, and in blood positive 1/20. At the end of May, patient was free of pain, and was up and around. By the beginning of June, no tumor or glands palpable. At the end of July, 1953, she felt normal, and had gained weight, going from 107 to 110 lbs. Aschheim-Zondek test positive till June 12, 1953.

On June 3, 1953, an X-ray examination showed irregular opacities in

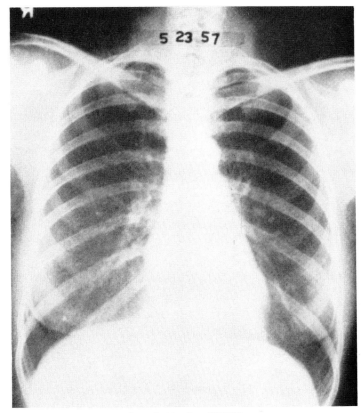

Case 9, No. 3 — 5/23/57

right lower lung field had decreased considerably. She recovered entirely in the months following and remained free of abnormal symptoms. Last heard of May 23, 1957. Last X-ray report: "*Chest:* The metastatic nodules previously noted in May, June, August, 1953, in the right 5th interspace, as well as in the left 6th interspace, are no longer in evidence." Patient was in good condition and normal working capacity.

CASE No. 10

Miss R. L., age—49.

Family History:

Father, Pancreas Ca; Mother, Breast Ca with bone metastases; both died.

Clinical Diagnosis: Chocolate cyst of left ovary, scirrhus carcinoma of right breast with regional lymph node involvement. Hyperparathyroidism, high blood pressure, angina pectoris.

Report of Hospital 2/18/47. Patient admitted.

Biopsy and Operations:

Patient has had low abdominal pain for many years—crampy and of colic nature, mostly marked after her periods. No metrorrhagia, no menorrhagia.

Onset of attack on the morning of admission was severe, compared to those in the past; there were cramps, nausea, vomiting. No temperature elevation. Pain had increased in severity. Had constipation for many years with hard movement requiring an enema. Pain radiated to pubis, but then was mostly in the RLQ.

Operation, February 19, 1947.

Findings: "There was a chocolate cyst of the left ovary, the size of a middle-sized grapefruit displacing the uterus somewhat to the right. Uterus was normal but contained subserous fibroid, somewhat larger than the size of a walnut, on its posterior wall. The right ovary was normal and contained at one pole a hemorrhagic cyst. The peritoneal cavity contained a good deal of greenish stained, non-odorous fluid with some brownish green flakes. A few reddish spots, of pinhead size, were noted on the uterine surface and the sclera of the pelvic colon, in all probability endo-metrical implants."

Pathological Report: "Left ovary with endometrial cyst: Left Fallopian tube endometriosis. Peritoneal fluid was sterile."

From "Pathology," Anderson, 1948, page 1143: "Endemetriosis of the tube signifies islands of endometrial character in the muscular wall of the tube developing by local downgrowth from tubal mucosa of abnormal endometrial character, or by local transformation of the islands of a tubal adenomyosis into endometrial character."

Report of Hospital to which patient was admitted 11/4/52

"Three weeks before admission, a mass was discovered at the Strang Clinic which was biopsied without result. One week later she was seen by the physician and presented an ill-defined hard tumefaction in the

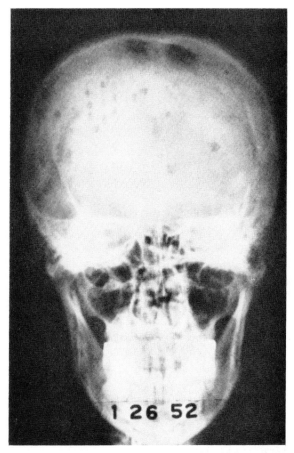

Case 10, No. 1 — 1/26/52

upper outer quadrant of her right breast with puncture mark of attempted needle biopsy. At the time, I was not sure how much the attempted needle biopsy was responsible for the tumefaction and since result of biopsy was negative, I waited one more week for possible changes in consistency. As there were none, hospitalization for biopsy was advised.

"At operation the day after entry, the mass was readily diagnosed as carcinoma which was confirmed by frozen section; therefore, a right radical mastectomy was performed."

Pathological Diagnosis: "Scirrhus ca of right breast with regional lymph node involvement."

Previous History:

1934 X-rays revealed calcium deposits or lesions in the skull, produced by seemingly parathyroid hypertrophy. Thirty-two deep X-ray treatments helped temporarily. In 1947 a chocolate cyst ruptured; patient was operated on in a Brooklyn Hospital for removal of left ovary and left tube. On November 5, 1952, there was a right radical mastectomy with spreading glands. When menstruation stopped in 1951, patient got estrogen hormones; menstruation returned and tumor developed one year later.

Condition when first seen, May 13, 1953: Patient gained too much weight and complained about shortness of breath with attacks of precordial pain. She could not stay long on her feet; there was frequent urination

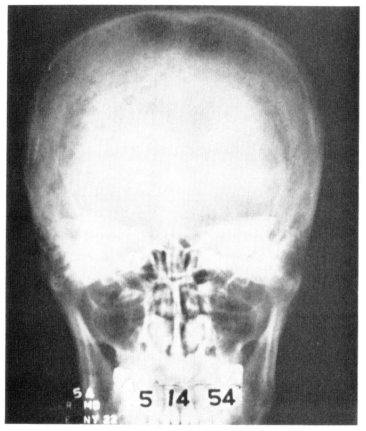

Case 10, No. 2 — 5/14/54

and high blood pressure; she was easily tired and exhausted. She looked nervous, restless and was easily excitable. Blood-pressure 178/102, 78 regular pulses, heart not enlarged, sounded weak. Lungs were free; there were several glands in right supraclavicular area. Abdomen was free, liver not enlarged, a little harder.

Treatment started immediately, July 28, 1953. Blood-pressure 138/94, 66 regular pulses, headaches reduced, less precordial pain, no menstruation. At the end of November, 1953, patient still complained of weakness in both legs, which showed some capillary bleedings. Vit. C.V.P. helped.

Against the menopause disturbances she took ovarian substance, 5 grn. each, two capsules, once a day up to the present which helps her against dizziness, perspiration and depression.

This case is a mixture of several pathological tissue symptoms. The abnormal metabolism caused on one hand various malignancies and on the other hand different deficiencies. The metabolic deficiencies were seemingly present first; the other disturbances are based upon these.

The calcium metabolism in serum was 8.8 to 9.9 mg% while phos-

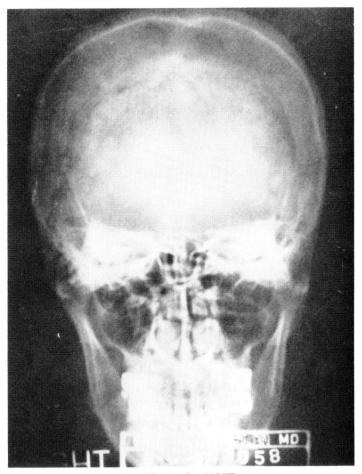

Case 10, No. 3 — 8/5/57

phorus was 3.8 to 4.2 mg%, both no longer characteristic during the treatment. Alkaline phosphatase was not examined. It was remarkable that the great arteries and the aorta did not show calcifications (see reports of X-rays 6/19/1956, 5/1/1957) and more remarkable was that "the skull became normal." (7/17/1956).

From "Pathology," Anderson, 1948, page 1081: "The increased parathyroid hormone mobilizes excess calcium from the bones, bringing about the skeletal changes described as osteitis fibrosa cystica. The blood contained an increased concentration of calcium and alkaline phosphatase, but a low level of phosphorus. The excess serum calcium tends to be precipitated in soft tissues, and may cause severe damage in such tissues as blood vessel walls and kidneys. Excessive amounts of calcium are excreted in the urine, and renal calculi are found in the majority of cases."

Tumors of Parathyroid Tissue: "Almost all cases of primary hyperparathyroidism are due to neoplastic overgrowth of functioning parathyroid tissue."

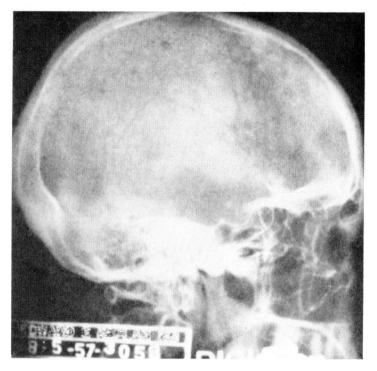

Case 10, No. 4 — 8/5/57

X-ray Reports

May 24, 1953.
X-ray Examination of the Skull (Both Directions).
X-ray Examination of the Chest (Both Directions).
Numerous small irregular defects are distributed over both parietal and upper frontal bones. (Difficult to see in reproductions).
The findings are compatible with the clinical diagnosis of hyperparathyroidism.
No pathological conditions of the lungs are revealed.

Hospital Report – Outpatient Dept.

July 17, 1956.
Blood: glucose - 112; serology - negative; CBC - normal; urinalysis - normal
X-ray of chest revealed the heart to be of aortic configuration, not increased; lung fields are clear, no metastic foci.
X-ray of the skull – normal.
May 1, 1957.
X-ray of the chest: The heart is of the aortic configuration, not increased in size with a para-vertebral aorta in evidence. The lung fields are fairly clear and well aerated. Thickening of the main interlobar fissure on the right side can be seen. No metastatic focci demonstrable.

CASE No. 11

Mr. E.B., age–31, married, three children.

Clinical Diagnosis: Right testicle Terratoma (Embryonal Cell Carcinoma) with regrowing mass in right inguinal area and many metastases in periaortic glands and both lungs.

Biopsy report: Embryonal cell carcinoma of testicle.

"In August of 1955 the right testicle was removed and a radical periaortic node dissection was done for an embryonal cell carcinoma of the testicle. All the nodes along the aortic chain were involved with metastatic cancer. Following the surgery he had extensive X-ray therapy to the back, chest and mediastinum. In March of 1956 an X-ray revealed the presence of metastatic nodules in the chest. At the time of his departure from here he was receiving additional X-ray therapy to the metastatic nodules in the lung.

"It is our feeling that this is a hopeless problem and any further treatment other than symptomatic relief as symptoms develop is unnecessary."

It started with enlargement of glands in the right groin in April, 1955. Then the patient found a lump in the right testicle. Two months later he noticed tenderness in testicle, swelling of the spermatic cord and quick growth of inguinal glands, more on the right side. On August II, 1955,

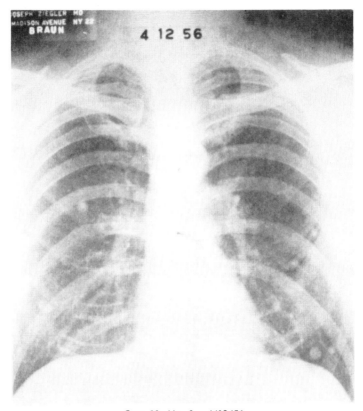

4 12 56

Case 11, No. 1 — 4/12/56

operation as described above was performed, followed by extensive X-ray treatments, altogether 82.

About mid-December, 1955, he felt a lump on dorsum penis, size of 8 cm in length and 2 cm in breadth. March, 1956, X-rays revealed metastases in both lungs.

Condition when first seen, April 13, 1956: There was a large tumor mass in right inguinal area, the pubic hairs at the right half of the abdomen were vacant, caused most probably by X-ray therapy. The abdomen was distended and resistant to pressure. It was therefore difficult to examine for mesenterial glands, spleen and liver. The chest did not show any dullness nor remarkable changes in breathing. The heart was not enlarged, the sounds weak but normal, blood pressure 100/70, pulse 84 regular, weight 184 lbs. Patient looked pale and was nervous, Hemoglobin 75%, 4.500.000 red blood cells, leucocytes 4.200, some cells showed toxic granules. From the chemical examinations it was remarkable that his basal metabolism was low, −17, and remained in ups and downs for a long time on the lower side, September 18, 1956 −21, January 24, 1957 −16, and July 9, 1957 —4, despite an intensive treatment of larger doses of thyroid and lugol solution. The tumor masses in the right groin disappeared in

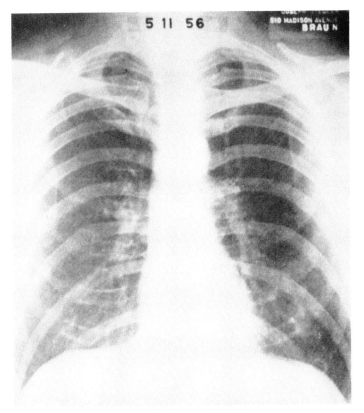

5 11 56

Case 11, No. 2 — 5/11/56

about 4 weeks; the penis tumor started to decrease about the same time but then disappeared entirely in about 5 days. According to my experiences the penis tumor was most probably not a metastatic tumor, but a more benign type responding to the treatment much later than the more malignant growth and their metastases. The lung metastases responded relatively quick; however, a much longer time is required to absorb the older settlements after the first disappearance of the fresh metastases. The description of the X-rays follows:

April 13, 1956 — X-ray examination of chest, P. A. and lateral views.

A number of rounded, mostly bean-sized opacities were seen in the lower half of the left lung field and a single one in the middle of the right lung field.

They were due to metastases.

The lung markings towards the left lower lobe were increased.

Some calcareous deposits were seen in both hila.

Note a suspicious area of translucency in the lower anterior portion of the 7th dorsal vertebra body.

May 12, 1956 — Control X-ray examination of chest, P. A. and lateral views.

The previously seen opacities in the left lung have decreased in number. The opacity in the right lung has nearly disappeared.

May 26, 1956 — Control X-ray examination of chest, P. A. and lateral views.

"Some of previously described opacities in the left lower lung field were smaller and some were no longer visible.

On the right side they were scarcely recognizable anymore."

April 30, 1957 — X-ray of chest, P. A. and lateral views.

A moderate amount of bihilar adenopathy was visualized with several nodules therein.

The pulmonary markings of both pulmonic fields were slightly accentuated.

The heart was not enlarged.

Trachea and both diaphragms were normal.

Both costo-phrenic sinuses were clear.

CONCLUSIONS:

Slight peribronchial thickening.

Last report, October 5, 1957: He is feeling fine, is working and is making good progress.

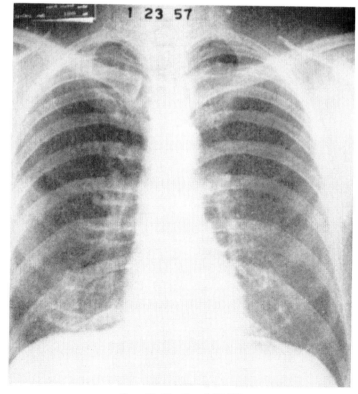

Case 11, No. 3 — 1/23/57

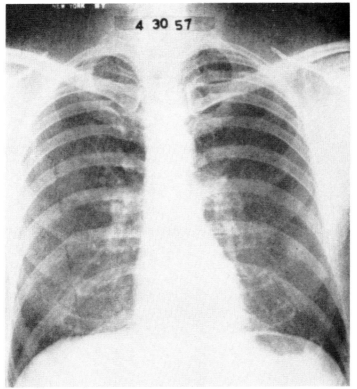

Case 11, No. 4 — 4/30/57

CASE No. 12

Mrs. V. G., age—28, married, one child.

Clinical Diagnosis: Spreading Melano-Sarcoma.

Previous History and Biopsy:

"The above-named patient was admitted to the hospital June 30, 1946, as the private patient of Dr. M. She complained of a growing mass in the left groin of two weeks' duration.

"The patient gave a history of having had a pigmented mole removed from her left ankle about one year previously. A few months later another "mole" appeared in close relation to the original site.

"A diagnosis was made of recurrent melanotic sarcoma of the left ankle with metastases to the inguinal glands.

"On July 1, 1946, excision of the melanoma and left inguinal node dissection were performed. Pathological examination revealed a diagnosis of melanoma with involvement of the inguinal nodes. Sections through the skin nodule showed that in the fibrous layer of the skin and elevating epidermis there was a small tumor nodule of a malignant type. The cells had some of the characteristics of a nevus, as they tended to grow in broad sheets and sometimes the nuclei were somewhat polygonal instead of rounded, and the whole seemed to be surrounded by a thin capsule, thus simulating nerve. This type of tumor is a malignant one; there are numerous mitoses. It has, however, some of the morphological characteristics which would indicate an origin from nerve endings. The nodes in the various groups were involved by tumor, only one of the smallest ones not showing metastases. The cellular tissue and fat were not involved."

Operation report: "Mrs. G. was operated upon in September of 1945 by another surgeon in New York for the removal of a small tumor of the left ankle. The original pathological diagnosis was benign. The later review of the sections, however, showed it to be a melanotic sarcoma.

"About three months ago patient noticed some swelling in the upper inner portion of the thigh which progressively increased. She was seen by me on June 27, 1946. At that time it was obvious that there was a recurrence of the tumor on the ankle and the swelling in the thigh was probably a metastatic gland from the original tumor. She was operated upon around July 1 by me, and an inguinal and sub-inguinal dissection was carried out together with a local excision of the tumor of the ankle. The pathological report of both tissues showed melanotic sarcoma."

"She has returned to her home in Alabama with a small open wound in the sub-inguinal region; there developed considerable induration and swelling at the site of the former enlarged gland. Whether this was purely a circulatory response to the removal of the lymphatic drainage in this area or a local recurrence immediately, I cannot say. Mrs. G. understood the seriousness of the situation. She came to convalesce and to see whether this local excision was sufficient. The dissection was carefully marked and examination of the upper limits in the inguinal region, both near the pubis and as high as the superior iliac spine showed no evidence of extension. The main tumor mass was low down, just below the femoral canal."

My previous History:

Patient noticed a non-healing skin wound over the left ankle, 1941 to 1945. In September, 1945, the non-healing skin area was excised at the Beekman St. Hospital, New York, biopsy showing melano sarcoma. In June, 1946, there was a recurrence of the tumor at the site of the operation on the left ankle, as well as appearance of several dark nodules in the left inguinal area. A second operation was performed at St. Lukes Hospital, New York, July 1, 1946. At that time the tumor at the inguinal site was excised and an extensive dissection of the left inguinal lymph nodes was made. Biopsy showed both to be melanotic sarcoma with obvious metastases

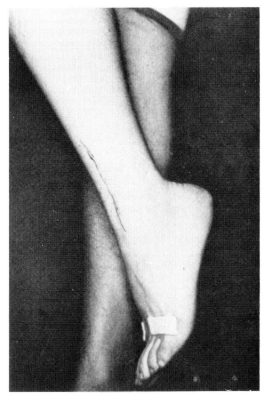

Case 12, No. 1

into the left inguinal area. Operation wound healed. At the end of August, 1946, two new recurrences occurred, one as large as a tomato above the femoral resection scar, a large dark subcutaneous mass, and the other as a hard nodule in the left adductor triangle below the scar of the last operation. Marked left ankle edema appeared. A hopeless prognosis was given to the patient's husband at this time.

Condition at time first seen in Gotham Hospital, New York, September 6, 1946: There was a large black subcutaneous tumor above the operation scar and a small node in adductor triangle.

After 3 months of treatment the tumor was barely palpable, the little node had disappeared. During the hospital treatment the tumor mass became red twice, swollen, hot and enlarged, lasting each time about two days. In January, 1947, no tumor could be found. Occasional ankle edema was present as well as frequent attacks of pain, both of which slowly disappeared in 1947.

In 1948 the patient went through a normal pregnancy with delivery of a healthy female baby in October, 1948. She remained well, free of any recedive and was last examined November 29, 1956. At that time she complained only that she has from time to time a swelling and soreness in left lower leg, especially ankle joint and foot. Then she limps a little and such a condition may last 5 to 10 days. The discomfort is limited to this place only, otherwise she is doing all her work; she took, in addition, singing lessons and was awarded with a prize. Through all the years her BMR remained low, about −25 to −11 despite large doses of thyroid and lugol solution. Only in the last years it was in normal range. In the differential count lymphocytes showed a variation from 18 percent to 49 percent.

Case was published with more pictures: Exper. Med and Surg., Vol. VII, No. 4, 1949.

Last examination, November 29, 1956: Patient looked well, felt fine; her only complaint was that she has a soreness and swelling in left lower leg, ankle joint and foot, from time to time. This is what remained from operation scars and tumor scars on that leg. No other remarkable findings were observed. Last heard from her friend on June 29, 1957, that patient is in good condition.

CASE No. 13

Mr. J. A., age—34, married, one child.

Clinical Diagnosis: Active melanosarcoma.

Biopsy and Operation Report:

"In March, 1950, he noted spots of blood on the sheet which seemed to come from a mole. It was sore and the patient saw his doctor at the Juneau Medical Surgical Clinic in Juneau, Alaska. The mole was removed by local excision and a piece of tissue was sent to the Virginia Mason Hospital; a malignant melanoma was diagnosed. Patient had no further treatment and noted nothing further until October 24, 1950, when he felt a lump under his right arm. He saw his doctor again, and he immediately sent the patient to this hospital for further treatment.

"Over the inferior angle of the right scapula there is a 2 x 3 cm. scar, in the right axilla two nodes are palpable; they are firm, movable, and about 1½ cm. in diameter. There are also a few nodes palpable in the left axilla but these are soft and appeared to be essentially normal.

"The Tumor Board examined the slides of the original lesion and it was their opinion that the original diagnosis of a malignant melanoma was correct; they recommended that this patient be offered the benefit of a right interscapulo-thoracic amputation, and that any remaining skin lesions which appeared to be enlarging, or which are in a position that they receive repeated trauma, be excised. The nature of the patient's disease was explained to him and he readily agreed to the proposed surgical procedure. Therefore, on November 17, the patient was taken to surgery where a right interscapulo-thoracic amputation was done. His post-operative condition was perfectly satisfactory. He received 4 pints of blood during the surgery and apparently withstood it very well.

"January 18, 1951. A new mole was excised under local anesthesia from the right flank. Pathologic study revealed a benign pigmented nevus. The next time, a fourth nodule was removed, on July 5, 1951. It was malignant."

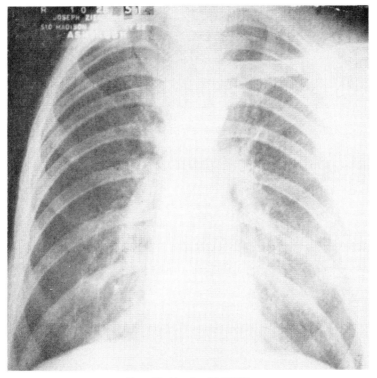

Case 13, No. 1 — 10/25/51
Right arm and shoulder are missing.

Condition when first seen, October 25, 1951: In the last three weeks, a new node appeared below the left ear. For several months he had coughing spells lasting two to three hours, eliminating after that a kind of whitish mucous.

Examination: Blood pressure 144 over 90, 72 regular pulses, heart not enlarged, sounded normal. Lungs showed bronchial râles all over, breathing reduced in left lower lobe.

At the region of the left upper half of sternocleido muscle, there was a large black swelling and there were three smaller glands. Two glands posterior to this mass and one farther below. November 3, 1951. The mass from the sternocleido muscle disappeared, and no glands were any longer palpable. Patient remained in good condition from then on, free of recedives and started his work about three months later.

Last report, October, 1957: Another patient from Portland, Ore., reported that he is in good condition.

Published: *Medizinische Klinik*, Germany, No. 5, pp. 175-179, 1954.

CASE No. 14

Rev. E. L. D., age—30, married, two children.

April 15, 1954

Clinical Diagnosis: Recurrent Melanosarcoma spreading over the body.

For many years patient had a small hard nodule on the posterior part of the neck, somewhat more to the left. Tumor started to grow and a small mole appeared outside.

May 14, 1954

The surgeon removed both on May 14, 1954. X-rays of the lungs were negative.

May 25, 1954

Patient went to Portland Clinic, Portland, Oregon, as new black nodes appeared. The doctor recommended radical operation of both axillas, the left half of the neck with removal of the muscles, and removal of the glands in the groins.

May 25, 1954

Pathological and Clinical Reports

The Portland Clinic

"I examined Rev. E. L. D. on May 25, 1954, at the request of his local surgeon. He brought with him a microscopic report, a copy of which you no doubt have."

Salem Memorial Hospital Pathological Report

"Sections of the skin show one area in the corium where there is a dense accumulation of brown pigment. This is largely contained within fairly large fusiform shaped cells. There are other cells in this same region which are small and have round nuclei. They apparently represent lymphocytes. The corium in this region appears to be thicker than normal. The pigmented cells do not show pleomorphism or the other usual findings of malignant degeneration. However, it is possible that the major part of this lesion is not included in these sections. For that reason additional sections of the skin will be examined later. The likelihood of the skin changes not being representative is further suggested by examining the deeper cyst-like structure which was lying in the sub-cutaneous fat. This actually represents a lymph node which is largely replaced by pigment containing epithelial cells. Where the pigment is less abundant these cells are in compact strands and cords without orderly pattern. They have fairly large and somewhat pleomorphic nuclei which are largely of the vesicular variety. Nucleoli are found in most of these cells and there are also mitotic figures. The pigment is exceedingly abundant in some areas so that it is difficult to distinguish nuclear detail. Obviously this change must represent metastatic spread of a maligant melanoma, and the likelihood is that the primary lesion is in the skin section described above."

P.D. Malignant Melanoma of Subcutaneous Lymph Node and Questionable Malignant Melanoma of the Overlying Skin.

First seen, May 27, 1954: There are several nodes at the neck, in both axillae and groins. Treatment immediately applied.

In a few weeks all glands and nodes disappeared and the patient remained in the best of health and working condition up to the present time.

The following resumé presents best his condition:

August 31, 1957.
"My vigor and strength is not only equal to that which I enjoyed prior to the summer of 1954, when you first met me at your office in New York, but I am now more vigorous and stronger than ever. The long 18 months to two years which we spent in following your orders have proved to pay off with the very best of health. Here is a brief resumé of my schedule:

Melanoma discovered, Salem, Oregon, May 14, 1954.
Therapy begun at Nanuet, N. Y., May 28, 1954.
Relaxing of diet in winter of 1954-55.
Enlargement of the right breast, April 10, 1955.
Resumption of stringent diet (by your order), May 10, 1955.
Return to ordinary foods, completely cured, July, 1956.

At present I am weighing 187 pounds, full of pep and health. I have worked harder this year than any year of my life, and eat a well-balanced diet of all normal, healthy foods."

CASE No. 15

Baby R. S., 8 months of age.

Clinical Diagnosis: Active Neurogenic Fibrosarcoma with glands.

Reoperation of larger block or amputation of left arm and shoulder advised.

Biopsy: St. Joseph Hospital, Elgin, Ill. Fascial fibrosarcoma, probably neurogenic, grade I.

Previous History Report: The Children's Memorial Hospital, Chicago, Ill.

"R. S. was brought to us by his parents for advice and treatment. They gave the history that the child had had a lump discovered on the left shoulder a few weeks before. This was excised in a hospital in Elgin, Ill., and the microscopic sections were said to reveal fibrosarcoma. They brought in a slide of the tumor and X-rays of the chest. The X-ray of the chest did not reveal any osseous metastasis. The slide was examined by me, by the pathologist at the Children's Memorial Hospital, and by the director of the tumor clinic at the University of Ill. We all agreed that it was a fibrosarcoma having some suggestion of a neural origin. I discussed it with Dr. S. and we decided that X-ray therapy would not be effective and might injure the epiphysis. The possibility of radical amputation of the arm and shoulder was likewise discarded as ineffective if the tumor had already extended sufficiently to make it necessary.

"We decided that wide local excision was the best procedure since the wound of the original surgery was rather small and the doctor evidently was not aware at the time of the type of tumor. We felt that reoperation was advisable to excise a larger block of the subcutaneous tissue, fascia and some muscle along with a little more of the skin. This would give a chance of eliminating any tumor cells which had been left behind after the original surgery. If the tumor has already metastasized by the blood stream or lymphatics, it is probably too late, but there is no evidence that this is the case."

First seen, July 25, 1950: The parents reported that they noticed a larger tumor at the left shoulder on June 20, 1950. On July 5, 1950, the tumor was removed in St. Joseph Hospital, Elgin. When the shoulder started to swell and the operation wound began to secrete, the physician assumed a regrowing of the tumor and recommended radical amputation. The physicians in Chicago decided otherwise. When more glands appeared at the posterior edge of the left sternocleido muscle, in left axilla among the swelling and tow glands at the left neck, the other physicians were pessimistic and recommended radical amputation. Parents refused.

Condition when first seen: At the left shoulder above the clavicle an operation wound very deep, 2½ inches long, covered with pus, was present; around the wound the skin and subcutaneous tissue showed hard infiltration, also the whole area of the left shoulder and axilla. After one

BABY R. S.

BLOOD:	7/27/50	8/11/50	8/28/50	10/9/50 AT HOME	10/23/50	11/6/50	11/27/50	12/11/50	1/17/51	3/10/51
Hemoglobin	64.5%	67.7%	87.1%	58%	62%	58%	58%	62%	60.2%	64.7%
Red Blood Cell	4,800,000	5,000,000	4,850,000	3,760,000	3,790,000	3,540,000	4,090,000	4,090,000	3,270,000	3,320,000
White Blood Cell	7,750	8,200	15,950	12,800	15,200	9,600	9,700	12,800	7,700	9,500
Neutrophiles	22	29	12							
Segmented	18	24	10	24	18	6	19	19	27	30
Juveniles	4	5	2	4	2	1	8	5		
Stab Form				3	5	1	1		1	1
Eosinophiles	6	4	2	2	3	6	5	2	2	1
Basophiles	3	1		2	3	1	1	4		1
Monocytes									4	6
Lymphocytes	69	66	86	67	72	85	66	70	66	61
	Hypochro-mia-nor-mocitic.	Ortho-chromic-normo-cytic. Marked lympho-cytosis.	Micro-1+ Ortho-chromic with few Greno-cyted cells.	Macro-few Hypoch.-2+ Sl. Poik. Sl. Polych. Basophilic Stippling present.	Micro-1+ Macro-few Hypoch-romia-2+	No abnor-mal lymph. Micro-1+ Macro-few Hypoch-romia	Micro-1+ Macro-few Hypoch.-2+	Micro-1+ Macro-few Hypoch.-2+		
URINE:										
Spec. Gr.		1.003	1.004							
Reaction		Faintly acid	Alk.	Alk.	Alk.					
Albumin		2 plus	—	—	—					
Pus Cells		2-3	1	—	—					
R. B. C.		rare	—	—	—					
Granular Casts		1	—	—	—					
Trichomonas		1	—	—	—					

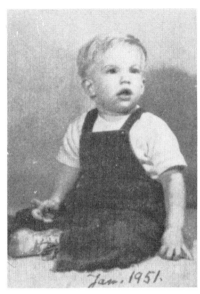

Case 15, No. 1 — 1/51

month the wound was closed and the glands had disappeared. X-rays of the lungs did not show bony or lung involvement. It was interesting that the baby refused at the beginning to drink the juices from the bottle, as he was used to the white color of the milk. After the mother had covered the bottles with white paper, the baby accepted the various juices eagerly, despite the different taste.

The different blood pictures with high lymphocytosis up to 86% can be seen in the table above, also the findings in the urine.

After a while the baby recovered entirely and grew up to a healthy, strong child.

Last report, end of July, 1957: The treatment was a lasting success.

CASE No. 16

Mrs. R. H., age—32, married, one child.

Family: mother had breast cancer with brain metastases.

Clinical Diagnosis: (Post operative.) Retro-peritoneal lymphosarcoma.

Biopsy and Operation Report:

"In answer to your request for information on Mrs. R. H., I can tell you that I operated on her on September 14, 1949, and found that she had retro-peritoneal lymphosarcoma."

Previous History:

Patient noticed in June, 1949, a lump in the left part of the abdomen near the navel. She had no pain. X-ray examination revealed the tentative diagnosis of a pancreatic cyst. September 14, 1949. Exploratory operation. University Hospital, Philadelphia. They found a large retro-peritoneal mass which could not be removed as it was localized around the large blood vessels. Twenty deep X-ray therapy treatments were applied in September and October, 1949. Two more masses disappeared after X-ray treatment for about six to seven months. Then she felt weak, tired, nervous, could not sleep, and a growing mass was palpable again in the left part of the abdomen near the navel.

Condition when first seen, September 17, 1950: Patient was depressed, pale, very nervous, and reluctant to be in a hospital. Examination revealed in the left lower abdominal quadrant a large mass with irregular surface, palpable at the depths of the abdomen just in front of the spine, extending downwards more to the left.

Gynecological examination, made September 23, 1950, found an irregular tumor mass at the above-described place but no other glands around. The treatment was immediately applied after her admission to the clinic on September 24, 1950. After one month the tumor mass was no longer palpable. Menstruation did not recur as the X-ray treatment produced an artificial sterilization. Instead of menstruation, she experienced nose bleeding which lasted about one week. The menstruation returned October 24, 1951, and has been both normal and regular since that time, lasting five days.

Follow-up examinations, until March 16, 1954, showed no recurrence of tumors, no glands; the patient remained in favorable healthy condition, doing all her housework.

Last report by phone, August 13, 1957: Patient is in best condition.

CASE No. 17

Miss J. P., age—10.

Clinical Diagnosis: Recurrent Osteofibrosarcoma (Giant Cell Tumor of left mastoid process.)

Biopsy Report: St. Vincent's Hospital, Staten Island, New York.

Osteofibrosarcoma (Review of this slide by consultants in pathology revealed giant cell tumor, of a borderline type, as a more likely possibility.)

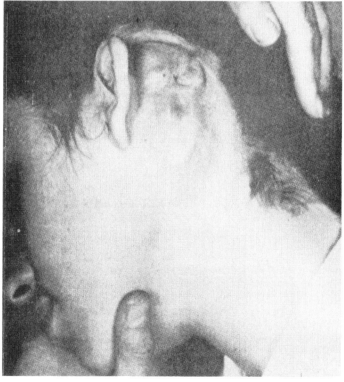

Case 17, No. 1 — 10/49

Previous History:

On September, 1939, patient was bitten on the left ear by a beetle. On April, 1946, a hearing test in school showed hearing in left ear to be reduced to 65 percent of normal. Otological examination on September 20, 1946, revealed a bony growth involving the left mastoid process. On November 21, 1946, tumor was removed at St. Vincent's Hospital, Staten

Island, N. Y. On January 18, 1947, left facial paralysis was observed, and on January 20, 1947, left aural canal was scraped but no change in paralysis occurred. On January 23, 1947, a radical operation was performed; more of the mastoid process was removed, along with more tumor tissue and the pressure on the N. facialis was relieved to a great extent.

Fifteen deep X-ray treatments were applied ending February 26, 1947.

Drainage remained, tumor regrew, and a hopeless prognosis was given to the child's parents by both radiologist and surgeon.

Condition at time when first seen, March 13, 1947: The child was pale, nervous, extremely irritable and apparently suffering continual pain over the whole left mastoid area as well as some referred pain to the neck and the head generally. Attacks of dizziness, loss of equilibrium and vomiting occurred when pain became intensified. There was a large suppurating cavity, eleven cm deep in the left mastoid area filled with gauze packing, which required changing every other day.

Case was published with pictures in Exper. Med. and Surg., 1949, Vol. VII, No. 4.

At the end of April, 1947, one and one half months later, the mastoid cavity was filled with granulation tissue and no secretion could be found. In the next few months, four separate abscesses occurred in the mastoid cavity with fever. Three were lanced by the family physician and the last opened spontaneously. By October, 1947, the cavity finally closed and has remained so up to the present. Nausea, vomiting, loss of equilibrium and severe headache persisted for several months, subsiding only after the fourth abscess opened. Each abscess formation eliminated some necrotic bone tissue. There have been no further signs of neoplastic activity in the last years. A school hearing test revealed 78 percent of loss on the left, 2 percent on the right. Patient is able to run and play normally with no impairment of the sense of equilibrium.

X-ray examination of the skull revealed May 12, 1947: The left mastoid and the lateral part of the left petrosus bone is missing. The remaining part of the os petrosum is irregularly outlined and condensed. The findings suggest a residue of the original osteo sarcoma. The skull showed no other pathology.

Last report, May 1956: Remained in normal condition, good pupil.

Bloodcounts (red counts)

	1/21/47	3/25/47	8/29/47	4/2/48
		71%	82%	60%
Hemoglobin	11.5 gms	12.0 gms	13.9 gms	10.2 gms
Erythrocytes	4.140.000	4.040.000	4.830.000	3.960.000
Leucocytes	19.600	8.850	11.050	15.150
Color Index		0.89	0.85	0.76

	7/19/48	10/18/48	11/30/48	2/21/49
	72%	70%	72%	72%
Hemoglobin	12.2 gms	11.9 gms	12.2 gms	12.2 gms
Erythrocytes	4.190.000	3.850.000	3.740.000	3.990.000
Leucocytes	11.900	15.200	14.700	16.950
Color Index	0.87	0.92	0.97	0.92

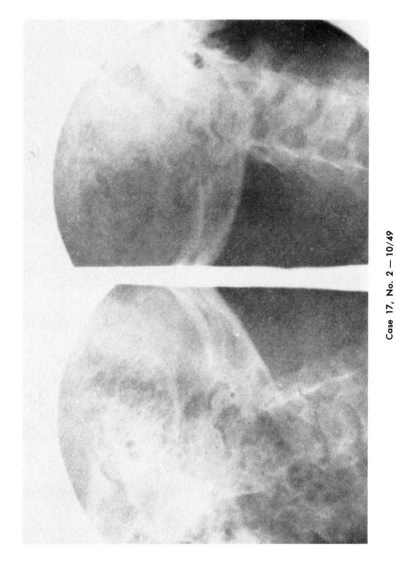

Case 17, No. 2 — 10/49
The right mastoid shows normal appearance of cells. The left mastoid
shows a large area of rarefaction extending into the squama.

	4/20/49	6/25/49	9/3/49
	76%	72%	71%
Hemoglobin	12.8 gms	12.2 gms	12.0 gms
Erythrocytes	3.830.000	4.130.000	3.620.000
Leucocytes	12.300	11.200	14.050
Color Index	1.0	0.88	0.98

Restoration of blood is much faster since liverjuice has been added to the therapy.

CASE No. 18

Mr. W. S., age—32, married, three children.

Clinical Diagnosis: Retroperitoneal lymphosarcoma, active, spreading, in glands all around, also bilateral broncheal.

Biopsy and Operation: Removal of retroperitoneal glands, appendectomy 6-29-51.

Findings: "There was a cluster of lymph glands in the right iliac region with the highest ones being the largest and the smallest ones being down towards the femoral artery. The largest gland measured approximately 5 cm in diameter. There was some slight edema of the retroperitoneal space surrounding the gland and the glands were soft and friable. The appendix was not remarkable. There were no other intra-abdominal or peri-aortic nodes."

Procedure: "Under spinal anesthesia the abdomen was entered through a low right rectus incision, the abdomen was explored. The peritoneum overlying the glands was incised and a removal of all enlarged glands was performed by means of blunt and sharp dissection, care being taken to preserve the iliac vessels and the ureter likewise was identified. After hemostasis, a small portion of oxycel was inserted into the bed from which the glands were removed. The peritoneum was approximated over the top of the area and the incidental appendectomy was performed with carbolization and inversion of the stump by means of a purse-string suture and the abdomen was closed in layers without drainage. Interrupted cotton was used throughout. The patient withstood the operation well and was returned to his room in good condition, having received one unit of blood while on the table."

Pathological Diagnosis: "Fibrotic appendix. Large cell lymphosarcoma."

Previous History:

In May, 1951, patient noticed a mass growing in abdomen, more to the right. Operated in June, 1951. Hospital in Cincinnati, Ohio. X-ray treatment followed.

In September, 1951, a new mass appeared in left lower quadrant, X-ray treatment applied, glands disappeared. A few months later new glands appeared, took spleen extract injections, 2 cc three times a week, prepared by the doctor. The patient used a partial diet, no salt, no sugar, no white flour. No improvement.

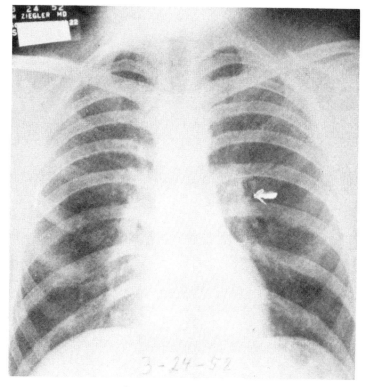

Case 18, No. 1 — 3/24/52

Condition when first seen, March 24, 1952: Patient complained about pain in lower back above sacro-iliac joints, sometimes more a kind of hypersensitivity. He observed from time to time new glands, was coughing in the last weeks.

Examination revealed a larger gland in left axilla, two small tumors in left lower quadrant, a few glands in right groin, more in the left. The place where he got the first mesenterial gland near the right iliac bone seemed to be free. Abdomen is soft, not distended, liver not enlarged, surface smooth. Heart not enlarged, sounds free, Bl.Pr. 118/68, 66 regular pulses, lungs present diffuse bronchitis in both lower lobes, no dullness. Patient looked normal, was calm outside but inwardly emotional and easily excitable.

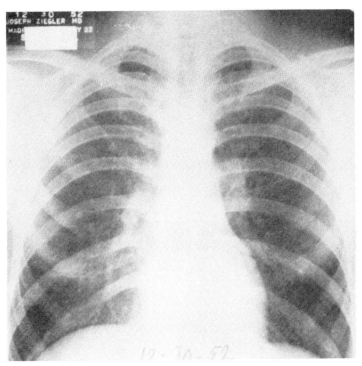

Case 18, No. 2 — 12/30/52

In the following months the glands disappeared. At the last examination on September 23, 1953, there were only two small hard glands left in left axilla, in right axilla one little hard node. Both groins and abdomen were free; the X-rays also showed scar formation left in both bronchial areas.

Since this treatment started, patient remained free of any recurrence or other discomfort after the restoration of his body in about 6 to 8 months. Since that time he felt better than ever before and was working full time and with good results. He himself and his family stayed on the diet most of the time as many other families do.

Reports of X-ray Specialist

March 25, 1952: X-ray examination of Chest, P. A. and Lateral Views. A. P. Film of Pelvis.

There was a definite enlargement of both hila especially the left one. (See also lateral views.) The lung tissue itself appears to be free.

No pathological conditions of the pelvis and the lower lumbar vertebrae are revealed.

December 31, 1952: Control X-ray examination of Chest, P. A. and Lateral Views. Lateral film of Skull. Films of both Mastoids.

The previously described enlargement of both hila is about the same as before, and therefore the process can be regarded as stable.

No pathological conditions of the skull and the mastoids are revealed. September 24, 1953: Control film of Chest.

The lung markings extending from the right hilum towards the middle and lower portions of the lung field have somewhat decreased, otherwise there was the same condition as before.

Last report, July 29, 1957: "I have been feeling really very well ever since I stopped sending in my treatment book and have been carrying on a full program of work."

CASE No. 19

Mr. W. H., age—38, married, three children.

Clinical Diagnosis: (Different diagnosis) Lymphoblastoma, or Hodgkin's Disease.

Biopsy Report: Lymphoblastoma—Mayo Clinic.

Previous History:

April, 1943. Patient noticed a swelling on the right part of the neck, went to Mayo Clinic; diagnosis lymphoblastoma, treated with X-rays. Later, glands appeared in both groins, right axilla, mesenterial and bronchial glands. Most glands disappeared after intensive X-ray treatment, but returned two months later. Repeated X-ray treatments were applied, six months later, then eight months later. The last treatment was applied in March, 1947. However, glands regrew and Mayo Clinic decided not to take any more biopsies, as it might have activated new spreadings. Patient was treated twice more; once in a clinic, and once by a doctor.

Condition when first seen, March 10, 1948: There was a large mass of lymph glands on the left side of the neck. Patient complained that he got tired very easily, had to sleep in the afternoon, had severe backaches down to the hip, more at morning than during the day. In a few months patient recovered, and the glands went down considerably. In the laboratory findings, there was a remarkably low basal metabolism, down to minus 22, later minus 18, in the following years up to minus 3 and minus 2. September 28, 1949. He complained about stiffness in the muscles when he sat awhile and started to read, the stiffness was more pronounced in both sides and calves, less in arms and fingers, but even the eyelids and other muscles showed some stiffness and tightness. Patient was, for awhile, reluctant to eat raw food and drink juices. Then, a new tumor mass appeared at the basis of the right sterno-cleido muscle, the size of a small tomato, hard, indurated, not growing and no other glands were palpable. X-rays of the lungs were negative, the abdomen, with liver and spleen, did not show anything remarkable.

Reexamination, January 30, 1950, showed a smaller, hard mass at the right sterno-cleido, which gave the impression that all was calcified. It was shrunken in the last year. General condition was good, appetite fair; patient had his normal weight, felt good, and was working.

Reexamination, March 21, 1950, showed the same favorable condition.

X-ray, February 13, 1951. There was an annular shadow seen in the lower region of the left hilum about 2cm in thickness which represented the partly calcified capsule around a very faint opacity. Several calcifications were seen above and below this area.

The findings point to the formation of partly calcified capsules around a very faint scar of an old tumor mass.

During the printing period I learned from the remarried widow that the patient died on July 8, 1953, more than five years after the beginning of the treatment. He remained always depressed and fearful. He gave up the treatment two years after he had started it, as he thought the liver was not sufficiently restored.

Patient followed different advices. He died after a long fast.

CASE No. 20

Miss K. D. N., age—11.

Clinical Diagnosis: Active lymphosarcoma, spreading.

Biopsy Report and former Treatment:

"You no doubt have heard from the patient's home physician, telling you that on November 26, 1954, a small 1 x 2 cm. nodule was removed from K.'s upper left arm near the insertion of the deltoid muscle. The nodule had been noted for about two months prior to that time. The pathological report by the doctor at the University of Minnesota Hospital was lymphosarcoma. On December 10, 1954, a physician removed about 12 nodes in a repeated node dissection and again the doctor's report was of evidence of a malignant *lymphoblastoma* which he preferred to classify as a lymphosarcoma. K. was studied in our hospital briefly, but a full survey was not performed because of chicken pox among the siblings in the family. Deep irradiation was carried out on an out-patient basis. The child received a total of 2700 air roentgens over a period of 16 days in nine treatments. X-rays of the chest failed to reveal any evidence of the malignancy when we last saw her in early January of 1955. Shortly after this period Mrs. N. took K. to New York to your care.

"I have just had a conversation with the family physician, who told me a little bit about your work. I am most interested in learning more of what you are doing and would appreciate any reprints you have that you feel might be informative to us. I also would want very much to follow K. upon her return home and would be only too glad to keep in touch with you concerning our follow-up care."

Previous History:

In September, 1954, the mother noticed a lump at left humerus, in the upper part. Patient was operated on November 26, 1954, Memorial Hospital, Litchfield, Minnesota. On December 6, 1954, glands in left axilla were removed. Mother reported there were 5 to 6 glands, all together about the size of a hand. Microscopic examination: malignant lympho-blastoma. Patient was sent for treatment to University Hospital, Minneapolis. X-ray treatment there could not prevent further spreadings to inguinal glands and other parts of the body. The mother mentioned, amputation was recommended and considered.

Condition when first seen on February 12, 1955: One node palpable at the first scar of left humerus, other glands, larger and smaller ones, in both groins, a larger mass was palpable in the middle of the abdomen (apparently mesenteric glands). Three other glands, one at the lower insertion of the sternocleido muscle and one at the left delta muscle, the third one at the scar in left axilla. Patient looked pale, had difficulty in taking food, was easily tired, weak, complained about pains in arms and legs, was listless.

Within three weeks the girl's general condition improved greatly, the abdomen was free, she had no pain, no complaints, could eat and drink and ran around like a normal child.

The family doctor was very interested in the case and examined the girl every month. The spleen was not palpable from the beginning, heart was normal and lungs were clear, temperature normal. Potassium, urea acid and urea nitrogen all were in normal range at the beginning, BMR −2. During the treatment we observed that the BMR went down to −10 and the potassium from 17.8 to 16.1 mg% in three weeks. The lowering of these findings we observe in malignancies frequently and I think that it is due to greater absorption of potassium and iodine into the different organs. One later report from the family doctor, on October 3, 1955, showed: "there were no lymph nodes palpable in the cervical region, axillae, or inguinal areas. Breath sounds were clear and normal over both lungs. Heart was regular; tones clear and no murmurs. No masses were palpable in the abdomen. Last medical report, February 6, 1957, shows no abnormalities."

According to the reports of the mother the girl is playing around like normal children, goes swimming and is a good pupil.

The blood-count frequently shows some little ups and downs in the red cells as well as in the percentage of lymphocytes. The urine presents, more rarely, little changes in traces of albumin and a small increase in pus cells mostly in the first days of a "flare-up." Both urine and blood regulate themselves to normal without any additional medication or necessary care except when there is a secondary infection present, an abscess absorbed or other complications set in.

Own report, September 2, 1957:

"I've been going to school regularly. I play basketball, skate, ride, bike and go swimming. I bake and sew an awful lot. I also do normal work and have been for over two years."

Physician's report, June 6, 1958: "Examination was essentially negative."

BLOOD:	2/15/55	2/22/55	3/1/55	3/15/55
Hemoglobin	78%	83%	76%	83%
Erythrocytes	4,000,000	4,510,000	4,080,000	4,040,000
Leucotcytes	10,100	4,400	4,200	5,600
Neutrophiles	87%*	57%	64%	52%
Lymphocytes	10%	40%	25%	30%
Mononuclears	2%	1%	5%	
Eosinophiles		2%	4%	18%
Basophiles			2%	

* Definite shift to left.

URINE ANALYSIS:	2/15/55	2/22/55	3/8/55
Reaction	Slightly alk.	Acid	Alkaline
Albumin	Positive 3	Negative	Negative
Sp. Gr.	qns	1.018	1.018
Casts	none	none	none
Leucocytes	masses	1-2	1-2
Erythrocytes	4-5	1-2	none
Epithelium	a few	a few	occas,

CASE No. 21

Mrs. H. W., age—58, married, two children.

Clinical Diagnosis: Lymphosarcoma, regrowing.

Biopsy Report and Operation: There were three operations.

    I operation—1952, September, Parson's Hospital, Flushing, L. I. Left axilla gland removed. Diagnosis: *melanosarcoma.*

    II operation—1953, April, Huntington Hospital. Again left axilla gland removed.

III operation—1953, November. Right axilla gland removed. Huntington Hospital.

Huntington Hospital Report

About six months prior to admission the patient developed a painless mass in the left axilla. This mass was surgically removed and a pathologic diagnosis of lymphosarcoma given to the patient. No further therapy was instituted. The patient remained well but under tremendous emotional distress until about two weeks ago when a recurrence of the axillary mass appeared. The mass rapidly increased in size and the axillary region was painful. There is, however, no radiation of the pain and no specific systemic complaints.

Operation: 4/21/53 — Excision of lymph node, left axilla.

Pathologist's Report: Specimen: Contents, left axilla.

             Microscopic Diagnosis: Giant follicular lymphosarcoma. (This diagnosis is made under the assumption that the bone marrow is not involved.)

Discharge Diagnosis: Giant follicular *lymphosarcoma*, left axilla.

Readmitted November 15, 1953. Discharged November 20, 1953.

Operation: 11/17/53 — Excision nodes of axilla, right.

Pathologist's Report: Giant follicular lymphosarcoma.

Discharge Diagnosis: Giant folicular lymphosarcoma, axillary lymph nodes, right.

Condition when first seen, April 16, 1954: Two larger masses were below the left mandibula. In addition, there were a few glands in left axilla. All these pathological findings disappeared within three weeks. Patient went off the diet as she thought she could return to work. October 21, 1954, she returned to treatment. A few small glands appeared in both groins. The glands in left groin disappeared in two weeks, while the glands in the right groin grew larger after a virus infection.

June 2, 1955. There was one larger and two smaller glands in right groin. They did not grow but got harder.

September 6, 1955. There was in the right groin one gland left, size of a plum of hard consistency.

Patient returned October 20, 1955. Numerous glands appeared in both groins, in the left adductor space. The abdomen distended, the liver enlarged, the surface free and even. Patient was told that she had to stick to the treatment for a longer period as I can otherwise not take the responsibility for the treatment.

January 24, 1956. Left groin free, right groin presented one hazel nut-like hard gland. Later all glands disappeared and also the scars were absorbed from the tissues where previously some glands and swellings had occurred. Patient continued the dietary regime more faithfully and remained free of all tumors and recurrences up to the present time.

Last Report: X-rays report taken at different times from pelvis, chest, skull, and spine, show essentially the following: "there is no evidence of any lung root or mediastinal adenopathy. There are hypertrophic arthritic changes in the mid-dorsal spine."

Last seen, May 16, 1957: No tumors, no glands palpable, liver seemingly in good condition, arthritis improved greatly.

Last Report, August 6, 1957: "I will continue your treatment the rest of my life, to keep well."

CASE No. 22

Mr. O. C., age—54, married, one child.

Clinical Diagnosis: Abdominal lymphosarcoma, subtotal occlusion. Inoperable case.

Biopsy Report: Lymphosarcoma.

Previous History:

December 10, 1953, patient had severe pain in the chest. Went to Montreal Hospital, where they found an obstruction in the large intestines. January 9, 1954, operation: tumor partly removed. After that 40 X-ray treatments were administered. No help, severe pain in abdomen, patient had great difficulty in passing stools, which could only be eliminated by enemas. 30 more deep X-ray treatments were recommended but were refused by patient.

Operation Report, January 9, 1954

Incision was made more to the right side. In the abdomen there was found at the hepatic curvature of the colon a large mass originating outside of the colon. Further below there are larger tumor masses composed of glands the size of a plum, also along the small curvature of the stomach, reaching the cardia. We think that we are dealing with a lymphosarcoma and found it inoperable in regard to the removal of the glands. Therefore we decided to perform an iliotransversostomy because there was a subtotal occlusion present. The coecum was found maximal distended, measuring about 12 cm in diameter.

Postoperative Diagnosis: Abdominal Lymphosarcoma.

First seen, April 2, 1954: Patient complained about pain in right lower abdomen and lower back. Lost 20 lbs. in the last few months, had 14 glucose infusions and 2 blood transfusions during stay at the hospital in Montreal.

We found in right lower abdominal quadrant a mass palpable like a small tomato fixed, painful on touch. Above that mass was a larger mass palpable, of about 3 inches in length and 2 inches in breadth. In addition, he had an abscess at the top of the nose and lower septum. Treatment started at once. May 1, 1954, patient showed a great improvement; the

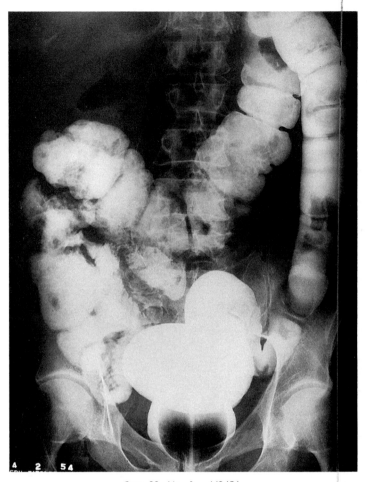

Case 22, No. 1 — 4/2/54

two tumors were no longer palpable. Passage of stools was easier, without pain. Patient gained weight, going from 109½ to 113 lbs. The enlarged liver showed an even surface, and the size was reduced. By July, 1954, patient was greatly restored, no pain, bowels normal, weight 125 lbs. In December, 1954, patient returned to work, had no pain, appetite was normal. In the right liver lobe a hard seemingly scar mass palpable existed. Patient looked normal and had regained all strength and working power. Last examination, February 14, 1957. No pain, good appetite, bowels normal and regular, no longer nervous, no headaches. He is careful with the diet, also when traveling.

X-ray Reports

April 2, 1954, Barium Enema:

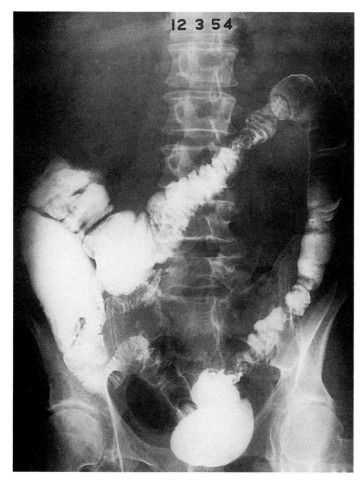

Case 22, No. 2 — 12/3/54

The barium fills the colon up to the ileocecal valve. Also some coils are filled.

The upper ascending colon below the hepatic flexure shows an irregular filling defect about apple-sized.

See also post-evacuation film.

There is no obstruction.

Further observation is recommended.

The findings are suggestive of a tumor.

December 3, 1954, Barium Enema:

The barium fills the whole colon up to the ileocecal valve and part of the ileal coils. Also the anastomosis between proximal transverse colon and ileum is visible.

No filling defect at the ascending colon is visible anymore.

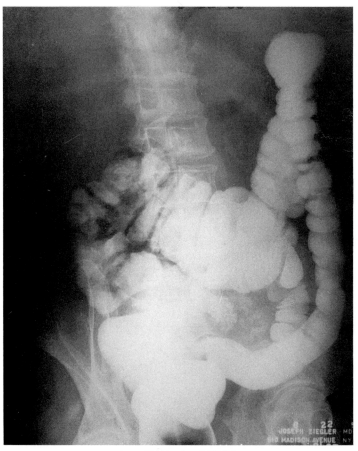

Case 22, No. 3 — 6/22/56

June 22, 1956, Barium Enema:
    The barium fills the whole colon up to the ileocecal valve and some
ileal coils.
    There appears to be a small walnut-sized filling defect at the medial
side of the upper ascending colon.
    Further observation is advisable.

CASE No. 23

Mrs. D. H. J., age—43.

Clinical Diagnosis: Myosarcoma followed by osteomyelitis, subtrochantheric pathologic fracture of left subtrochantheric area. Left thigh presenting extensive scar masses from operations as well as from cancer with consecutive infections.

Biopsy Report, Medical College of Virginia, Richmond, Va.:

"The relative past history disclosed the fact that she had a myosarcoma removed from her left hip in 1924. Subsequent operations were required. Intensive X-ray therapy was used. She had developed an osteitis of osteomyelitis in the area of her fracture. After several consultations, it was decided that this fracture should be fixed with internal fixation. A Jewett nail was used for this purpose. Following operation she developed a tremendous skin slough at the site of previous aggravating operations. She continued to drain from this site where she had previously for years bad drainage . . . I felt that she should not have further surgery at the time . . ."

Previous History:

1923   Diagnosis: Myosarcoma (according to biopsies).
1923   Growth on left upper femur removed.
1923   Removal of recidives from same spot.
1924   Removal of recidives from same spot. X-ray treatments begun.
1925   Removal of the whole mass of scars again at the same place. Since that time wound has remained open.
1928   Skin grafted on open wound.
1929   Removal of piece of bone at same place. Wound healed and remained closed until 1940.
1940   The scar mass ulcerated again. Bone inflammation and destruction set in.
1941   All scar masses removed and skin grafted. Treatment with penicillin and antibiotics until 1944.
1944   Small bone splinters removed.
1945   More small bone splinters eliminated.
1946   Another skin graft attempted. Wound remained in status quo until May 25, 1951, when patient fractured leg.
1951   Long metal plate 2/3rds of entire length of femur was inserted and nailed to bone with silver screws at Medical College of Virginia. The muscle and skin did not heal.
1952   Removal of necrotic masses.

First seen, September 15, 1952. Treatment immediately applied.

Patient was bed-ridden; there was a large ulcerated area, extending over nearly the entire lateral surface of the left thigh. In the depth of the ulcera-

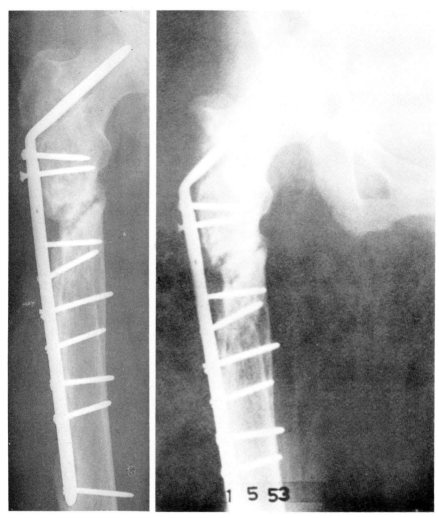

Case 23, No. 1 — 9/15/52   Case 23, No. 2 — 1/5/53

tions, a greater part of the metal plate could be seen. There was abundant secretion of pus. Severe pain. Bursitis with slight swelling in left hip joint. She could hardly walk on crutches.

March, 1953. Almost the entire ulcerated area is closed. There is good growth of fresh bone tissue closing the pathological fracture. The power of the new growing bone tissue was so great that it broke three screws into pieces. The surrounding muscle and tissues have been restored. In the following years the fragments of the broken screws were separated further and the plate shifted upwards and outwards, causing pain in walking. As the pain increased, I advised her to have the metal plate and the screws removed from her leg.

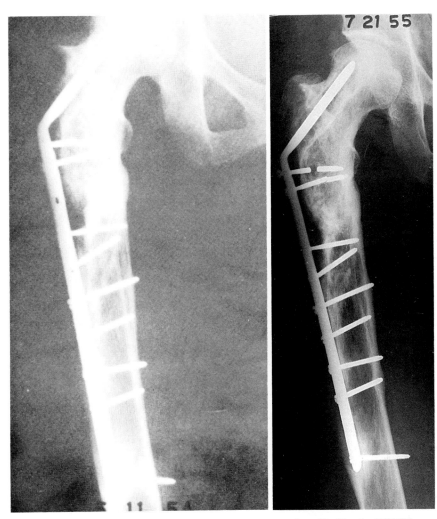

Case 23, No. 3 — 5/11/54   Case 23, No. 4 — 7/21/55

Specialist's Report from Richmond, Va.

"We operated on her, May 29, 1956, at which time an incision was made over the old previous incisions and the old, hard, leathery granulation tissues, exposed the plate and removed the plate with the screws. There was another screw broken which we found to be present but which did not show up on the X-ray. I was able to get the remaining portion of one of the screws out of her leg but I was not able to remove two of the portions of screws which had broken off. I hesitated to do this because of the precarious healing and the osteomyelitis made the bone very hard and brittle. I was afraid that I would cause damage which would not be reparable, particularly if she should fracture her femur. Incidentally, on

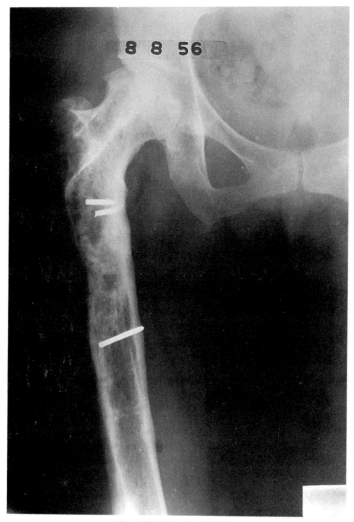

Case 23, No. 5 — 8/8/56

examining her, the drainage sinus, which she had, went directly to the
plate; in fact, it could be seen by looking in the hole with a lamp. I told
her and her family that anything you had ordered previously or wish to
order for her, I will be glad to see that she gets. I advised them to bring
things from home in order to help her. Incidentally, this was the worst
case of osteomyelitis that I have ever seen, particularly which has had X-ray
treatment, fracture and many operations."

Interesting in this case is the fact that patient had from the beginning
a basal metabolism of −33. The blood pressure was low, 104/52, later
114/82, and she had 76 regular pulses. We succeeded to bring the BMR
to −7 in June, 1953; later, to −3 and +4. The potassium content in blood

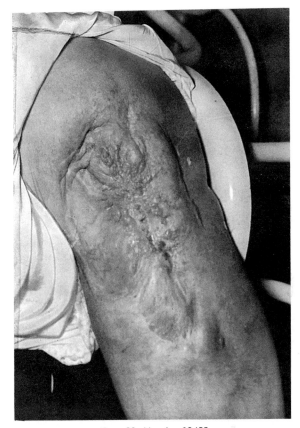

Case 23, No. 6 — 12/55
Left thigh presenting extensive scar from operations as well
as from cancerous consecutive infections.

serum could be restored much quicker to or near normal. Patient was last seen July 20, 1955. Later reports, up to July, 1957, show that she is in good condition, free of pain and able to follow her normal activities.

This case shows remarkably the tremendous power of healing which is inherent in the body by nature. It breaks big metal screws to extend the bone. Its granulation tissue kills parasites, bacterias and cancer cells, eliminates them and produces first hypertrophic scar tissues, later normal or near normal various tissue layers again. In order to achieve this task, it is necessary to support the body with a maximum of living chemical substances contained in fresh food to transform it in the powerful creative granulation tissue with all its biologic potentialities.

From this case we learn what overwhelming forces nature has created to produce life and to maintain it. We physicians should use the same force to heal far advanced defects and degenerative formations such as cancer.

In physics one begins to understand those forces and to use them. In biology, however, all body functions are so intricately regulated and interwoven that it is much more difficult to recognize their value and to apply these secret forces of Nature.

CASE No. 24

Mrs. H. S. J., age—54, married, two children.

Family History:

Two brothers had the same disease (Paget Bone Disease) and died later of sarcoma with metastases. One sister had lymphosarcoma and died.

Clinical Diagnosis: Paget Bone Disease.

Biopsy and Clinical Findings:

January 3, 1949, gland from right neck removed, was cancerous gland, origin unknown.

Biopsy:

Cancer formation, origin uncertain. Then abscess formation and re-growth. February 5, 1949. "A week ago she had an abscess on the right side of her neck incised by another physician and has now come to me for the redressings. She looks well but the neck lesion has not become smaller and the tonsillar involvement persists. *The abscess was sterile.* The possibility of a new growth cannot be eliminated unless biopsies are taken and patient has been so informed."

Previous History:

After her second delivery, the ankle joints started to swell; she had had trouble with her feet all her life. Ten years ago, she started to put on over-weight. She took nine grains of thyroid a day, and felt better for a while. "When losing weight, I always feel better." She had an early menopause, which started at 35 years of age. Sometimes trace of sugar in urine.

Condition when first seen, March 30, 1948: Patient was bedridden, could not stay on her feet, was so weak that she could not feed herself, had flashes and perspiration, atrophic skin on both hands, and paraunguitis. All teeth in her lower jaw bone became loose; she had a total upper plate. X-ray showed typical osteitis Paget with considerable bending of right tibia to the anterior part. Cortex was thickened, and showed a number of lanceolate cystlike structures. The medullary cavity was clearly outlined.

May 10, 1948. She could walk, felt much stronger, right knee joint was more easily movable, and felt much easier in her whole body. A much lighter treatment was applied, because there was no direct symptom of cancer, but more of a preventive treatment to avoid the transformation of the Paget Disease into cancer, as had happened to her two brothers. However, January 3, 1949, she complained that three weeks earlier a row of glands appeared on the right neck all along the sternocleido muscle. Patient first refused a biopsy which was done later in another clinic. The glands disappeared, but later, a regrowth was observed, February, 1949.

During the following months the glands disappeared, and no new

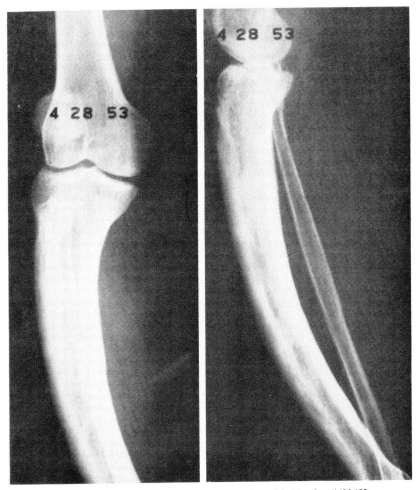

Case 24, No. 1 — 4/28/53   Case 24, No. 2 — 4/28/53

glands reappeared again. Within a few years, she became much stronger. By January, 1952, she was able to take up most of her daily housework. When after that time, fresh calf's liver juice was added to her treatment, she was able, within a few months, to take up her normal, daily housework, and the laboratory findings showed that the alkaline phosphatase went down from 6.7 Bodansky units within four months to 2.32 and was later, February 9, 1956, 1.24. Hands and fingers were no longer crooked and had straightened out. The right tibia, however, remained crooked, but according to the observation of the patient, was bent outwards to a lesser degree. She could work and walk like any other normal person, but observed, sometimes, after longer work hours, some discomfort in the right knee joint.

X-ray findings: March 30, 1948. Tibia: The right tibia showed extensive bowing accompanied by cortical thickening, which suggest strongly the presence of Paget's Disease. X-ray of the skull advised. January 10, 1952. The right tibia showed a considerable bending to the anterior and lateral side. The cortex is considerably thickened, showing a number of lanzeolate cystlike structures.

The medullary cavity is clearly outlined.

There is some hälisteresis of the tibia and femur condyles and of the fibula.

No pathological conditions of the left side were seen.

The findings point to an advanced Paget's disease.

The later X-rays made 1953 and 1954 showed almost the same condition.

Last Report, August 2, 1957:

"I feel fine and take care of a fairly large house, do all my own work and also help my son in his business for 2 to 3 days a week. I seem to have lots of energy and do *not* tire very easily. I still stay on the diet you have prescribed and also take juices every day. I have not had an ill day in a long time."

CASE No. 25

Mr. J. N., age—52, married, one child.

Family History: Negative.

Clinical Diagnosis: Tumor mass in aortic window, February, 1952.

Biopsy: Impossible.

Previous History:

Patient was a heavy smoker till one month ago; in younger years, he liked good wine, too. Within the last several months he noticed some pain in the heart area, not really precordial pain, and it was difficult for him to cough and to clear his throat. Deep breathing was also painful. He perspired easily and freely, and was very sleepy when he ate a little more than usual. He felt weakness in the upper back, and in the last three months had a pain in the left knee. Wasserman reaction, negative.

Condition when first seen, July 8, 1947: The heart was enlarged, one finger to both sides. Sounds were normal, blood pressure 108 over 76;

there were 52 to 54 regular pulses. Lungs showed a slight bronchitis. The gums were swollen, receding. Pupils normal, deep and superficial reflexes normal, liver four fingers below rib arch, a little harder, than according to the age, surface smooth. Abdomen was not distended, no free fluid. In half a year, he felt much better, free of pain and other disturbances. X-rays, negative.

Returned February 22, 1952, with complaints about general weakness, nervousness, disturbed sleep, painful cough and difficulty in eliminating mucus, pain in upper back.

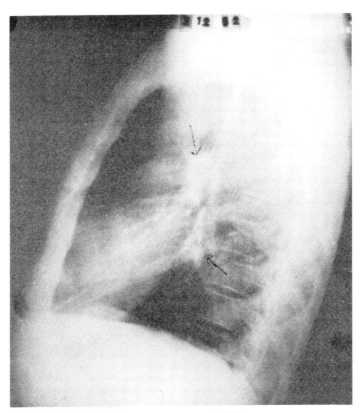

Case 25, No. 1 — 7/12/52

New X-ray Examinations

June 6, 1952: Both hila were enlarged, especially the right one.

A number of calcerous deposits were seen in both hila.

The heart was enlarged to both sides. The aortic arch was somewhat elongated.

There was a moderate congestion of the lung vessels. June 19, 1952. The P. A. film showed both hila enlarged.

The lateral view showed an enlargement, especially of the left hilum which also was somewhat higher located than the right one.

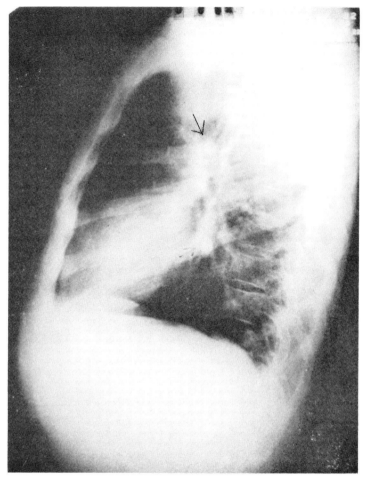

Case 25, No. 2 — 9/6/52

Note that there was a moderate congestion of the lung vessels July 12, 1952. A comparison of this film with the previous ones showed that the enlargement of the hila had decreased as seen on the P. A. and lateral views. Also the congestion of the lung vessels was diminished.

The transverse diameter of the heart was about 1 cm less than before. Otherwise there was the same condition as before.

September 7, 1952: There is a further increase in calcifications in the hila which was best seen in the lateral view as compared with the previous films. This increase affects the number as well as the size of calcifications.

January 24, 1953: There was the same condition as before.

The condition was to be regarded as stable.

May 23, 1954: There was about the same condition as before.

February 4, 1957: The scar masses of both hila were reduced to a small amount, also the calcified spots.

Last Report, August 2, 1957: Free of symptoms, feels well, doing his regular work.

This case is included despite the fact that in such cases a biopsy is impossible because it demonstrates remarkably well that some tumor masses become sometimes seemingly larger by production of connective tissue and calcifications. These abnormal amounts of scar masses and calcifications show in the following years considerable reductions. In this case it took about 5 years to accomplish this task.

The same observations we can see in cases of tuberculosis, arthritis and other chronic infections as well as in benign and malignant tumors. They do not permit any conclusion as to the type or origin of the former tumor mass. Whatever the cause may be — it disappears. (In a case like No. 23 it may take many years more to transform such extraordinary leathery scar formations in bones to or near normal.)

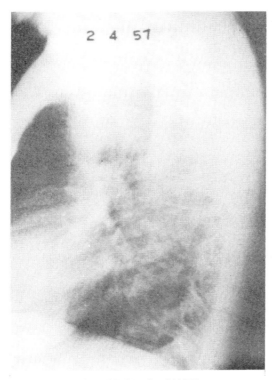

Case 25, No. 3 — 2/4/57

CASE No. 26

Mrs. E. M., age 58, married, one child.

Clinical Diagnosis: Regrowth of malignant tumor of the right parotis. Chronic Osteoarthritis.

Biopsy Report, The Rochester General Hospital, Pathological Report:

"Tumor parotid region. Several small irregular muscles of quite firm nodular greyish white tissue. Microscopic: Maligant mixed tumor of the parotis with marked lymphoid stroma."

Previous History:

Beginning 1946, the patient observed a mass in the right parotid gland; was sent to Rochester General Hospital, March 13, 1946. She was operated there and the tumor mass was removed.

In March, 1948, she again felt a tumor mass below the right ear and also another one at the other parotid gland. The family doctor advised another operation but the patient refused.

Condition when first seen, September 19, 1949: The right parotid gland presented tumor mass, the size of a walnut and some swollen glands below the mandibular angle. On the left parotid, she presented in front of the ear a round, hard movable mass, the size of a hazelnut. There were no glands on the left side.

The combined dietary regime started immediately in my clinic.

In addition to some minor arthritic changes, she had for two years menopause trouble with frequent perspiration, hot flushes and attacks of depression and fear. The menstruation was normal until the age of 56 years.

After about 4 weeks of treatment the right tumor was smaller and softer. The left tumor remained, however, hard and more rounded. Both tumors were now movable.

After four months, both tumors were much reduced, no glands palpable, menopause troubles reduced to a minimum. Some discomfort of osteo-arthritis, which were localized by X-rays; in sixth cervical vertebrae, left sacro-iliac joint, right hip joint and left thumb.

After one year, patient had no disturbances from menopause or arthritis any longer, and from the tumor masses only two small hard scars were left.

May 4, 1955, patient had no pain and no discomfort whatsoever. The right parotid gland presented a little hard scar below the ear, the left parotis showed a more lengthy hard scar, running in front of the ear.

Last seen, July 30, 1957. Patient is now 66 years old. Complains that she observed in the last weeks slight swelling in both parotid glands. She was on a partial diet for several years, till 1956, and all was well. Then she went on a 3 months' trip to Europe mid-1956 and was off the diet entirely.

I found on both parotid glands on the lower part a swelling the size of a hazel nut, harder than the normal tissue, no glands around. Patient looks well, no other arthritic complaints, abdomen not distended, liver enlarged, little harder than compatible with the patient's age.

This case is presented to show that we physicians have to advise people who suffered from malignant recurrences, farther developed arthritis and hardening of the arteries, diabetes, etc., to stay during the rest of their lifetime on a milder diet and to avoid especially most different types of fat (except fresh butter) and salt.

CASE No. 27

Mrs. H. D., age—68, married, one child.

Clinical Diagnosis: Adenocarcinoma of both thyroid and sigmoid.

Biopsy and Previous History:

Following is a summary of her admissions to St. Vincent's Hospital, Portland, Oregon.

First admission: 5/21/40 to 5/29/40
   Diagnosis: Toxic nodular goiter.
   Operation: 5/23/40. Thyroidectomy.
   Pathological report: Carcinomatous adenoma of the thyroid gland.

Second admission: 2/24/42 to 3/2/42
   Diagnosis: Carcinoma of the thyroid.
   Operation: 2/25/42. Removal of nodule from left side of thyroid gland.
   Pathological report: Recurrent or metastatic carcinoma, primary in the thyroid gland.

Third admission: 3/9/46 to 3/29/46
   Diagnosis: Carcinoma of the recto-sigmoid, grade 1 to 2.
   Operation: Partial bowel resection; end-to-end anastomosis.
   Pathological report: Adenocarcinoma of the sigmoid, grade 1 to 2.

Fourth admission: 6/3/46 to 6/7/46
   Diagnosis: Aberrant thyroid.
   Operation: Thyroidectomy.
   Pathological report: Aberrant anaplastic malignancy, probably secondary to carcinoma of the thyroid.

Fifth admission: 7/16/47 to 7/18/47
   Diagnosis: Chronic cervicitis with erosion; papilloma of the cervix.
   Operation: Excision of papilloma of cervix and biopsy.
   Pathological report: Chronic cervicitis with erosion; papilloma of the cervix, benign.

Sixth admission: 3/5/48 to 3/6/48.
   Diagnosis: Cardiospasm.
   Operation: Esophagoscopy.
   Pathological report: Nothing abnormal.

Seventh admission: 12/14/48 to 12/19/48
   Diagnosis: Recurrent adenocarcinoma of thyroid.
   Operation: 12/15/48. Thyroidectomy.
   Pathological report: Recurrent adenocarcinoma of the thyroid, (°Hurthle
   cell type).

Condition at time first seen, April 19, 1949: Patient complained about high blood pressure since years fluctuating between 178 and 200, we found 192/90, 88 regular pulses, heart enlarged 1½ fingers to the left, second vessel sounds accentuated, lungs free. Around the thyroid there were many scars and two smaller nodes, the size of a hazelnut. Abdomen not distended, liver four fingers below ribs, a little harder. In left lower quadrant two tumors palpable of lemon size connected with each other. Basal metabolism very low, −41 which could only be slowly increased.

During the following years all tumors disappeared. Patient felt well and stronger, blood pressure went down to 168/80. Gynecological and rectal examinations made July 21, 1952, showed scar masses and stringlike formations but no tumors or any active processes. The nodes in thyroid and parathyroid were no longer palpable. Reexamination July, 1952, found the patient in good condition, blood pressure 168/80, pulse 64 regular, abdomen not distended, liver almost normal size but a little harder, probably according to the patient's age, basal metabolism −6. Patient was instructed that she would need thyroid and potassium therapy for the following years.

Last Report: From reports of other patients in July, 1957, we know that the patient is in good condition.

CASE No. 28

Mrs. T. A., age 47, married.

Clinical Diagnosis: Carcinoma of thyroid gland.

Biopsy Report:

"She was readmitted to Memorial Hospital on November 19, 1945, with a diagnosis of a tumor of the thyroid gland. She presented a firm mass in the right lower neck, measuring 5 x 6 cm, which moved upwards on deglutition. The patient states that she noted the mass three weeks previous.

"A clinical diagnosis of carcinoma of the thyroid gland was made. An aspiration biopsy of the mass was reported as "Carcinoma." Radiograph of the chest showed no evidence of substernal extension and there was no evidence of metastasis. BMR was −6 and 0.

"A radical thyroidectomy combined with neck dissection was advised but refused by the patient."

Previous History:

Patient complained that she became very nervous in the last two to three months. She suffered from heart palpitation, was easily tired, had difficulty in going up stairs, and in doing any hard work. Below her throat, a tumor mass developed and was growing in the last weeks more rapidly. She gained weight, and complained about her flabbiness which hung down in folds from her arms and abdomen.

Condition at time when first seen, March 12, 1946: She complained that she was terribly fearful of cancer and against any operation. She was easily upset, depressed, sleepless, had rheumatic pain, more before rain, and bad cramps during menstruation. Blood pressure was low, 102 over 68, she had 60 regular pulses. Basal metabolism 0 and −6. Menstruation painful, lasting longer, mostly ten days. Treatment was immediately applied. Tumor mass disappeared in about six weeks, but the general condition improved slowly in about one year.

In August, 1947, she suddenly showed a terrible vaginal bleeding from a submucosal fibroma which had to be removed immediately. Operation confirmed the diagnosis. A specialist performed a partial hysterectomy. Since that time, patient remained free of recidives and other disturbances. She had no complaints, and could do her usual work as in her best time.

She was last seen, May 8, 1953.

Last Report, July 29, 1957: Patient without symptoms, well and working.

CASE No. 29

Miss A. L., age—47, single.

DIAGNOSIS: Adenocarcinoma of right breast, Grade III. Right radical mastectomy. Metastases in 5th and 6th thoracical vertebrae.

1944—Partial hysterectomy.

March, 1945—Right radical mastectomy. Mayo Clinic. "On March 29, 1945, member of our surgical staff removed the carcinoma of the right breast, carrying out a right radical mastectomy. The pathological examination

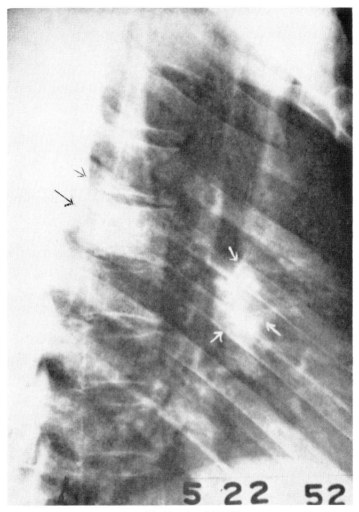

Case 29, No. 1 — 5/22/52

revealed an adenocarcinoma, grade 3, with marked involvement of the axillary glands. In November, 1945, a small nodule appeared on the right upper anterior chest wall, and on November 15, this was removed. On pathologic examination this proved to be inflammatory fat. On December 5, 1946, Miss L. again underwent surgery here. At this time the doctor performed a dilation and currettage because of metrorhagia. The examination of the scrapings showed the late proliferative phase of the menstrual cycle."

June, 1949—Paresis in left arm.

October, 1949—Pain in both shoulders.

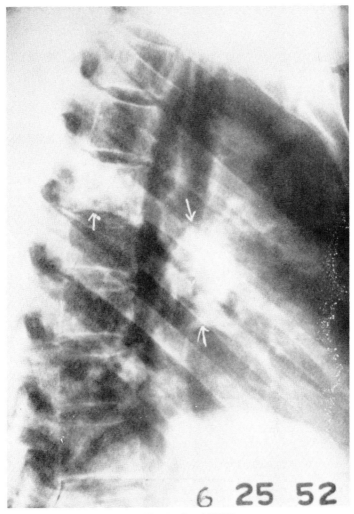

Case 29, No. 2 — 6/25/52

November, 1949—Metastases in 5th and 6th thoracical vertebrae and both adjacent ribs. Diagnosed in Illinois Research Cancer Clinic, Chicago. Deep X-ray treatment; male hormones, then 20 injections of Krebiozen.

February, 1951—Artificial sterilization.
Because of progressive deterioration she sought treatments in several clinics all over the country.

May 22, 1952—First seen: Complaints of very intensive pain in upper back, both arms, shoulders; very weak, extraordinarily nervous. She wrote her "own death sermon."
In six months restored to full working power; free of pain. Has been working up to the present (August, 1957, last report).

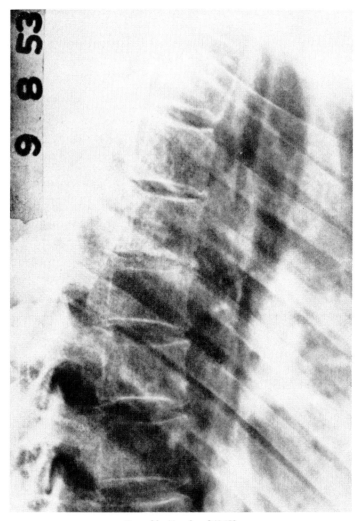

Case 29, No. 3 — 9/8/53

X-rays

May 23, 1952—Fifth dorsal vertebra shows several dense confluent opacities distributed over the posterior two-thirds. The structure of the vertebra for the most part was lost. The adjoining intravertebral spaces were narrowed in and there was a very slight gibbus.

The osteoplastic process involved also part of the vertebral end of the right 5th rib and the neural arches.

The findings point to an osteoplastic carcinosis.

The intrevertebral space betwen 4th and 5th lumbar vertebrae was narrowed in at the right side. Here also some spur formation was seen.

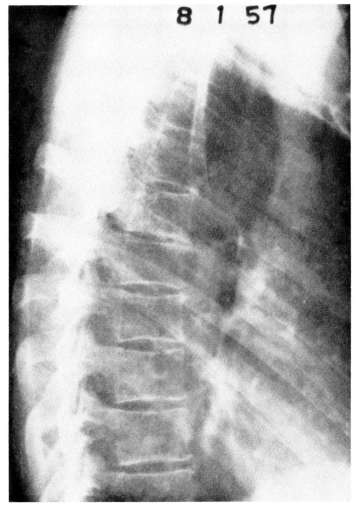

Case 29, No. 4 — 8/1/57

Some osteosclerosis at the adjacent portions of the above-mentioned vertebrae were noted.

The findings point to an osteoarthrosis deformans but there was also some suspicion of an osteoplastic carcinosis.

June 26, 1952—The lateral view of the dorsal spine showed that the process of calcification of the 5th dorsal vertebra had progressed anteriorly along the lower border.

Some calcifications were also seen in the right transverse process. Otherwise there were the same conditions as before.

April 9, 1953—It was seen from the lateral view that the process of calcifica-

tion seen previously in the anterior portion of the body of the 5th dorsal vertebra had reversed itself and there was again a rather normal bony structure.
No definite alterations were seen at the fifth rib.

September 8, 1953—There were only some small irregular areas of calcification seen in the left and posterior portion of the 5th dorsal vertebra.
The intervertebral space between the 5th and 6th dorsal vertebrae was partly obliterated.
No other pathological conditions were seen.

February 16, 1954—There was only a slight calcification seen in the posterior portion of the 5th dorsal vertebra.

December 2, 1954—The 5th dorsal vertebra showed in the lateral views some tiny calcifications.
Otherwise no pathological conditions were revealed except that the intervertebral space between 5th and 6th vertebrae was partly obliterated.
The restoration as shown in the X-rays proves that the bone substance could be restored within one year after the absorption of the pathological substances. We see now an almost normal tissue formation on the more or less involved previous pathological bone substances.
This seems to prove that cancerous bone tissue cannot only be transformed to scar formation, but also restored to normal bone structure.

Last examination and X-ray, August 1, 1957: No pathology — working normal as nurse.

CASE No. 30

Mrs. L. W., age—47, married, one child.

Clinical Diagnosis: Adenocarcinoma of right breast with diffuse axillary lymph node involvement and recurrence after radical mastectomy.

Biopsy and Operation:

Patient was first seen in Walter Reed Hospital, May 25, 1945. Radical mastectomy was performed with axillary lymph node dissection followed by severe wound infection due to hemolytic staphylococcus and alpha hemolytic strectococcus. Blood transfusion 1000 cc. Reexamination October 1, 1946: There was some evidence of bronchitis but no evidence of tuber-

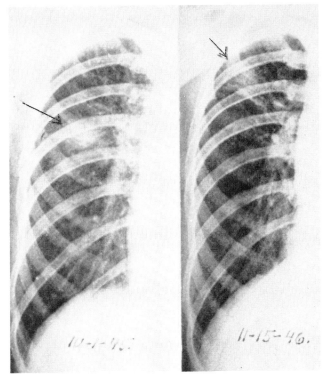

Case 30

10/1/45 — An ill-defined focus at base of right upper lobe.

11/15/46 — Instead of the previous focus there are a few fibrotic
strands left with elevation of the lower border of upper
lobe.

culosis. Loss of weight down to 123 lbs., blood pressure 110/80, pulse 70
irregular, some extra systoles. Skin discoloration from X-ray treatments.
X-ray of chest: There was a clouding in the upper mid-third of the right
lung, which involved the intralobular pleura. The lesion had the appearance
of X-ray infiltration but was not necessarily metastatic in nature. Family
was advised no further treatment would be of any benefit.

Pathological Diagnosis: Adenocarcinoma of breast with diffuse axillary
lymph node involvement.

Condition at time first seen, October 29, 1945: Patient cachectic, sub-
icteric, cyanotic, had severe cough dyspnea, increasing *left* adenopathy,
extreme weakness, persistent nausea and vomiting, abdominal distention
and enlarged liver. No adenopathy was found in right axilla.

X-ray of chest showed infiltrating process in right upper lobe, probably
not metastatic in nature, but more likely a deep X-ray infiltration.

Patient was sitting in bed for the first week because of dyspnea. Treatment applied immediately. Within one week nausea and vomiting disappeared, but cough and weakness remained.

In January, 1946, glands in left axilla disappeared, patient recovered within one month. After one year on this treatment, patient gradually resumed a normal life and diet, but without salt and fat.

Reexamination October, 1949, with X-rays of skull, spine, chest, showed no signs of metastatic involvement. Shadow in the right upper lungfield appeared less marked than on first examination in October, 1945.

In regard to this case, we would like to state that in our opinion the patient was in a nearly terminal state caused either by the effect of deep X-ray or by a progressive active carcinomatosis or by both, so that although the patient benefited greatly by the treatment, we cannot determine in this case exactly what underlying disease process was influenced by the treatment in the best way. The case is presented because such combination of circumstances occurs frequently in our cases as partly demonstrated here, and requires immediate aid and strictest detoxication by day and night.

Last Report, 1957: Remained well and is working.

This case was published in *Exper. Med. and Surg.*, Vol. VII, No. 4, 1949.

See a similar case in American Journal of Medicine 21: 211-226, Fatal Pulmonary Insufficiency due to radiation effect on lung. (Year Book of Pathology, 1957, p. 44.)

CASE No. 31

Miss E. C., age—61, single.

Clinical Diagnosis: Anaplastic carcinoma of the right breast with axillary metastases and a regrowth in the cartilage of the fifth rib.

Biopsy Report:

"Anaplastic carcinoma with axillary metastases, with grade III malignancy."

"The microscopic sections show a cellular anaplastic growth composed of large hyperchromatic pleomorphic epithelial cells with numerous mitoses. No attempt at gland formation is seen. Sections of the lymph nodes show almost complete replacement by tumor . . ."

Previous History:

On March 20, 1947, patient was operated on for right radical mastectomy with removal of the axillary contents. Seven years before X-ray treatment was administered for goiter with no result; therefore, she was operated on for removal of the greater part of the thyroid glands, Peralta Hospital, Oakland, California.

Since that time Miss C. constantly took small doses of thyroid, despite the fact she developed symptoms of beginning myxedema.

Condition when first seen, June 26, 1947: Patient showed a larger swelling which was localized at the fifth right rib near sternum. There were a few small glands in right axilla. Patient complained about pain in right arm and soreness in the muscles, especially in the biceps area; she presented an atrophic, shiny skin, and both lower lids were swollen. Blood pressure in the beginning, 154 over 92, the pulse 54 regular.

June 26, 1947, admitted to Cancer Clinic: The combined dietary regime was begun immediately and within five weeks the tumor and the glands disappeared and the other symptoms were greatly reduced. In due time she recovered entirely. The last report shows that she had retired from her profession as teacher. She is in a good healthy condition; there was no recurrence and essential disturbances.

Last Reports, Christmas, 1955 and August 5, 1957: She is in very good health; "I am doing normal work, almost as easily as I did ten years ago . . . I am still careful of my diet."

CASE No. 32

Mrs. M. H., age—44, married, no children.

Family: mother died of cancer of hip bone, one sister died of breast cancer with bone metastases.

Clinical Diagnosis: Recidives of breast carcinoma.

Biopsy and Operation Report, The Greenwich Hospital Association, June 12, 1952:

"The patient was operated upon on March 16, 1949, for carcinoma of the left breast. At that time, she had a very small original lesion, which, on microscopic examination, revealed very definite malignancy; a left radical mastectomy was done. Microscopic examination subsequently revealed the axillary lymph nodes were free of metastases. From this procedure she made a completely uneventful recovery. In March of 1950, there were noted several small shoddy nodes in the left axilla which were removed on March 16, 1950, and microscopic examination again revealed negative findings.

About February 25, 1951, she again noticed a small lump in the left axilla. She had been examined by her doctor routinely at his office on February 15, 1951, at which time, the axilla was entirely negative. This small mass on the left axilla had been completely asymptomatic. She had the node removed on March 5, 1951, which showed metastatic carcinoma, probably of breast origin.

After the third operation, she had some deep X-ray treatments, April, 1951."

Condition at time first seen, June 12, 1952: There was another lump which appeared May, 1952, and a new gland was found in the right axilla. Examination revealed a new node in left axilla, the size of a walnut, just in the scar where the second and third operations were done. The other examination did not show any abnormality, except that the left arm was a little more swollen than the right one. Circumference in the middle of the right upper arm, 10 inches; at the left, 10½ inches. Patient suffered from migraine headaches from the age of 23 years. Menstruation was irregular, lasting one week. Before menstruation time, some discomfort and spasms. Patient also complained about an unhappy sex life. June 5, 1953. Tumor and glands disappeared. Later we found at the place of the tumor, a small, very hard, most probably calcified scar formation. Her migraine headaches and attacks of fear and depression did not recur from 1953 on. Last examination, February 4, 1957: There was no symptom or sign of any malignancy. X-ray reports and laboratory findings showed no pathological conditions. Interesting in that case is that the examination of the gynecologist, Dr. V. R., showed: "the external genitalia, the vaginal walls and cervix are normal. The uterus is atrophied, angulated, smooth in outline and contour. The adnexa are not palpable. Opinion: The bleeding in this case is due to fibrosis uteri. This is a decidedly benign condition and needs no surgery of any kind. I would suggest some hormonal therapy, possibly some Testosterone or Oreton."

Last Report, July 27, 1957: "She is going to work 5 days a week and keeps house besides."

CASE No. 33

Mrs. M. E., age—62, widow, one child.

Clinical Diagnosis: Paget's Disease, right breast.

Biopsy Report, N. Y. Infirmary, 12-5-47 A6854:

Specimen of breast tumor taken from areolar area. Mammary carcinoma infiltrating skin.

Previous History:

Was seen first at American Oncological Hospital, Philadelphia, because of lump and ulceration of right breast below nipple. The right nipple was somewhat retracted and indurated. Below the lateral areola edge was a firm palpable mass. X-rays of the lungs were negative.

Condition at time first seen, December 5, 1947: Right nipple retracted, below nipple an open ulcer formation and larger infiltrating mass. Patient had refused operation. Treatment started immediately. After four weeks, January, 1948, the infiltration was barely palpable; the ulcer was covered with a fine crust, and appeared to be healing. Nipple is still retracted. February, 1948, no infiltration was felt and ulcer was closed. Nipple slightly retracted. November, 1948, nipple partially everted, no other changes.

Since that time there have been no complaints, no signs of recurrence locally or generally. No other treatment was used before or later. X-ray examinations of skull, chest, spine and pelvis taken October, 1949, were negative.

Last Examination, June 1, 1955: Patient is doing all housework, drives a car, remained in good condition.

Last Report, August 6, 1957: "I am in very good health and am doing all my work." This patient had no other treatment before she was first seen nor later. This case is demonstrated for that purpose.

Case has been published with pictures: *Exper. Med. and Surg.*, Vol. VII, No. 4, 1949.

CASE No. 34

Rev. J. F. McL., age—64, married, four children.

Clinical Diagnosis: Recurrent basal cell carcinoma and other carcinoma types.

Biopsy Report:

Made each time before and after operations, mostly basal cell carcinoma or epithelioma, twice squamous cell carcinoma, grade II (10/10/1947 and 7/20/1949) and once epidermoid carcinoma of dorsum nasal septum 6/28/46, infiltrating the different layers of the nose and surrounding tissues.

Previous History:

1937 to 1938—Skin cancer on nose, burned with radium.

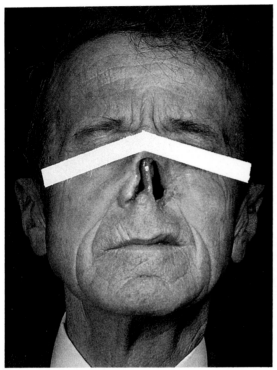

Case 34, No. 2 — 4/3/51

Case 34, No. 1 — 12/3/49

1939 to September, 1943—Treated by skin specialist with different methods.

1943, September—Came to Memorial Hospital. Removed diseased part and did plastic.

1945, January—Came back. Removed diseased part again, and used false piece of nose.

1946, May—When he returned for plastic, found some trouble, removed it and did plastic.

1947, December—Returned because of a new infiltration. Found new trouble and removed that.

1948, April—Came for check up. Plastic surgeon said, "All is well" and does not need to return.

1949, July—Returned again. All 4 biopsies were positive, and the surgeon removed the whole nose, July 20, 1949.

Condition at time first seen, August 10, 1949: Removing the bandage, I saw the place of the nose covered with pus, blood and secretion. Some of the pus flew into his mouth. This was a tragic sight.

Treatment started immediately, August 10, 1949. The patient showed a large ulcerated open area, the far exposed areas of the mucous membranes were swollen and red, showed some ulcer formations; these were partly covered with pus, which ran down into the upper pharynx and mouth.

This secretion ceased in three to four months; the mucous membranes returned to a normal condition. The nose could be replaced by a plastic one in December, 1949. The artificial nose is attached to glasses. (See picture.)

The patient had no recurrence up to 1956 and was able to carry on his work. The first photo was taken December 3, 1949, after all involved parts were cured. The second photo was taken occasionally, April 3, 1951.

Last Report, July 28, 1957: Patient's wife reports that he had the gallbladder removed October, 1954, and the physicians found at that time that he was suffering from hardening of the arteries. October, 1955, his son, an M.D., changed the physician and the young new physician administered Thorazine, Metrozol and Quinidine.

According to my own experiences Thorazine produces new growths in 4-8 months; it also did in this case. A growth was removed from the ear in July, 1956. In my opinion, Thorazine stimulates the liver, directly or indirectly, and removes most of the reserves of the liver, necessary to prevent recurrences. I have observed in 4 other cases recurrences when Thorazine was applied by others. It helped, similar to the contrary hormones, to stimulate the body the first months but has the unfavorable consequences later.

The patient is now 73 years old; he retired in May, 1956. Except for reduced memory, he is bodily in a normal condition. No other recurrences have been reported up to the present.

This case was published in: Medizinische Klinik, No. 26, Munich, Germany, June 25, 1954.

CASE No. 35

Mr. G. G., age—27, married, no children.

Clinical Diagnosis: Basal cell carcinoma with undiagnosed complications.

In 1938, patient first noticed a pimple or wart on neck; it grew, became an ulcer, which later grew slowly. He entered the Army in August, 1944, despite the ulcer.

BIOPSY, August 28, 1944, in Fort Riley. Biopsy was made, report: Basal cell carcinoma of skin, below and posterior to right mastoid, removed by block dissection.

RECURRED, April 1945: A large lump reappeared at the site of right mastoid; no second biopsy was taken. Patient was sent to a hospital in

Denver in September, 1945. October, 1945, X-ray therapy was suggested but was turned down by X-ray specialist. Surgery in Walter Reed Hospital suggested, but this was refused by patient; he also refused surgery in Bronx Hospital.

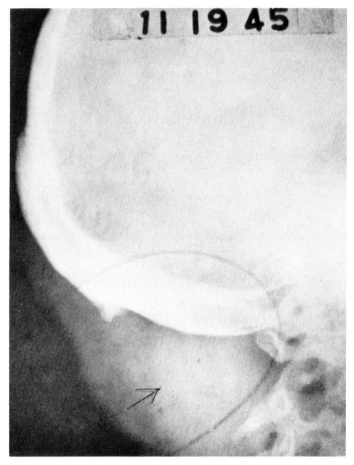

Case 35, No. 1 — 11/19/45

FIRST SEEN, October 20, 1945: Diffuse swelling of face, neck — extreme pain, dizziness, loss of equilibrium; no signs of acute inflammatory lesions, or redness. During last few weeks at home, pains had increased terribly. His face became more and more swollen and cyanotic. The left eye was closed by swelling; the right eye could hardly be kept open. There was no temperature. Two men helped him walk to the office; he was crying from pain and his head covered with a wet towel. Complaints: "Terrible drawing and pulling pain in my head; I stumble, have no equilibrium, my hair is falling out."

Below the right proc. mastoideus, there was a hard mass as large as a small fist, not movable but fixed on the base of the skull. Above there was an operation scar 3 inches long. The entire face was swollen and cyanotic. Right corner of mouth hung down, caused by facial paralysis and general swelling of the face. The left eye was entirely closed. The right eye could

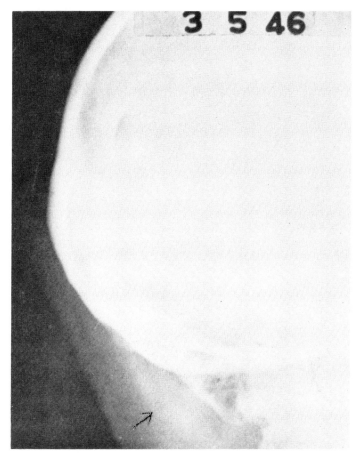

Case 35, No. 2 — 3/5/46

be somewhat opened. The right cornea and conjunctival reflex was very weak. Pupils responded normally to the light and distance. There was no imbalance of eye muscles as far as they could be tested. Deep tendon reflexes more active. No Babinski; anesthesia on right auricle and in a circle around it. Pulse 98, not quite regular. Urine normal, partial agranulocytosis, lymphocytosis. X-ray showed a large bulging tumor mass. Reexamined by specialist who took some photos of the tumor. Diagnosis of several neurologists uncertain — probably a sinus thrombosis. Treatment started immediately.

In four weeks, the tumor mass almost disappeared. Face was no longer swollen, facialis restored. The mouth was even, the deep, drawing pains appeared rarely, and the hair stopped falling out. At intervals there was some pain and some difficulty in keeping equilibrium. Circulation and motility were first restored in face in about 3 weeks. In February, 1946, circulation and strength returned to both hands. Later, in about six months, circulation and strength returned to both legs as well, so that patient could walk normally. The final improvement was the restoration of his sexual function.

He went back to light work July, 1946, for 3 to 4 hours a day, but was advised to wait for 1-1½ years before returning to his heavy work as a longshoreman.

February, 1947, no complaints, except that he has no normal sensitivity on and around the right ear. Urine normal, blood normal. Strong, took full-time easy job. New X-rays negative.

April, 1948, went back to normal work and has been working since.

February, 1950, no complaints — except some overweight — 223½ lbs.

Interesting may be that after 3 years of dietary regime, patient gave up the diet. No pregnancy occurred during the first 11 years of marriage. After both he and his wife were advised to return to the diet, pregnancy occurred 4 months later. January, 1952, his wife wanted another baby; according to my advice, both returned to the diet and new pregnancy occurred. Both children are normal.

October, 1954, his gallbladder was removed.

November, 1956, hemorrhoids were removed.

Last Examination, August 8, 1957: Patient is now in good health, free of any disturbances and lives partly on the diet with his family.

Patient was demonstrated July, 1946, in Senate Subcommittee, where 5 of my cured cancer patients were shown for the first time in American history.

CASE No. 36

Mrs. C. W., age—61, married.

Clinical Diagnosis: Basal cell carcinoma of right upper lip.

Biopsy Report: Gotham Hospital, New York City, and Lankenau Hospital, Philadelphia.

Diagnosis: Basal Cell Epithelioma.

Microscopic Examination: Sections show alveoli of closely packed epithelial cells in subcutaneous tissue.

Previous History:

Many years ago there was a little wart below patient's nose. It got larger and began to itch; the last four months it formed into an ulcer which grew deeper and deeper.

Condition at time first seen, February 3, 1946: There is a slowly progressing rodent ulcer 1½ to 2 cm at junction at right nostril and upper lip, forming a deep crater.

Patient saw two specialists before. Both hesitated to apply X-rays, radium, or to cut or burn it out because there was only a thin layer of tissue left separating the crater from the mucous membrane of the mouth. They were afraid to perforate the septum and would in that case have to remove the whole right upper lip.

Treatment started immediately.

Subsequent History:

Healing of the ulcer became apparent in 6 weeks, forming good granulation tissue. In July, 1946, the ulcer was closed, forming a fine superficial scar. In July, 1948, there were no longer any signs of recurrence, glands or other disturbances in motility of the lip, speech and while eating. Since that time the patient has remained symptom-free and no sign of recurrent tumor occurred.

Last Report, July 24, 1957: "I have not had any recurrence of my former ailment for which you so successfully treated me."

This case was published in *Exper. Med. and Surg.*, Vol. VII, No. 4, 1949, with pictures.

CASE No. 37

Mrs. L. O. divorced, no children, age 49.

Clinical Diagnosis: Recurrent basal cell epithelioma, sole, left foot.

She was first seen in her home confined to bed, November 25, 1945. Her troubles started in 1929 when a little red spot was noticed on the sole of the left foot. This was treated with silver nitrate, but it continued to grow — first slowly, then more rapidly.

In February, 1944, in St. Vincent's Hospital the infiltrated part was cauterized with several methods, but a tiny spot was left. Therefore, X-ray treatment was recommended. After two treatments the specialist gave up to avoid further irritation. Then the tumor grew again and opened to become a discharging ulcer, the size of a quarter.

She was again admitted to St. Vincent's Hospital. On October, 1945, biopsy was taken. Diagnosis: "Basal Cell Epithelioma, sole, left foot." The tumor was removed and covered with a full thickness graft from the left thigh.

Patient lost weight (from 103 lbs. to 82 lbs.), was more than three months in bed, became terribly nervous and sleepless. The entire foot was swollen and terribly sensitive to touch; it was painful when moved or when hanging down as she walked on crutches to the bathroom. In the middle of the left sole there was a deep ulcer in the form of a rectangle $2\frac{1}{2}:1\frac{1}{2}$ cm in size. Treatment was begun November 25, 1945. By the end of December, after four weeks, the ulcer was almost closed, the foot no longer swollen. The patient had a good appetite, began to walk with a cane and to be up and around; her weight rose to 91 lbs. At the end of January, 1946, the former ulcer showed a scar retracted to a little below the skin level. No pain, no other complaints. She had gained further in weight up to 101 lbs. and walked without the use of a cane.

Patient was last seen, July, 1957. Her left foot and sole were quite normal; she can dance; has no other complaints; the scar is now almost on a level of the skin. It is interesting to note that the patient has returned to regular food since the end of 1946 without any restrictions; she even smokes and drinks moderately, at present, a great risk for a former cancer patient.

Last Report, July, 1957: No recurrence, feels very well.

CASE No. 38

Sister M. M., age—44.

Clinical Diagnosis: Regrowth of left kidney sarcoma.

Biopsy Report, Sacred Heart Hospital, Allentown, Pa.:

"I operated on her 2-19-45. Our pre-operative diagnosis when she was admitted 2-17-45 was an ovarian cyst; however, on entering the abdomen I found a large tumor extending from pelvis to diaphragm. This tumor was not an ovarian cyst but retroperitoneal. I opened the posterior layer of the periotoneum, carefully avoiding injury to the descending and transverse colon. The gradually shelling out the tumor arrived at a broad pedicle springing from the left kidney. Then did a removal of the tumor including the left kidney. Made a stab wound into the retroperitoneal space of the left lumbar region, placing a penrose drain into same. Now closed off the retroperitoneal space by closure of posterior peritoneal layer. The tumor was the size of a large hand-dip-basin, while the kidney was about normal in size. The pathological examination was reported as a mass 45 cm with kidney attached. The actual weight of the tumor was twenty-three pounds (exclusive of weight loss in removal). Microscopic examination revealed tumor to be small, round and spindle-cell sarcoma. I would not be surprised if we were having a recurrence, in fact, rather surprised that same has not recurred before this, and although I could not find any gross mass, the Sister Superior and I concluded to subject her to deep therapy."

Previous History:

She had deep X-ray therapy from July 16 until August 4, 1946 (18 treatments), then again last summer, June 24 till August 24, 1947 (42 treatments). She could no longer stand these treatments, as she had frequent vomiting, dizziness, secondary anemia, weakness and loss of weight (10 lbs.). The standard treatment with iron pills, liver injections, vitamins and Stilbestrol remained ineffective. She was in menopause, suffering from hot flushes and perspiration. Stomach was very often upset and she suffered from bad constipation.

First seen, October 29, 1947. She looked very pale and complained about distended abdomen and left leg, swollen to a circumference of about 25 inches, at the thigh, which she could hardly bend or move. In left lower abdominal quadrant, there was a large tumor mass, size of two fists, palpable, a little below the old operation scar. The first two months during the treatment she was very weak, tired, but started to improve in the last three weeks. She had the typical reaction pain in almost all bones and joints, also in the neck, right ear and around the abdomen. From then on, she improved and recovered. September, 1948, she felt much stronger, no tumor could be felt, the leg was normal in size and motility. There was one remarkable exception: She could type but could not write with a pen or pencil. She recoverd entirely in March, 1949, felt only from time to time pain the right kidney area. May 20, 1949, she recovered also mentally and said, "Now I feel that nothing will grow any more in my body." It took her more than 1½ years to recover from fear and anxiety. She reported on June 20, 1954, the following: "I have been feeling all right for the past years. Due to circumstances I could not keep up the special diet. However, I try to eat plenty of vegetables, fruit and fruit juices. I gained weight and to make sure that not another growth had appeared, I was checked by doctors in Wedron, Illinois, and also here in our hospital about a year ago. The examinations checked "negative." I have been able to do my work all along since my visits to you, either in school till 1949 and from then on as laboratory technician."

Report, December 5, 1955.

Last Report, July 28, 1957: "I have been feeling fine all along and do my full day's work in our laboratory here at St. Mary's Hospital. I have a good appetite and did not lose any weight. There isn't any evidence of a new cancerous growth."

CASE No. 39

Mr. L. G. W., age—75, married, four children.

Clinical Diagnosis: Prostate carcinoma with metastases in lumbar spine. Arteriosclerosis and high blood pressure.

Previous History:

Five to six years ago he was examined at Memorial Hospital for prevention, all was negative. Next year he was examined in Life Extension Institute, where all again was negative. However, from 1950-1951, he observed severe pain in the lower back, loss of weight, frequent urination, especially at night and was examined by two urologists. His wife was informed that there was an enlarged prostate condition with metastatic findings in lower spine and pelvis. Therefore no operation was possible, no observation nor biopsy necessary, prognosis serious. The medical report from August, 1951, says: "there is a change in the density of the pelvis and lumbar spine which is suggestive of metastatic disease."

Condition when first seen in my cancer clinic, May 20, 1952: Patient complained about prostate condition of 15 years' duration. He had to urinate at night 3 to 4 times; in the morning it was very difficult for him to urinate and he had to wait several minutes, but during the daytime the stream was mostly free and a little stronger. In previous years he also observed some dizziness and eye trouble. The previous treatment had consisted of several types of female hormones, which enlarged his breasts, but did not help him otherwise. The blood pressure was 182/94, he had 64 not quite regular pulses. Rectal examination revealed a very large prostate tumor mass with a nodular surface on the left side. The heart was enlarged to both sides, about 1 finger to the right and more than one finger to the left side. Both vessel sounds were accentuated. The findings of the radiologist on the X-ray taken June 5, 1952, reads as follows: "The upper two-thirds of the sacro-iliac joints, especially the left one, are partly obliterated. In the surroundings there are a number of irregular areas of translucency extending also into the sacral regions. In addition, there are also several areas of osteosclerosis.

"At the lower portion of the spinal processes of the second, third and fifth lumbar vertebrae, there are osseous defects with irregular hazy borders.

"These alterations point to metastases of an osteolytic and osteoplastic character."

In the beginning, the urine showed albumin plus 2, trace of sugar leucocytes 20-25 per HPF and a few red blood cells. Some specimen showed also hyaline casts and a few granulated casts.

The combined dietary regime was immediately applied May 20, 1952. During the following months the patient recovered, pain in lower back and left lower quadrant disappeared; he gained weight, and X-ray examination showed a decrease in the osteoplastic processes, especially in both sacro-iliac joints. On July 10, 1953, a re-examination of the X-ray showed:

"The previously seen osteoplastic process in the region of both sacro-iliac joints has decreased. The joints themselves are again better outlined.

"No signs of metastases are revealed.

"The arthritic process of the spine is about the same as before."

During the following years the urination became more difficult. An urogolist had to dilate the urethra several times and this did not help enough. Suprapubic prostatectomy was performed November 1, 1955, with bilateral scrotal vasectomy. The weight of the prostate was 250 gms. The pathological report reads as follows:

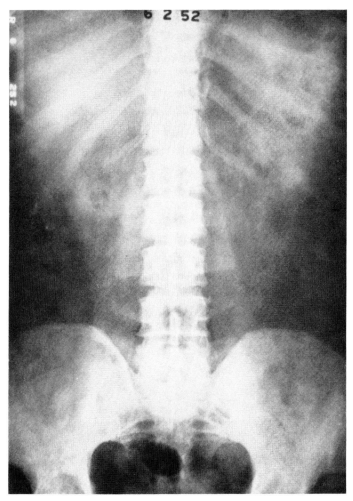

Case 39, No. 1 — 6/2/52

"Section shows tissue to be composed of numerous dilated tortuous alveoli, lined by cylindrical epithelium, resting in a dense fibrous stroma. Some of these alveoli are cystic and filled with a pinkish secretion. Others have ruptured and coalesce with one another.

"The stroma shows infiltrations with small round cells and a few eosinophylic leucocytes.

"*No malignant changes noted.*

"Diagnosis: Chronic fibro-adenomatous hyperplasia."

Last Report, August 1, 1957: After the first 3 months of treatment he is working up to the present — age 81 years.

X-ray Reports

June 5, 1952:
    X-ray examination of lumbar spine and pelvis.
    Mention p. 1 of history (bottom).

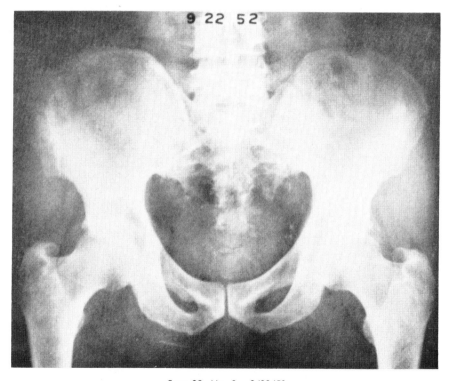

Case 39, No. 2 — 9/22/52

September 22, 1952:
    A. P. film of pelvis.
    A. P. and lateral view of lumbar spine.
    The osteoplastic process in the region of both sacro-iliac joints has again partly increased.
    Otherwise there is the same condition as before.
November 15, 1952:
    X-ray examination of pelvis and lumbar spine.

Although the condition in general is the same as before, it must be
noted that the regions of both sacro-iliac joints are partly better
outlined and that the process can be regarded now as stabilized.
July 9, 1953:
Control X-ray Examination of pelvis and lumbar spine in both
directions.

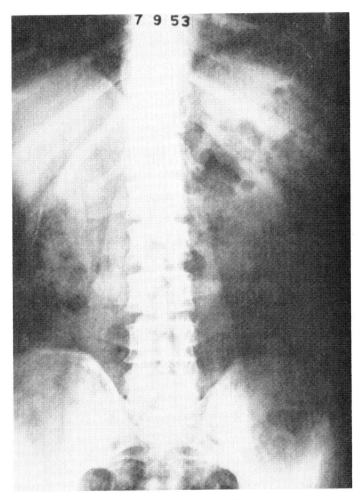

Case 39, No. 3 — 7/9/53

The previously seen osteoplastic process in the region of both sacro-
iliac joints has decreased. The joints themselves are again better
outlined.
No signs of metastases are revealed.

The 4 X-ray findings are combined here to show that the osteoplastic process is first increasing, preparing the way for the bony restoration processes — it can be regarded as hyperproduction of bony tissue for defense or a higher degree of healing power (with the subsequent restoration).

The last X-rays (November, 1957) show only osteosclerotic changes.

CASE No. 40

Mr. L. J. R., age—59, single.

His sister was cured here of a regrowth of thyroid cancer. He lives with her. There are several other cases of cancer in the family.

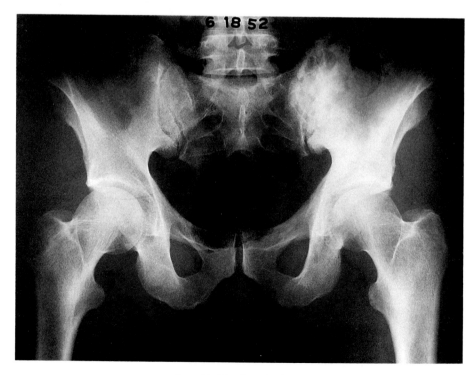

Case 40, No. 1 — 6/18/52

Clinical Diagnosis: Cancer of prostate, metastases in left sacro-iliac joint.

Biopsy Report:

Four years ago, physicians found an enlargement of the prostate with an irregular surface. Biopsy and operation recommended. When, in following years, metastases developed on both sides of the left sacro-iliac joint, physicians thought that a biopsy was no longer necessary.

Previous History:

It started early in 1948 with frequent urination. Later, the stream of the urine became smaller, and at times, especially in the morning, he had to press stronger; sometimes he had to wait till it started to flow; other times it came slower.

Condition at time when first seen, March 25, 1952: He complained about difficulty in urination, but catherization was not yet necessary. Patient had no other treatment, except massage of the prostate in the last year. Rectal examination revealed an enlarged prostate enlarged in all directions, with hard consistency, and some harder nodules on the surface. The prostate extends so far that the finger cannot reach the upper end. Blood pressure was 146 over 92, there were 64 regular pulses, heart was not enlarged, abdomen was not distended, liver not enlarged but harder,

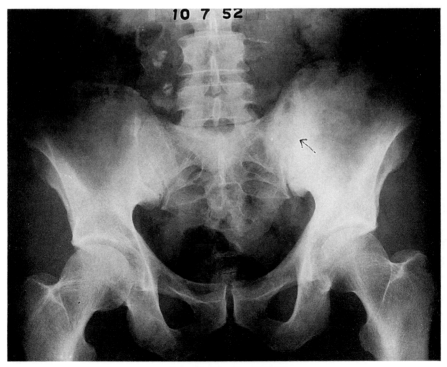

Case 40, No. 2 — 10/7/52

surface free. During the following months, the frequency of urination decreased to normalcy at daytime, and 4 times at night. In the next few years, the enlargement of the prostate went down considerably and urination was reduced at night to three times. The prostate remained a little enlarged, the surface was smooth, and nodes no longer palpable. He was sent to specialist for reexamination. He found the prostate enlarged to a smaller degree, surface smooth, no glands, on the back a larger atheroma, a smaller one on the anterior part.

During the treatment, the alkaline phosphate was examined almost every month. It went up and down from 11.2 to 21 Bodansky units. I cannot find any connection of these findings with the degree of the disease (in some cases it came down to normal).

X-rays:

June 18, 1952:

"In the region of the left sacro-iliac joint there are a number of irregular and partly confluent dense opacities which are partly interrupted by areas of translucency. The process involves more the iliac bone than the sacrum and extends downwards towards the acetabulum. The upper portion of the joint is obliterated. A number of calcified glands are seen at the right side of the 4th and 5th lumbar vertebrae. The lumbar spine shows no pathological condi-

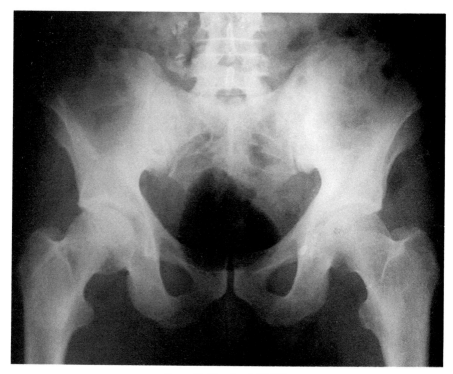

Case 40, No. 3 — 3/25/53

tions. Conclusion: The process in the region of the left sacro-iliac joint must arouse the strong suspicion of metastases mostly of the osteoplastic type, but also of the osteolytic type."

July 24, 1952:

"A comparison of this film with the one taken on June 18, 1952, shows that in the upper portion of the left sacro-iliac joint lateral to the joint space there is now a new area of calcification where there was previously an irregular area of translucency. Otherwise there is about the same condition as before."

September 10, 1952:

"The process of calcification in the region of the left sacro-iliac joint and the left iliac bone has increased as compared with the previous film. At the same time the areas of translucency have diminished."

December 10, 1953:

"There is a slight increase of calcification in the surroundings of the left sacro-iliac joint. Otherwise there is the same condition as before."

The following X-rays show further calcification and bone restoration. Last Examination, July 7, 1957: Prostate further reduced, no nodes palpable. Urination only at night more frequent. There are no glands. Patient looks well, works hard all the time.

Date	Bodansky Units Serum Alkaline Phosphatase		Date	Bodansky Units Serum Alkaline Phosphatase	
1953—August	19	14.9	1956—January	21	12.8
1954—January	20	12.0	April	30	21.0
February	18	12.8	July	16	17.4
March	25	13.2	August	9	12.8
April	9	17.4	October	22	18.0
July	1	12.0	1957—January	7	16.8
July	22	12.8	March	4	14.4
September	2	11.2	April	22	13.6
October	19	12.0	June	24	12.2
December	6	14.0	November 18		12.8
1955—February	14	11.2			
March	28	13.6			
June	13	9.6			
July	22	13.0			
September	6	11.6			
October	10	12.0			
November	7	13.2			
December	5	12.8			

CASE No. 41

Mrs. G. G., age—55.

Clinical Diagnosis: Bronchogenic carcinoma, total right pneumonectomy. Indication of active spreading cancer.

Biopsy Report: Bronchogenic carcinoma in right lung.

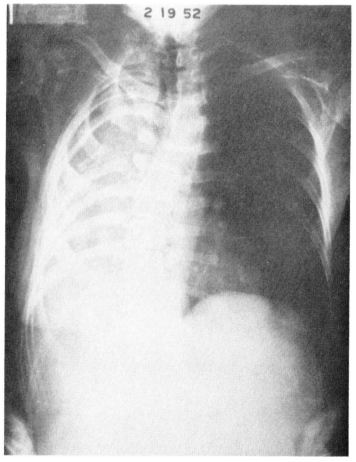

Case 41, No. 1 — 2/19/52

Previous History:

After a routine examination at Women's Infirmary, she was sent to Memorial Hospital, New York. Bronchoscopy and biopsy revealed malignancy. October, 1949, total right pneumonectomy. June, 1950, severe anemia, loss of weight from 130 to 115 lbs. Cough increasing. August, 1950, four blood transfusions in Memorial Hospital. High fever of seven weeks' duration. Underlying cause unknown. Further loss of weight to 97 lbs. Family was told cancer would probably develop in remaining lung and that Mrs. G's life numbered months at best.

First seen, October 7, 1950: Patient had high fever, could not endure further X-ray treatments because of weakness. Shortness of breath, was confined to chair day and night. Had extreme difficulty in eating. Cough was dry and hard; it was difficult for her to eliminate mucus and some

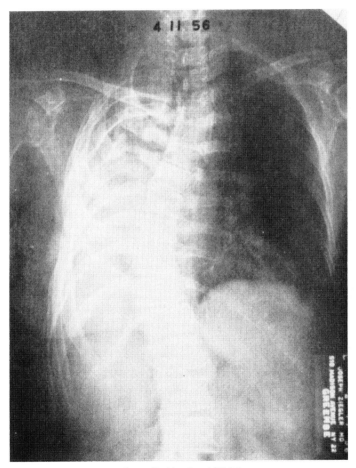

Case 41, No. 2 — 4/11/56

pus. There were a few small hard glands in left and right axilla, origin doubtful. Blood pressure 98/62. 106 regular weak pulses. Lungs: Over the right upper lobe, transferred breathing audible. Left lung shows hoarse inspirium and prolonged rough experium. After one week, eczema eruption on third right intercostal space, right shoulder and humerus. Further loss of weight. January, 1951, patient was free of pain, no cough, no sputum, could eat, drink and sleep in bed. Started to help at home. During the following years she remained free of malignancies and other disturbances. She also suffered less from osteo-arthritis and kypho-scoliosis of long standing. At present, she reports that she has been doing her work as housewife for years and enjoys relatively good health.

X-ray Findings:

> May 14, 1952: There was a rather homogenous opacity occupying the entire right lung. Operative defect of the sixth right rib. The dorsal spine showed a scoliosis toward the right side.
> April 11, 1956: Note that the scoliosis has increased; there are now more ossifications seen at the posterior region of the sixth rib.
> Last Report, August, 1957: Good condition.

CASE No. 42

Mr. J. P., age—47, married, two children.

Clinical Diagnosis: Bronchiogenic carcinoma inoperable. Suspicion of neoplasma pressing on spinal cord.

Biopsy Report, March 24, 1954:

"Bronchial washings from left lobe: One smear has a few nests of very bizarre cells, moderately increased in size with large, deeply stained nuclei. The other constituents are some mucus and pus. Diagnosis: Positive for malignancy."

Previous History, September, October, 1953:

Patient felt very tired and started to cough. First diagnosis, laryngitis. November, 1953, he observed pain in right lower neck and more cough. January, 1954, he had terrible coughing spells, was treated with a strict diet, X-rays taken were negative. Throat specialist found nothing in the larynx, ordered bronchioscopy. This was taken in General Hospital, Paterson, New Jersey, March 24, 1954, but was negative.

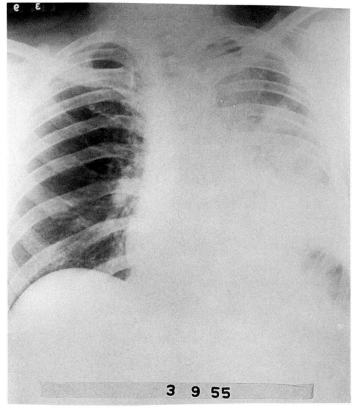

Case 42, No. 1 — 3/9/55

X-rays showed at that time a tumor in the left lung. Patient was sent to a specialist for surgery. This specialist, however, found the tumor inoperable and sent him for deep X-ray treatment to another physician. Patient regained his voice after the X-ray treatment and did not cough until December, 1954. At that time, the left leg started to have pain, became heavy, and lost the sense of feeling.

The report from St. J. Hospital, 3/3/55, reads as follows:

"We are probably dealing here with early cord compression from the neoplasm in the left lung. This may be by direct extension at the upper dorsal level. In order to prevent the dire effects of rapidly developing paraplegia I would recommend that the patient be hospitalized for spinal fluid study and myelography. If necessary, laminectomy and decompression should be carried out. However, we would consider the possibility of radiotherapy if the patient can be under careful observation and if there is no rapid progression of his signs."

"X-ray dorsal vertebra: There is a minimal degree of levoscoliosis of the upper dorsal vertebra. There is minimal spur formation along the

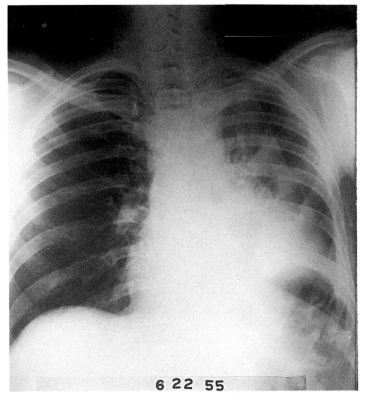

Case 42, No. 2 — 6/22/55

mid-dorsal vertebrae. The pedicles are intact and there is no evidence of osteolytic metastases. The interspace appears normal.

"Myelogram: Three c.c. of pantopaque was instilled in the lumbar region. The dye column was followed through the upper lumbar and entire dorsal vertebra. No obstruction was encountered. No impingement of the dye column was seen. Upon reaching the level of C7-D1 the dye broke up into multiple globules. The dye was scattered again in a caudal fashion and again no lesion was seen."

Condition at time first seen February 20, 1955. Patient had "awful" pain in the left lower chest and left axilla and severe coughing spells. There were also pains on the right side of the neck and in the lower part of the back; the patient was confined to bed and could hardly walk to the toilet without help. Weakness and pain in both legs were severe. He could be calmed down partially only with frequent enemas, and frequent doses of three tablets: aspirin, niacin, vitamin C. The first week, none of the neighboring patients could sleep as he was crying and moaning day and night.

After five days, coughing spells and pain in left chest were reduced, but the pain in lower back and right leg increased to terrific intensity, lasting almost ten days. After this time, the right leg was stiff, very weak,

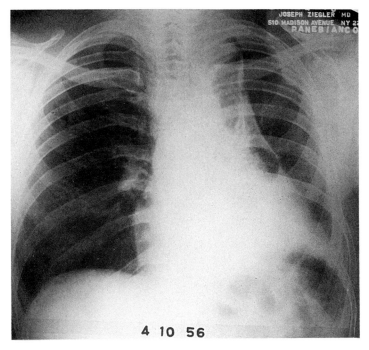

JOSEPH ZIEGLER MD
510 MADISON AVENUE NY 22
PANEBIANCO

4 10 56

Case 42, No. 3 — 4/10/56

could not be bent, showed increased reflexes, and positive Babinski while the left leg would not feel either cold or warm. Locally there was the upper lumbar spine which was very painful on touch or pressure, despite the fact that all direct examinations of spinal fluid, myelogram, X-rays, etc., did not reveal any positive signs of neoplasm in or near the spinal cord. The clinical diagnosis, however, became in time clearer in that direction.

In the next two years, the lung tumor was, according to the clinical findings and roentgenological pictures, reduced to a scar mass. There was still some breathing restored in the area of the left lower lobe. The right lung, the heart, and mediastinum remained in normal condition. The spinal cord condition, however, made longer clinical appearances and symptoms and also some difficulties. The right leg remained partially stiff, less movable, and weaker. Patient walked for about two years with a cane. Later he went for shorter distances without. The reflexes on the right side became weak at the patella and achilles tendon, and Babinski reflex remained positive. The left foot showed partially increased reflexes, the foot presented a very strong defense reflex. Sensitivity was only partially restored on both legs. It is interesting that, even now, patient reports every time that the sensitivity for touch, pain, cold, or warm increases on the right leg, there is less on the left.

Last Report, August, 1957: Patient helps his wife in the store, as he is no longer able to continue his vocation as barber, since the left leg doesn't permit him to stay a longer period on his feet.

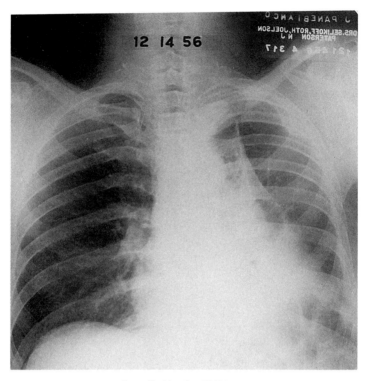

Case 42, No. 4 — 12/14/56

CASE No. 43

Mr. R. B., age—47, married, no children.

Clinical Diagnosis: Left submaxillary gland tumor, metastases in right upper lung lobe.

Biopsy Report, Memorial Hospital:

"Mixed Salivary Gland Tumor."

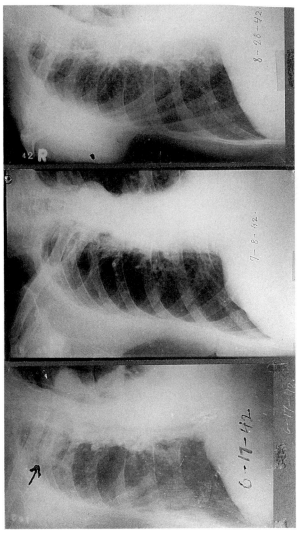

Case 43 — 6/17/42 - 7/8/42 - 8/28/42

Previous History:

A left submaxillary gland tumor was removed in Memorial Hospital in February, 1942. Three months later, patient expectorated bloody sputum and developed an irritating cough. Had bad taste in mouth and severe pain in the right lung. Breathing became difficult. He could not lie down or sleep in bed. Bronchoscopy performed by physician. His findings: The walls of the trachea appeared to be thicker than normal. The right upper lobe bronchus showed considerable congestion on the lower wall. The narrowing of the main bronchus was more noticeable after passing the opening of the upper lobe bronchus.

Condition when first seen, June 17, 1942: Patient was nervous, looked pale, tongue coated, heart not enlarged, blood pressure 120/72, 88 regular pulses, weight 146. There was slight dullness in right infraclavicular area and mid-scapular region of right lung. Inspiration was harsh, expiration prolonged, no râles. Three tablespoons sputum a day, dark yellowish to red in color, of jelly-like consistency. In two weeks, the expectoration was easier, also the breathing, still pure blood in sputum, weight 156 lbs. In four weeks, patient was sleeping in bed, less nervous, breathing normal, very little sputum, without blood. Pain in left lung had disappeared. End of August, 1942, no cough, no sputum, normal breathing, weight 160 lbs.

September, 1942, patient went back to work.

X-ray findings, June 17, 1942: An irregular opacity with varying degree of intensity, occupying upper right lung field. Some streak-like shadows extended from the right hilum upwards. Dorsal scoliosis extended towards the right side. After five weeks, July 22, 1942, the opacity had nearly completely disappeared, only some fine strands extended toward the hilum.

Patient at work since mid-September, 1942. Had no recurrence in 5½ years. He died on June 1, 1948, according to the report of his mother, of a coronary thrombosis attack, within 15 minutes. He had been the owner of a tavern, a heavy smoker and a "moderate" drinker.

This case is presented in memory of the event that he was my first cancer patient in the United States.

CASE No. 44

Mrs. J. D., age—45, married, three children.

Clinical Diagnosis: Regrowth of adenocarcinoma of upper rectum with metastases in lower abdomen.

Biopsy Report:

"Tissue Rectum": "A section of rectum with anal canal and anus 14.0 cm. long. It had been cut open and when spread out 9 cm. broad. At a distance of 5.5 cm. above the anus, is a round, raised, firm, nodular dark red growth, 4.3 cm. in diameter and 0.8 cm. high. In its center is an ulcerated depression, 2.2 x 4 cm. No glands were found in the surrounding tissue."

Histological Examination: "Within a stroma of a dense fibrous tissue are great numbers of closely approximated atypical glandular structures lined with columnar epithelium exhibiting malignant characteristics. Many of these structures are long, slender and branching, some are large and irregularly shaped. They penetrate into the muscle, but do not reach the peritoneum.

Pathological Diagnosis: Adenocarcinoma of the rectum, grade 2, malignancy."

Operation Report reads: "March 22, 1946, I performed one stage abdominal perineal procto-sigmoidectomy, with partial preservation of the sphincter mechanism for the carcinoma of the upper rectum. I also did a bilateral salpingo-oophorectomy. She had no metastases at the time of operation. Although there was a small amount of fluid present in the pelvis, which is indicative of some lymphatic glandular disturbance."

"This patient has done quite well, considering, but at the time that I examined her in July, 1948, she had a recurrence of a carcinoma outside of the rectal wall, which means that the recurrence is metastatic. I will be interested to know how she progresses on your line of treatment."

Condition at time first seen, May 27, 1948: Abdominal examination did not reveal any pathological findings. The patient only complained about pain and soreness in the lower abdomen, and increasing difficulty in eliminating stools. The enemas became more and more painful and difficult. She was still in the menopause condition (post-operative menopause) with flashes and perspiration.

Rectoscopic examination revealed recurrence of cancer growth and in addition some metastases outside of the rectal wall, July, 1948.

The combined dietary regime was immediately applied. She improved relatively quickly and the gynecological examination, September 16, 1949, by specialist, revealed the following:

"Abdomen reveals two incisions. The external genitalia are normal. The vaginal wall and cervix appear normal though there is some atrophic change. There is no palpable mass felt in the pelvis at all. There is some thickening in both adnexae areas and this is probably due to the operative procedure. Uterus not palpable. I see no evidence of any pelvic disease."

During the following years, no active cancer could be found, no glands or any other metastatic disturbance. The patient had, however, an acute infection of the urinary bladder several times. The function of the rectum and anus was remarkably restored.

X-ray Report:

In an X-ray examination of January 26, 1952, of Mrs. J. D., I see no evidence of metastases in the lower two dorsal vertebrae, lumbar vertebrae, pelvis or upper ends of the femora. The sacro-iliac joints are clear. There is no narrowing of the intervertebral discs.

In the flat plate of the urinary tract the kidneys are faintly outlined and normal in size and position. I see no calculi in the kidneys, ureters or bladder.

In the intravenous urogram both kidneys are excreting normally and promptly. The pelves and calices of both kidneys are fairly well filled. I see no evidence of pathology or obstructive uropathy. The upper portion of each ureter is outlined and appears normal. In the upright position there is moderate ptosis of the right kidney. There is no ptosis of the left kidney.

This is a negative intravenous urogram.

In the report of August 1, 1956, patient informed us that she was mostly feeling fine.

Last Report, August 7, 1957: "I will say that I am feeling better than I have for a long time and I am doing all my house work."

CASE No. 45

Mr. H. H., age—64, married, two children.

Family, negative.

Clinical Diagnosis: Adenocarcinoma of sigmoid colon. Obstruction, necessitating operation.

Biopsy Report and Pathological Findings:

Colon: Extensively infiltrating and ulcerating anaplastic adenocarcinoma, with evidence of metastases to the fatty mesocolon.

Previous History:

Never sick before, except for headaches; they stopped in the last months, which we observed several times as precursal signs of cancer development.

It started April, 1954, when he first noticed a pinkish discharge with his stools. There were great accumulations of gas and the elimination of stools became more difficult and was mixed with bloody mucus and some pus. A rectoscopy by a specialist remained negative. Barium enema also did not reveal any filling defect or other pathology. Later X-rays in July presented a filling defect 8 to 9 inches above the anus. Specialist recommended operation.

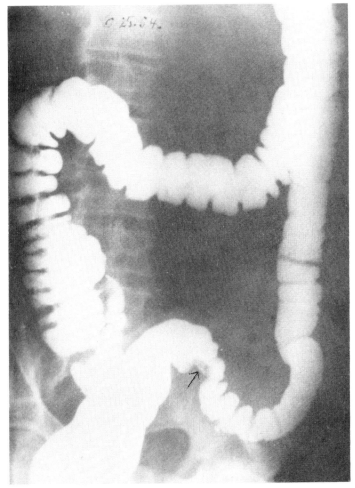

Case 45, No. 1 — 6/25/54

Condition when first seen, July 16, 1954: Patient complained about pain in lower abdomen, indigestion, discomfort from gas, difficulty in eliminating stools; he was forced to use frequent enemas. Treatment started immediately. Patient was deeply depressed, refused operation. In two to three weeks, the elimination of greater amounts of mucus with blood discontinued, and stools became more formed.

August 5, 1954. The patient complained that the allergic headaches returned twice a week, not so severely as before. This condition we observed also in other cases: that allergic reactions return when the body is sufficiently detoxified. October 24, 1954. Sigmoid wipings: "Cellular and mucoid debris and cellulose fibers. No tumor cells seen."

After six to seven months the patient observed that the stool was thin like a pencil without mucus or blood and without pus. He felt urge for stool elimination six to eight times a day, sometimes more. The best relief given him by the treatment was with castor oil by mouth and castor oil enema.

On April 18, 1955, the X-ray report revealed that there was a stricture where the cancer ulcer formation was localized before. He found the cancer not extended, but, on the contrary, reduced; however, there was a partial obstruction which had to be removed. Patient agreed to the operation which was performed at end of April, 1955. After the operation the patient recovered in due time and remained free of symptoms or any disturbances from colon and abdomen since that time.

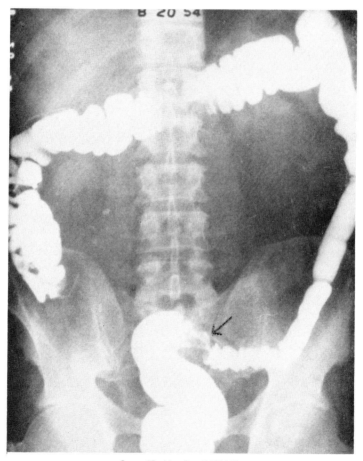

Case 45, No. 2 — 8/20/54

X-ray findings, June 25, 1954: "A barium enema filling defect at the sigmoid colon, compatible with an annular neoplasm."

X-ray findings, August 20, 1954: "A barium enema flows freely without obstruction from rectum to cecum. At the distal sigmoid a segment of the colon is seen showing narrowing of the lumen, a filling defect and destruction of mucosal pattern. These changes are characteristic of carcinoma of the sigmoid."

April 19, 1955: "The enema fills the rectum and distal sigmoid which are being dilated by the enema. After sometime also the proximal sigmoid is filled out between them there is a ring-like deep indentation. Another stop is seen at the sigmoid — descending junction and only traces of barium are flowing into the descending colon.

Besides the stenosis there are most probably also widespread adhesions."

Last Examination, August 2, 1957: No symptoms of cancer. Good

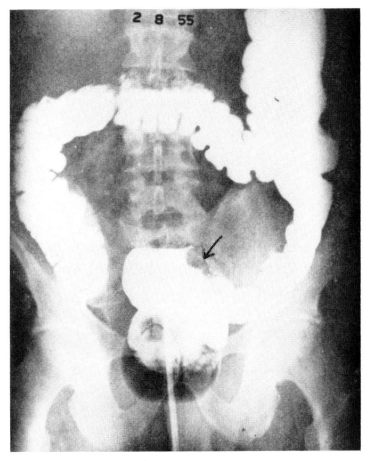

Case 45, No. 3 — 2/8/55

appetite, normal bowel movements, normal weight. November 28, 1957, no symptoms from the intestinal tract, but showed some discomfort from old age arteriosclerosis.

CASE No. 46

Mrs. E. B., age—48, married, two children.

Clinical Diagnosis: Cervix carcinoma with involvement of the vaginal vault, more induration to the left vaginal vault, quite nodular. There is also induration in the recto-vaginal septum.

Biopsy Report (University of Oregon Medical School Hospitals and Clinics):

Squamous cell carcinoma, vaginal smears showed evidence of definite cancer cells.

Previous History:

It started January, 1946, with discharge from the vagina. Was sent to the University Clinic in Portland. There she got deep X-ray treatments for two months. In April, 1948, a gynecologist found new tumors, but advised that no more X-rays should be given at present.

First seen, June 16, 1946. Patient had vaginal discharge, slightly creamy and watery. No blood. Was depressed and fearful, lost 10 pounds in recent weeks. Menstruation ceased March, 1946, after two months of deep X-ray treatment. Gynecological examination showed no cervix, but a crater covered with pus, uterus a little shrunken, ligamenta lata enlarged and harder on the left side. Some nodules in the left vaginal vault and towards the rectum. Abdomen free, liver and spleen not enlarged, no glands in the inguinal areas nor abdomen. Blood pressure and other organs were normal. Weight 137½ lbs. In her report of July 15, 1954, she wrote that she was examined July 14, 1954. The physician could not find any abnormal condition. She had no other treatment whatsoever in the meantime. She wrote: "I took the diet and medications faithfully eighteen months." Then she discontinued medication and diet gradually. "At the present time, I am eating everything just as anyone else. My weight is now 142 lbs. My appetite is good and my bowel conditions excellent."

Last Report, July 22, 1957: "I am glad to report that so far I have been feeling fine and up to last December (1956) when I had my last examination, there had been no change in my well-being."

CASE No. 47

Mrs. V. B., age—36, married, two children.

Family, negative.

Clinical Diagnosis: Cervix carcinoma, inoperable case.

Biopsy and Operation Report:

Report of specialist: "She had not been in my office in over a year until February 3, 1947, at which time she gave a history of irregular menstruation with some bloody stain each day which had persisted for several months.

"On examination, I found the cervix covered with a growth which on biopsy proved to be squamous epithelial carcinoma. It was an inoperative case, so I turned her over to our leading radiologists."

Previous History:

At the first delivery, seventeen years ago, she had a bad hemorrhage. Menstruation was not regular; she hemorrhaged often twice a month, each time lasting seven to nine days. Finally, a fibroid tumor was discovered. She was operated on in 1947, and the uterus was fixed in a normal position. Then she had another pregnancy, with normal delivery and no abnormal hemorrhage.

February, 1946, patient observed slight discharge from the vagina which became darker and more bloody. Examination by gynecologist revealed the findings mentioned above. Biopsy taken: See above.

February and April, 1947, patient had radium and X-ray treatments, which could not be continued. Discharge discontinued for a while, but the last six weeks the discharge returned, containing blood and more pus. Artificial sterilization performed at that time.

Condition at time first seen, September 3, 1947: Gynecological examination revealed a large ulcerated cervix mass covered with blood and pus, easily bleeding on touch. Therefore, no further examination was called for. At the same time, patient had some hyperinsulinism which was corrected with the regular treatment in five weeks. Patient felt free of discharge and free of pain, July, 1949. She started to get cramps in the chest and upper abdomen with a burning sensation. She kept on eating, but "nothing did me good." Her nervous excitement and depression became worse. She couldn't sleep, was tearing, menstruation had not returned since the deep X-ray treatments. Hot flashes appeared with bad palpitation. Larger potassium doses helped again without additional sex hormones, as I observed on several patients that additional sex hormones reactivated the cancer condition. I was and am very hesitant to give the cancer patients the same or contrary sex hormones a year or longer before they are entirely free of symptoms and general disturbances.

Report of the Gynecological Examination, September 16, 1949: Examination of Mrs. B. reveals no evidence of any pelvic or abdominal palpable recurrence. The vaginal wall is completely fibrosed. There is no area of erosion whatsoever. The entire pelvic findings are similarly negative. There is slight sensitivity in the right adnexal area but there are no areas of thickening, nor pelvic mass. Nothing definite was felt in the upper abdomen.

"I therfore would consider this patient at present free from any recurrence in the pelvis and in the abdomen."

In the following years, patient felt good and remained free of any recurrence or pathological disturbance.

On June 23, 1954, she wrote the following: "I am delighted to tell you I am feeling wonderful. I would say my physical condition is probably better than it has been since the birth of my first child twenty-four years ago. I had a complete physical a few months ago and the only trouble anywhere was a spastic condition in my stomach; however, that is all right now. No, I have not had any recurrence of my former condition."

Last Report, August 5, 1957: Very good condition, bodily and mentally. "I am in wonderful health. I have not had any cause to be concerned or anxious about my old condition."

CASE No. 48

Mr. E. M., age—51, married, no children.

Family history, negative.

Clinical Diagnosis: Squamous cellcarcinoma of left kidney, left ureter, recurrence in urinary bladder.

Biopsy Report and Operation:

"He was first admitted December 4, 1946, with a provisional diagnosis of tumor of the ureter. The next day following admission a ureterectomy, left, was performed. The pathological diagnosis on the procedure was reported as squamous cell epithelioma of pelvis, of left kidney, grade II, papillary type, left ureter, following squamous cell epithelioma of pelvis of left kidney. He gave a history of having left nephrectomy for malignancy four months prior to his admission and not until one month ago did he discover blood in his urine. He was dismissed on the 19th with an uneventful post-operative recovery. He had no complications of any sort.

"On his second admission, two years later, December 5, 1948, provisional diagnosis was carcinoma of the bladder. On December 6th, biopsy

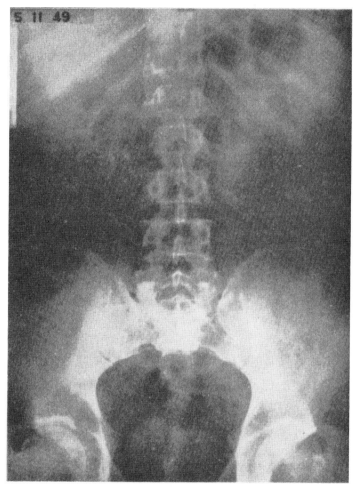

Case 48, No. 1 — 5/11/49
5 minutes after injection

and fulguration of the bladder with implantation of radon seeds were performed. Pathological diagnosis revealed papillary squamous cell epithelioma, grade II. He again had an uneventful post-operative course and was dismissed December 20, 1948."

Condition when first seen, May 9, 1949: Patient complained about attacks of spasms and sharp pain in the bladder, very often passing blood and pus, and a growing mass of glands in left groin. Examination revealed enlargement of the prostate with smooth surface. He reported that the prostate was massaged for five years, once a month. Urination was frequent and painful. In the left lower quadrant, there were two smaller tumors palpable. Treatment started immediately. After two weeks, the bleeding stopped; after six months both tumors in left lower quadrant were no longer palpable, and the glands in the left groin entirely disappeared. Renewed cystoscopic examination revealed scar formation only. Urine was free, after two months, and remained so, up to the last report, July 20, 1952. There was also a new cystoscopy made, which was negative. Patient was, after six months, able to take up his daily work and remained in his occupation free of further recurrences up to the present time.

May 11, 1949: X-ray Kidneys (Intravenous Pyelography).

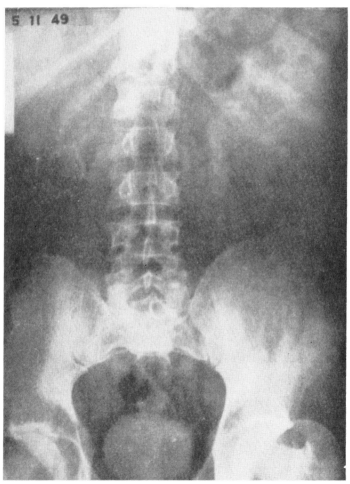

Case 48, No. 2 — 5/11/49
15 minutes after injection

5-15-30 min. films: Shows normal calices, pelvis and ureter on the right side. The urinary tract on the left side is not visualized. The bladder is filled showing a regular outline.

Conclusion: Normally functioning right kidney.

May 12, 1949: Mr. M. was here today for bladder observation. A 16 F.B.B. scope was passed (for cystoscopy) with ease under local anesthesia.

A urine specimen was obtained. This revealed 5-6 w.b.c. per h.p.f. — and no r.b.c. The gross specimen was also negative for occult blood. Examination of the bladder on the right side was essentially negative. The right ureteral orifice was normal and functioning satisfactorily. The bladder neck was also negative. On the left side in the region of the ureteral orifice there was an area of slough which was washed away. This left crater-like depression of redness. This apparently is the area which was operated upon and implanted with radon seeds. No orifice on this side. Examination revealed no evidence of recurrence of the bladder tumor.

The posterior urethra was negative. No residual urine was also found on a check-up. It appears that Mr. M. is well controlled to date and was advised to have his periodic checks.

Last Report, August 5, 1957: "I am proud to state that I am working every day and have been, since I was in New York in 1949. I am feeling fine."

CASE No. 49

Mrs. F. H., age—53, married, one child.

Clinical Diagnosis: Cancer of the urinary bladder. Migraine headache.

Biopsy Report (Toronto Hospital, Canada):

"A cystoscopic examination was carried out on the 6th of August, 1955, and showed the presence of multiple pedunculated, papillary tumors scattered throughout the bladder. They totalled about eight or nine in number and each had a well-defined stalk and each tumor appeared to be well epithelialized. The separate growths measured about 1 x 2 cms and each was papillary. There was no infiltration of the base observed. Each bladder tumor was resected and a second resection was accomplished ten days after the initial examination and treatment.

"I was anxious to have Mrs. H. complete the examination by having an intravenous urogram done; however, she was considerably upset by my findings and wished to continue further treatment in New York or nearer to home.

"The surgical pathology report from the Toronto Western Hospital reads as follows:

"Section shows papillary masses of fairly well differentiated tumor cells of transitional cell type. A few mitotic figures are seen."

Diagnosis: Transitional cell carcinoma of bladder (grade 2).

Previous History:

She was never sick before except for migraine headaches, which were more severe during menstrual periods. She was not relieved from the migraine headaches during and following the time of her menopause. That is, according to my experiences, an exceptional condition.

May, 1955, patient first noticed blood in the urine without having pain. She remained free of pain and had no other abnormal symptoms. While on vacation she travelled to Canada where she observed quite a bit of constant bleeding in the urine. Cystoscopic examination revealed carcinoma of the bladder. The urologist in the Toronto Hospital recommended removal of the bladder and insertion of the ureters into the abdominal wall. Patient refused the operation, and wanted to see another authority in Walter Reed Hospital, who also confirmed the necessity of the operation. Patient refused.

Condition when first seen, September 8, 1955: Treatment started immediately. Patient was depressed, very nervous, and had, during the first days, severe migraine headaches, so that she could hardly eat anything. Such attacks were lasting 8 to 10 days at home. In the Cancer Clinic she had only one attack lasting three days and a second one lasting no longer than one day. After one week, she had only one light bleeding lasting only a few hours. She was discharged after four weeks of intensive treatment, free of pain, free of bleedings and free of migraine headaches which always brought about a kind of depression and fearful feelings. When she was free of migraine headaches and observed that no further bleedings occurred, she became hopeful and said, "Life starts again for me." Patient continued the treatment at home. She returned in June, 1956, for further observations. Cystoscopy revealed the following: "I was impressed by the very good general condition of the patient. At cystoscopy, I found a small scar at the site of the previous biopsy. No tumor in bladder seen but a very small papilloma at the sphincter region on the right side. As we discussed this case over the telephone, we both felt it would be best for the patient not to do anything with this small papilloma, just to watch it as it definitely did not look like a malignancy."

Patient returned May 16, 1957. After a period of six weeks not on the diet, migraine headaches returned, but in a milder form. However, the patient was afraid that with the migraine, the cancer may also have returned, despite the fact that the urine remained always normal.

Reexamination with cystoscopy revealed the following: "Urine yellow, turbid, no macroscopic hematuria. 3 tumors which had the size of a cherry were seen at the right side of the bladder; a small reddish area was seen above the left ureteral orifice. This area was coagulated. Biopsy taken of tumor medial to right ureteral orifice (#1), another biopsy taken from a tumor at the sphincter region at 11 o'clock (#2). Both these tumors were fulgurated and destroyed. The third tumor was lateral to the right ureteral orifice at the lateral bladder-wall, near the sphincter at about 9 o'clock. This tumor was fulgurated also. Complete hemostasis obtained, no other pathology in bladder seen."

New Biopsy Report: "Specimen consists of a few small pieces of soft, friable, greyish white tissue, removed from the bladder for biopsy study."

Microscopic Diagnosis, May 23, 1957: Papilloma.

"No malignant changes noted."

Last Report, August 11, 1957: "I am pleased to tell you that I am feeling fine and enjoying a normal life again. No more migraine headaches and I have more strength and endurance than I have had in years."

Specialist writes, September 21, 1957: I cystoscoped Mrs. F. H. on September 19, 1957. "There was no tumor in the bladder found, even the scars of the previous operations could not be seen. A pronounced cystitis colli (trigonitis) was present, both ureteral openings were normal in size, position and outline."

CASE No. 50

Mrs. E. P., age 71, married, four children.

Clinical Diagnosis: Adenocarcinoma of uterus and metastases in urinary bladder and vagina.

Biopsy Report: Adenocarcinoma of body of uterus.

Previous History:

"10 to 12 years ago, she started to have difficulty in holding her urine. March, 1952, a sudden, profuse bleeding from vagina started; brought to St. Francis Hospital in Trenton, New Jersey. Examination there revealed tumor of uterus inoperable, therefore no special treatment recommended other than sedation. September 1953, again taken the same hospital where they applied 20 deep X-ray treatments. Further X-ray treatments had to be discontinued because of abundant hemorrhage. 3 blood transfusions necessary. February, 1954, patient could not retain urine. Examination revealed a large opening from the urinary bladder into the vagina. In addition, large tumor masses all around."

Condition at time first seen, March 30, 1954: External genitalia extensively swollen and skin partly ulcerated. Outside large eczematous condition from constantly dropping urine. There was little bleeding, but the patient was very weak, and had to sit in a chair most of the time. Treatment immediately applied. After two and a half weeks of treatment she felt much better, could keep the urine for three hours at night, when lying down, and went to toilet without a drip. She could not pass urine in the natural way for the past six months. During the daytime, she passed urine every one to two hours, but in addition there was some leakage. May, 1955, the swelling of the external genital organs disappeared and the tumor

URINE ANALYSIS TABLE
Case No. 50

Date	4/6/54	4/13/54	4/22/54	4/27/54	7/27/54	11/4/54	1/11/55	3/30/55	3/18/57
Reaction	alk.					alk.	alk.	neutral	pH 9
Spec. Grav.	1010	1006	1003	1003	1010	1014	1010	1008	1011
Albumin	3 plus	1 plus	2 plus	3 plus	2 plus	2 plus	—	—	—
Sugar	—	—	—	—	—	—	—	—	—
Acetone	—	—	—	—	—	—	—	—	—
Diac. acid	—	—	—	—	—	—	—	—	—
Casts	—	—	—	—	—	—	—	—	—
Leucocytes	10-15	4-5	1-2	2-3	1-3	none	1-3	3-4	none
Erythrocytes	masses	60-65	2-3	1-2	1-2	none	none	1-2	none
Epithelium	many	a few	a few		a few	many	occ.	a few	a few

masses around the vagina and both ligamenta lata were greatly reduced. In the next year, her general condition recovered almost to normal, but the fistula to the vagina did not improve, and drainage was reduced to a certain degree only. Gynecological examination, June, 1956, revealed only large fistula from the urinary bladder to vagina. Operation for the vesico-vaginal-fistula was also now impossible because of the great amount of scars all around the vagina and urine bladder. Patient was seen a few months ago, is doing some housework, and she accepted her fate with the fistula, which is the only after effect which remained from the disease.

Last Report, August 5, 1957: "I am feeling just fine and do help my daughter as much as she will let me. I have not an ache or pain. I have the feeling that the whole thing may clear up. I have voided lately several times in a natural way in the daytime."

APPENDIX I
Restoring the Healing Mechanism in other Chronic Diseases
by Charlotte (Lotte) Gerson Straus

The title of this book is *A Cancer Therapy - Results of Fifty Cases*. In the course of the book, Dr. Gerson explains the underlying ideas and proves his theories by the results which he obtained. However, the title seems to restrict his therapy to the treatment of cancer. The reason Dr. Gerson chose to present his therapy to the medical profession and to the public as a treatment for cancer specifically was because cancer, of all chronic conditions, presents the most complete degeneration, poisoning, and destruction of the human body. The aim of this therapy is to restore the body's healing mechanism, the functions of all its organs, and the future maintenance of health. Since this could be achieved in the most severe, terminal cancer cases as presented here, it follows that the same therapy could achieve restoration and healing in other, less destructive chronic conditions. "In all textbooks, we find that single biological processes have been studied and overestimated statements made about them. The symptoms of the disease have become the main problem for research, clinical work, and therapy. Medical science has eliminated the totality of the natural biological rules in the human body, mostly by dividing research and practice into many specialties. . . . It was forgotten that every part is still only a piece of the entire body." (*Cancer Therapy*, p. 13)

The specialization of research and medical practice may be an outgrowth of the microbe theory of disease. It became fixed in the minds of researchers that there must be a specific cause for each disease. But as Dr. Gerson expresses it, cancer is not specific. It is a degenerative condition of the total metabolism, including damage to the liver and all essential organs, which then makes it possible for cancer to develop. Similar damage also precedes other chronic diseases. "All degenerative diseases, such as mental diseases, arthritis, hardening of the arteries, heart (coronary) diseases... all show liver damage." (M. Gerson, Radio Interview)

According to Dr. Gerson's observation, "The food is taken into the body through the digestive canal but sometimes the digestive system lacks the ability to break it up from one intermediary substance into the next. These normal intermediary substances remain in the blood stream and cause abnormal substances to be formed if they are not digested to their end product and fully eliminated. Through accumulation and backing up, these abnormal substances finally exert a harmful influence on the organism. Individual factors, special weakness of a set of tissues previously damaged, will determine which tissues will finally react or which organs will be affected unfavorably. For example, we can see that disturbances of the fat metabolism may lead to psoriasis if only a certain feature of the fat metabolism is abnormal; but when the fat metabolism is disturbed as a result of a general decrease in the oxidizing power, as happens in arteriosclerosis, then the tissues of the arteries will show the damage." (M. Gerson, unpublished article)

Thus, similar disturbances can cause different degenerative diseases. According to Dr. Gerson's many years of experience, when the liver and all essential organs function fully, whether originally or when restored after disease, the body can eliminate all chronic disease and maintain health. All the body's defenses must be reactivated, including its immunity, inflammation reaction, enzyme function, dissolving of lumps and scars, carrying off of waste or dead matter, etc.

These are sweeping statements, not in accordance with orthodox medical thinking—"specialization," local treatment such as surgery, drug therapy, and radiation. Surgery, radiation, and chemotherapy do not restore the full, normal function of the entire system in cancer patients but tend to further damage the liver and other essential organs. In other degenerative conditions too, the orthodox approach is either symptomatic (i.e., aspirin to relieve pain in arthritis, anti-clotting agents and dilating drugs in coronary disease to avoid blockage of arteries) or local (i.e., the replacement of a sick hip-joint, or the removal of a sick kidney). This symptomatic approach does not restore normal organ function. With a total therapy, by reactivating all organs, sick kidneys can be brought back to function; blood clots can be dissolved and prevented from forming again; arthritic processes can be dissolved and carried off and bones restructured, etc., etc.

According to Dr. Gerson's research, the beginning of all chronic disease is the loss of Potassium (K) from the cells and invasion of Sodium (Na) into the cells—and with it water. This causes edema and the resulting malfunctions—loss of electrical potentials in the cells, improper enzyme formation, reduced cell oxidation, etc. The building of almost all enzymes requires K as a catalyst (activating agent) and is inhibited (slowed or stopped) by Na (Dixon and Webb, *Enzymes*, pp. 422-423). The extent of these malfunctions then determines how and to what extent the system is affected and where the symptoms will occur. Obviously, previous damage, weakness, or trauma are also determining factors. In order to initiate healing then, it is essential to remove excess Na from the cells, re-introduce large amounts of K, and detoxify the system of accumulated intermediary substances and other toxins. This is best accomplished by large amounts of K from fresh fruit and juices, detoxification through the kidneys and by enemas, and reactivation of the liver by special liver therapy. If this were only a theoretical assumption, it would not be worth mentioning. However, in Dr. Gerson's many years of experience with all types of chronic disease, this process worked in practice. Degenerative diseases could be reversed, eliminated, and the body healed.

In the process of restoring the body's functions, its own healing activity will take over in eliminating the specific symptoms. The body will activate enzymes to carry off arthritic swellings, lumps, and bony processes. It will reactivate its immune responses to attack tuberculosis or other chronic infections and inflammations. It will dissolve old scars and adhesions, ulcerative processes, absorb pus, eliminate allergies. In muscular dystrophy, normal enzyme activity can be restored and new muscle is formed. In multiple sclerosis, myelin sheaths are healed and further deterioration is stopped (dead nerve tissue cannot be re-activated, of course). In mental diseases, abnormal blood chemistry is eliminated and brain cells again function normally. In diabetes, much of the pancreas can be reactivated so that usually within a month insulin can be discontinued. Kidneys which no longer function can be restored to near normal. Kidney dialysis machines and organ transplants become unnecessary. In certain patients some weaknesses in the system remain. They have to be recognized and certain types of foods have to be permanently prohibited. There are too many chronic diseases to mention here, but it can be said that even obscure, unrecognized conditions can be relieved. As we have said before, the body will heal itself when given the right substances and help in detoxification. Local or symptomatic treatment does not heal. Excising a tumor or irradiating it does not heal cancer. Nor does aspirin heal arthritis nor insulin diabetes.

A normal, healthy body has its own healing mechanism—immune

response to germ invasion, healing inflammation, mending of broken bones and skin, elimination of toxicity, etc. In chronic disease, these defenses have been lost or damaged.

This inability to heal is caused by various malfunctions including loss of normal mineral balances, poisoning of essential organs due to toxicity, and incomplete digestion and elimination. In order to initiate healing, the first and constant care of the physician is to detoxify the body, especially the liver-bile system. Coffee enemas are the principal means of detoxifying. The caffeine was found to dilate the bile ducts and stimulate discharge of accumulated toxins. Frequent intake of freshly pressed raw fruit and vegetable juices stimulated the kidneys to detoxify the body. Since the juices are extremely rich in minerals, enzymes, and vitamins, they begin the process of returning these substances to the seriously depleted organs. It is not possible to simplify this process by giving, for example, only water to supply the fluid and pills containing vitamins, minerals, and enzymes. The severely toxic and damaged system is unable to absorb and utilize just concentrated preparations. Pills and concentrated substances have a tendency to irritate the severely ill patient further and cause him to lose more of his own already depleted reserves.

As an extension to this reasoning. Dr. Gerson opposed fasting as a detoxification procedure. True, in heavy over-eaters, fasting may be of some use. However, it should not be applied in chronic diseases because deficiencies are always present. Fasting does not restore the urgently needed minerals and vitamins to the organs. Enemas, freshly squeezed juices, and much raw and freshly prepared food achieves detoxification much more quickly and efficiently than fasting. At the same time, this approach helps the body restore the deficient organs and thus restore its healing ability.

Initial evidence of the healing process brought about by the Gerson therapy takes various forms. For instance, edemas go down with astonishing rapidity; skin afflictions recede and heal quickly; in areas of old scars, adhesions, lumps, or bone deformations, "healing" often begins as a hyperemia, i.e., the body produces dilated blood vessels with redness and tenderness in the affected area. The newly oxygenated blood, now freshly supplied with enzymes and other healing substances, is brought into the damaged or sick areas. This may alarm the patient and sometimes even the doctor not familiar with this therapy and its "healing reaction" (see flare ups, p. 201). This healing reaction can be frightening and misinterpreted if long forgotten scars or poorly healed injuries flare up along with the flare ups expected for the major condition being treated. "These reactions have even caused an occasional patient to give up the treatment when he was within reach of excellent results." (Max Gerson)

It must be kept in mind that in a body in which the healing mechanism is being reactivated, the healing cannot be done selectively. The healing mechanism will attack all chronic problems. All old dormant and active diseases are eliminated. (See Case No. 6 where syphilis disappeared along with the cancer without the use of any specific anti-syphilis drug or antibiotic.)

In the 1930's Dr. Gerson had not brought his treatment to the point where he was able to obtain consistently good results in the treatment of cancer. However with this less intensive treatment, in Dr. Gerson's own words in 1932:

"My results with the Gerson Therapy have been very satisfactory is arthritis deformans. X-ray examination shows that the structure of the diseased bones changes with the use of the Gerson diet. The compacta becomes denser and more sharply outlined. Subjectively, the patients' symptoms improve, their motility and ability to work returns. In these cases, it is particularly important to restrict protein intake.

"Epilepsy reacts very favorably. Previously in 1900 the two French scientists, Toulouse and Richet, used the saltless diet in cases of epilepsy with good results. With the addition of phosphorus-enriched cod-liver oil and strictly limited protein intake, healing was speeded visibly. Mental disease was helped. Neurasthenia was greatly improved. Even in cases of neurasthenia *with* male impotence, potency returned. On the other hand, patients with unusually strong libido returned to a more normal condition.

"In the tremendously extensive area of skin diseases, the saltless therapy is extremely valuable—i.e., in acne, eczema, urticaria, prurigo, pemphigus, etc., as already stressed by Luithlen. However, the use of the Gerson therapy in lupus vulgaris and psoriasis is a first and is extremely effective, even in severe cases with already partial sclerodermy. It is particularly interesting to note the scar-dissolving effect of the treatment in old scars and adhesions as well as in cases of Keloid acne.

"Multiple sclerosis responds well. The ulcerations or scar tissue are absorbed and healed. However, where there is destruction of nerve tissue, obviously this cannot be restored.

"Many other chronic diseases respond extremely well to the Gerson therapy even though in many cases their origin is obscure or unknown. Exophthalmic goiter (Grave's disease) responds well. However patients must be given proteins after about four weeks or weakness and loss of weight may result.

"Dysmenorrhea, vaginal discharge, atypical menstrual periods (of 21 days or 5 to 6 weeks) return gradually to normal cycles of 28 days.

"The use of the therapy in kidney disorders should be obvious. It is also important to note that diseases of the respiratory organs, such as asthma, respond very well. Bronchiectasis, also chronic cases, react well without exception.

"One important field of application of the therapy is in heart and circulatory diseases where the results are excellent, also in arteriosclerosis and connected kidney diseases. In these cases, it is important to limit protein intake.

"It is interesting to note here that in almost all cases of serious migraine, the presence of paradentosis was noted. This always disappeared together with the migraine. I found later that the presence of paradentosis was often true in cases of severe arthritis deformans, too."

Thus, in Dr. Gerson's own words, we have a survey of chronic diseases which could be helped and healed by his method-as used in the early 1930's. The purpose of this addition to the book is to outline in more detail the treatment used for chronic diseases other than cancer.

With the start of the Gerson therapy, all of the usual drugs have to be discontinued. This includes not only the highly toxic pain killers often administered to terminal cancer patients but also chemotherapeutic agents, cytotoxins, blood thinners, vasodilators, cortisone, antihistamines, and others too numerous to mention. These drugs are materials foreign to the body. They place an additional burden on the liver which must eliminate foreign materials. Also these drugs contribute nothing positive toward rebuilding the diseased organs. The purpose of the therapy is to reduce and eliminate the load of toxic materials which have accumulated. Obviously one must not add to this load.

For cancer patients, even in advanced stages, pain relief was promptly obtained by the use of coffee enemas, given every two hours in some cases. In the first few days of the therapy, it was sometimes necessary to add "pain relief." In these cases Dr. Gerson allowed the use of the following, used together: one tablet of aspirin (5 gr.), one Vitamin C (100 mg) and one Niacin (50 mg) up to four times in the course of 24 hours. These "three pills" also produced restful sleep. Their action is surprisingly effective once spasms and edema are eliminated through large doses of potassium given immediately at the start of the treatment with de-toxification. The relief obtained through the use of the constantly given coffee enemas is quickly noted by the patients and they often voluntarily take more than the number prescribed. This practice should be encouraged as no harm can come of it. In fact, the only danger to the cancer patient can arise from insufficient de-toxification—not enough enemas—and the possible poisoning of the liver (see hepatic coma, p. 198).

Insulin is a substance normally manufactured by the body and is not toxic. In diabetics, it must be continued at the beginning of the therapy. The blood and urine of these patients must be carefully monitored as the therapy progresses, because the pancreas starts to function again. Often insulin dosage can be cut in half within 10 days of the start of the therapy and can be entirely eliminated within a month in most cases.

Dietary adjustments made for diabetic patients were to reduce the number of baked potatoes given from two to one a day, to use grapefruit juice for breakfast instead of orange juice, and to give more green juice than apple and carrot juice.

In coronary disease Dr. Gerson added two tablespoons of cold pressed linseed oil (food grade) to the medication. The linseed oil promptly reduces the cholesterol level in the blood. In combination with the remainder of the therapy, the danger of clotting is eliminated even though all drugs such as blood thinners and capillary dilators were discontinued. The same amount of linseed oil was also added to the diet of cancer patients. Dr. Gerson made this addition to the therapy just after the publication of the present book. This explains why it was not described in the book. It must be mentioned here, since he subsequently used it regularly and with such excellent effect in helping to reduce the high cholesterol level in cancer and arteriosclerosis patients. In cancer patients it also speeded up the reduction and absorption of the tumors.

In cases of multiple sclerosis, egg yolks were used rather early in the treatment (in cancer patients, yolks could not be given for over a year). In arthritis patients, protein had to be held at a low level for longer periods of time while in goiter it had to be added after three to four weeks. In muscular dystrophy, special attention had to be paid to re-establishing the iodine metabolism and especially in fatty hypertrophy cases, large doses of thyroid were necessary. Let us understand again that cancer does not respond to the earlier, less stringent therapy but must be treated exactly as outlined on pp. 235-248. It is important to note that with the "strictest cancer diet," other chronic diseases respond more rapidly than with the less intensive treatment. It is also self-defeating to become too lax in the application of the treatment, with the rationalization that "a little bit of this or that won't hurt." This is not correct. "A little bit" interferes with absorption and detoxifi-cation. "A little bit more" will erase all benefits. Therefore, when we outline below the earlier, less intensive therapy a patient can use for non-neoplastic chronic diseases, we must stress the following:

1. Forbidden foods and stimulants (p. 238) cannot be introduced into the diet with the exception of some fresh berries and safflower oil.

2. Detoxification must be carried on regularly, although 2 to 3 coffee enemas a day are sufficient.

3. The amount of fresh juices can be reduced to 4 to 5 glasses a day plus one glass of citrus juice (always freshly prepared just before drinking). Also, carrot and apple juice may be mixed in the course of preparation with the green leaf juice, and a centrifugal type juicer may be used. In order to speed up healing, more juices and. press-type juicers are recommended.

4. The special soup and menus should be adhered to (p. 244). After initial improvement, usually the patient can go back to work and adjust his lunch to include soup (brought from home in a vacuum bottle), fresh juice, a baked potato, fresh mixed salad, and fruit. Much fresh fruit should be eaten during the day.

Aside from the addition of linseed oil to the dietary treatment since the first publication of this volume, some other things require special mention. Fluoridation of the water supply has become very common in many communities. Since fluorides are among the most powerful enzyme inhibitors and since healing requires the reactivation of enzymes, it is obvious that fluorides must be eliminated from all food and water supplies as much as possible. In areas where water is fluoridated, patients should use spring water or distilled water for making soup, teas, and even for enemas. Fluoridated toothpastes or enzyme inhibiting toothpastes must be avoided along with other toxic substances such as insect sprays, paint sprays, underarm deodorants, and toxic or pore-clogging grooming substances.

After an initial period of only vegetarian foods, certain milk products become part of the therapy. These include buttermilk, yogurt, and pot (cottage) cheese. Dr. Gerson's intent was to have the patient use only defatted, unsalted products; At present, buttermilk is often "cultured" instead of churned, is sometimes made from whole milk, and is often salted. When buttermilk is added to the patient's diet after the first three to six weeks, care must be taken that it has no fat content and that no salt is added (read list of ingredients). Pot cheese (or cottage cheese) similarly must be made of skim milk without added cream or salt. Yogurt means only natural yogurt, without flavoring additions, fruit, or sweeteners, and should be made from defatted milk. If any of these items is not available without fat or salt, it is better to omit it and use one of the others in its place.

(Continued on next page)

The Less Intensive Gerson Therapy
for Non-Malignant Diseases
(should not be used in the treatment of cancer)

See: Allowed and forbidden foods; preparation of foods and juices, pp. 237-247. Forbidden foods are the same, except fresh berries may be used occasionally, also safflower oil may be used in salad dressing.

First 3 to 4 weeks: no animal proteins whatsoever. Time depends on severity of condition and patient's response.

If water supply is fluoridated, use spring or distilled water for making soup, teas, stewed fruit, etc.

For the preparation of juices, a centrifugal type juicer may be used, although it is not as effective as the press-type. Juice may be made of a combination of carrots, apples, green leaves, etc. instead of making carrot-and-apple juice and green-leaf juice separately.

Breakfast, lunch and dinners: see sample menu, pp. 244. Between meals: juice and fresh fruit as often as possible.

Medication:
    1 tablespoonful of 10% solution of potassium compound (p. 246) in each glass of juice (6-8 a day)
    1 tablet of niacin, 50 mg., three times a day, with meals
    2 capsules Vitamin E (made of mixed tocopherols, not acetate) 400 I.U. each, or equivalent, in the morning
    1 drop lugol's solution in glass of juice, morning and night (total: 2 drops full strength, or equivalent)
    2 tablets Pancreatin, Lilly 1001, three times daily with meals
    2 capsules Vitamin A (from fish liver oil), 25,000 units each, or equivalent, at night before retiring
    500 mg. Vitamin C twice daily, morning and night
    Injection of Crude Liver Extract, Lilly 370; 3cc, 3 times a week, intramuscularly
    2 tablets defatted, dessicated liver with each meal
    4 tablets 3 times daily of brewer's yeast (or 2 rounded tbsp. daily)
    2 capsules Acidol (see p. 236a & 246) before each meal

No other medication should be used except for pain relief *after enema has been tried first*: 1 aspirin, 1 Vitamin C (100 mg.), 1 niacin (50 mg.). This medication no more than 4 times in 24 hours.

Enemas: Two coffee enemas daily, preferably three, after meals (not at bedtime). Take additional coffee enema immediately if in pain or discomfort of any kind.

After 3 to 4 weeks, depending on severity of condition and on patient's reaction, add defatted, plain yogurt, 2 cups daily, or one cup plus ½ Ib. uncreamed, unsalted cottage cheese. Mix with yogurt and onions, chives, garlic, etc. or mix with fruit, raw or stewed, and honey. If these proteins cause renewed symptoms or disturbances, omit again. Two level tablespoons of bee pollen may be used daily.
Depending on condition, add lean fish, boiled or broiled, after 4 - 6 months. Start with the use of a small portion once a week; add more only if no trouble is noted. If renewed symptoms occur, omit immediately.

An intensive Gerson Therapy is indicated in cases of serious degeneration or intoxication (including previous long term drug usage) such as (pp. 81, 82, 210):
  1. intoxication during pregnancy
  2. tuberculosis
  3. osteoarthritis
  4. mental disease & bodily aesthenias
  5. spastic conditions, especially angina pectoris
  6. asthma
  7. malignancies
  8. spinal cord degenerative changes

APPENDIX II

The Cure of Advanced Cancer by Diet Therapy:
A Summary of Thirty Years of Clinical Experimentation*
Max Gerson, M.D.

Reprinted by permission of *Physiological Chemistry and Physics and Medical NMR*, Meridional Publications, Route 2, Box 28 A, Wake Forest, North Carolina 27587

Thirty years of clinical experimentation has led to a successful therapy for advanced cancer. This therapy is based on the concepts (1) that cancer patients have low immuno-reactivity and generalized tissue damage, especially of the liver, and (2) that when the cancer is destroyed, toxic degradation products appear in the bloodstream which lead to coma and death from liver failure. The therapy consists of high potassium, low sodium diet, with no fats or oils, and minimal animal proteins. Juices of raw fruits and vegetables and of raw liver provide active oxidizing enzymes which facilitate rehabilitation of the liver. Iodine and niacin supplementation is used. Caffeine enemas cause dilation of bile ducts, which facilitates excretion of toxic cancer breakdown products by the liver and dialysis of toxic products from blood across the colonic wall. The therapy must be used as an integrated whole. Parts of the therapy used in isolation will not be successful. This therapy has cured many cases of advanced cancer.

Ladies and Gentlemen:

I came here on vacation, I didn't come here for a lecture. I didn't bring anything. So, I wrote down some things since I was asked to tell you first how I arrived at the cancer treatment. It is a funny story.

When I was a physician for internal diseases in Bielefeld [Germany] in 1928, one day I was called to see a lady. I asked her what was wrong with her but on the telephone she didn't want to tell me. So I went there, a little outside of town. Then I asked her "What's wrong?" She told me she was operated on in a big clinic nearby and they found a cancer of the bile duct. I saw the operation scar. She was running a high fever, was jaundiced. I told her, "Sorry, I can do nothing for you. I don't know how to treat cancer. I

*Publisher's Note. This is a lecture given by Dr. Gerson in Escondido, California, in 1956. Dr. Gerson died in 1959. Socioeconomic and political perspectives are discussed in the book *Has Dr. Max Gerson a True Cancer Cure?* by S. J. Haught, (now published as *Cancer? Think Curable: The Gerson Therapy*, Gerson Institute, 1983). Gerson Institute, 1572 Second Ave., San Diego, CA 92101

have not seen results, especially in such an advanced case where there is no longer the possibility of operation." So, she said, "No, doctor, I called because I saw the results in your treatment of tuberculosis and arthritis in various cases. Now, here is a pad and you write down a treatment. On that table over there, there is a book, and in that book, you will be good enough to read to me aloud the chapter called 'The Healing of Cancer.' "

It was a big book of about 1,200 pages on folk medicine and in the middle there was that chapter. I started to read. That book was edited by three schoolteachers and one physician. None of them practiced medicine. So they put together that book. I read that chapter. In it there was something about Hippocrates who gave these patients a special soup. I should like to tell you, we use that soup at the present time! That soup from that book, out of the practice of Hippocrates—550 years before Christ! He was the greatest physician at that time, and I even think the greatest physician of all time. He had the idea that the patient has to be detoxified with the soup and with some enemas and so on.

I read and read but finally I told the lady, "Look, because of my tuberculosis treatment physicians are opposed to me. Therefore I'd like not to treat you." Again she insisted, "I'll give you in writing that you are not responsible for the outcome of the treatment and that I insisted that you do so." So with that signed statement, I thought, all right, let's try.

I wrote down the treatment. It was almost the same which I used for tuberculosis patients[1-7] which I had worked out and used at the University Clinic in Munich with Prof. Sauerbruch. After the work at the University Clinic the treatment had been established and had been found effective.[8,9] I thought that maybe it will be effective in cancer too. It is always written in scientific books that tuberculosis and cancer are both degenerative diseases where the body has to be detoxified. But this latter thought was written only by Hippocrates.

I tried—and the patient was cured! Six months later she was up and around in the best condition. Then she sent me two other cancer cases. One of her family with a stomach cancer where it had been found during an attempted operation that there were metastasized glands around the stomach—also cured! And I had to cure then, against my will, a third case. I expected to have still more opposition from the medical profession. The third case was also a stomach cancer. It was also cured. Three cases were tried and all three cases were cured!

I have to tell you that up to this day, I don't know how this happened, how I stumbled into that, how this was achieved. At that time I always said that I didn't know why they were cured. I didn't know enough about cancer and it was such a difficult problem to go into. But once it was in my head and in my hands and in my heart, I could no longer separate myself from that problem.

Some time later I was in Vienna. I had left Germany due to the political upheaval at the time of Hitler. There in Vienna I tried six cases and in all six cases, no results—all failures. That was shocking. The sanatorium where I treated my patients was not so well organized for dietary treatments. They treated other diseases by other methods and didn't pay much attention to diet. So, I attributed the failures to that.

Then I came to Paris. In Paris, I tried seven cases and I had three results. One of the cases was an older man. He had a cancer of the cecum where the colon starts, 70 years old. Another case was a lady from Armenia. This was a very interesting case. I had to work against the whole family. There were many physicians in the family, and I had plenty of trouble. But, anyway, I came through in that case. She had cancer of the breast which regrew. Every time the family insisted that she was "so much down." She weighed only 78 pounds. She was skin and bones and they wanted me to give her egg yolks. I gave her small amounts of egg yolks—the cancer regrew. Then they insisted that I give her meat, raw chopped meat. I gave her this and the cancer regrew. The third time, they wanted me to give her some oil. I gave her the oil and the third time the cancer regrew. But, anyway, three times I could eliminate the cancer again and cure. And still I had no idea what cancer was. If somebody asked me about the theory, just what it was I was doing, I had to answer, "I don't really know myself."

Some time later I came to this country. I couldn't get the cancer problem and the cure of the first three cases out of my mind. I kept thinking "It must be possible, it would be a crime not to do it." But it wasn't so easy. When I came here, I had no clinic. I didn't even have a license to practice medicine. When I had taken the exams and could take patients, I had to treat them at home and that was hard work. The patients didn't like to obey the diet, to do it at home. They were accustomed to save kitchen time and not to work hard to make all the juices necessary for the treatment as it had been worked out.

Now the treatment for tuberculosis was a saltless diet, mostly fruit and vegetables, vegetables cooked without added water, steamed in their own juices, with a heavy pot, no aluminum. The cover had to be heavy and fit well so that the steam could not escape. Then they had to have most of the food raw, finely grated. They had to drink orange juice, grapefruit juice, and apple and carrot juice. This had to be produced in a special machine—a grinder and a separate press—because I found that in centrifugal juicers or liquefiers, I couldn't obtain the kind of juice which cured patients.

At first, I had thought that liquefiers would be the most wonderful thing. All the material was there, nothing was lost. But it didn't work. Then I found out through a physicist that in the liquefier, in the center, there is positive electricity and in the fluid there is negative electricity. This electricity kills the oxidizing enzymes. And that is also true for the centrifugal juicer and the other apparatus. The juice must therefore be made by a grinder and a separate press-if possible, made of stainless steel.

The patients must drink a lot of those juices. They have to have the Hippocrates soup. I can't go into all the details. The evening would not be long enough for that. But very important for the detoxification are enemas. I felt that the detoxification as suggested in the book of Hippocrates was a most important part.

Finally, I had a clinic. The patients saw that also the more advanced cases and even some terminal cases, very far advanced cases, could be saved. They brought me more and more of these terminal cases. I was forced into that. On the one side the knife of the AMA was at my throat, and on my back I had only terminal cases. If I had not saved them, my clinic would have been a death house. Some of the cases were brought on stretchers. They couldn't walk. They could no longer eat. It was very, very difficult. So, I really had to work out a treatment that could help these far advanced cases.[10,11] Again, I was forced into it.

On the need of where to put the emphasis: reading all the literature, I saw that all the scientists treat the symptoms. These, I thought, are only symptoms. There must be something basic behind them. It has to be impossible that there are symptoms in the brain, others in the lungs, in the bones, in the abdomen and in the liver. There must be something basic, or else this is impossible.

Already, through my work with tuberculosis, I learned that in tuberculosis and in all other degenerative diseases, one must not treat the symptoms. The body—the whole body—has to be treated. But that is easily said. How will you do it? Little by little I came to the conclusion that the most important part of our body is the digestive tract. For all our intake to be properly digested, and for the other organs of the digestive tract to function right and help in the digestion to the end product—and at the same time eliminate all the waste products—*all* the toxins and poisons which must be eliminated so that nothing will accumulate in our system, I thought that this was the most important thing in the tuberculosis treatment. It must be the same in all the other degenerative diseases, too. And still, up to the present, I am convinced that cancer does not need a "specific" treatment.

Cancer is a so-called degenerative disease, and all the degenerative diseases have to be treated so that the whole body at first is detoxified. In my tuberculosis work again, I saw that the liver plays the important role. It eliminates the toxins from the body, prepares them so they can enter into the bile ducts, and can thus be eliminated with the bile-that is not an easy job. In addition, the liver helps to prepare the stomach juice with the help of the visceral nervous system. The liver helps to prepare the pancreas, trypsin, pepsin, lipase, the digestive enzymes—all that is regulated with the help of the visceral nervous system. The liver has many, many more very important functions. One of them is the reactivation of the oxidizing enzymes as we know through Rudolf Schoenheimer. He did the work along these lines. It would go too far to go into that at this time. It is very important to note that oxidizing enzymes are at a low level of function in cancer patients.

Now let us anticipate the theory. During these years the idea occurred to me that there are two components in cancer which are of particular importance. One is the whole body, the general component. The other is a local one, the symptom. The treatment has to be applied to the general component. When we are able to bring this into balance, the local one disappears.

What is the general component and what does the treatment have to do to bring it into balance? I should like to devote this evening mostly to that question. The general component is the digestive tract and the liver. The digestive tract is very much poisoned in cancer. How can we handle that? Detoxification is an easy word, but it is very difficult to do in cancer patients. These cases, when they are far advanced, can hardly eat. They have no stomach juice, the liver doesn't function, the pancreas doesn't function, nothing is active.

Where do we begin? The most important first step is the detoxification. So let us go into that. First, we gave some different enemas. I found out that the best enema is the coffee enema as it was first used by Prof. O. A. Meyer in Goettingen. This idea occurred to him when together with Prof. Heubner he gave caffeine solution into the rectum of animals. He observed that the bile ducts were opened and more bile could flow. I felt that this was very important and I worked out coffee enemas. We took three heaping tablespoons of ground coffee for one quart of water, let it boil for three minutes, then simmer 10 to 20 minutes, and then gave it at body temperature.

The patients reported that this was doing them good. The pain disappeared even though in order to carry through the detoxification, we had to take away all sedation. I realized that it is impossible to detoxify the body

on the one hand and put in drugs and poisons on the other, such as sedation medication—demerol, codeine, morphine, scopolamine, etc. So, we had
to put the medication aside which again was a very difficult problem. One
patient told me that he had one grain of codeine every two hours and he got
morphine injections... how can you take these away? I told him that the
best sedation is a coffee enema. After a very short time he had to agree with
that. Some of the patients who had been in severe pain didn't take coffee
enemas every four hours as I prescribed—they took one every two hours.
But no more sedation.

After just a few days there was very little pain, almost none. I can give
you an example. A lady came to me not so long ago. She had cancer of the
cervix and then two large tumor masses around the uterus. The cervix was
a large crater, necrotic, producing blood and pus, and the poor lady could-
n't sit any more. The condition was inoperable. She had been given X-rays
and vomited any food she took in. She couldn't lie down anymore. She could
not sit. She walked around day and night. When she came to my clinic the
manager told me, "Doctor, you can't keep her here. This moaning and walking day and night is keeping the other patients from sleeping." After four
days she was able to sleep with no sedative whatsoever—which had not
helped her much anyway. The sedation had worked for perhaps half an
hour or so. After 8 to 10 days, she asked me for just one thing: let her omit
that night enema at 3 or 4 o'clock in the morning. These patients who
absorb the big tumor masses are awakened with an alarm clock every night
because they are otherwise poisoned by the absorption of these masses. If
I give them only one or two or three enemas, they die of poisoning. I did not
have the right as a physician to cause the body to absorb all the cancer
masses and then not to detoxify enough. With two or three enemas they
were not detoxified enough. They went into a coma hepaticum (liver coma).
Autopsies showed that the liver was poisoned. I learned from these disas-
ters that you can't give these patients too much detoxification. So I told this
lady that for *one* night she could sleep for seven hours—but only for one
night. I wouldn't risk more! When I didn't give these patients the night enemas, they were drowsy and almost semi-conscious in the morning. The
nurses confirmed this and told me that it takes a couple of enemas till they
are free of this toxic state again. I cannot stress the detoxification enough.
Even so with all these enemas, this was not enough! I had to give them also
castor oil by mouth and by enema every other day, at least for the first week
or so. After these two weeks you wouldn't recognize these patients any
more! They had arrived on a stretcher and now they walked around. They
had appetite. They gained weight and the tumors went down.

You will ask, "How can such a cancerous tumor go down?" That was a difficult question for me to understand. I had learned in my treatment of tuberculosis patients that I had to add potassium, iodine, and liver injections to help the liver and the whole body to restore the potassium. Now as far as I can see this is the situation. At first we give the patient the most salt-free diet possible.[12] So, as much salt (sodium) is removed from the body as can be. During the first days, 3 grams, 5 grams, up to 8 grams a day of sodium are eliminated while the patients receive only about one half gram of sodium content in the diet and no sodium is added.

The patients are given thyroid and lugol solution.* I learned first through the so-called Gudenath tadpole experiment that iodine is necessary to increase and help the oxidation ability. Then we gave the patients large amounts of potassium.[12] It took about 300 experiments until I found the right potassium combination. It is a 10% solution of potassium gluconate, potassium phosphate (monobasic), and potassium acetate. From that solution the patient is given four teaspoons full 10 times a day in juices. That large amount of potassium is introduced into the body.[12] At the same time 5 times one grain of thyroid and 6 times three drops of lugol solution, Vz strength. That's 18 drops of lugol which is a large dose. Nobody was observed to develop heart palpitations from that, even if some patients told me that they could previously not take thyroid because they would develop heart palpitation. And all allergies disappeared! Some patients claimed that they could previously not take one teaspoonful of lemon juice or orange juice—they were allergic. But when they are well detoxified and have plenty of potassium, they are not allergic. Allergies and other hypersensitivities are eliminated.

When introduced into the system, thyroid and lugol solution go immediately into the cancer mass. These ripe cells take it up fast and they perhaps grow a little faster but they soak in more with great greed—as much as they can—together with a little bit of sodium, probably. But then there isn't much sodium left. So then these cells pick up potassium and the oxidizing enzymes and die by themselves. You have to realize that cancer cells live essentially on fermentation but potassium and oxidizing enzymes introduce oxidation. And that is the point at which we can kill cancer cells because we take away the conditions which they need to continue to live.

But now we have to deal with a mass of dead cells in the body, in the blood stream—and they have to be eliminated wherever they may be. And that is not so easy! The ripe cells, the mature cells are very abnormal. These are much more easily killed than the other cells which are unripe,

*Lugol's solution is iodine plus potassium iodide.

not yet mature, and not so well developed. And there are other cancer cells in lymph vessels. These are clogged at both ends by cancer cells. No blood and no lymph can reach them. There are cancer cells in the glands. They are hidden there, protected from regular circulation. So it isn't easy to reach these. At first it is only the big mass which is killed. But this dead mass now has to be absorbed wherever it is—perhaps in the uterus, perhaps in the kidney, or in the lung, or in the brain—this has to be absorbed. This absorption is only possible through the blood stream. I call this "parenteral digestion." Enteral digestion is in the intestinal tract. Parenteral digestion takes place outside of the digestive tract, through the blood stream. It becomes important then to continually carry on detoxification day and night in order to bring the parenteral digestion to the highest point, even to a "hyperfunction." How can this be done?

I found that in order to bring the parenteral digestion to the highest function, it is necessary to start with the soil. Our soil must be normal, no artificial fertilizers should be used, no poisons, no sprays which go into the soil and poison it. Whatever grows on a poisoned soil carries poison too. And that is our food, our fruit and vegetables. I am convinced that the soil is our *external* metabolism. It is not really far removed from our bodies. We depend on it. But our modern food, the "normal" food people eat is bottled, poisoned, canned, color added, powdered, frozen, dipped in acids, sprayed—no longer normal. We no longer have living, normal food, our food and drink is a mass of dead, poisoned material, and one cannot cure very sick people by adding poisons to their systems. We cannot detoxify our bodies when we add poisons through our food which is one of the reasons why cancer is so much on the increase. Saving time in the kitchen is fine but the consequences are terrible. Thirty or fifty years ago cancer was a disease of old age. Only elderly people whose liver was no longer working well—was worn out—became sick. They contracted cancer when they were 60 to 70 years old and cancer was a rare disease. Everybody knows that. And now one out of four, even going on one out of three, dies of cancer. Now in the second generation it is even worse. The poor children get leukemia more and more. There is no country which has so much leukemia as this country, no country in the world. That is our fault. Ice cream is made with invert sugar. Coca-Cola contains phosphoric acid. Is it surprising that children get degenerative disease? These things constitute our external metabolism.

Now let us consider our digestive tract. As part of the digestive tract, the most important thing is that we restore the function of the liver—the tissue and the function of the liver. That is very hard work. We give the patients (including also the tuberculosis patients) liver injections, and since most of these patients need an increase in the red blood cells, we add some vitamin B_{12}. They receive 3 cc of crude liver extract together with 100 mcg of B_{12}. In addition when I found that our fruit and vegetables no longer have the normal content of potassium and not enough of the oxidizing enzymes, I looked for the best source of potassium in the best composition and the best supply of oxidizing enzymes. I found that to be calves liver. But we cannot give the patient calves liver because it contains too much fat and cholesterol. As you know, fat and oils cannot be given. Therefore we give these patients freshly pressed calves liver juice,* which is made in a special way with equal parts of carrots. Liver alone cannot be pressed. We take ½ pound fresh calves liver (not frozen) and ½ pound of carrots to make one glass of 200 cc (approx. 8 oz.) of fresh juice. The patients, the far advanced cases, get two glasses a day, even three glasses, and they like it!

All this is done in the effort to restore the enteral digestion. When that functions, we add stomach juice (Acidol Pepsin) and we add pancreatin not coated. The cancer patients cannot digest the coated pancreatin. The pancreatin is given five times a day, three tablets each time. So they always have plenty of trypsin, pepsin, lipase and diastase in their systems. The blood can carry this around and digest the tumor masses wherever they may be.

Now, since I am running out of time, I should like to tell you what we do to prove that this treatment really does work on cancer.[13,14] Number one, the results. I think I can claim that I have, even in these far advanced cases, 50% results. The real problem arises when we cannot restore the liver. Then there is no hope. The liver—the restoration of the liver, and its functions—are so important that some of the patients whose livers cannot be restored die some six months to 2½ years later from cirrhosis. Autopsies show no cancer cells in the body. They did not die from cancer. They died from a shrunken liver. Since I give more liver juice and I give more for promoting the parenteral digestion, these cases of a shrunken liver are rare.

I think I could do a lot to improve the results. I do not want to go into the problems that patients face when they go home and the family physician tells them that they need not "eat that cow fodder." Or the family thinks they cannot carry through this treatment because it is too much work as it takes one to one and a half years to restore the liver. The liver cells are renewed in four to five weeks, five to six weeks in older patients. To restore such a liver, you would need 12 to 15 new generations of liver cells. That is 1½ years. But the most important part of the treatment, I have learned, is to give the patients a new functioning liver.

* See Appendix III, page 421

Now, for the proof of this theory. I had the idea to make an animal experiment in which we connected two rats—one cancerous rat and one healthy one. We cut them open along the side and connected a blood vessel, then sewed them together. The blood from the healthy rat circulated in the sick one day and night and cleared up the sick body. Thus we showed that with a healthy normal metabolism you can cure cancer. You can cure the cancerous rat with the healthy body of the normal rat. But we are in the early stages of this type of experiment. There was one patient whose husband wanted to be connected to his wife because other very poor condition. But she said no, she didn't want to have him immobilized so long, next to her, with extensive nursing day and night. When she was first brought in to me, she had a very bad liver with probably hundreds of metastases, also in the rest of the body. I had told them that I didn't believe I could do anything for her, so the husband had offered his healthy body. But, even as it is, she is still living and improving. At any rate, with this type of experiment we have had no experience on human beings, only on rats.

Our next step to prove the theory was by taking tiny tissue samples from the liver by liver punctures. When time goes on and the patient recovers, the liver shows microscopically and chemically that recovery has taken place. This is done by microchemistry. There is an increase of the potassium content and iron, and now we can even trace the content of cobalt.

For ten years, I examined the potassium content in the serum of human beings and I made about 200 curves. But these are not characteristic. On the other hand, if we take a little tissue—a little mucous membrane or muscle tissue—with the improvement of the patient, the tissue also shows a return to the normal potassium content.[12] This is of tremendous importance.

* * *

Two months ago when I planned to come here for my vacation, the parents of this little boy wrote me and asked me for treatment for leukemia. Here is the little boy. He was treated with blood transfusions, had between 50 and 60 thousand white blood count and his red blood count was down to 1,400,000. He lost eight pounds in one week, couldn't eat or drink. I started the treatment about six weeks ago. Since that time, the boy is up and around, he can ride his bicycle, he is active and gained a total of five pounds. The blood count is normal. Lymphocytes are 6,500; hemoglobin is 73; 4,500,000 red blood cells—from 1,400,000! And here is the little boy. (The mother adds: I want to tell you doctor, he really likes the liver juice,* he doesn't want to eat chocolate.) You see, the liver juice,* the chil-

* See Appendix III, page 421

ly like it and ask for more. In the clinic where the parents had taken the child, they were told nothing could be done for him but I feel that now we can save this child. (Applause)

I have here another patient: Mr. Eyerly. Could you come here? Mr. Eyerly came here to see me. He lives in Salem, Oregon. The man had cancer of the prostate and it had grown into the urine bladder. He went to the University Clinic at Portland, Oregon, to a famous urologist. He diagnosed the metastasis into the urinary bladder and said that they could do nothing. Besides, the cancer had grown into the pelvic bones. This was two years ago. The physicians, including the family doctor, all told him that he could live only 4 to 6 weeks, especially since all bones of the pelvis were full of cancer. He looked terribly ill when he came to me. His wife brought him with a nurse. He had made his last will and did not expect to live. Now we cured that. It was especially difficult. I should like to thank his wife. She prepared the treatment with the greatest devotion. She was wonderful and we could rely on her. In a family where there is real devotion in the application of this treatment, we can even save these far advanced cases. Of course, we cannot save all of them but we can save more than we sometimes even consider possible. (Question from the audience: How long did it take?) In the urinary bladder, it didn't take but a few weeks and there was no longer any blood and pus, nor in the stools either. But in the pelvis there were hundreds of spots, and that takes a long time because the body transforms this cancer first into so-called osteoplastic areas, not an osteolytic process which is bone reducing. With my treatment more bone is produced. The body produces more bone, and then the hypertrophic bone is transformed into normal bone tissue. Then there is no more pain. Now the patient can get around and is even the manager of a company.

By chance I had these two patients here and could show them to you.

Post-Lecture Questions and Answers

Q. Can fibroid tumors be dissolved in the same manner?

A. Fibroid tumors are mostly benign. Benign tumors take 10 to 20 times as much time to absorb as malignant tumors. This goes for adhesions and scars. Fibroid and benign tumors are dissolved only very slowly because they are not abnormal. It is difficult for the parenteral system to bring its digestive powers to bear on these benign tumors. But when they turn malignant, then they are quickly dissolved.

Q. (from a doctor) Dr. Gerson, when I visited your hospital in 1946 your housekeeper was drinking fresh carrot juice. She had had an inoperable cancer of the pancreas. Please tell us about her. She was doing very well for such a bad condition.

A. She is living and in good condition now, 10 years later.

Q. Is cancer a state of reaction of unrestrained excessive factors of certain hormones working on various degenerated organs or tissues?

A. No, I don't think so. There is much more, and to answer that question I have to go deeper into the problem. We have to separate the state of
pre-cancerous condition from the state where the cancer appears. In the
pre-cancerous condition, all is prepared. The liver is sufficiently damaged
and the other organs of the intestinal tract are damaged enough and then
later the symptoms appear. Until then we have the pre-cancerous condition
and this condition cannot be cured with hormones and enzymes, etc. We
can to a certain degree stimulate the liver with hormones. We can stimulate the liver with cortisone. We can stimulate the liver with adrenaline
etc., but then we take out the last reserves. We empty the liver instead of
refilling it. What we have to do in cancer—a degenerative, deficiency disease—is to refill the organs which are empty and poisoned. Therefore it is
almost a crime to give cortisone and the other stimulants which will take
away the last reserves and improve the condition for a short while only.

Q. Why are all berries prohibited?

A. Some of the patients are hypersensitive, especially in the beginning,
against berries which are a little difficult to digest. Therefore I cut them
out.

Q. Are tomatoes OK?

A. Tomatoes are OK.

Q. Soy products and soy beans are forbidden. But is lecithin forbidden,
which is made from soy beans?

A. Since soy beans contain fats, I had to forbid them. Cancer patients
are not able for a long time to digest fats to the end products. When some
intermediate substances are left in the body, they work as carcinogenic
substances. Therefore we had to cut out fats, oils, and goods containing
them for a long time.

Q. What metabolic tests do you do before and after to further prove
recovery systematically as well as clinically?

A. I examine in all these cases the urine, the complete blood count, basal
metabolism or protein-bound iodine, and potassium in serum and tissue.
To see how the liver functions, I found it best to examine the end product
of the protein metabolism, urea nitrogen and uric acid. When these are normal and stay normal, then I assume that the patient is all right. But potassium in serum does not give a characteristic picture and makes it difficult
to judge. The patient can be cured yet the serum potassium still shows low

dren real because the tissues take it away. In some of the cancer patients when they arrive as terminal cases, potassium is above normal! One of the physicians asked me once, "Are you crazy? With the potassium above normal, you give such big doses of potassium?" And I said, "Yes, sir, I am not crazy. The patient is losing the potassium.[12] That is how it is increased in the serum."

Q. How harmful is coffee as a drink?

A. Coffee as a drink can be used by the patients only when they take the castor oil because coffee increases the motility of the stomach so the castor oil moves more quickly out of the stomach. But otherwise, coffee as a drink disturbs the function of the capillaries and therefore it has to be cut out.

Q. Would not detoxification be advisable in the majority of illnesses? Is this not comparable to what is called "a cleansing program?"

A. We have to detoxify the body in *all* degenerative diseases, in acute diseases too. But not to the extent as is required in cancer. Even most of the arthritis cases are not so toxic. I found that almost all of the arthritis cases have a weak liver or damaged liver. This is also true of coronary disease.

Q. Are vitamin and mineral supplements OK?

A. No, they are wrong because calcium and many other minerals cannot be added so easily. They bring the system out of harmony. With calcium you can produce cancer. I was forced in three cases of hemophilia to give calcium to bring the blood to coagulate. I did it but the cancer regrew and I lost all three cases. No calcium, no magnesium, no other minerals. I tried it. There must be harmony in our body under the law of totality. One should not change the mineral metabolism, especially not in cancer. Only the two most important minerals potassium and sodium must be balanced. This is the need of the cancer patient.

Q. In John Gunther's book, *Death Be Not Proud*, mention is made of your treatment as used on Gunther's son. Spectacular results were obtained at first but then there was a relapse and the patient died. Could you have cured this case without the regular MD's interference?

A. I will tell you why this poor boy died. He had a terrible brain tumor growing out of the skull, larger than my fist. I cured that. It's written in the book. But after that, the boy had an eczema and this eczema was of a special type which can usually be cured by giving the anterior lobe pituitary extract, a hormone. The family doctor, Dr. Traeger, said, "Why don't you give it to him?" But I told him that this is a terrible risk and I don't like to take such a risk with the life of that boy. When we give the pituitary, like many other hormones we may kill. But finally I gave in and it was my fault.

And for a long time after that I couldn't sleep nights. I gave him the hormone and the tumor regrew. I can add to that, that more than 12 years ago now, there appeared an article by a professor in Chicago that cancer patients benefit from administration of sex hormones. I gave it first to three patients, then to five. They reacted well for the first two to three months. Then I gave it to 25 more. They all reacted well for three to four months but after five months they went downhill. I lost 25 of my best cancer cases. Only six I could save again. That was the disaster from the hormone treatment. The Gunther boy was another disaster. That was not necessary. I want to reemphasize that we must not give the cancer patient "a little something" for temporary relief. I learned that the hard way.

Q. Your treatment worked in advanced cases of cancer of the liver?

A. If more than half to three-quarters of the liver is gone, you can't restore its function enough to save the patient. You may save them for half a year to a year, but then the liver may shrink and the patients die of a shrunken liver, cirrhosis of the liver. The liver is such an important organ that when it has to eliminate its own cancer, this has to be done by the healthy liver tissue. But the process of elimination can damage the healthy liver tissue if we don't detoxify constantly day and night, especially in these cases.

Now about three or four months ago a case came to me from Philadelphia. She told me when her son and brother brought her in that she had suffered from cancer of the rectum. At first the doctors didn't want to operate, then they couldn't. It was too late. Then she spent a half year at the Hoxey Clinic, and then she came home with a liver full of cancer, and hard as a board. I told her son and brother that this was too much, it wouldn't go. Take her home and make her comfortable. But they insisted I must try. And I did. And she is doing well! She can eat and drink, and the anterior part of her liver is a scar, hard as though it were calcified. Probably there is enough liver left. The son asked when they took her home after eight weeks, "You see, why didn't you want to take her?" At least for four weeks, every two hours and sometimes even every hour, she took coffee enemas—and castor oil enemas twice a day! She had so much gas and eliminated such large amounts of evil-smelling masses. When she left, we had to paint the room. It couldn't be washed off the paint.

(Comment by M.C.: I may say that I have looked through a lot of these places in a general way. I have been through Dr. Gerson's sanatorium on three different occasions and spent each time eight or ten days. I saw cases come in there by ambulance, on stretchers—just like Dr. Gerson said—hopeless metastatic cancers of the liver, the intestines, with obstructions, getting morphine every three to four hours. To my amazement within ten days these same patients would be walking around, free from pain. I was so amazed I couldn't understand it. It was so incredible that I made my son who was a senior in medical school come back with me to see these things. But it was not only cancer. I saw cases there of other degenerative diseases of all types.)

Q. Is folic acid treatment contra-indicated during treatment of cancer?

A. Yes, folic acid did damage.

Q. Can arthritis be cured by the same treatment which you use for cancer?

A. Yes. The treatment is not specific. It is not a specific treatment for cancer.

Q. How do you account for the fact that many skin cancers and some other cancers can be surgically removed and they never regrow or recur, even though no metabolic changes have been made?

A. Some patients have only temporary damage of the liver and the liver is then able to restore itself. But that is not in a majority of the cases. Sometimes if you remove, say a breast cancer, the removal of these toxins and poisons which the cancer itself generates is sufficient in some cases to relieve the temporary damage from the liver. Then the liver can recover. But these are the exceptions. And it is not basic. Also some of these patients get recurrences later. Many of my patients, after an initial operation, had stayed well for three or sometimes even five years. Then the cancer recurred. They were inoperable and orthodox medicine was helpless.

Q. Would it not be advantageous for the cancer patients to remain permanently on a vegetarian diet for the rest of their lives?

A. That depends on how far the liver can be restored. If it can be restored entirely, after say 1½ years, we tell the patients only to avoid fats and salt. Otherwise they are free. Many of them lead normal lives. But I'd like to say that about 75% like to stay more or less on the diet, and some even convince the other members of their families to stay on it with them. For instance, we have a photograph here in Escondido of Mr. Walter Wagg. He had a 100% incurable disease, progressive muscular dystrophy. He had been in the best clinics and could get no help. I cured him. Then his wife wanted to have another baby and they were able to have one. Later he came to where I was spending my vacation and showed me his wife and the baby. He told me that the whole family sticks to the diet and said he would stay with it as long as he lived since he is in such fine condition.

Q. What can be done for impaired lymph circulation following surgery in one arm for what was diagnosed as cancer?

A. It is very difficult to absorb these scars so that the lymph circulation can be restored, a very difficult task. It takes years.

Q. What is your conception of a prolonged fast or periodical three-day fast?

A. You can't let the cancer patient fast. In the cancer patient the body is so depleted, if you let them fast they go downhill terribly.

Q. What would you consider more important, diet or balanced emotions?

A. The balanced emotional condition is very important but without the diet and the detoxification you cannot heal.

Q. Would Parkinson's disease respond to a treatment similar to that for cancer?

A. What is destroyed in the central nervous system—and Parkinson's disease is a disease of the basal centers—is destroyed forever. But you are able to help the arteries in the brain with the treatment, and you can stop the progression, and you can restore what is not yet entirely destroyed.

Q. Does anemia contribute to cancer?

A. Sometimes it is a pre-condition to cancer, especially a certain type of anemia, not the so-called secondary anemia.

Q. Can too much vegetable juice cause alkalinity?

A. No.

Q. Dr. Otto Warburg advises increased intake of oxygen.

A. Oxygen would not go into the system so easily. You must have oxidizing enzymes, you must have more potassium, you must have the conditions under which oxygen can function.

Q. What vitamins are OK to take with your treatment?

A. With the vitamins we have a similar situation as we saw with the hormones. I damaged patients with vitamin A, vitamin E, vitamin B and B_6. Patients get really damaged. Vitamin A and D is picked up by the cancer cells immediately. Niacin we can use, that is B_3.

Q. What do you think of deep manipulation?

A. Cancer patients should not be massaged. Rubbing of the skin to open the capillaries and to help the body to stimulate the circulation is very valuable. We give the patient a rub two or three times a day before meals with a solution of ½ glass water with two tablespoons rubbing alcohol and two tablespoons of wine vinegar. To rub the whole body is very refreshing and helps the circulation.

Q. Can a person with a colostomy take the same type of coffee enema as a regular patient?

A. Yes.

Q. What are the principles of the coffee enema?

A. It opens the bile ducts. This is the principle.

Q. How can we prevent cancer?

A. Cancer must be prevented by preventing damage to the liver. The basic measure of prevention is not to eat the damaged, dead, poisoned food which we bring into our bodies. Every day, day by day, we poison our bodies. The older people still have a better liver and resistance from the food they had when they were young. They younger people get worse and the babies, now the second generation on canned baby foods, are still worse. They get leukemias. First of all, eat as much as you can of raw food, keep the potassium level up, and take some iodine.

NOTES AND REFERENCES

1. F. Sauerbruch, A. Herrmannsdorferand M. Gerson, "UeberVersuche, schwere Formen derTuberkulose dureb diatetische Behandlungen zu beeinflussen," *Muench. Med.Wochenschr.*, 2, 1 (1926).

2. M. Gerson. *ibid*, 77, 967 (1930).

3. —, "Phosphorlebertran und die Gerson-Herrmannsdorfersche Diat zur Heiling der Tuberkulose," *Dtsch. Med. Wochenschr.*, 12, 1 (1930).

4. F. Sauerbruch, A. Herrmannsdorfer and M. Gerson, *Muench. Med. Wochenschr.*, 23 (1930).

5. M. Gerson, "Wiederherstellung der verschiedenen Gefuehiqualitaeten bei der Lupusheilung," *Verh. Dtsch. Ces. Inn. Med.*, 43, 77 (1931).

6. —, *Diattherapie der Lungentuberkulose*, Deuticke, Vienne, 1934.

7. —, "Einiges ueber die kochsalzarme Diat," *Hyppokrates Z. Einheitsbestr., Cegenwartsmed.*, 12, 627 (1931).

8. F. Sauerbruch, *Das War Mem Leben*, Kindler und Schiermeyer Verlag, Bad Woerischofen, 1951, pp. 363- 371. This contains an account of how the author learned of Gerson's work by an accidental conversation on the train with one of Gerson's cured TB patients, which led to a large scale successful trial of the Gerson TB therapy at the Sauerbruch clinic.

9. E. Urbach and E. B. Le Winn, *Skin Diseases, Nutrition and Metabolism*, Grune and Stratton, New York, 1946, pp. 4, 65-67, 530-537. This contains a comprehensive review (in English) of the successful use of the Gerson therapy to cure tuberculosis of the skin.

10. M. Gerson, "Dietary considerations in malignant neoplastic disease. A preliminary report," *Rev. Castroenterol.*, 12,419 (1945).

11. —, "Effects of a combined dietary regime on patients with malignant tumors," *Exp. Med. Surg.*, 7,299 (1949).

12. F. W. Cope, "A medical application of the Ling association-induction hypothesis: The high potassium, low sodium diet of the Gerson cancer therapy," *Physiol. Chem. Phys.*, 10, 465 (1978).

13. M. Gerson, "Diattherapie boesartiger Erkrankungen (Krebs)," in *Handbuch der Diatetik*, Scala, Ed., Deuticke, Vienna, 1954, pp. 123-169.

14. —, *A Cancer Therapy: Results of Fifty Cases*, Third Ed., Gerson Institute, 1572 Second Ave., San Diego, CA 92101, 1977. This is a comprehensive description of the Gerson method of cancer treatment written both for the physician and for the layman.

(Revised September 8, 1978)

APPENDIX III

Discontinuing the Raw Liver Juice for Gerson Patients

In late 1989, it became necessary to discontinue the use of raw liver juice in the treatment of Gerson Therapy patients at the Mexican Gerson hospital. This important decision was reached due to urgent negative developments.

In this book, *A Cancer Therapy*, Dr. Max Gerson stresses the importance of the liver in health and healing. He discusses his use of the raw liver juice at length. However, even though all the livers used at the Mexican hospital came from U.S. growers and slaughterhouses, it became evident in late 1989 that a nationwide epidemic existed in U.S. stockyards in those young animals. The veal calves were all infected with campylobacter (c. jejuni and c.fetus subspecies fetus)

The decision to discontinue the raw liver juice was based on a number of outbreaks of campylobacter gastroenteritis (infectious diarrhea) at the hospital in up to 50% of the patients. Campylobacter was cultured from stools of affected patients. Veal liver was found to be the source of bacteria. {Erythromycin which is a mildly toxic antibiotic, is the drug of choice for treatment of campy and can usually clear it.}

At that time, there appeared to be a nationwide U.S. stockyard epidemic of these bacteria. The Gerson Institute contacted Dr. Tauxe of the CDC, (Centers for Disease Control, in Atlanta, GA) to learn what was known about the increased spread of "campy" (campylobacter) infections. Campy is now known to be twice as common as the more familiar and ever present salmonella. Many sources contribute to this overall incidence of campy, including even tap water. CDC recorded 41,343 treated cases over a 5 year period ending in 1986. Raw meat products, possibly also rare steak and beef tartare contribute to the incidence of campy.

Dr. Gerson added raw liver juice to his dietary therapy in 1950. He had noted in the years just preceding this action that his results were "not as good". Several examinations revealed that the patients were suffering from poisoning by the newly introduced DDT (in 1944). By the end of the 40's,

DDT was found in the fat of beef, in butter, even in mother's milk. "It was cumulatively stored in body fat." (Gerson, p. 167, A Cancer Therapy). Since cancer patients often lose weight quite rapidly, the previously stored DDT is released from the fat tissue into the blood stream and contributes to the body's toxicity. It is virtually impossible for the body to eliminate the severely toxic pesticides.. However, Dr. Gerson found that the raw juice of young calves' livers achieved this detoxification. When he added the liver juice to the patients' regimen, he saw that his results improved again.

In order to overcome the loss of this benefit as much as possible when it became imperative to stop the use of the raw liver juice, the hospital's scientific staff replaced each liver juice with carrot juice supplemented by two 500 mg desiccated liver tablets or capsules. In addition to the liver capsules, the patients receive 600 to 2,000 mg of Coenzyme Q-10 (CoQ-10) daily. This coenzyme contains many of the important nutrients found in raw liver. While this was not quite as effective as the raw liver juice, it had a different advantage. After patients return home, procuring the fresh raw liver twice a week and making the liver juice was a complex, time consuming and very expensive process. When the requirement was no longer made, more patients remained on the program, so the somewhat reduced results in some patients was made up by numerous patients who were able to stay on the program rather than having to give it up.

It is interesting to note that campy is a relatively weak, opportunistic bacterium. The veal animals must already be weakened from years of their mother's hormone injections and antibiotic treatments to be so severely infected. It is also of interest that Charlotte Gerson, who regularly visited the Mexican Gerson hospital at that time, regularly drank the liver juice the patients were served. She did not develop any infections. It must be assumed that a normal healthy immune system is capable of resisting the campy. Since a strong immune system is able to overcome malignant tissue, it must be assumed that the cancer patient's immune system is weakened and cannot deal with campy any more than it can overcome cancer.

Name and Author Index

423

Subject Index